Multi-Dimensional Project Breakdown Structures – The Secret to Successful Building Information Modeling (BIM) Integration

Xavier Leynaud
Paul D. Giammalvo, Ph.D.
Jean-Yves Moine

Copyright 2019©

Authors/Editors:	Xavier Leynaud, France Paul D. Giammalvo, Ph.D., Indonesia Jean-Yves Moine, France
Editor / Publisher:	DBC Publishing, Richmond, VA 23150
ISBN Numbers	ISBN-13: 978-1-948149-12-9 ISBN-10: 1-948149-12-5

Table of Contents

List of Figures

Multi-Dimensional Project Breakdown Structures –
The Secret to Successful Building Information Modelling (BIM) Integration

11

Preface

This book has come about through a chance meeting of three people from different parts of the world, with the same interests and core belief that the use of multi-dimensional (relational- or object-database) work breakdown structures are preferable to the use of flat-file or single-dimensional work breakdown structures. Our basic premise, theory, or hypothesis is by looking at our projects from a minimum of three (and preferably more) dimensions or perspectives that it will help us pick up these missing scope elements.

The three authors do not agree 100% on all items; we do agree the leading cause of project failures, claims, change orders, litigation and unhappy clients, and contractors alike are the inability to easily define a project's scope from the earliest conceptual phases of a project through project completion. Scope definition is happening too late in the project definition and design phases and results in missing too many critical elements.

This book started life as a series of blog postings initiated by Jean Yves Moine but expanded with inputs from other professional parties. As the concept evolved and expanded, adult learners from the six-months-long, graduate level students started contributing; and at a point, the three primary authors agreed this collective work was important enough to publish an explanation with the hopes it will attract more people interested in expanding on the ideas and concepts being offered.

To keep the dialog open and continuing, and in hope of attracting Millennials to participate in the discussion, we have created a Facebook Group (https://www.facebook.com/Multi-dimensional-Project-Breakdown-Structures-593192384497323/) and a LinkedIn Group (www.LinkedIn.com/groups/10437665) where we can continue to expand on the growth, particularly given the 15-dimensional model being developed by OmniClass in support of Building Information Modeling, (BIM) with the interesting work of theoretical physicist Anthony Garrett Lisi, with his 8-dimensional model of the universe. To gain a better understanding of the driver behind this book watch these two TED-talk videos - https://youtu.be/y-Gk_Ddhr0M and https://bit.ly/2NBxgMt.

Enjoy the book … but more importantly … keep the discussion alive by sharing examples of how you are using Multi-Dimensional Breakdown structures in your line of work and how it is helping you better define scope.

Acknowledgments & Forward

****

This book is dedicated to the memory of Jack and Ralph Masiello, of Masiello Construction, Shrewsbury, MA, USA; two general contractors who gave me a start as a carpenter apprentice and shaped a portion of my career growth and success.

As Work Breakdown Structures (WBS) and Systems Engineering have long been an interest when I chanced upon Jean Yves Moine and Xavier Leynaud, it seemed only logical we combine our ideas to see where the concepts may take us. While originally our attempts to link WBS to Quantum Physics seemed pretty far-fetched, with the growing use of Virtual and Augmented Reality, the relevance between WBS structures and Lisi's 'Theory of Everything' is becoming stronger by the day.

A special thanks to Dr. Phillippe Ruiz, who was consulted on the development and calculation of Eigenvalues and Eigenvectors. And, a special thanks to our editor, Dr. Dawn D. Boyer.

Dr. Paul D. Giammalvo

****

This book is dedicated to four people that helped me discover and understand project management, e.g., Paul Barclay, Amar Bhambhra, Don Puney, and Michel Laignel, as well as my wife, Alexandra, who always supports me and to my young twins, Constance and Aurore, hoping they will be able to read it one day.

I had the chance to discover project management in a French offshore engineering company named Bouygues Offshore (later acquired by Saipem). I was under the direct supervision of Puney and Bhambhra, who taught me real planning (with drawings and contract in hand) on the larger project they had signed at that time that was led by Barclay. I had the chance to dive deep into project-management methods under the supervision of Laignel, who had massive experience in the field of planning during the buildings of nuclear plants in France. Laignel was in charge of planning at the method department of the same company. Those earlier experiences gave me the capacity to understand deeply the world of project management as it applied to mega-construction projects, and with my software engineer background, to start thinking about planning models.

I had never practiced software engineering because project management was my passion at that time, but I was mindful of relational models that were the founding principle of the 3-D WBS. Later, during my career as a manager of services for a consulting company dedicated to project management, I hired and managed Jean-Yves, and we become friends. He started to develop a full picture of what I had in mind. Our collaboration improved the concept method so much, in time, this gave Giammalvo (the lead editor) the desire to work with us to birth this book. I was so impressed with the request I accepted without hesitation for bringing my experience to this book.

I hope you will enjoy reading this book and readers appreciate the power of the concept. It considers the full effectiveness of 3-D WBS as the missing link in the field of interfaced project management.

Xavier Leynaud

****

First, I would like to thank Xavier Leynaud who shared with me his knowledge about the multi-dimensional breakdown structures of project management and trained me for project planning since 2001.

Thanks to Dr. Paul D. Giammalvo who pushed me to this fantastic adventure since 2011 and made me dream with all his ideas and added developments of the method.

Thanks also to Thomas Bacus, Bernard Vajente, Alexis Bilon, Sylvain Le Muet Delays, and Stephen Devaux who helped me to progress in the understanding of the subject.

Jean-Yves Moine

****

Introduction

The world of construction has become increasingly automated through the use of Building Information Modeling (BIM) and Virtual Reality (VR), particularly during the early design phases, it is apparent those responsible for executing the projects – the owners and contractors project managers, cost estimators, schedulers, document controllers, and project controllers – are not yet caught up with architectural and engineering counterparts. To ensure the work is consistent with, complementary to and supportive of the use of BIM, VR and evolving technological advances must be included in the management of the project, including the use of drones, time-lapse photography, and driverless equipment. From the perspective of being a practical resource for use by project practitioners today, the authors will be sticking with three-dimensional (3-D) models, understanding as we move into the world of Virtual Reality in planning and scheduling projects, the authors believe in the FUTURE, we will see the use of these databases to produce Tesseract models of the project.

The Purpose of This Book?

While there are no shortage of 'project breakdown structures,' which have been around for many years now (i.e., Work Breakdown Structures, (WBS); Cost Breakdown Structures (CBS); Contract Work Breakdown Structures (CWBS), etc.), this book has been written to demonstrate early experiments to integrate these various 'flat file' or 2-D coding structures into 3-D models, just as 3-D BIM can turn traditional 2-D drawings into 3-D graphics. Taking it one step further, Virtual Reality (VR) enables us to 'walk through' a project while still in the design phases. The objective of the authors is to demonstrate how designers or project managers or both can do the same with scope, time, cost, resources, and/or other project variables. This book captures and shares the experiences of three early believers and exploratory experimenters in the integration of two-dimensional project coding structures in three (or more) dimensions.

Key Definitions

The following terms are used throughout this section. To understand and appreciate the authors' proposal, it is essential these definitions are reviewed before proceeding:

- Virtual Reality (VR): the computer-generated "simulation of a three-dimensional image or environment that can be interacted with in a seemingly real or physical way by a person using special electronic equipment, such as a helmet with a screen inside or gloves fitted with sensors."[1]
- Augmented Reality (AR): the integration of digital information with the user's environment in real time. Unlike *virtual* reality, which creates an artificial environment, *augmented* reality uses the existing environment and overlays new information on top of it.
- Systems Dynamics (SD): is an area of mathematics used to describe the behavior of complex dynamical systems, usually by employing differential equations or difference equations. When differential equations are employed, the theory is called continuous dynamical systems.
- Project Breakdown Structures (PBS): A project breakdown structure is any hierarchical alpha or alpha-numeric coding structure which identifies the components which go into a project permanently or those attributes, products or services which are required to support the administrative or support functions of a project. Commonly referenced Project Breakdown Structures include, but are not limited to:

  - ✓ LBS (Location Breakdown Structures)
  - ✓ PBS (Product Breakdown Structure)
  - ✓ FBS (Functional Breakdown Structure)
  - ✓ ABS (Activity Breakdown Structure)
  - ✓ OBS (Organization Breakdown Structure)
  - ✓ CBS (Cost Breakdown Structure)
  - ✓ RBS (Resource Breakdown Structure)
  - ✓ CWBS (Contract Work Breakdown Structure)

As you can see, there are many more methods to be developed for various databases to communicate with one another. For this book, the basis for the initial examples of Project Breakdown Structures have come from the actual documents commonly used by project managers, however any combination of 3 or more of these coding structures can be used to filter, group, and sort in a way which enables projects to be viewed or understood in multiple dimensions. They also can be combined or permutated to create new PBS not explicitly identified in this book.

---

[1] *Technology Terms Flashcards | Quizlet. (n.d.). Retrieved from quizlet.com/68691426/technology-terms-flash-cards/*

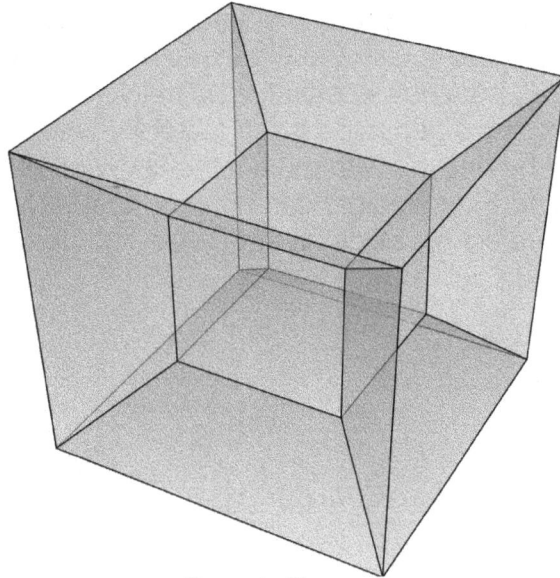

Figure 1 : Tesseract

"In geometry, the tesseract is the four-dimensional analog of the cube;[2] the tesseract is to the cube as the cube is to the square.[3] Just as the surface of the cube consists of six square faces, the hypersurface of the tesseract consists of eight cubical cells. The tesseract is one of the six convex regular 4-polytopes.[4] The tesseract is also called an 8-cell, C_8, (regular) octachoron, octahedron, cubic prism, and tetracube (although this last term can also mean a poly-cube made of four cubes). It is a four-dimensional hypercube, or 4-cube, as a part of the dimensional family of hypercubes or 'measure polytopes.'[5] For those unfamiliar with these terms, before getting too far into the book, it is recommended you take a few minutes to review these YouTube videos:

Unwrapping a tesseract (4-D cube aka hypercube)
  Retrieved from: https://www.youtube.com/watch?v=BVo2igbFSPE

A Journey into the 4th Dimension - Perspective [Part 1][6]
  Retrieved from: https://www.youtube.com/watch?v=4TI1onWI_IM

---

[2] *And He Built A Crooked House by Robert A. Heinlein. (n.d.). Retrieved from goodreads.com/book/show/3791158-and-he-built-a-crooked-house*
[3] *Figure of Tesseract from Wikipedia: Retrieved from https://en.wikipedia.org/wiki/Hypercube*
[4] *Tesseract - Wikipedia. (n.d.). Retrieved from en.wikipedia.org/wiki/Tesseract*
[5] *Wikipedia Definition of Tesseract. Retrieved from en.wikipedia.org/wiki/Tesseract*
[6] *A Journey into the 4th Dimension - Perspective [part 1 ... (n.d.). Retrieved from youtube.com/watch?v=4TI1onWI_IM*

Visualizing 4-D Geometry - A Journey Into the 4th Dimension [Part 2][7]
Retrieved from: https://www.youtube.com/watch?v=4URVJ3-D8e8k

- Eigenvectors and Eigenvalues- where λ is a scalar known as the eigenvalue or characteristic value associated with the eigenvector v. geometrically, an eigenvector corresponding to a real, nonzero eigenvalue point in a direction that is stretched by the transformation and the eigenvalue is the factor by which it is stretched.[8] As much of this book will be dealing with multi-dimensional matrices, an understanding of how Eigenvalues and Eigenvectors can be used to analyze the relationships between the various project break down structures can be understood and applied.[9]

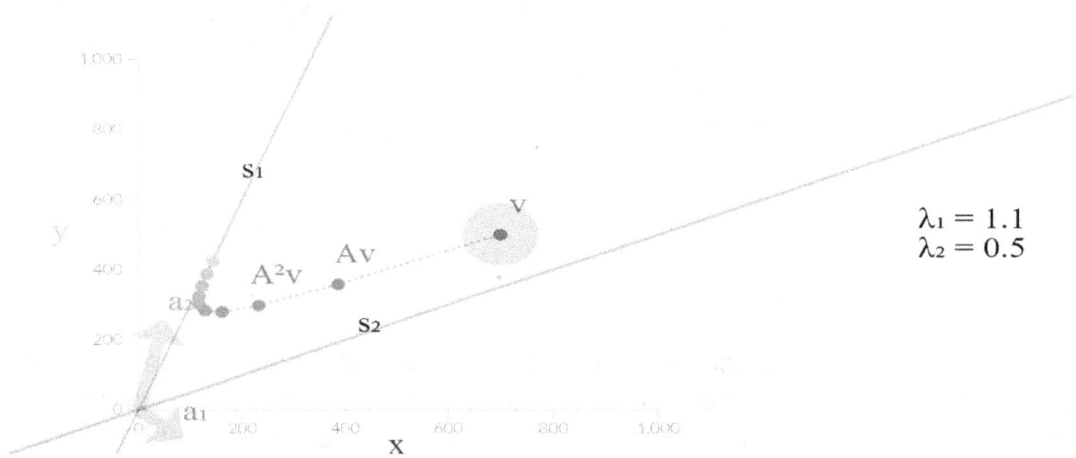

$$\lambda_1 = 1.1$$
$$\lambda_2 = 0.5$$

Figure 2: Illustrating the use of Eigenvalues and Eigenvectors for Analyzing Multi-Dimensional Matrices

Definitions of Building Information Modeling: For this book, recognizing there are opinions about what components go into a BIM, the definitions for the different components of Building Information Modelling are adapted from the BIM model.

---

[7] Journey into the 4th Dimension - Perspective [part 2 ... (n.d.). Retrieved from youtube.com/watch?v=4TI1onWI_IM
[8] Eigenvalues and Eigenvectors. (n.d.). Retrieved from en.wikipedia.org/wiki/Eigenvector,_eigenvalue,_and_eigenspace
[9] Powell, V. & Lehe, L. (n.d.) "Eigenvalues and Eigenvectors Explained Visually." Retrieved from setosa.io/ev/eigenvectors-and-eigenvalues/

3-D	4D	5D	6D	7D
	SCHEDULING	**ESTIMATING**	**SUSTAINABILITY**	**FACILITY MANAGEMENT APPLICATIONS**
• Existing Conditions Models 　- Laser Scanning 　- Ground Penetration Radar (GPR) conversions • Safety & Logistics Models • Animations, Renderings, Walk-throughs • BIM-driven Pre-fabrication • Laser-Accurate BIM-driven field layout	• Project Phasing Simulations • Lean Scheduling 　- Last Planner 　- Just-In-Time (JIT) Equipment Deliveries 　- Details Simulation Installation • Visual Validation for Payment Approval	• Real-time conceptual modeling and cost-planning (DProfiler) • Quantity extraction to support details cost estimates • Trade Verifications from Fabrication Models 　- Structural Steel 　- Rebar 　- Mechanical / Plumbing 　- Electrical • Value Engineering 　- What-if scenarios 　- Visualization 　- Quantity Extraction • Prefabrication Solutions 　- Equipment Room 　- MEP systems 　- Multi-trade, Pre-fabrication 　- Unique architectural and structural elements	• Conceptual energy analysis via DProfiler • Detailed energy analysis via Eco-Tech • Sustainable element tracking • LEED tracking	• Life-cycle BIM Strategies • BIM As-Builts • BIM embedded Q&M manuals • COBie data population and extraction • BIM Maintenance Plans and Technical Support • BIM file hosting on Lend Lease's Digital Exchange System

Figure 3: Definitions for Building Information Modeling used in this book.

This BIM model[10] was chosen as it seems to be the most expansive and is the model which most closely represents or is consistent with the concept of the hypercube or tesseract model.

1D	2D	3-D	4D	5D	6D	7D
Scratch Point	**Vector**	**Shape**	**Time**	**Cost**	**Performance**	**Facility Management**
Research • Existing conditions • Regulations • Weather simulations • Sun Orientation • Functional Program **Implementation** • Consulting • BIM Execution Plan • Server Depository • Software **Concept Design** • Strategies • Area Estimation • Cost Estimation • General Volumetry • Accessibility • Viability	**Production** • 2-D Drawings • Documentation • Views and Plans **Implementation** • BIM Object Creation • Parameterization • File Management • Communications **DS Development** • Room Data Sheets • List of Deliverables • Scope Definition • Materials • Structural Loads • Energy Loads **Sustainability** • Life-Cycle Estimation • Construction Solutions • Primary MEP systems • Energy Production • LEED Strategies	**Representation** • Renderings • Walk-throughs • Laser Scanners **Implementation** • BIM Object Creation • Visual Programming • Clash Detection • Model Checker **Final Documentation** • Detailed Design • Assemblies • Structural Design • MEP Design • Specifications **Sustainability** • Insulation Values • Sun Protection • Daylight Requirements	**Production** • Model Federation • Virtual Construction • Scheduling • Project Phasing • Time-Lining • Construction Planning • Equipment Deliveries • Visual Validation **Systems** • Pre-Fabrication • Structural Construction • MEP Construction **Simulations** • Life-Cycle Simulation • Sun Simulation • Wind Simulation • Energy Simulation • LEED check	**Production** • Quantity extractions • Details Cost Estimation • Fabrication Models **Contracts** • Fees Comparison • Trade Selection • Logistics **Sustainability** • LEED Evaluation • Life-Cycle Cost • Comparative Study	**Results** • Known Alternatives • Assortment • Audited BIM Model (BPA Project) • To Be Optimized **Value Engineering** • Simulations • Energy Performance • Systems Performance • Construction Performance • Architectural Performance **Save Estimation** • Comparative Cost • Construction Benefits • Owner Benefits • Timing Risk • Selected Items to be Optimized **Re-Design** • Certified BIM Model	**Applications** • Life-cycle BIM strategies • BIM As-Builts • BIM embedded Q&M Manuals • COBie data population and extraction • BIM Maintenance Plans & Technical Support • BIM File hosting on Lend Lease's Digital Exchange System

Figure 4: Impacts that BIM has on Project Management, Cost Engineering and Project Controls

---

[10] *Origins of BIM, Bimpanzee Blog (nd). Retrieved from bimpanzee.com/about-building-information-modeling--bim-.html*

Figure 4 provides for early evidence of the direction the future of 'Project Management,' 'Project Controls' and 'Cost Engineering' (Engineering Economics) seems to be evolving. This 'birth-to-death' or 'total life-span management' of all assets from conception through obsolescence and disposal becomes more important as the issues of sustainability become more pronounced.

Individual Discussion and Comments

The three authors' individual opinions, perspectives, and/or clarifications are offered here:

Xavier Leynaud

The only difference between the multi-dimensional WBS and generic coding structures lies in their links to one another. If all one does is create coding structures, but there is no relationship or connection between them, then all you have are a bunch of sort codes. When you structure the sort codes together (through the activities or lower levels of the WBS), now one can begin to see and to analyze relationships between them … e.g., one can analyze float in two dimensions using the 'forward pass' / ' backward pass' information, one can analyze the distance between any two or more activities – not in just a single dimension – but in three dimensions.

This is important. With the proliferation of Building Information Modeling (BIM), project managers are going to see an increasing use of multi-dimensional sorting capabilities combined with the electronic data interchange between the design databases (3-D CAD); scheduling databases (4-D CAD); cost-estimating databases (5-D CAD); and risk-simulation databases (6-D CAD). This book will be one of the first to explore the use of these coding structures to integrate these divergent databases.[11]

When Leynaud first worked on the concept Moine developed, it was because Leynaud was 'fed up' with the hierarchical approach implied by most of the WBS and the resulting discord about standardization. Leynaud studied management software engineering in his youth. He was fascinated with relational-database models, and eager was to find a way to model data elements. Leynaud wanted to respond instantly to requests within his company by researching others' solutions to this same problem.

Leynaud worked primarily with Artemis, within the structured codification environment of the oil and gas industry (Mobil and Exxon). He was actually using the process without knowing it was a 3-D approach to the project work planning and management. Leynaud met Moine, and together they pushed the concept into new frontiers (in addition to increasing the speed to develop schedules). In particular, what is very important for Leynaud was the following:

---

[11] *Leynaud Xavier: President of Xavier Leynaud & Associés noted how he evolved into the process*

- Two of the three types of codification, the Activity Breakdown Structure (ABS) and Product Breakdown Structure (PBS) can or should be able to be standardized in the company without conflict with other systems. This is why adopting standardized coding structures (e.g., OmniClass or Norsok) are strongly advised.
- Location Breakdown Structure (LBS) is specific to each project and can support the installation of the product (LBS could follow guidelines in its definition – in particular – the uniqueness of each area referred by each code – no overlap)[12]
- Different levels of each of the structures could be mixed at a different stage of the project and defending the use of the 'WBS to create the project WBS (you can have a detail difference in your WBS for procurement and manufacturing because you manufacture some items for example), and the approach is still coherent.'[13]

Creating a mix with the Organizational Breakdown Structure (OBS) to share the work results in a more difficult interface than the fundamental dimension of the WBS component via the specific branch of code (that led to creating an allocation of the package, reducing those gaps to simplify the interface). Without knowing it, Leynaud had been implementing the method for years. Adding the full model developed by Jean-Yves, they succeeded in standardizing codification within the company. No more frozen hierarchical Work Breakdown Structure (WBS)! Just ABS, PBS, FBS, and rules to create the LBS. This resulted in packages with very few gaps between each of the dimensions (or no large logic gaps for a client company sub-contractor with high levels of specifications, functional testing, and commissions).

The 'Flat File' WBS was a thing of the past because 3-D WBS allowed 'relational' components instead of only hierarchical. This works with many projects, especially with those computerized, financial-management systems called Enterprise Resource Planning (ERP), (which imposes a 20+ digits codification) to link everything, when an anonymous code is more significant if the four codes are composing the 3-D were used.

Dr. Paul D. Giammalvo

The evolutionary trend is clearly towards multi-dimensional WBS structures (Relational and Object-Oriented Databases versus Flat Files). The formal use of multi-dimensional WBS/CBS started in 1973 with 'Master Costs,' which became 'UniFormat.'[14] This structure looked at buildings' components, such as foundations, sub-structures, and super-structures. Recognizing there needed to be another way to look at costs, Construction Specifications Institute (CSI) developed two different paths in

---

[12] *Cubix Project Management - 3-D Work Breakdown Structure Method. (n.d.). Retrieved from breakdown233.rssing.com/chan-12384124/all_p1.html*

[13] *Cubix Project Management - 3d3-D Work Breakdown Structure Method. (n.d.). Retrieved from breakdown233.rssing.com/chan-12384124/all_p1.html*

[14] *CSI's UniFormat (1973). Retrieved from arc-solutions.org/wp-content/uploads/2012/03/Charette-Marshall-1999-UNIFORMAT-II-Elemental-Classification....pdf*

1975 with the creation of MasterFormat.[15] The Norwegians adapted what CSI started explicitly for off-shore oil and gas with Norzok Z-014.[16] The authors are urging Information Technology (IT) and Telecommunications clients to recognize the value and importance of standardizing the WBS, but to also value, create, and use multi-dimensional WBS (3-D WBS).

Where the authors don't agree totally is with object-oriented databases. Assuming the number of fields has no limit, there may not be a need for limiting the coding structures to only three dimensions or having to combine them. As the development of BIM evolves, there is an expectation of the 15 OmniClass Tables, including the actual codes, automatically being built into each object. Unless both owners and contractors adopt these standardized coding structures, they will have to write conversion macros to convert the data for cost, duration, and productivity into the OmniClass Table Codes.

Jean-Yves Moine

As a consultant, I created a blog which illustrated what Leynaud and Giammalvo had in their heads to illustrate their ideas. I worked to improve and develop the method and educate our trade members and continued to be a consultant for this book with a great passion!

Additional Quotes Supporting the Use of Multi-Dimensional WBS

"With 3-D WBS, new users, as well as experienced schedulers, have time to talk about interface coordination while meeting project actors, instead of spending their time behind their computer. Less keyboard, more paperboard! The 3-D WBS is a key for project planning efficiency!" - Xavier Leynaud, Head of Planning & Load Management HEU Projects, Alstom Power Hydro

"As Project coordinator, I was pleased to try out the 3-D WBS method for the development of the railroad schedule of the tramway of Tours. By my knowledge of the Tramway activity, we were able to structure, in very little time, a robust and effective framework of the schedule, which is still in use in our project management." - Doris Leroy, OPC – SYSTRA

"I had the opportunity to work with the 3-D WBS method as it was being developed as a prototype tool. Within the framework of one of the parts of the Ballard building site, the French Pentagon, we were able to make the schedules on Primavera P6 very quickly in a rough draft of 12 different buildings (new, heavy, and light

---

[15] CSI's MasterFormat (1975). Retrieved from csinet.org/numbersandtitles
[16] NORSOK STANDARD, SCCS. (Oct. 2002), Z-104. Retrieved from https://www.standard.no/pagefiles/951/z-014.pdf

rehabilitation). This method is more refined and effective according to the knowledge of the project or the project's managers, and it requires close cooperation with the planners." - Alexis Bilon, Planning Unit Manager – Bouygues Batiment

"The factorization of the Project's tasks following the three Axis Activities, Products, and Zones, then the automated development in 3-D allows a dramatically efficient project planning. It was easy to build examples of an application to an IT project within the framework of an agile predictive method waterfall. Innovating, effective, efficient, and educational!" - Sylvain Le Muet Delays, Project Manager IT - Project Management Institute

History of Multi-Dimensional Project Breakdown Structure

Introducing MasterFormat

The idea or concept of multi-dimensional Work Breakdown Structures (WBS) or Cost Breakdown Structures (CBS) is not new. After World War II, building construction specifications began to expand, as more advanced materials and choices became available.[17] The Construction Specifications Institute (CSI)[18] was founded in 1948 and began to address the organization of specifications using a numbering system similar to the Dewey Decimal System used by libraries. The purpose or objective of this effort was to ensure that a specification appeared once and only once in any set of contract documents, thus helping to eliminate redundancy or conflicting information in the contract documents, and thus reducing claims and disputes.[19]

In 1963, CSI published a format for construction specifications, with 16 major divisions of work. These 16 divisions were built around work packages traditionally or customarily sub-contracted by prime contractors to specialty sub-contractors (e.g., Site work, Concrete, HVAC, Electrical) or prime contractors would supply their workforces (e.g., general building, masonry, finishes, doors, and windows).

Below are listed the 16 original MasterFormat divisions. For the current version, down two sub-levels, you can download it in Excel format here via this online page: constructupdate.com/sheets/construction-cost-estimate-template-download.xls

---

[17] *Introduction - Pmworldlibrary.net. (n.d.). Retrieved from pmworldlibrary.net/wp-content/uploads/2018/04/pmwj69-Apr2018-Giammalvo-E*

[18] *Masterformat | Wiki | Everipedia. (n.d.). Retrieved from everipedia.org/wiki/lang_en/MasterFormat/*

[19] *Mapping ERP "Chart of Accounts" to Building Information ... (n.d.). Retrieved from pmworldjournal.net/article/mapping-erp-chart-of-accounts-to-building-inf*

MasterFormat Level 1 Code Structure	Uniformat Level 1 Name
Division Number	Name
1	General Requirements
2	Site Construction
3	Concrete
4	Masonry
5	Metals
6	Wood and Plastics
7	Thermal and Moisture Protection
8	Doors and Windows
9	Finishes
10	Specialties
1	Equipment
12	Furnishings
13	Special Construction
14	Conveying Systems
15	Mechanical
16	Electrical

Figure 5: Original 1963 MasterFormat Divisions

A 1975 update published by CSI used the term MasterFormat as the formal name for this trade-based coding structure. The last CSI MasterFormat publication to use the 16 divisions was in 1995 but is no longer supported by CSI.[20] In November of 2004, MasterFormat expanded from 16 divisions to 50 divisions, reflecting innovations in the construction industry and expanding the coverage to a larger part of the construction industry. Changes were facilities construction, e.g., petrochemical process plants, power plants, and other industrial facilities. (Updates were published in 2010, 2012, and 2014.[21])

Introducing UniFormat

In the early- to mid-1970s, around the same period that MasterFormat was evolving within CSI, the U.S. General Services Administration (GSA; Uniformat 2002 Update[22]), in conjunction with the United States-based American Institute of Architects (AIA), commissioned Hanscomb Associates, Inc., to create a standardized construction cost-coding structure, originally named 'Master costs.' The GSA and AIA renamed this

---

[20] MasterFormat | Wiki | Everipedia. (n.d.). Retrieved from www.everipedia.org/wiki/lang_en/MasterFormat/

[21] MasterFormat | Wiki | Everipedia. (n.d.). Retrieved from www.everipedia.org/wiki/lang_en/MasterFormat/

[22] U.S. General Services Administration. Retrieved from: https://portal.ct.gov/-/media/DAS/Office-of-School-Construction-Grants/Task-188---Required-Forms-Regarding-Plan-Review-and-Approval/FORM-SCG-2020-UNIFORMAT-II-classification-for-building-cost-estimating-4-24-17-KD.pdf

'UniFormat,' which enabled capture and summation of costs by building components. ASTM International began developing a standard for classifying building elements (1989), based on UNIFORMAT, and renamed to UNIFORMAT II.[23,24]

Below is an example of top levels of the two-level UniFormat Coding Structure:

UniFormat Level 1 Code Structure	UniFormat Level 1 Name	UniFormat Level 2 Code Structure	UniFormat Level 2 Code Name
A	Structure	A11	Foundations
		A12	Basement Construction
		A21	Super-Structure
B	Exterior Construction	B11	Exterior Walls
		B12	Exterior Glazing & Doors
		B13	Roofing
C	Interior Construction	C11	Partitions, Doors, and Specialties
		C12	Access / Platforms
		C13	Interior Finishes
D	Services	D11	Conveyance Systems
		D21	Plumbing
		D22	HVAC
		D31	Fire Protection / Alarm
		D41	Electrical Service, Distribution & Emergency Power
		D42	Lighting and Branch Wiring
		D43	Communications, Security & Other Electrical Systems
E	Equipment & Furnishings	E12	Equipment & Furnishings
F	Special Construction, Demolition, and Abatement	F11	Special Construction
		F12	Building Demolition & Abatement
G	Sitework	G11	Sitework – Building Related
		G12	Other Sitework – Project Related
Z	General Conditions	Z11	Project General Conditions
		Z12	Contractors OH & P

---

[23] Introduction - Pmworldlibrary.net. (n.d.). Retrieved from www.pmworldlibrary.net/wp-content/uploads/2018/04/pmwj69-Apr2018-Giammalvo-E

[24] Charette, R. P. (n.d.) UniFormat II. Retrieved from: www.uniformat.com/index.php/using-uniformat-ii/building-design-management#astme1557

Figure 6: Uniformat 2002 Update

As can be seen, by the example above, this breakdown structure enables those using the codes to see the project by the major components that go into any structure. From the perspective of the contractor, this coding structure roughly breaks the project down by sub-contractor. These components may be done uniquely by the general or prime contractors' workforce, yet still, represent a unique skill set.

Around 1995, the Construction Specifications Institute (CSI) USA and Construction Specifications Institute (CSI) Canada agreed to assume responsibility to maintain, update, and expand on UniFormat. By combining the UniFormat coding structure with MasterFormat, the result was a two-dimensional model, Uniformat-based on the parts of a structure, and on which MasterFormat is trade-based.

Introducing NORSOK Z-04

In 1989, the Norwegian Petroleum Directorate (NPD), STATOIL, (Den Norsok Stats oljeselskap a.s.) Saga Petroleum and Norsok Hydro collaborated to create a standardized Cost Coding Structure (CCS) or Cost Breakdown Structure (CBS). This document was updated in 1992, 2002, and 2012.[25] The team tasked with creating this standardized, cost-coding structure started by analyzing what other organizations had created, (e.g., PMI, AACE, CSI, et al.), which led the team to adopt the concept behind MasterFormat (Work Results) and UniFormat (Element or Module based).

While both Master and UniFormat were designed specifically for general construction, the Norsok Z014 team found them unsuited to offshore oil and gas, which had a heavy emphasis on piping, electrical, and mechanical systems, but was relatively light on many of the (then) 16 Divisions (e.g., Division 08- Doors and Windows or Division 09- Finishes).[26] While the concept behind what CSI had achieved made sense, the work results and elements or modules were unique. This method requires those using the CSI codes to customize the structures, as well as the names, associated with each of the coding structures. The Construction Specifications Institute started with a single-dimensional model called MasterFormat that, when combined with the US General Services Administration's UniFormat, provided a capability for sorting in two dimensions.

---

[25] Resource: standard.no/en/sectors/energi-og-klima/petroleum/norsok-standard-categories/z-stand-cost-coding/z-0142/.
[26] Graphics are from the original version of the Standard Cost Coding System (05/92); graphics were eliminated in the newer versions as the coding structures have been updated and expanded.

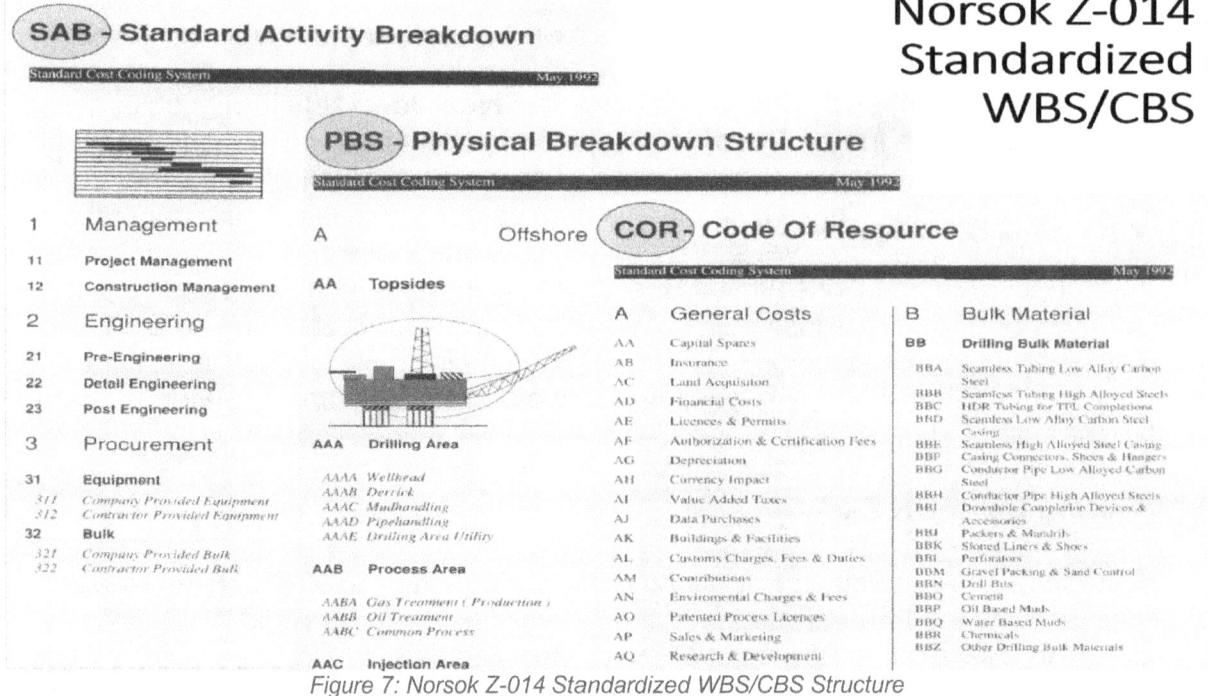

Figure 7: Norsok Z-014 Standardized WBS/CBS Structure

The Norwegian government expanded this to include a three-dimensional model specifically used for offshore and near-onshore oil and gas structures.[27]

1. Standard Activity Breakdown Structure (SAB)
2. Physical Breakdown Structure (PBS)
3. Code of Resource (COR)

Following the Norsok Z-014 approach, the Standard Activity Breakdown Structure (SAB) is roughly equivalent to MasterFormat or OmniClass Table 22, 'Work Results' or 'Deliverables.' Physical Breakdown Structure (PBS) is comparable to CSI's Uniformat or OmniClass Table 21, which represents the 'Component' or 'Element.' Code or Resource (COR) does not have a comparable CSI structure (CSI is only two dimensional, not three), but is the equivalent of the OmniClass Table 23, 'Products.'

Around 2000, CSI – in collaboration with ISO and the International Construction Information Society – produced OmniClass, which provided 15 different tables used to sort or to view the work or costs on projects. This book takes the multi-dimensional concept to the next level, demonstrating how to use multi-dimensional views to identify missing-scope elements, producing better CPM schedules, more accurate cost estimates, and eliminating (or at least mitigating) one of the leading causes of cost and time over-runs along with the ensuing claims.

Introducing OmniClass

---

[27] *Norsok Standard. SCCS. (2002) Retrieved from build-project-management-competency.com/wp-content/uploads/2009/12/Z-014-Norwegian-Standard-wbs-cbs.pdf*

The OmniClass Construction Classification System (known as either OmniClass or OCCS) originated around 2000[28] as a collaboration between the International Standards Organization (ISO), the Construction Specifications Institute (CSI), the Electronic Product Information Cooperation (EPIC), the International Construction Information Society (ICIS), and other trade-related organizations. "It incorporates other extant systems currently in use as the basis of many of its Tables – MasterFormat™ for work results, UniFormat for elements, and EPIC (Electronic Product Information Cooperation) for structuring products."[29] The OCCS is a means of organizing and retrieving information specifically designed for the construction industry. OmniClass is useful for applications in the area of Building Information Modeling (BIM), from organizing reports and object libraries to providing a way to roll up or drill down through data to get the information that meets your needs.[30] OmniClass draws from other extant systems in use to form the basis of its Tables wherever possible: MasterFormat™ for work results, UniFormat™ for elements, and Electronic Product Information Cooperation (EPIC) for products. OmniClass was designed to provide a standardized basis for classifying information created and used by the North American architectural, engineering and construction (AEC) industry, throughout the full-facility, life-cycle from conception to demolition (or reuse). OmniClass encompasses the different types of construction that make up the building environment. OmniClass is intended to be the means for organizing, sorting, and retrieving information as well as deriving relational computer applications.

OmniClass consists of 15 hierarchical tables, each of which represents a different facet of construction information. Each table can be used independently to classify a particular type of information, or entries on it can be combined with entries on other tables to classify more complex subjects. OmniClass provides a basic structure of information about construction grouped into three primary categories composing the process model: construction resources, construction processes, and construction results. These categories are then divided into 15 suggested Tables for organizing construction information. The OmniClass Tables correspond to this arrangement of information:"[31]

- Tables 11-22 to organize construction <u>results</u>
- Tables 23, 33, 34, and 35, and to a lesser extent 36 and 41, to organize construction <u>resources</u>, and
- Tables 31 and 32 to classify construction <u>processes</u>, including the phases of construction entity life cycles.

The framework for object-oriented information implements the basic approach of

---

[28] *Introduction - Pmworldlibrary.net. (n.d.). Retrieved from pmworldlibrary.net/wp-content/uploads/2018/04/pmwj69-Apr2018-Giammalvo-E*

[29] *Mapping ERP "Chart of Accounts" to Building Information ... (n.d.). Retrieved from pmworldjournal.net/article/mapping-erp-chart-of-accounts-to-building-inf*

[30] *About OmniClass. (n.d.). Retrieved from omniclass.org/about/*

[31] *Introduction - Pmworldlibrary.net. (n.d.). Retrieved from pmworldlibrary.net/wp-content/uploads/2018/04/pmwj69-Apr2018-Giammalvo-E*

ISO 12006-2 but uses table entries as defining points (or characteristics) for object-oriented information organization. The 'object-oriented' approach describes the characteristics of things without imparting a grouping preference or hierarchical order. In the object-oriented approach, the object is central, acting as a basis for characteristics or properties that describe that object. An object thus described can then be grouped with similar objects using a classification arrangement like OmniClass.

The framework established by ISO/PAS 12006-3 enables computers to store and relate data in an object-oriented manner. The foreword to ISO/PAS 12006-3 indicates, "… while ISO 12006-2 is a standard that reflects many years of refinement of classification systems, ISO/PAS 12006-3 represents not so much new thinking, but a new implementation of established information modeling practice using a new ISO process which aims to bring new work of this kind into use as quickly as possible."[32] OmniClass Tables provide users with a variety of viewpoints of that data and is a useful approach to establishing relationships between objects.[33]

The 15 inter-related OmniClass tables are:

15 OmniClass Tables with Definitions		
Table 11	Construction Entities by Function	Construction Entities by Function are significant, definable units of the built environment comprised of elements and inter-related spaces and characterized by function.
Table 12	Construction Entities by Form	Construction Entities by Form are significant, definable units of the built environment comprised of elements and inter-related spaces and characterized by form.
Table 13	Spaces by Function	Spaces by Function are basic units of the built environment delineated by physical or abstract boundaries and characterized by function.
Table 14	Spaces by Form	Spaces by Form are basic units of the built environment delineated by physical or abstract boundaries and characterized by physical form.
Table 21	Elements (includes Designed Elements)	An Element is a major component, assembly, or "construction entity part which, in itself or combined with other parts, fulfills a pre-dominating function of the construction entity" (ISO 12006-2). Predominating functions include, but are not limited to, supporting, enclosing, servicing, and equipping a facility.

---

[32] Introduction and User's Guide - OmniClass. (n.d.). Retrieved from omniclass.org/tables/OmniClass_Main_Intro_2006-03-28.pdf
[33] Introduction and User's Guide - OmniClass. (n.d.). Retrieved from OmniClass.org/about.asp

15 OmniClass Tables with Definitions

		Functional descriptions can also include a processor activity. A Designed Element is an "Element for which the work result(s) have been defined." (ISO 12006-2). This Table is the OCCS version of Uniformat.
Table 22	Work Results	Work Results are construction results achieved in the production stage or phase or by subsequent alteration, maintenance, or demolition processes and identified by one or more of the following: the particular skill or trade involved; the construction resources used; the part of the construction entity which results; the temporary work or other preparatory or completion of work which is the result. This table is the OmniClass version of MasterFormat.
Table 23	Products	Products are components or assemblies of components for permanent incorporation into construction entities.
Table 31	Phases	Life cycle phases are often represented by two terms used somewhat interchangeably in our industry. For clarity and standardization, OmniClass defines these terms: Stage: A categorization of the principal segments of a project. Stages usually are Conception, Project Delivery Selection, Design, Construction Documents, Procurement, Execution, Utilization, and Closure. Phase: A portion of work that arises from sequencing work by a predetermined portion of a Stage. For purposes of usage in OmniClass classifications, a Stage is a higher-level of categorization, and a Phase is a subordinate level of titling within a Stage.
Table 32	Services	Services are the activities, processes, and procedures relating to the design, construction, maintenance, renovation, demolition, commissioning, decommissioning, and all other functions occurring about the life cycle of a construction entity.
Table 33	Disciplines	Disciplines are the practice areas and specialties of the actors (participants) that carry out the processes and procedures that occur during the life cycle of a construction entity.
Table 34	Organizational Roles	Organizational Roles are the functional positions occupied by the participants, both individuals, and groups that carry out the processes and procedures which occur during the life cycle of a construction entity. Table 34 can be combined with Table 33 – Disciplines, to provide a full classification of each participant

		15 OmniClass Tables with Definitions
		in the creation and support of a facility.
Table 35	Tools	Tools are the resources used to develop the design and construction of a project that does not become a permanent part of the facility, including computer systems, vehicles, scaffolding and all other items needed to execute the processes and procedures relating to the life cycle of a construction entity.
Table 36	Information	Information is data referenced and utilized during the process of creating and sustaining the built environment.
Table 41	Materials	Materials are substances used in construction or to manufacture products and other items used in construction. These substances may be raw materials or refined compounds and are considered subjects of this table irrespective of form.
Table 49	Properties	Properties are measurable or definable characteristics of construction entities.

Figure 8: OmniClass Tables 2017

OmniClass was designed to be a standard for organizing all construction information.[34] The concept for OmniClass was derived from internationally accepted standards developed by the International Organization for Standardization (ISO) and the International Construction Information Society (ICIS) sub-committees and work groups from the early-1990s to the present. ISO Technical Committee 59, Sub-committee 13, Working Group 2 (TC59/SC13/WG2) drafted a standard for a classification framework (ISO 12006-2; more information below) based on traditional classification but also recognized an alternative 'object-oriented' approach, which was to be explored further.[35]

The ISO workgroup, TC59/SC13/WG6, developed an electronic framework (ISO/PAS 12006-3; more information below) for tagging and managing of objects and their attributes. These standards, ISO 12006-2: Organization of Information about Construction Works - Part 2: Framework for Classification of Information, and ISO/PAS (Publicly Available Specification) 12006-3: Organization of Information about Construction Works - Part 3: Framework for Object-oriented Information, define methods of organizing the information associated with construction and affiliated

---

[34] *Introduction and User's Guide - OmniClass. (n.d.). Retrieved from omniclass.org/tables/OmniClass_Main_Intro_2006-03-28.pdf*
[35] *Introduction and User's Guide - OmniClass. (n.d.). Retrieved from omniclass.org/tables/OmniClass_Main_Intro_2006-03-28.pdf*

industries. The standards also promote a standard object-modeling definition for addressed concepts. Of these two standards, ISO 12006-2 has a more immediate impact on OmniClass. "The OCCS Development Committee has closely adhered to this standard in establishing and defining the tables that makeup OmniClass."[36]

The Construction Industry Project Information Committee (CPIC) of the UK, formed to create UniClass, has successfully used this standard by publishing a usable version of UniClass in 1997. United Kingdom authors will likely assess OmniClass as they update the publication. In addition to the application of ISO 12006-2 in UniClass, the object-oriented framework standardized by ISO/PAS 12006-3 has been adopted by ICIS members in their Lexicon program. Both standards are followed by groups in several other countries developing similar classification standards, including Norway, Netherlands, and the UK, "in concert with the Nordic chapter of the International Alliance for Interoperability (IAI) and the Japan Construction Information Center (JACIC), currently working to develop the Japan Construction Classification System (JCCS)," modeled in part on OmniClass.[37]

The OmniClass Construction Classification System (OCCS) Development Committee believes following ISO standards will promote the ability to map between localized classifications systems developed worldwide. It is the Committee's hope organizations in other countries will pursue initiatives similar to OmniClass and also strive to be ISO-compatible, thereby enabling the smoother exchange of data "between them. As stated by ISO in the text of ISO 12006-2,

Provided that each country uses this framework of tables and follows the definitions given in this standard, it will be possible for standardization to develop table by table in a flexible way. For example, Country A and Country B could have a common classification table of, e.g., elements, but different classification tables for work results without experiencing difficulties of 'fit' at the juncture.[38]

Why are Multi-Dimensional Project Coding Structures Important?

To be able to create relational or object-oriented databases, each object (row) needs to have one or more coding structures (fields) that enable the objects to be filtered, sorted and viewed by one or more of these codes. These are the three

---

[36] *Introduction and User's Guide - OmniClass. (n.d.). Retrieved from omniclass.org/tables/OmniClass_Main_Intro_2006-03-28.pdf*
[37] *Introduction and User's Guide - OmniClass. (n.d.). Retrieved from omniclass.org/tables/OmniClass_Main_Intro_2006-03-28.pdf*
[38] *Introduction and User's Guide - OmniClass. (n.d.). Retrieved from omniclass.org/tables/OmniClass_Main_Intro_2006-03-28.pdf*

concepts or models being introduced and advocated in this paper: a three-dimensional model (used for most of the examples), an eight-dimensional model based on theoretical physics research, and a 15-dimensional model, developed by OmniClass. While one can apply the three-dimensional model using all three coding structures, one can look at three coding structures at any time. To see multiple dimensions, users will need a Virtual Reality software that can produce a Tesseract Model from the data.

The Multi-Dimensional Work Breakdown Structure Method

There are many hierarchical structures:

- LBS (Location Breakdown Structure)
- PBS (Product Breakdown Structure)
- FBS (Functional Breakdown Structure) – can also be designated as SBS (System Breakdown Structure)
- ABS (Activity Breakdown Structure)
- OBS (Organization Breakdown Structure)
- CBS (Cost Breakdown Structure)
- RBS (Resources Breakdown Structure)
- CWBS (Contract Work Breakdown Structure)

The question is: how all these tree structures are mixed?

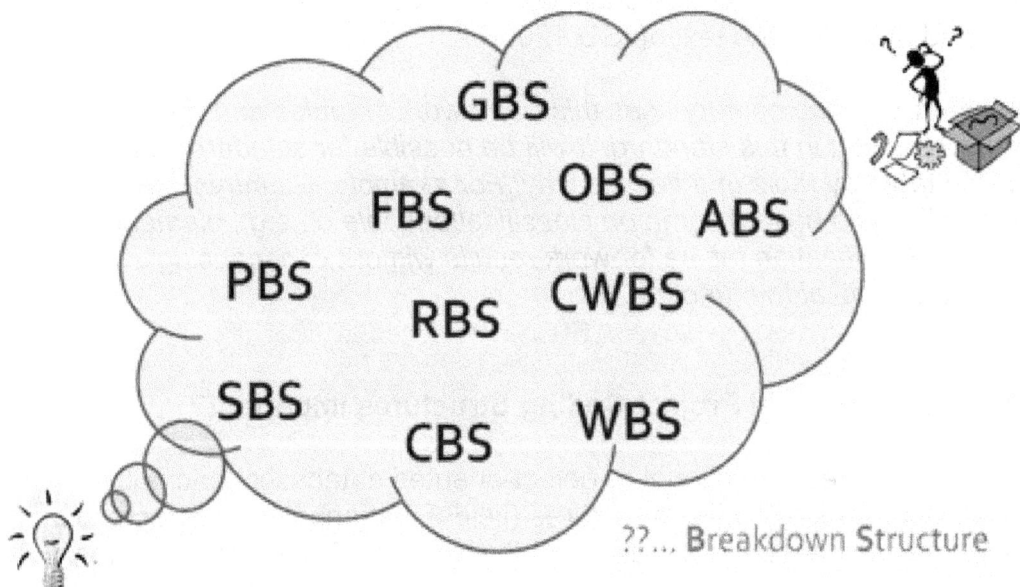

Figure 9: Tree structure without logical Structure

The goal of project management is to give answers to questions mentioned in the functional octopus below. It is a functional analysis of project management needs.

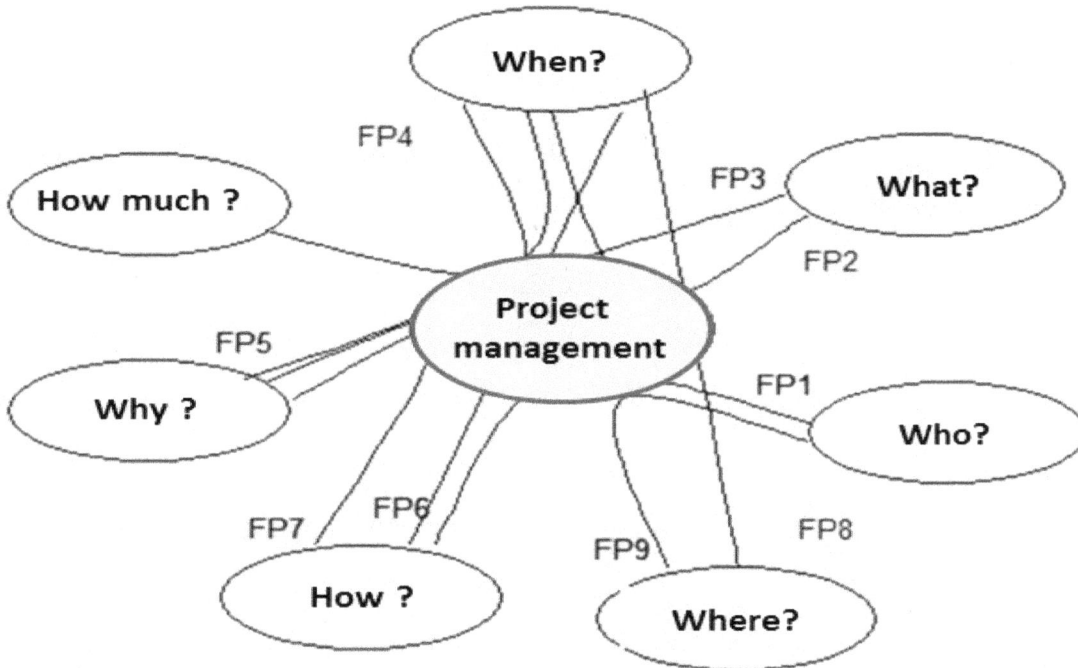

Figure 10: Project Management Octopus (Management Mapping)

For instance: Who does what? How much is the cost of what? Where is done what? It seems all the tree structures that compose the Project must answer to one question. The question is, "Do the combined breakdown structures define exactly 100% of the project with nothing missing and nothing additional or extra?" The Unfolded Tesseract is used as an example in this case.

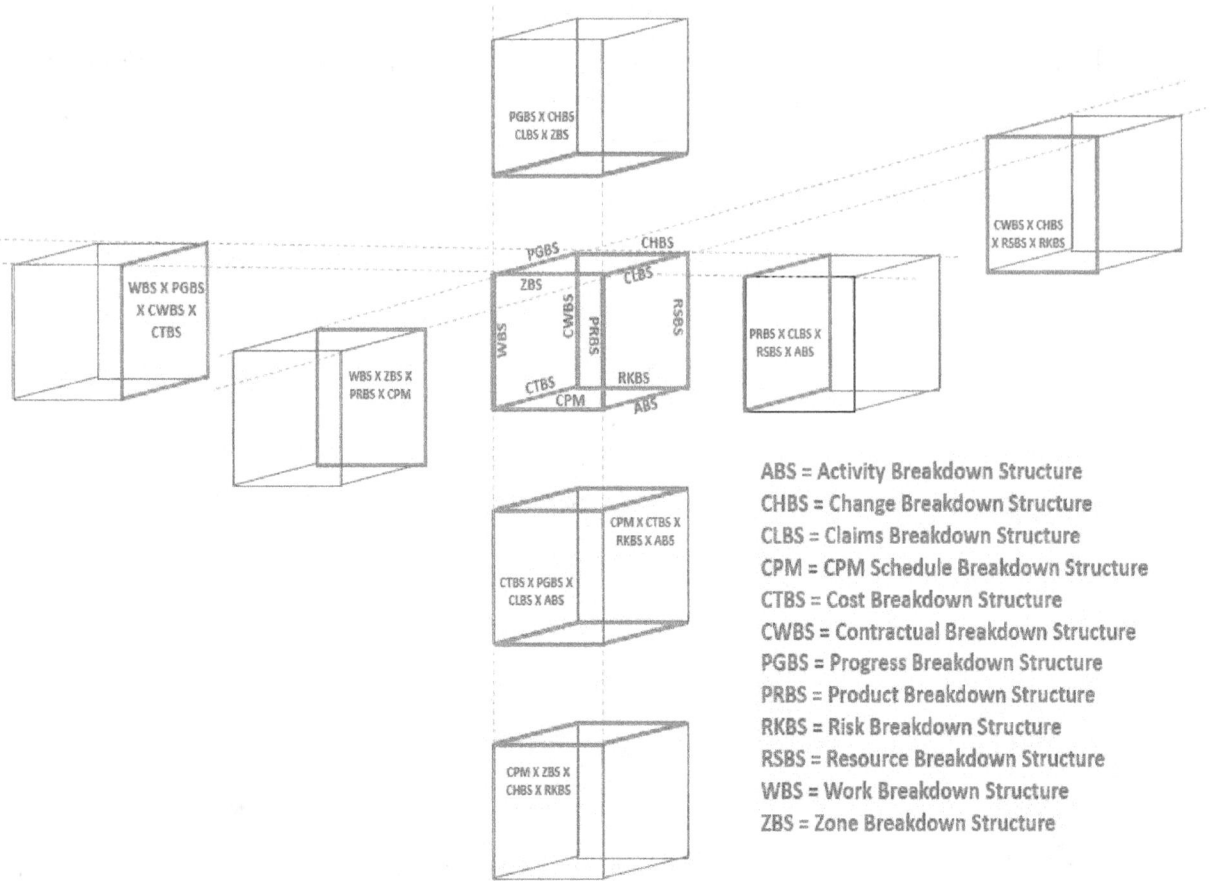

ABS = Activity Breakdown Structure
CHBS = Change Breakdown Structure
CLBS = Claims Breakdown Structure
CPM = CPM Schedule Breakdown Structure
CTBS = Cost Breakdown Structure
CWBS = Contractual Breakdown Structure
PGBS = Progress Breakdown Structure
PRBS = Product Breakdown Structure
RKBS = Risk Breakdown Structure
RSBS = Resource Breakdown Structure
WBS = Work Breakdown Structure
ZBS = Zone Breakdown Structure

Figure 11: Unfolded Tesseract showing the various Breakdown Structures

There are many Documents produced in support of any project. For this example, the list of documents was taken from PMI's PMBOK Guide, 6th Edition, Figure 4.1 Table of Documents, page 86.

Project Management Plan	Project Documents	
1. Scope management plan	1. Activity attributes	19. Quality control measurements
2. Requirements management plan	2. Activity List	20. Quality metrics
3. Schedule management plan	3. Assumption Log	21. Quality report
4. Cost management plan	4. Basis of Estimates	22. Requirements

Project Management Plan	Project Documents	
		documentation
5. Quality management plan	5. Change log	23. Requirements traceability matrix
6. Resource management plan	6. Cost estimation	24. Resource breakdown structure
7. Communications management plan	7. Cost forecasts	25. Resource calendars
8. Risk	8. Duration estimates	26. Resource requirements
9. Procurement management plan	9. Issue log	27. Risk register
10. Stakeholder management plan	10. Lessons learned register	28. Risk report
11. Change management plan	11. Milestones list	29. Schedule data
12. Configuration management plan	12. Physical resource assignments	30. Schedule forecasts
13. Scope baseline	13. Project calendars	31. Stakeholder register
14. Cost baseline	14. Project communications	32. Team charter
15. Performance measurement baseline	15. Project schedule	33. Test and evaluation documents
16. Project life-cycle measurement baseline	16. Project schedule network diagram	
17. Project life-cycle description	17. Project scope statement	
18. Development approach	18. Project team assignments	

Figure 12 - List of Project Documents

To validate the unfolded tesseract model, shown in Figure 11 (Tesseract), the test was whether or not the combinations and permutations of the Breakdown Structures illustrated above produced the required documents. If the answer is yes, the model is a valid construct. If the answer is no, the model is missing one or more potential breakdown structures or some combination or permutation other than those shown.

HOW MUCH?
-Basis of Estimate
-Cost Estimate
-Cost Forecasts
-Risk Registers/Updates

WHY?
-Business Case
-Assumptions

WHERE?
-Contract Documents
-Plans & Specifications

WHAT?
-Scope Statement
-WBS

FOR WHAT?
-Stakeholder Register
-Stakeholder Analysis

WHEN?
-CPM Schedule
-Milestone List
-Duration Estimates
-Calendars
-Schedule Forecasts
-Risk Registers/Updates

HOW?
-Activity Lists
-Activity Attributes
-Resource requirements
-   Resource Assignments
-Quality Metrics

WHO?
-Team Assignments
-Team Charter
-Team Evaluations
-Control Accounts

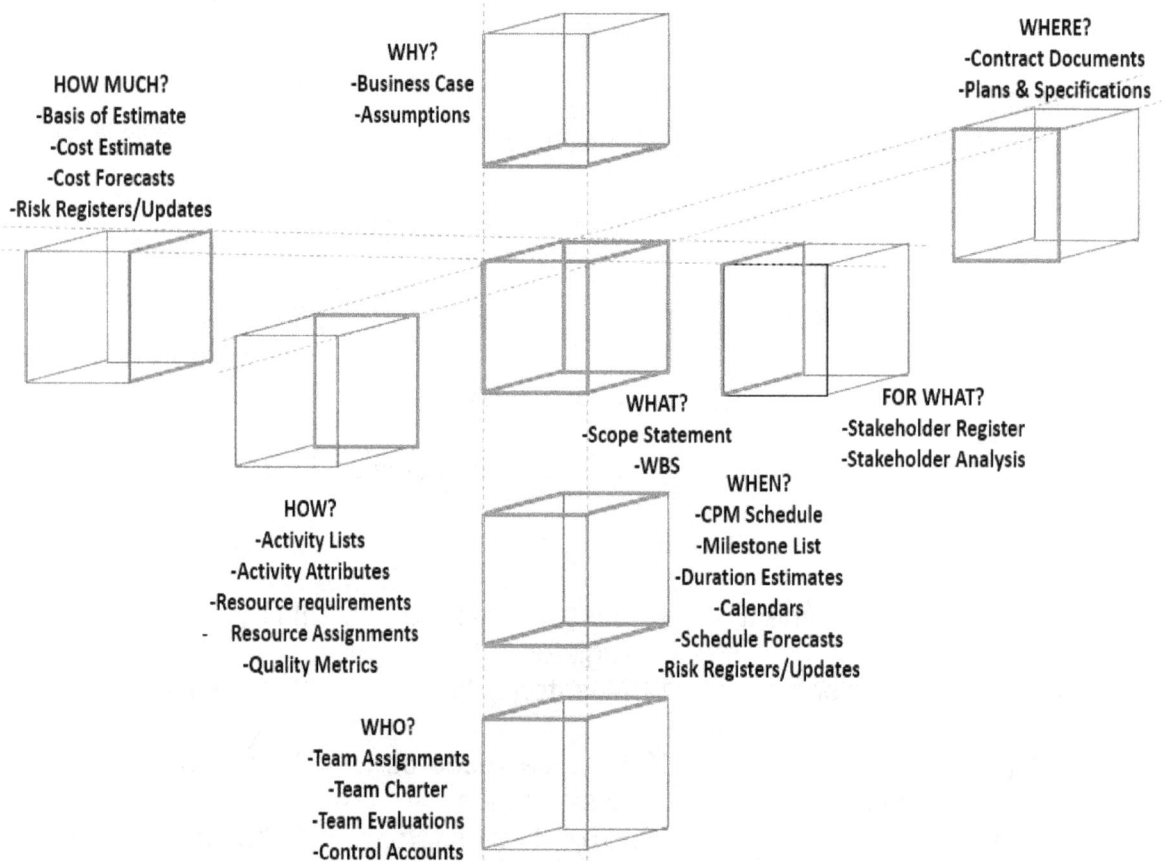

Figure 13: Mapping Typical Project Documentation to the Breakdown Structures

The Work Breakdown Structure

Three-Dimensional Work Breakdown Structure Definition

The 3-D WBS method (3-D) has its definition of the WBS that is quite different from the usual definitions. It is a hierarchical tree structure of Work; it means "the whole of work to be carried out within the framework of a project,"[39] but in the 3-D WBS method, the last levels of the WBS are the Tasks included in the WBS. The 3-D WBS crosses between the three-tree Structures (primary structures): Locations, Products, and Activities.

---

[39] *Cubix Project Management - 3-D Work Breakdown Structure Method. (n.d.). Retrieved from breakdown233.rssing.com/chan-12384124/all_p1.html*

One can write: 3-D WBS = LBS x PBS x ABS with:

- Product Breakdown Structure (PBS) axis is composed of:
    o Functional Breakdown Structure (FBS): working units, process units) Note: the FBS can also be called System Breakdown Structure (SBS).
    o PBS can be ("pure" Products: equipment, materials, civil work components, deliverables)
- ABS (Activity Breakdown Structure) axis that is composed at least of:
    o Phases,
    o Actions
    o Disciplines.
- LBS (Location Breakdown Structure) axis that is composed of:
    o Physical locations,
    o Virtual locations.

The above formula means a scheduled task, or one part of the WBS, is a summation of the LBS (Location Breakdown Structure); PBS, (Product Breakdown Structure) and the ABS, (Activity Breakdown Structure). Each elementary tree-structure (LBS, PBS, ABS) also has some Primary structures, for instance, Physical and Virtual location for the LBS. Remember that a Product belongs to a Location.

The PBS has a characteristic; which means it can be instantiated (an occurrence of a concrete instance). An instantiated product is the prolongation of a generic Product – the clone of a generic Product – because the activities necessary to carry out instantiated products are the same as those of the generic Product from which they arise. For example, if a project integrates a product viaduct, and in the project, there are three viaducts, one can identify the Viaduct product in three instantiated products: viaduct #1, viaduct #2, and viaduct #3. The activities necessary to carry out each one of these viaducts are the same since they are identical viaducts.

The Work Breakdown Structure (WBS) Cube

The following figures show a primary tree structure projected on one axis.

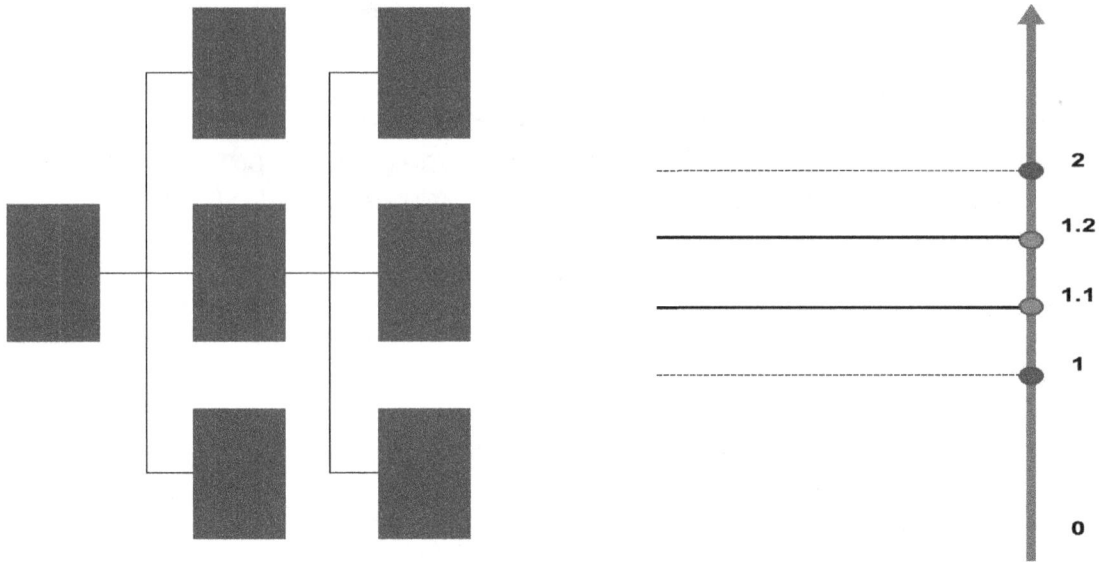

Figure 14: Tree structure projected on one axis

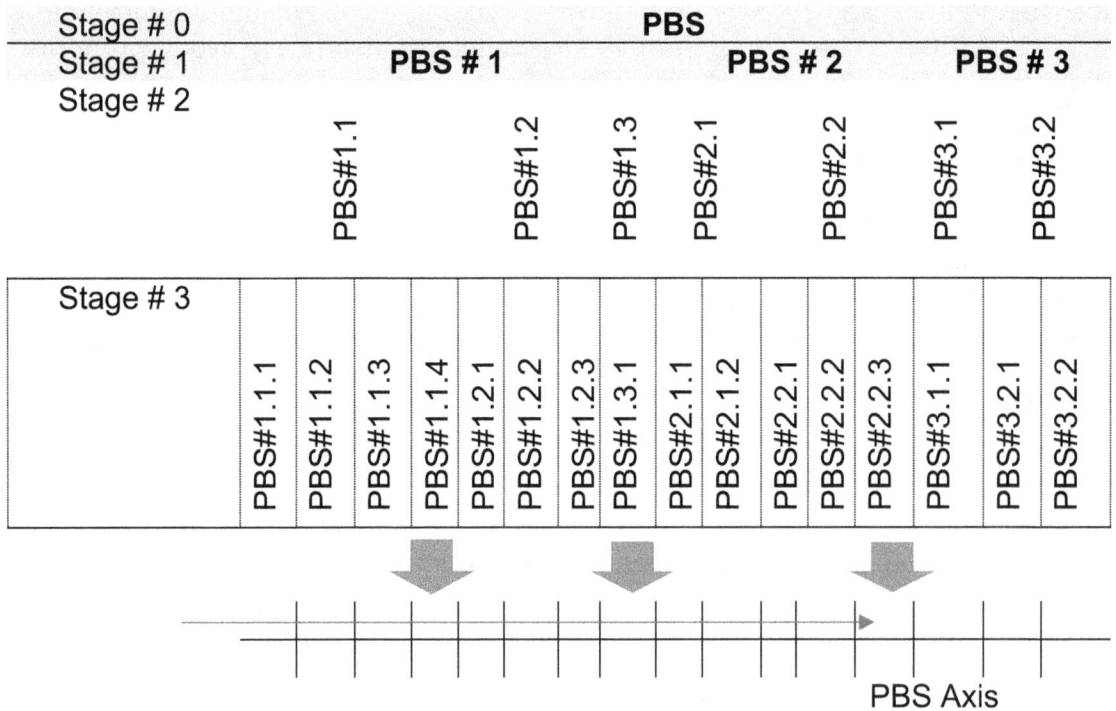

Stage # 0	PBS							
Stage # 1	PBS # 1			PBS # 2			PBS # 3	
Stage # 2	PBS#1.1	PBS#1.2	PBS#1.3	PBS#2.1	PBS#2.2		PBS#3.1	PBS#3.2

Stage # 3															
	PBS#1.1.1	PBS#1.1.2	PBS#1.1.3	PBS#1.1.4	PBS#1.2.1	PBS#1.2.2	PBS#1.2.3	PBS#1.3.1	PBS#2.1.1	PBS#2.1.2	PBS#2.2.1	PBS#2.2.2	PBS#2.2.3	PBS#3.1.1	PBS#3.2.1	PBS#3.2.2

PBS Axis

Figure 15: One-Axis PBS Sample

Note that tree structures are detailed in chronological order (following planning logic). If two tree structures are projected, one obtains a square including little squares inside the overall square. If we project three tree structures, one obtains one cube, including little 3-D cubes inside the overall cube. There is a chronology in this projection. There are three tree structures composing the WBS. Thus, there are three Axis, and in the space, it forms one cube: the WBS cube.

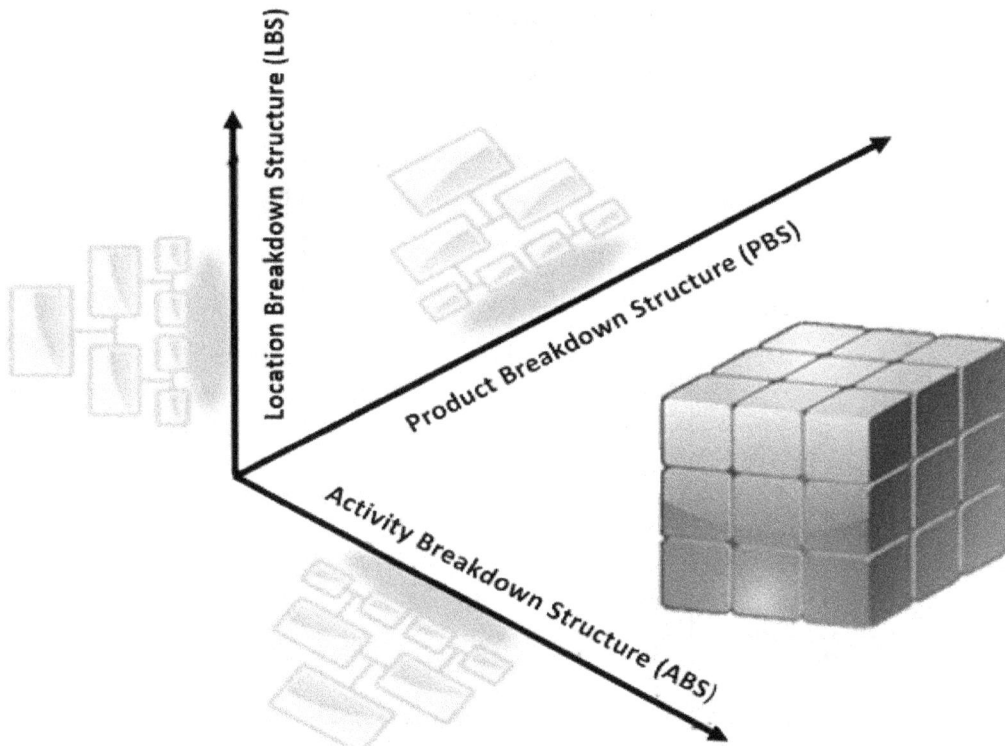

Figure 16: The WBS cube

Another view of the WBS cube is shown as follows.

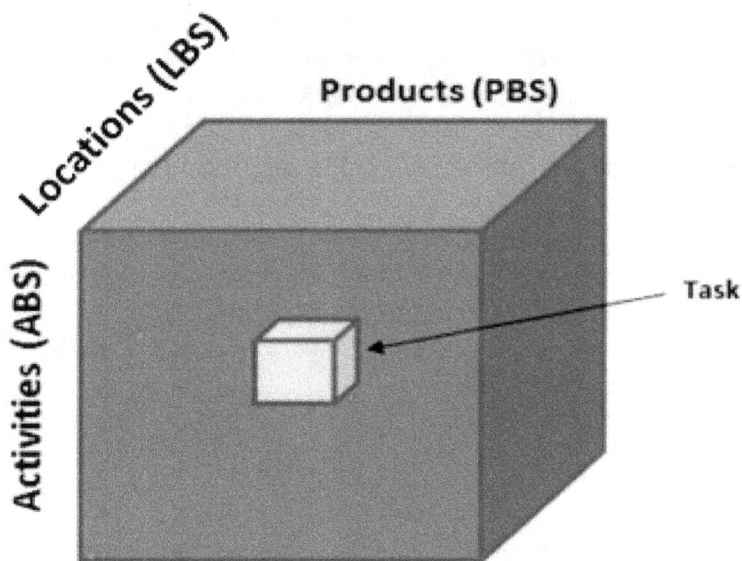

Figure 17: The tasks in the WBS cube

A classical view of the 3-D WBS is shown below:

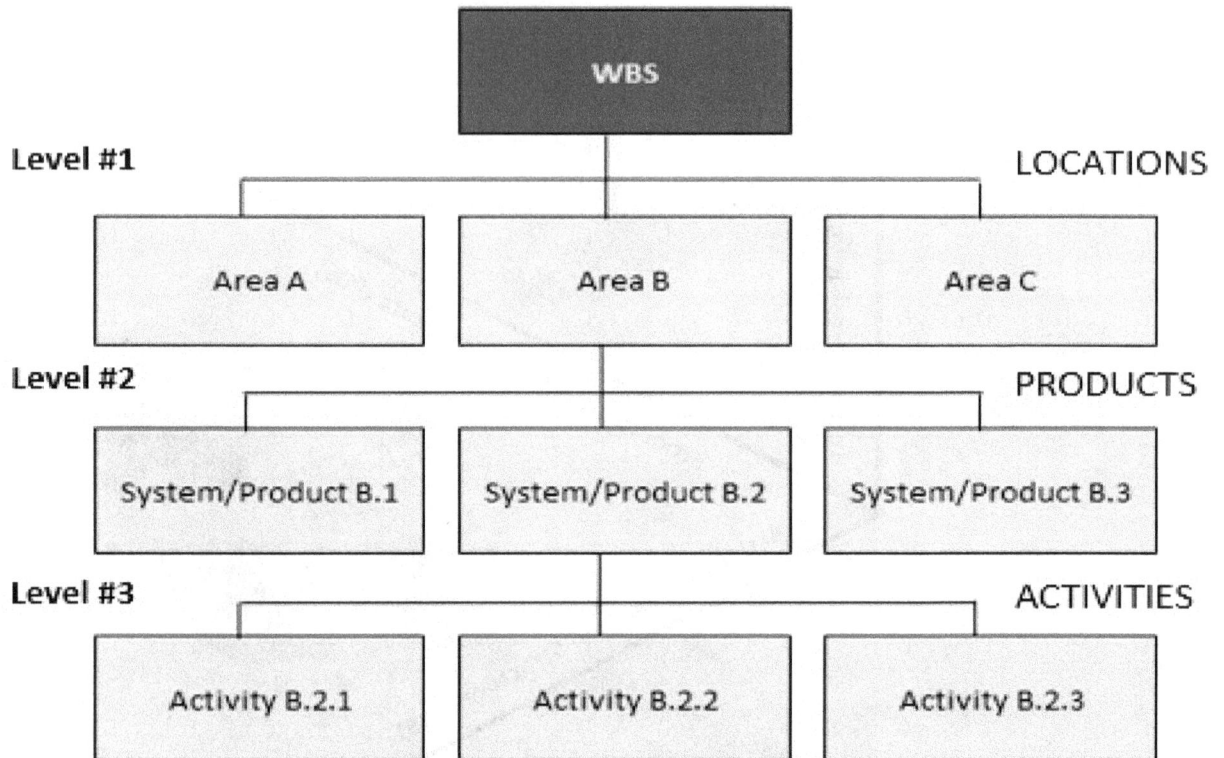

Figure 18: Another view of the 3-D WBS

A WBS can be read in standardized English: "in all projects, in the construction phase, for instance, Products (PBS) are constructed/installed (ABS) somewhere (LBS). It forms the WBS."[40] Because we are working with a relational database rather than a flat-file database, the WBS levels can be reversed. For instance, at the first level, the Locations are illustrated; at the second level, one can see Products; and at the third (last) levels, one can see Activities. Alternatively, one can have the same result with Activities at first level, Products at the second level, and Locations at the last level.

The Task is not the Activity; a task is a concatenation between one Activity, one Product, and one Location, whereas an Activity is a part of one task, it is an action. "There are three dimensions to describe a WBS and tasks. For instance: Location A-Track-Installation is a task, and Installation is an action."[41]

---

[40] Work Breakdown Structure for Tangible Drilling Cost In ... (n.d.). Retrieved from pmworldlibrary.net/wp-content/uploads/2014/12/pmwj29-dec2014-Wibowo-WBS-T

[41] Work Breakdown Structure for Tangible Drilling Cost In ... (n.d.). Retrieved from pmworldlibrary.net/wp-content/uploads/2014/12/pmwj29-dec2014-Wibowo-WBS-T

The Work Breakdown Structure (WBS) Matrix

The schedule's tasks are described in the WBS matrix, developed by the authors. The list of tasks provided by an algorithm extracts the tasks from the WBS cube, and the WBS matrix is this algorithm. A simplified version of the WBS matrix is shown below.

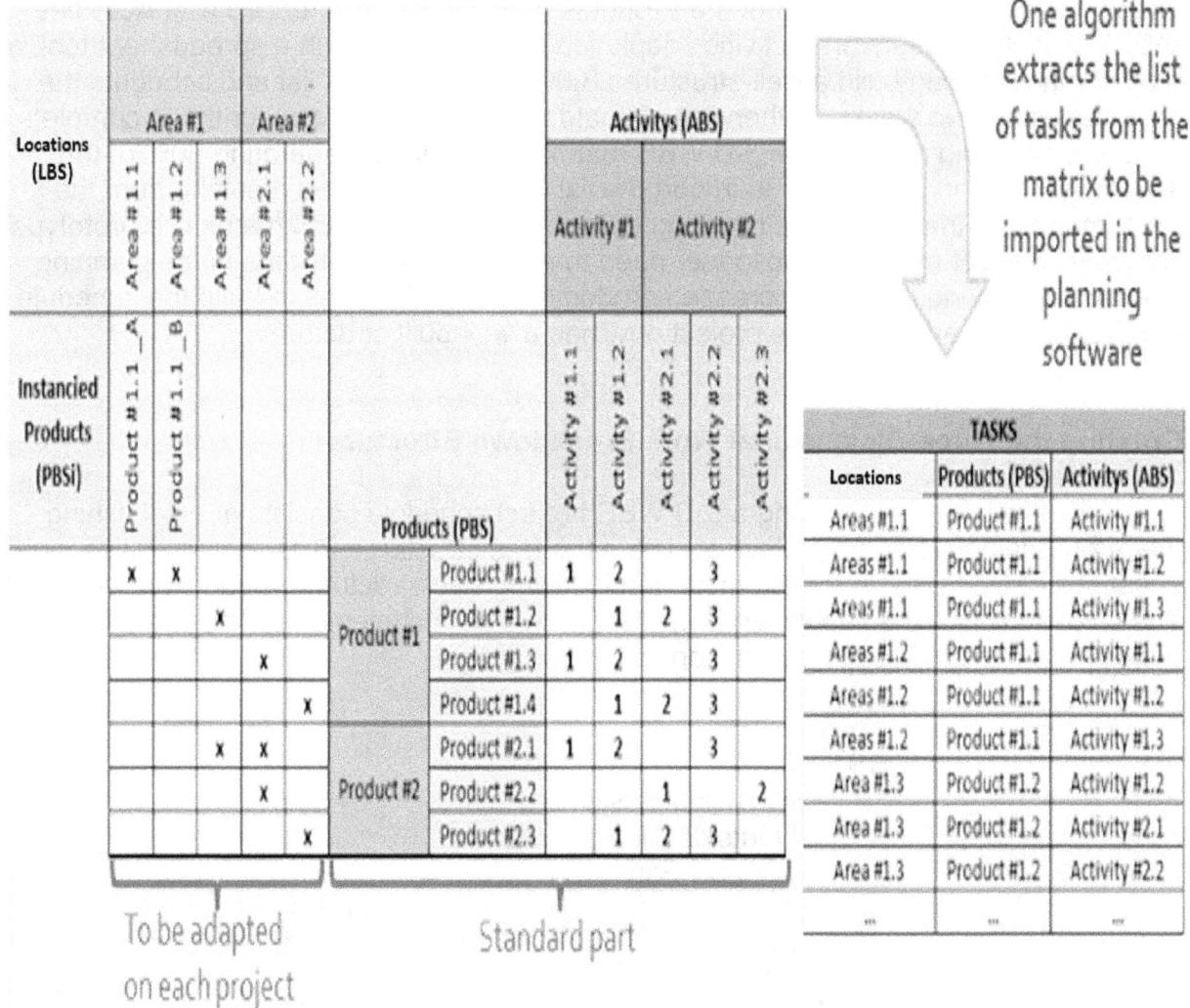

One algorithm extracts the list of tasks from the matrix to be imported in the planning software

TASKS		
Locations	Products (PBS)	Activitys (ABS)
Areas #1.1	Product #1.1	Activity #1.1
Areas #1.1	Product #1.1	Activity #1.2
Areas #1.1	Product #1.1	Activity #1.3
Areas #1.2	Product #1.1	Activity #1.1
Areas #1.2	Product #1.1	Activity #1.2
Areas #1.2	Product #1.1	Activity #1.3
Area #1.3	Product #1.2	Activity #1.2
Area #1.3	Product #1.2	Activity #2.1
Area #1.3	Product #1.2	Activity #2.2
...	...	...

To be adapted on each project / Standard part

Figure 19: The WBS matrix

Activities (ABS) are deployed on Products (PBS), and Products are assigned in a Location (LBS). Products are instantiated (similar to cloning) before being assigned somewhere (LBS); they are instantiated to become unique, with a specific name. An instantiated Product is the same than the generic Products regarding planning, and is the same as the Activities used to produce it, but are assigned in another Location.[42] This WBS matrix can be completed within a Microsoft Excel spreadsheet program; by adding an algorithm in Visual BASIC for Applications (VBA), the spreadsheet extracts the tasks from the WBS matrix by analyzing the correspondences, with all the necessary attribute codes (Contracts, Disciplines, LBS, PBS, ABS levels #1, 2, and 3), and duration.

Activities are scheduled because there are 'order numbers' in the WBS matrix. These numbers are on the row of the Products (PBS), cross-referenced with Activities (ABS). The successors are Activities deployed on Products. With a spreadsheet tool, a project manager can build a well-structured 3,000 (or more) task list and schedule the calendar within two weeks. Otherwise, it could take as long as two months to complete the same planning matrix. The 3-D WBS matrix is capable of generating 80% of the schedule. The principal task is to import the list of tasks scheduled resulting from the WBS matrix treatment, into the planning software.[43] The 3-D WBS matrix is a prototype software. Project managers no longer need to methodically enter data in the planning software. The benefits result increased productivity up to 10 times to build the schedule. Another positive attribute is the project now has a well-built structure.

Creating the Three-Dimensional Work Breakdown Structure

The first stage of building a 3-D WBS project schedule consists of establishing the reference points of the project; to define the tree structures Products, Activities, and Locations of the WBS. In the example, the following tree structure products are defined. The instantiation of the supply fan is present in two distinct elements. These elements prolong the generic product supply fan.

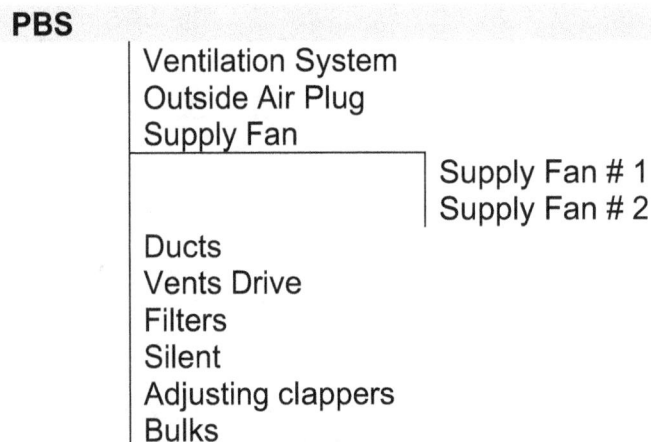

PBS

Ventilation System
Outside Air Plug
Supply Fan

Supply Fan # 1
Supply Fan # 2

Ducts
Vents Drive
Filters
Silent
Adjusting clappers
Bulks

Figure 20: Products

---

[42] *3-D Work Breakdown Structure Method - PM World Library. (n.d.). Retrieved from pmworldlibrary.net/wp-content/uploads/2013/04/pmwj9-apr2013-Moine-3-D-Work*
[43] *3-D Work Breakdown Structure Method - PM World Library. (n.d.). Retrieved from pmworldlibrary.net/wp-content/uploads/2013/04/pmwj9-apr2013-Moine-3-D-Work*

The second tree structure to be created is one of the activities (illustrated below).

ABS

| Basic Design
| Detail Design
| Consultations
| Purchase Order
| Supply
| Installation
| Equipment Tests
| System Tests

Figure 21: Activities Tree Structure Example

The last WBS tree structure, the Locations to be defined, is illustrated below. Note the Location ventilation is a virtual location, whereas other Locations are geographical.

LBS

| Ventilation
| Area # 1
| Area # 2
| Area # 3

Figure 22: Activities Tree Structure Example

The WBS matrix of 3-D WBS method makes it possible to generate a schedule by using the lower levels of the elementary tree structures Activities, Products, and Locations. It is often necessary to define two tree structures for each one of these three elementary tree structures: 1) a physical tree structure, and 2) a virtual tree structure, as well for the Activities, the Products, and the Locations.

The elementary tree structures are composed of the project definition; the task remains to cross them (intersect) within the WBS matrix. The first stage of the phase of the structuring of the project consists of intersecting the Products and the Activities. One will deploy Activities on each Product to completion. This is illustrated in the following figure. For the ventilator, there must be consultations, placement of an order, supply (vendor delivery), installation, and finally, testing. To deploy an Activity on a Product, it is enough to put an 'X' in the matrix below.

PBS	Basic Design	Detail Design	Consultations	Purchase Order	Supply	Installation	Equipment Tests	System Tests (ABS)
Ventilation System	X	X						X
Outside Air Plug			X	X	X	X	X	
Supply Fan			X	X	X	X	X	
Ducts			X	X	X	X	X	
Vents Drive			X	X	X	X	X	
Filters			X	X	X	X	X	
Silent			X	X	X	X	X	
Adjusting Clappers			X	X	X	X	X	
Bulks			X	X	X	X	X	

Figure 23: Example of Crossed Off Activity Matrix Indicating Completion on a Product

Crossing out the matrix listed tasks results in a list of the following tasks. These tasks are grouped by Products.

Ventilation System

Ventilation System - Basic Design
Ventilation System - Detail Design
Ventilation System - System Tests

Outside Air Plug

Outside Air Plug - Consultation
Outside Air Plug – Purchase Order
Outside Air Plug – Supply
Outside Air Plug – Installation
Outside Air Plug – Equipment Tests

Supply Fan

Supply Fan - Consultation
Supply Fan – Purchase Order
Supply Fan – Supply
Supply Fan – Installation
Supply Fan – Equipment Tests

Ducts

...

Vents Drive

...

Filters

...

Ventilation System

Silent

Adjusting Clappers

Bulks

...

...

...

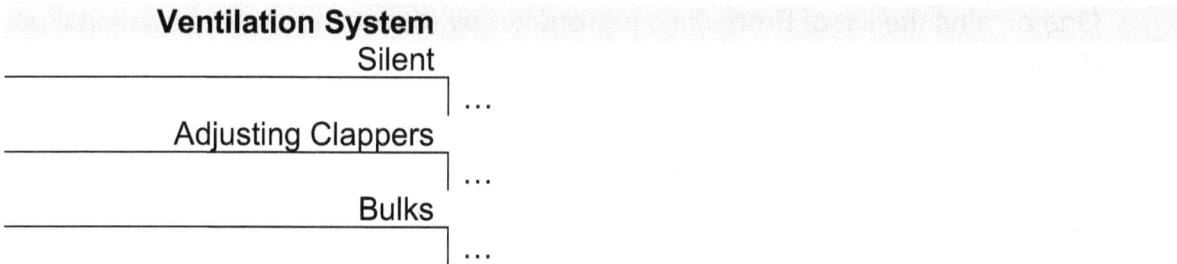

Figure 24: Checked Off Tasks Within Products List Groupings Example

The second stage of the phase of structuring and the development of the WBS consists in crossing the Products and the Locations. Assign the Products to Location. Consider a Location as a group of Products. With this intention, add X's in the matrix to define the assignments; only reason on the lower levels of the tree structures. The generic product supply fan cannot be affected at a Location, whereas its instantiated products could be affected since they are located at the lower level of the Product Breakdown Structure.

There are two tree structures products: 1) a virtual tree structure and 2) a physical tree structure. The Product ventilation system is a virtual element, whereas all the other Products are equipment, which is a physical element.

LBS

PBS	Ventilation	Area # 1	Area # 2	Area # 3
Ventilation System	X			
Outside Air Plug		X	X	X
Supply Fan				
Supply Fan # 1		X		
Supply Fan # 2		X		
Ducts		X		
Vents Drive		X		
Filters		X		
Silent		X		
Adjusting Clappers		X		
Bulks		X	X	X

Figure 25: Assignment of the Products to the Locations

One obtains the list of Products congregated by (associated with) Locations, as demonstrated below:

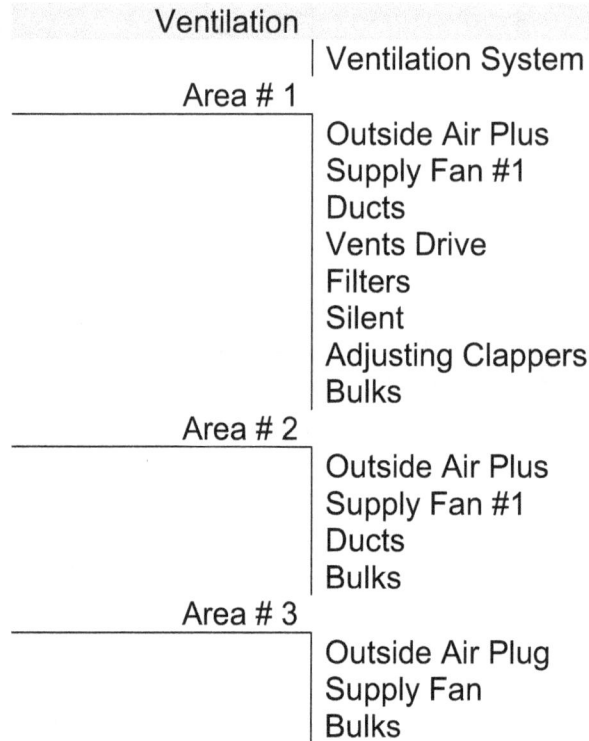

Ventilation
| Ventilation System
Area # 1
| Outside Air Plus
| Supply Fan #1
| Ducts
| Vents Drive
| Filters
| Silent
| Adjusting Clappers
| Bulks
Area # 2
| Outside Air Plus
| Supply Fan #1
| Ducts
| Bulks
Area # 3
| Outside Air Plug
| Supply Fan
| Bulks

Figure 26: List of Products Congregated by Zones

At this stage, the structuring of the WBS is finished. The analysis of the preceding matrices makes it possible to spearhead a list of structured tasks. Note the wording of the tasks is explicit: Location, Product, and Activity. Tasks are grouped by Locations and Products. This tree structure is in the classical sense of the term called WBS (hierarchical tree structure). This WBS extends until the lower level tasks of the schedule are completed in the WBS 3-D method). The Activities, Products, and Locations are also task dimensions; these last elements are integral parts of the definition of the tasks.

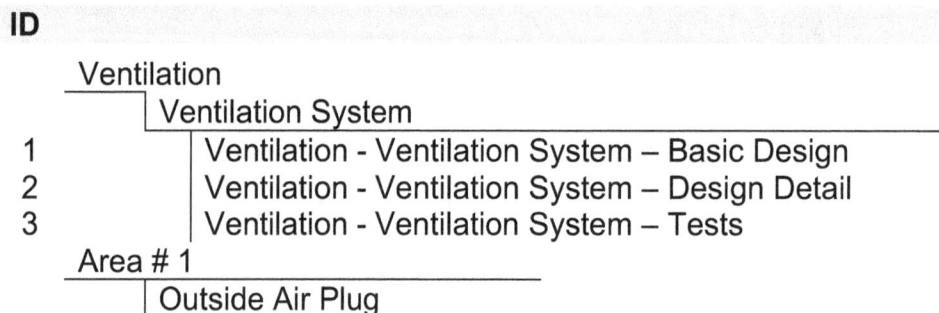

ID

Ventilation
| Ventilation System
| 1 | Ventilation - Ventilation System – Basic Design
| 2 | Ventilation - Ventilation System – Design Detail
| 3 | Ventilation - Ventilation System – Tests
Area # 1
| Outside Air Plug

ID			
	Ventilation		
		Ventilation System	
4			Area # 1 – Outside Air Plug – Consultation
5			Area # 1 – Outside Air Plug – Purchase Order
6			Area # 1 – Outside Air Plug – Supply
7			Area # 1 – Outside Air Plug – Installation
8			Area # 1 – Outside Air Plug – Equipment Tests
		Supply Fan	
9			Area # 1 – Supply Fan – Consultation
10			Area # 1 – Supply Fan – Purchase Order
11			Area # 1 – Supply Fan – Supply
12			Area # 1 – Supply Fan – Installation
13			Area # 1 – Supply Fan – Equipment Tests
		Ducts	
14			…
		Vents Drive	
		Filters	
		Silent	
		Adjusting Clappers	
		Bulks	
	Area # 2		
		Outside air plus	
		Supply Fan # 2	
		Ducts	
		Bulks	
	Area # 3		
		Outside air plus	
		Supply Fan # 2	
		Bulks	

Figure 27: The WBS or list of tasks structured

Primary Benefits and Ideas – Exhaustivity and Coherence

The reasoning to create the WBS provides two main benefits – exhaustivity and coherence. Exhaustivity is ensured by the systematic cross of the Axis that enables the project manager to recognize if the result (intersection) is - or – is not a part of the project. The exhaustivity of each Axis is a condition to the validity of the benefit, but each of the Axis' exhaustivity is much easier to ensure that trying to build a WBS from scratch or, by analogy, to another project. Ensuring exhaustivity of an LBS Axis is generally easy. The trick is not to generate lower level entries in the LBS that contains others.

Ensuring exhaustivity of the ABS Axis is generally easy because ABS is advised to be standardized in the company. An ABS results from the Quality Assurance policies and practices of the company. As most companies have ISO 9001:2008[44] standard processes, this practice can be easy to implement and deploy. The only additional matter to consider is a requirement in the ABS coming from a contract specificity. For example, a particular test in the factory that may not be unusual, but is unique in itself, as a contractual requirement. This will not be part of the standard process of the company illustrated in the standard ABS, so must be added.

Last, the PBS Axis, which is probably the most difficult of all concerning exhaustivity, because standard PBS most of the time does not exist in the company. When Standard PBS coding exists, codes are often not corresponding to the need of the whole project. Either the standard PBS is oriented as a 'study,' an oriented 'fabrication,' or is defined as site work. In one example, there were non-resolved company issues about PBS. To resolve the issues, a common solution was to break down the PBS into two different codes, the 'pure' PBS that contained the physical and virtual product(s) and the FBS. The resulting codes could be standardized. Exhaustivity can be a concern, but resolved, because of the part of the scope is usually found outside the product of functions the company normally handles. Control is relatively easy if the scope of work of the project is well defined.

Coherence is automatically ensured by the decomposition process, as the structure is bijective[45] to each other; thus, the coherence of the resulting WBS is ensured. The trick of the decomposition process is the creation of a non-existing work package. It is important to verify the work packages exist by comparing the scope of work of the project, the contract, the technical specification and any documents that can be used to do so. This control should be quality ensured before the next step.

---

[44] *International Organization for Standardization. (n.d.) Retrieved from iso.org/about-us.html*
[45] *One-to-one correspondence is a function between the elements of two sets, where each element of one set is paired with an exact (matching) elements of another set; each element of the other set is paired with exactly one element of the first set. (Wikipedia)*

Creating the Schedule

The process to build a schedule is illustrated below:

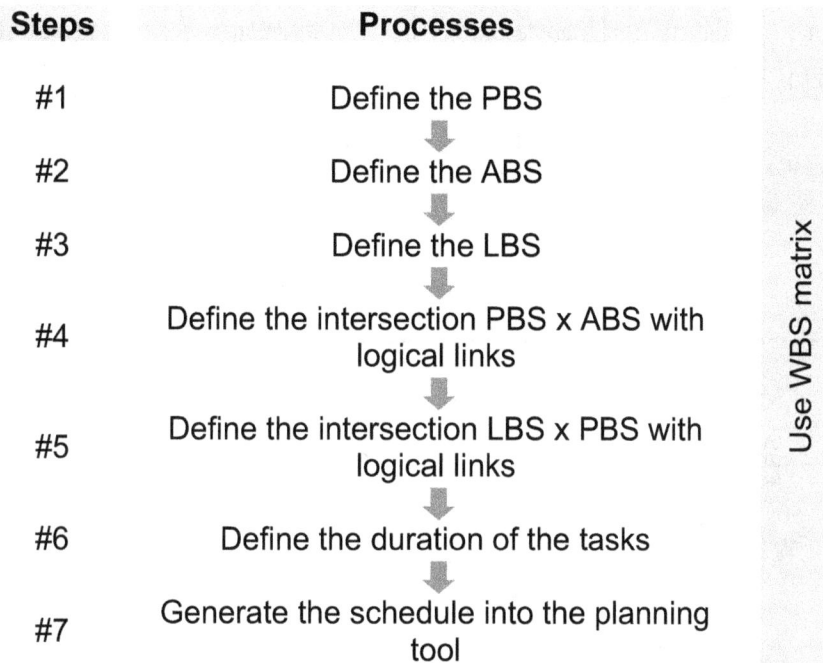

Steps	Processes	
#1	Define the PBS	
#2	Define the ABS	
#3	Define the LBS	Use WBS matrix
#4	Define the intersection PBS x ABS with logical links	
#5	Define the intersection LBS x PBS with logical links	
#6	Define the duration of the tasks	
#7	Generate the schedule into the planning tool	

Figure 28: Process to Build a Schedule

Note that to build a schedule, it is not enough to simply have a list of tasks. We also need to know the definitions of the relationship as well as the duration of the tasks. The duration of the tasks are functions of three dimensions.

3-D WBS 'V' Lifecycle

The 3-D WBS 'V' lifecycle[46] of the project can be imagined if one remembers there is only one project cube. Imagine WBS cubes in each phase of a project (level #1 of the ABS) as one viewpoint – or another representation of the project. The illustration in figure 29 shows a 3-D 'V' life cycle of one project.

---

[46] *3-D Work Breakdown Structure Method - Pmworldjournal.net. (n.d.). Retrieved from pmworldjournal.net/wp-content/uploads/2013/04/pmwj9-apr2013-Moine-3-D-Wor*

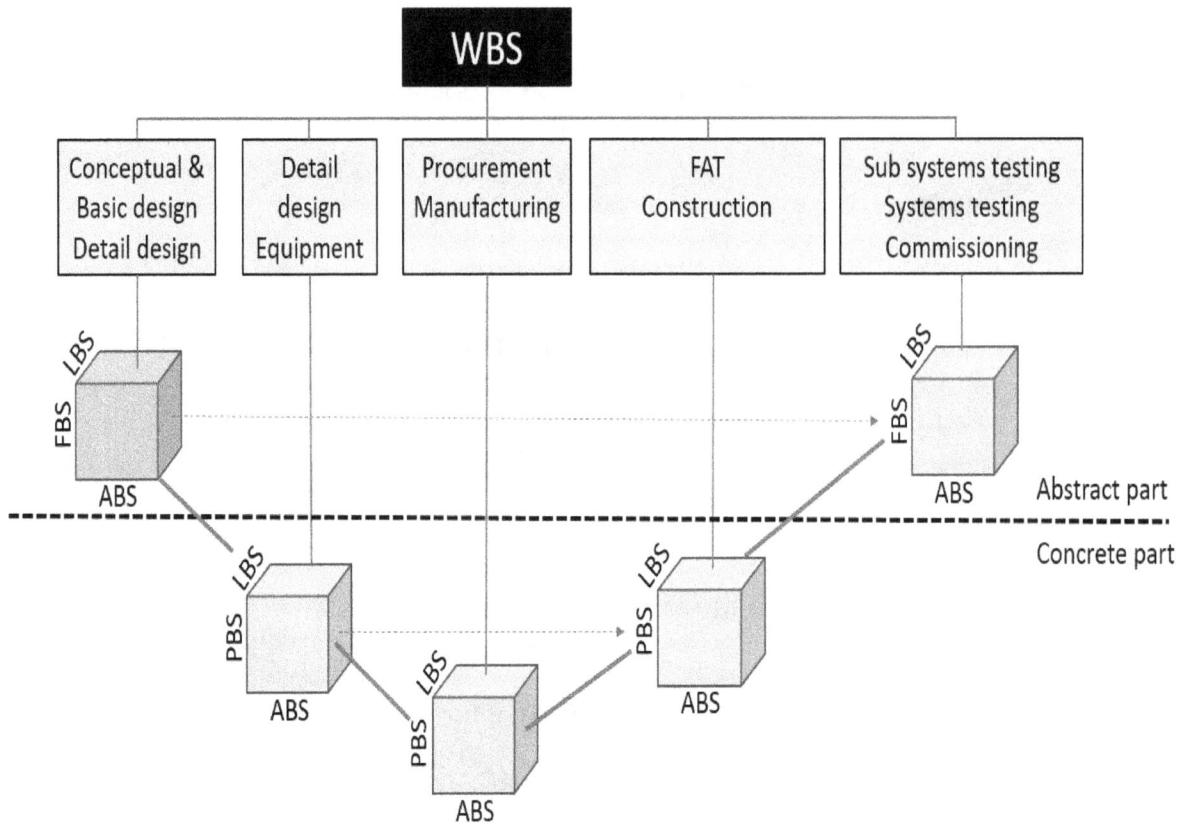

Figure 29: 3-D 'V' Life Cycle of one Project

In this case, the ABS is following a classical V life cycle. The following explanation will include in parentheses, the type of structure involved, e.g., ABS, PBS, LBS. For the first design phase (ABS) that corresponds to the top left of the 'V,' identify the functional systems (SBS) by big zones (LBS). When followed down the 'V' lines, the design phases (ABS) are detailed; next, identify the sub-systems (FBS) by more precise Location (LBS) to document the design phase (ABS). Enter the specification phase (ABS) to produce the specification of the products (PBS). Enter the procurement and manufacturing phases (ABS) of these products (PBS) while going up in the 'V' line. These products (PBS) must be installed or be part of an installation (ABS) somewhere (LBS) during the construction phase (ABS level#1)."

Near the end of the project, one tests the individual (ABS) products (PBS) and performs the pre-commissioning (ABS), the commissioning (ABS) of sub-systems (FBS), and the systems (FBS) in a general Location (LBS). At the end of the project, we test (ABS) the overall Product (PBS) in all the Locations (LBS). As the LBS, PBS, and ABS increase in accuracy within the construction phase, they become increasingly concrete. The example is shown in the 3-D V lifecycle in Figure 29 (3-D V Life Cycle) contains:[47]

---

[47] *3-D Work Breakdown Structure Method - PM World Library. (n.d.). Retrieved from pmworldlibrary.net/wp-content/uploads/2013/04/pmwj9-apr2013-Moine-3-D-Work*

- Hierarchical links between the WBS cubes and the phases (ABS level #1),
- Logical links inside the WBS cubes and between WBS cubes,
- Functional links between opposites WBS cubes (on the same row).

The 3-D 'V' lifecycle of the projects' guaranteed that goals identified are tested at the end of the project. The process guarantees completeness of the scheduled tasks.

3-D 'V' Lifecycle of a Building Construction Project

Illustrated below is an example of the 3-D V lifecycle of a building construction project.[48] Notice there is always three dimensions for the Work (ABS, PBS, LBS).

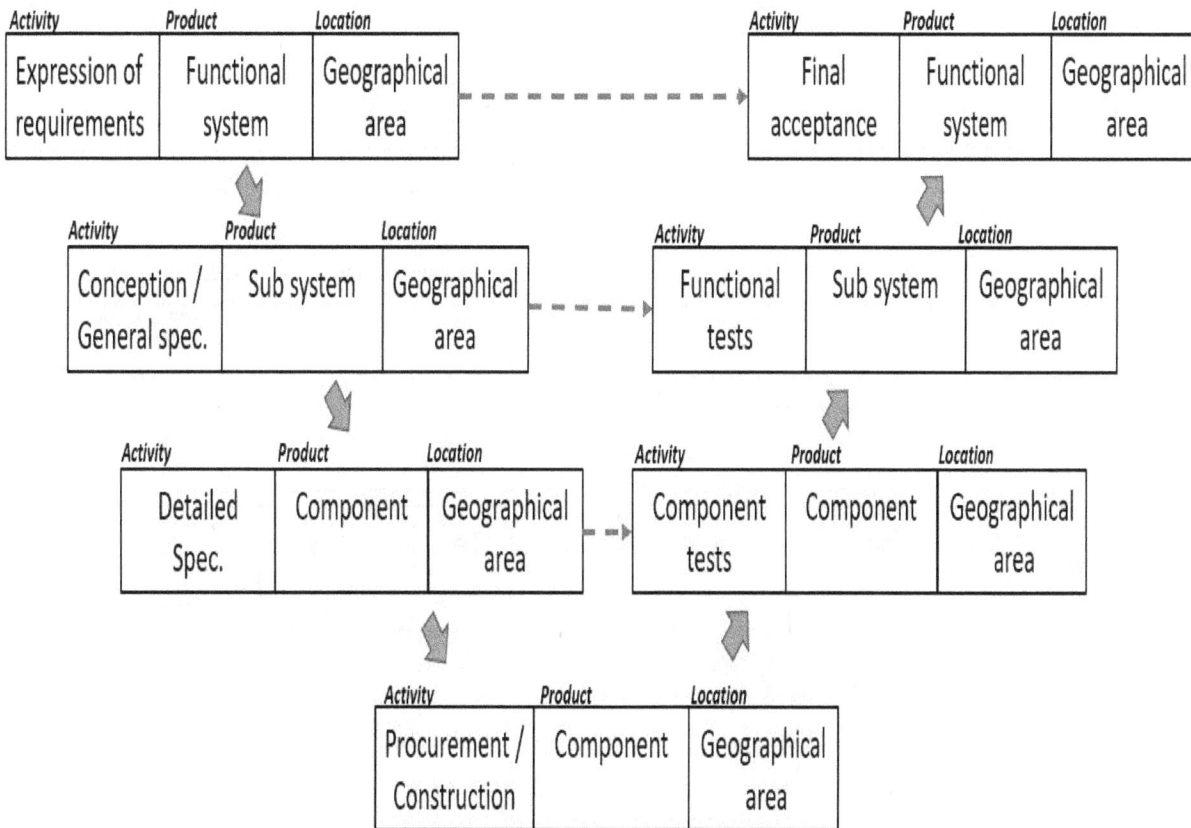

Activity	Product	Location
Expression of requirements	Functional system	Geographical area

Activity	Product	Location
Final acceptance	Functional system	Geographical area

Activity	Product	Location
Conception / General spec.	Sub system	Geographical area

Activity	Product	Location
Functional tests	Sub system	Geographical area

Activity	Product	Location
Detailed Spec.	Component	Geographical area

Activity	Product	Location
Component tests	Component	Geographical area

Activity	Product	Location
Procurement / Construction	Component	Geographical area

Figure 30: 3-D V Lifecycle of a Building Construction Project.

---

[48] 3-D Work Breakdown Structure Method - PM World Library. (n.d.). Retrieved from pmworldlibrary.net/wp-content/uploads/2013/04/pmwj9-apr2013-Moine-3-D-Work

In the previous Figure 30:

- The activities are an Expression of Requirements, Conception/General Specifications, Detailed Specifications, Procurement/Construction, Component Tests, Functional Tests, and Final Acceptance.
- The Products are Functional System, Sub-System, and Components.
- The locations are Geographical areas.

3-D 'V' Lifecycle of an Engineering, Procurement, Construction Project

A 3-D V lifecycle of an Engineering, Procurement, Construction (EPC) project is illustrated below. The project starts and finishes with abstract items (Locations, Products, Activities), and in the middle of the cycle are physical items on the three Axis, for other types of projects.

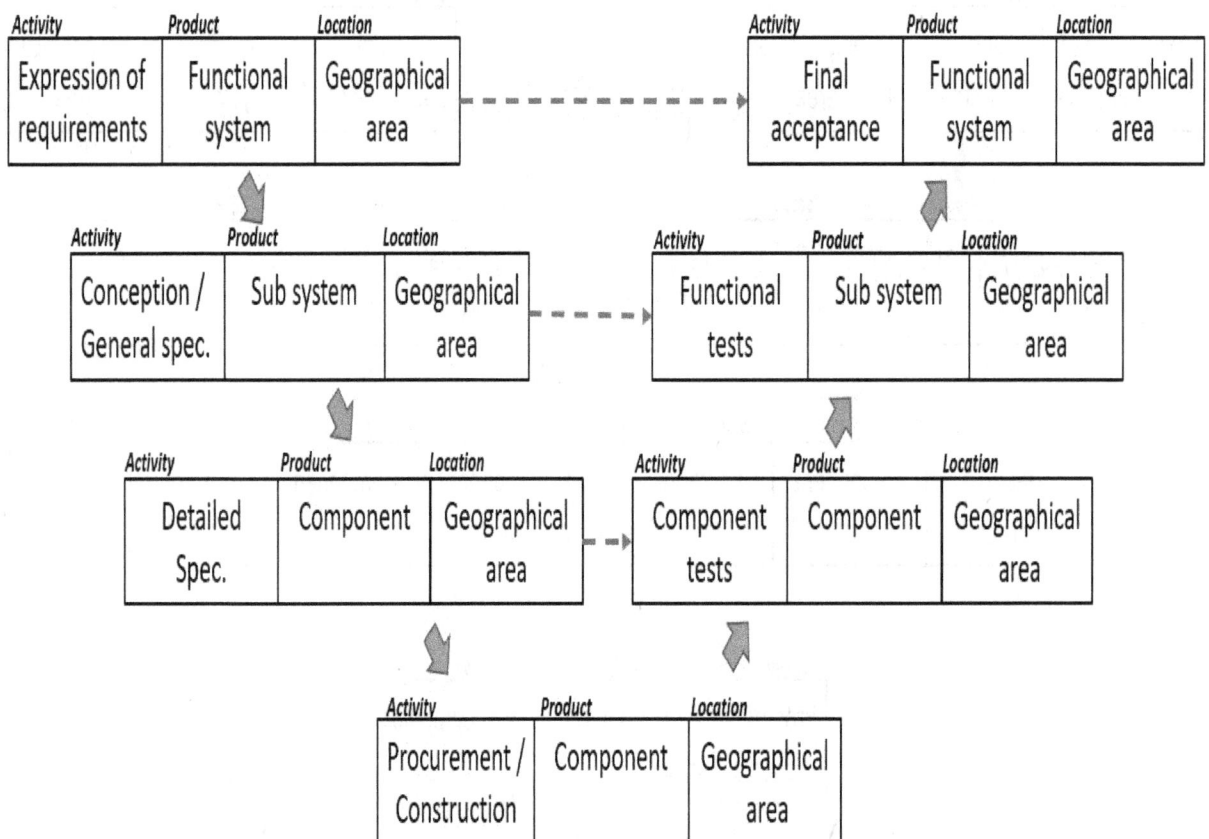

Activity	Product	Location
Expression of requirements	Functional system	Geographical area

Activity	Product	Location
Final acceptance	Functional system	Geographical area

Activity	Product	Location
Conception / General spec.	Sub system	Geographical area

Activity	Product	Location
Functional tests	Sub system	Geographical area

Activity	Product	Location
Detailed Spec.	Component	Geographical area

Activity	Product	Location
Component tests	Component	Geographical area

Activity	Product	Location
Procurement / Construction	Component	Geographical area

Figure 31: 3-D V Lifecycle of an Engineering, Procurement, and Construction Project (Sample)

In the previous Figure 31:

- The activities are an Expression of Requirements, Conception/General Specifications, Detailed Specifications, Procurement/Construction, Component Tests, Functional Tests, and Final Acceptance.
- The Products are Functional System, Sub-System, and Components.
- The locations are Process Unit and Geographical areas.

3-D 'V' Lifecycle of a New Product Development Project

Below is an illustration of the 3-D 'V' lifecycle of a New Product Development (NPD) project from start to finish with abstract items (Locations, Products, Activities), and in the middle of the cycle, documentation of Physical items on the three Axis, as well as another type of Projects.

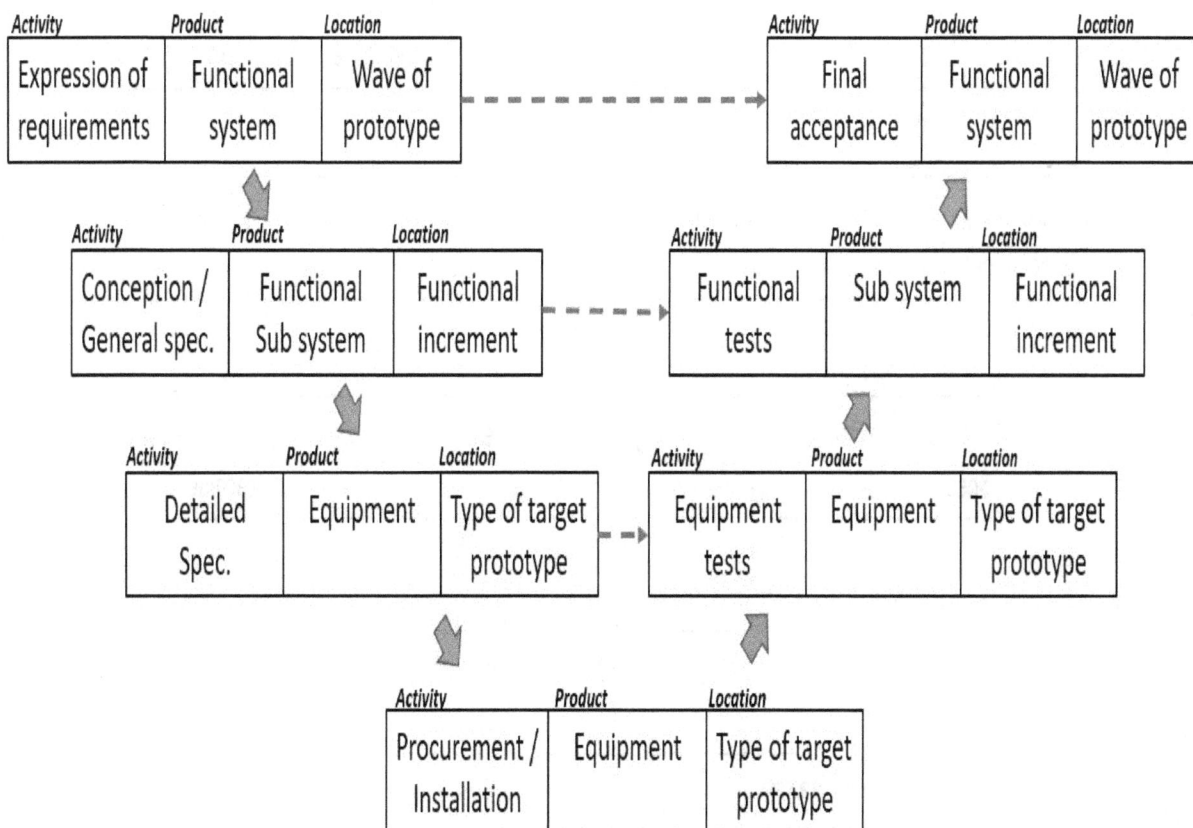

Activity	Product	Location
Expression of requirements	Functional system	Wave of prototype

Activity	Product	Location
Final acceptance	Functional system	Wave of prototype

Activity	Product	Location
Conception / General spec.	Functional Sub system	Functional increment

Activity	Product	Location
Functional tests	Sub system	Functional increment

Activity	Product	Location
Detailed Spec.	Equipment	Type of target prototype

Activity	Product	Location
Equipment tests	Equipment	Type of target prototype

Activity	Product	Location
Procurement / Installation	Equipment	Type of target prototype

Figure 32: 3-D V Lifecycle of New Product Development Project

In the preceding Figure 32:

- The activities are Expression of Requirements, Conception/General Specifications, Detailed Specifications, Procurement/Construction, Component tests, Functional tests, and Final Acceptance.
- The Products are Functional System, Sub-System, and Equipment.
- The locations are Wave of Prototype, Functional Increment, and Type of Target Prototype.

3-D 'V' lifecycle of an Information Technology Project

The 3-D 'V' lifecycle of an Information Technology (IT) project is a practical application of the 3-D WBS 'V' lifecycle. The illustration below shows elements analyzed are also tested at the end of the project.

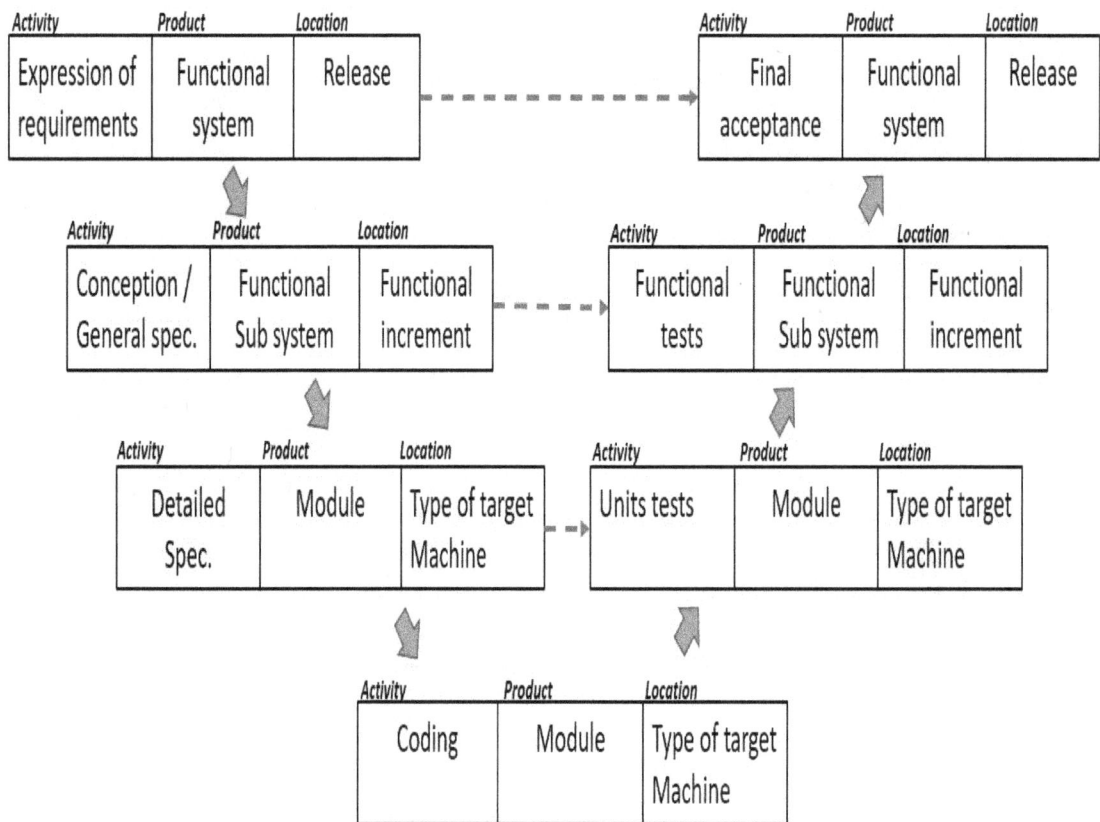

Figure 33: 3-D Lifecycle of an Information Project Sample

In each software version, there are new features. There are also releases, which are a group of incremental versions. In the preceding figure:

- The activities are Expression of Requirements, Conception/General Specifications, Detailed Specifications, Procurement/Construction, Component Tests, Functional Tests, and Final acceptance.
- The Products are Functional System, Functional Sub-System, and Module.
- The locations are Release, Incremental Versions, and Type of Target Machine.

At the highest levels of this 3-D 'V' lifecycle: Activities, Products, and Locations are abstracts; there are macro-activities, functional systems, and incremental versions (a group of new functionalities, on the highest levels of LBS). At the lowest levels of this 3-D 'V' lifecycle, there are Activities, Products, and Locations, which are more concrete. One can find accurate Activities like coding, concrete Products (modules), and the type of target machine (e.g., Smartphone, operating systems, client/server) in a concrete Location (physical). The closer the schedule is to the coding phase (lowest level of the V lifecycle), the more detailed it must be.

Technical Interface Management with 3-D WBS

The ability to identify and manage technical interfaces is improved with the 3-D WBS method. Using 3-D WBS, every task can be modeled within the three dimensions of the cube and appropriate coordinates applied on each Axis. Interfaces have the same properties and can be described using a double-point reference on each Axis (one for each side of the interface). The double-point reference can then be analyzed by using the following three principles. The principles rest on the scaled distance between corresponding tasks for each of the Axis of the WBS cube (LBS, PBS and ABS).

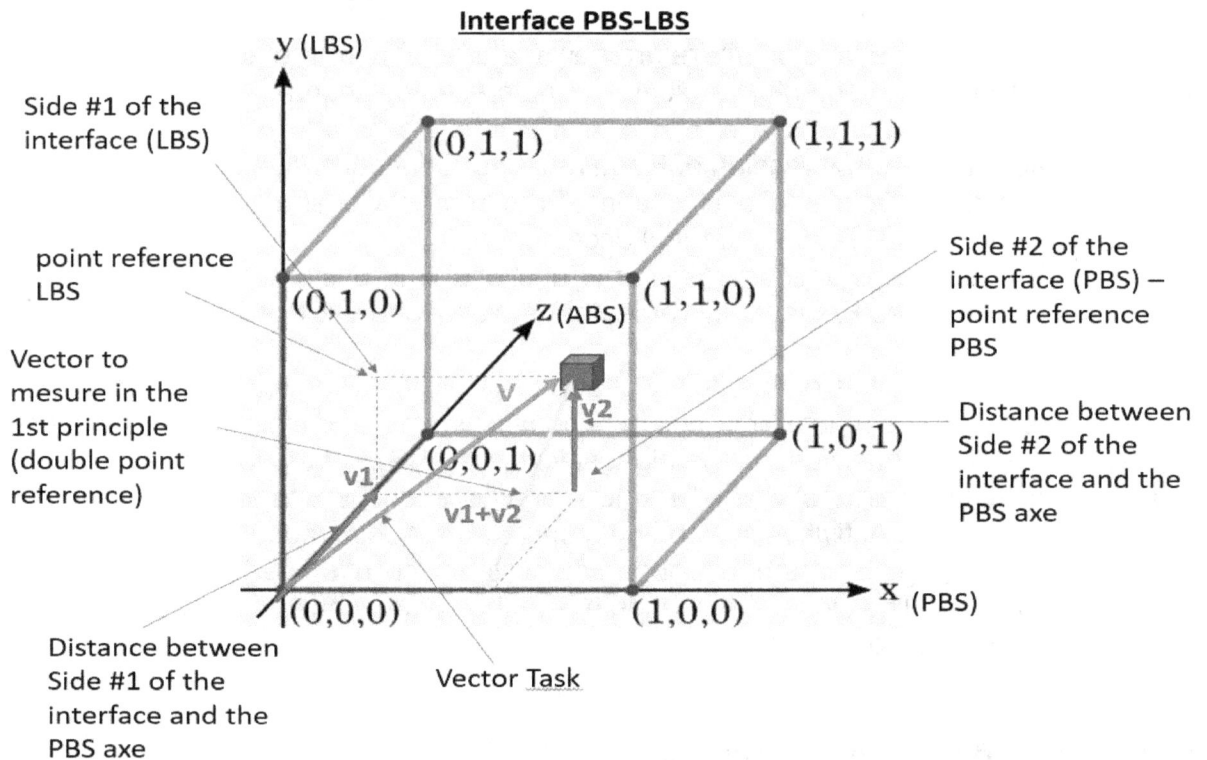

Figure 34: First Principle Illustration

1st Principle: The further away the reference point of each side of the interface is on the PBS Axis, the more complex and critical are the codes and elements for planning. The reference points will probably identify a task that has multiple responsibilities. The result is more complex and will be explained in the OBS part.

2nd Principle: The closer the reference point of each side of the interface is on the ABS Axis, the more critical in terms of planning. This is due to the weakness of available margins in the planning between two close elements of the ABS. Project managers only have a small amount of time between engineering and procurement, but that issue is not the case between the engineering and commissioning stages.

Interface PBS-LBS

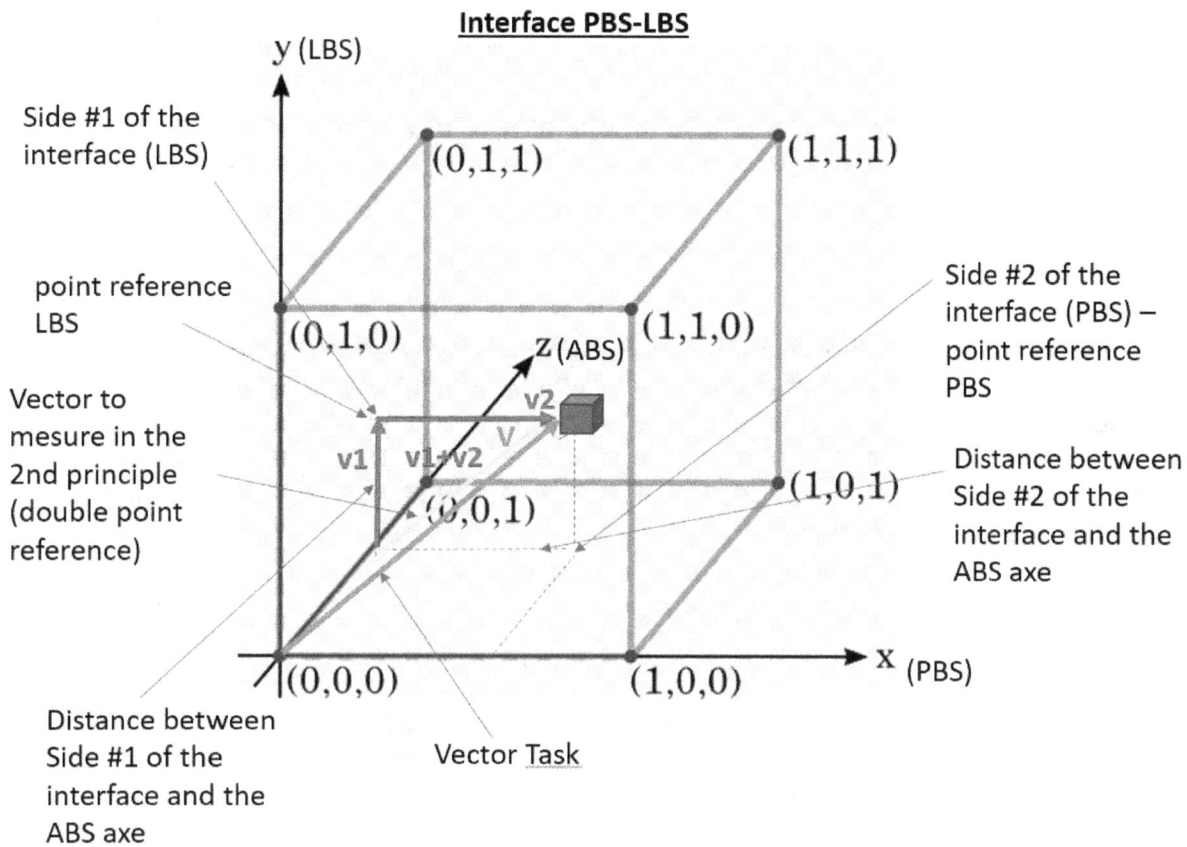

Figure 35: Illustration of the 2nd principle

3rd Principle: Per LBS rules, the distance between the points depends on the nature of the PBS/OBS couple-reference points. The complexity can be reduced and standardized for some reference points and can be cross-checked with Return of Experience (REX) from the project and from interface managers (if known).

Interfaces (and modifications) with Command Control are usually deep in technology and tough to understand; each interfaced element can be far apart on the PBS/FBS Axis. Interfaces are critical in planning because of the need for one design to interact and be based on or connected to others' designs and quality-assurance loops. The resulting activities each have a corresponding code from one to another on the ABS Axis. Activities are grouped in a location that can be far from one to another on the LBS Axis. As a consequence, the specification must be available early in the planning process, which is a risk, while the same is true in integration.

An important consideration for using WBS 3-D is available predictions at the beginning of the project, which would eliminate difficulties in managing the interfaces. By adding the WBS 3-D coordinates to the interface management system and developing a standard for qualifications, this improves the control of documentation, planning, and general project tasks. This also can be a simple, efficient tool to score (rank or rate) the interface for risk management. Predictions improve the management risk by focusing on and reviewing high-scoring interfaces. By extending this concept to each discipline, department, and employee involved in the project management (cost, documentation, contract), the identification of interface provides an innovative aspect to the 3-D WBS methodology.

The 3-D Gantt

In this diagram, the 3-D Gantt, the Locations (LBS) and Products (PBS), are projected on the axis of the WBS cube. Activities (ABS) are deployed on Products in one Location. The position of the Activities is on a scheduled calendar; each Activity has a duration. The ideation of time is also included in the three Axes of the projected cube. The position of the Locations, the Products, and Activities on each of the WBS cube axes is a function of time.

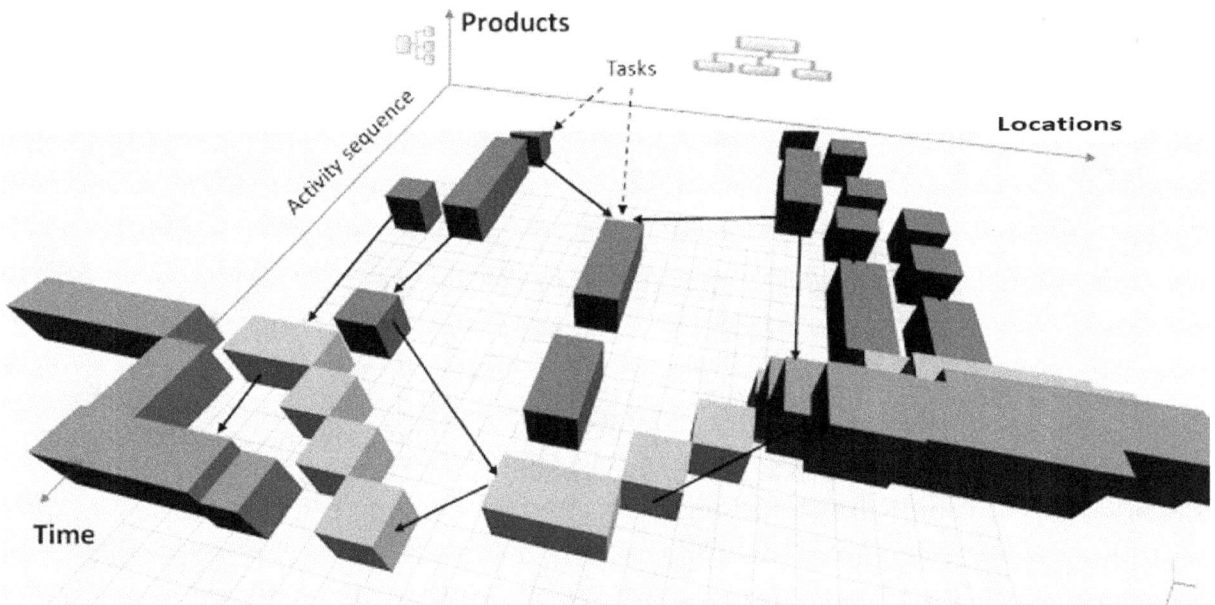

Figure 36: Representation of 3-D Gantt

"Compared to a classical Gantt diagram, with an axis for tasks and an axis for time, the 3-D Gantt allows to better visualize the logical links of schedule. The logical links are not superposed anymore in 3-D."[49]   Below (Figure 37) is an illustrated, classical (2-D) Gantt diagram, for a communication project (Tri / Trimester = quarters).

---

[49] *3-D Work Breakdown Structure Method - PM World Library. (n.d.). Retrieved from pmworldlibrary.net/wp-content/uploads/2013/04/pmwj9-apr2013-Moine-3-D-Work*

Task Name	Tri 1, YYYY	Tri 2, YYYY	Tri 3, YYYY
	Jan Feb Mar Apr	May Jun	Jul Aug

1. General

2. All systems – General Design

3. Telephone System – Detail Design

4. Radio System – Detail Design

5. Communication System

6. All Equipment – Procurement

7. All Systems – Install and Test

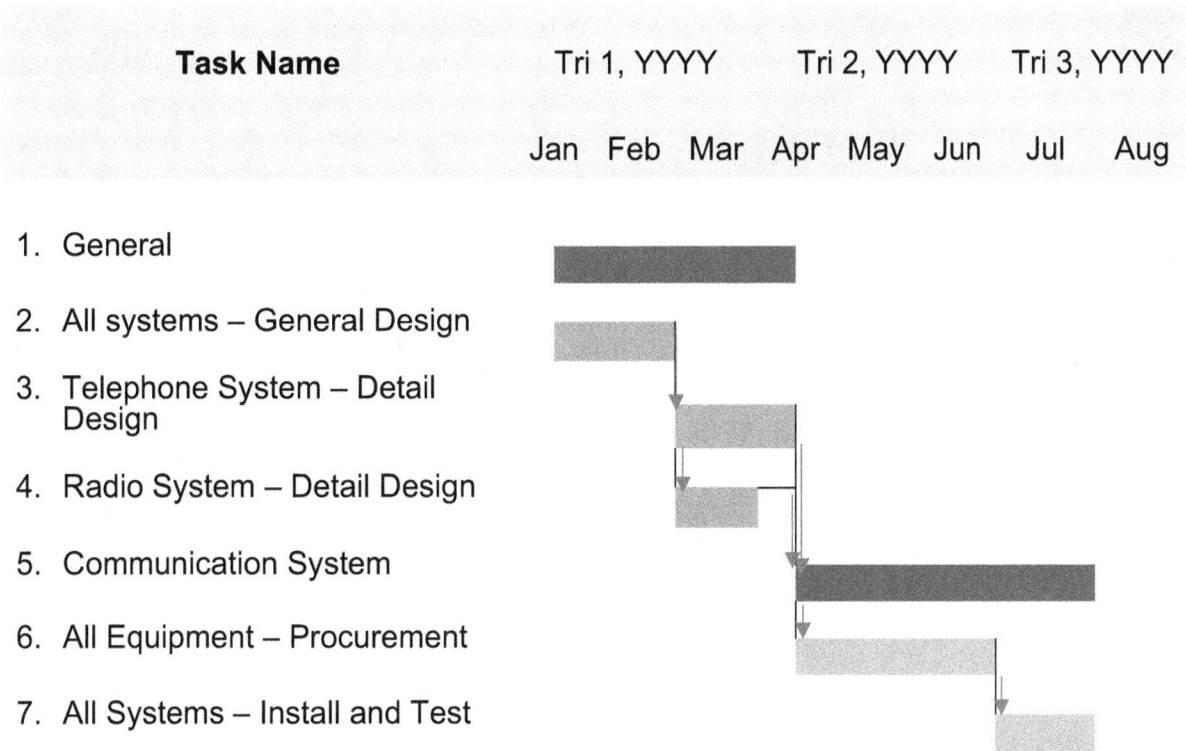

Figure 37: Gantt Diagram for a Communication Project.

The following shows the same project, but in 3-D, with the 3-D WBS method.

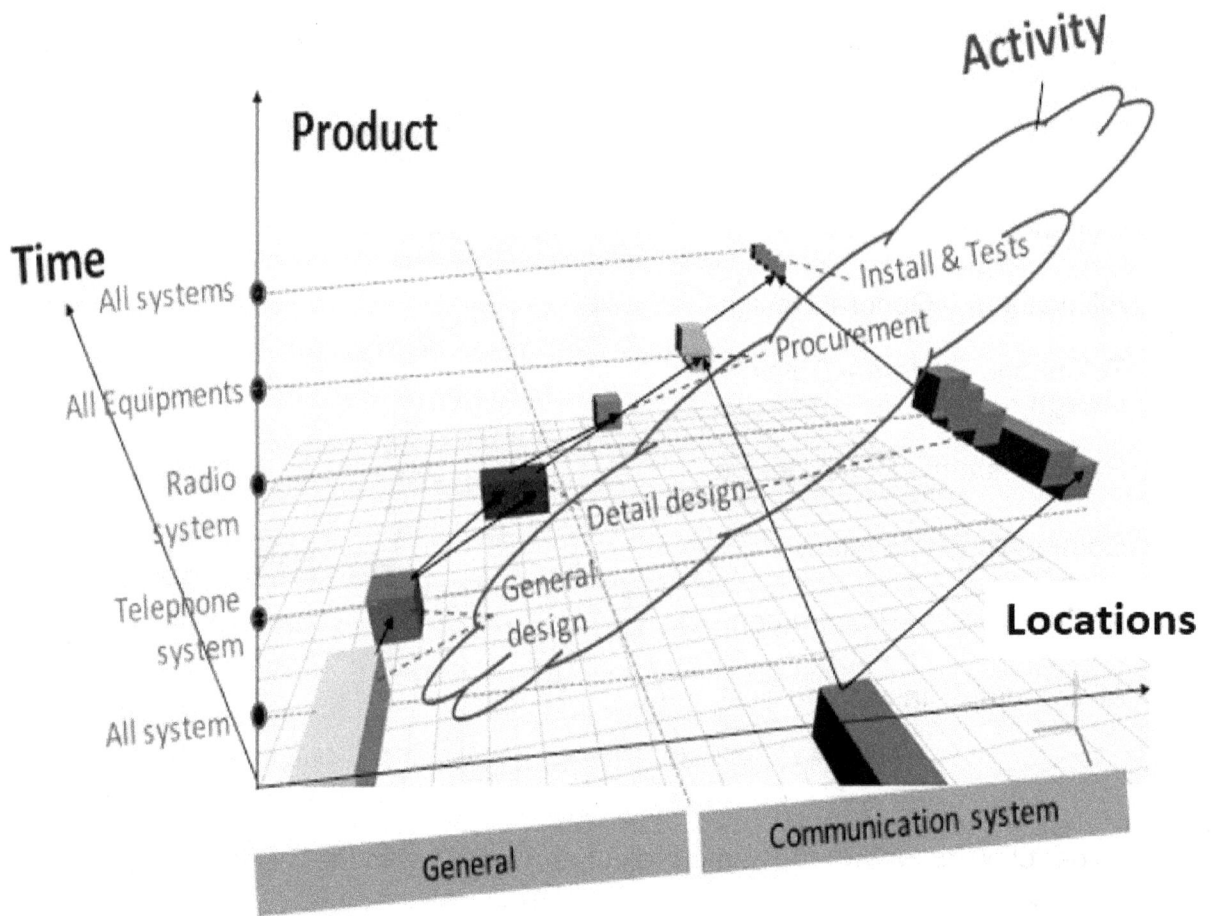

Figure 38: Sample of the 3-D Gantt

This concept is introduced to underline the possibilities that offer the model. 3-D Gantt is just a concept, difficult to apprehend today, but that can be developed in the future using the rising power of BIM tools.

The Organization Breakdown Structure

The OBS represents the responsible entity for the tasks. While it is a dimension for the 3-D WBS model, the OBS can then also be viewed as an attribute or property of the tasks.

Organization Breakdown Structure

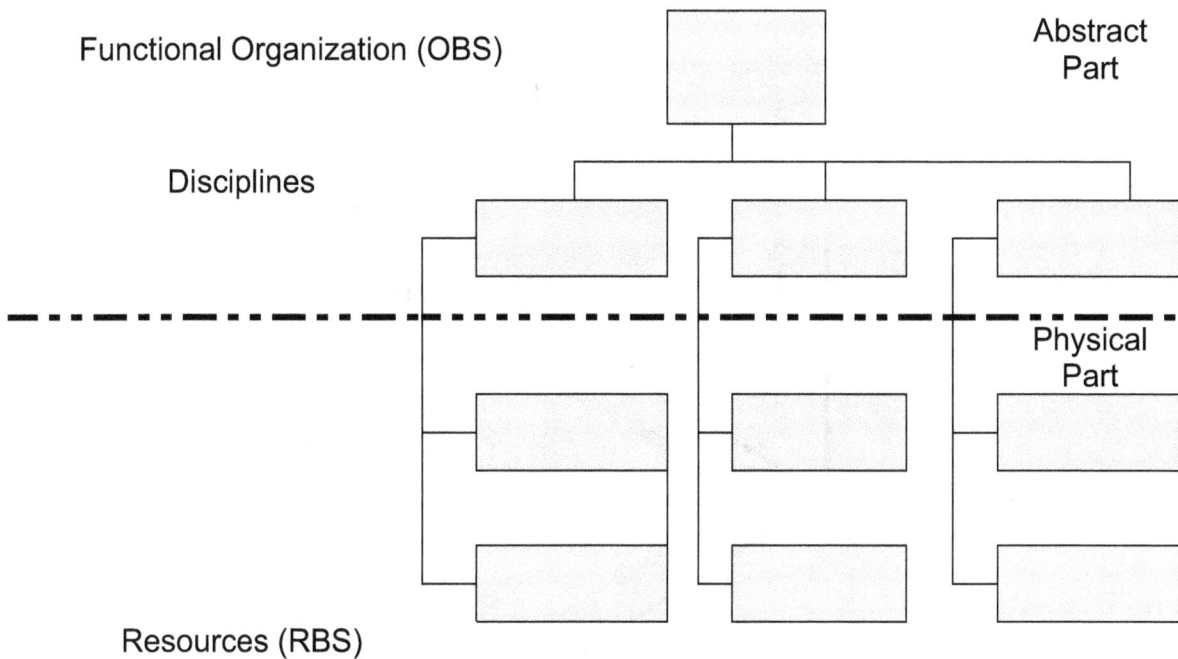

Functional Organization (OBS)

Abstract
Part

Disciplines

Physical
Part

Resources (RBS)

Figure 39: Organizational Breakdown Structure (OBS)

The Organization Breakdown Structure (OBS) is composed of a:

- Company's Breakdown Structure (CBS)
- Contract Work Breakdown Structure (CWBS)

The CWBS is 'designated,' knowing that the CWBS is known only in the future. The CWBS will also vary, depending on the phase of the project (ABS), of the nature of the project (PBS in its larger definition as a combination of pure product and system), and of the location of the work (LBS) to be executed following the contract. The OBS is developed in continuity with the RBS (Resource Breakdown Structure).

RBS is either:

- Human

and/or

- Material resources,

Material resources are Physical and virtual Products and represent an instantiation of the WBS (e.g., if two generators are needed, instantiate that option in this Axis). It is also composed of the Disciplines breakdown. One representation of the OBS is shown below. It integrates internal OBS, the CWBS, and the RBS.

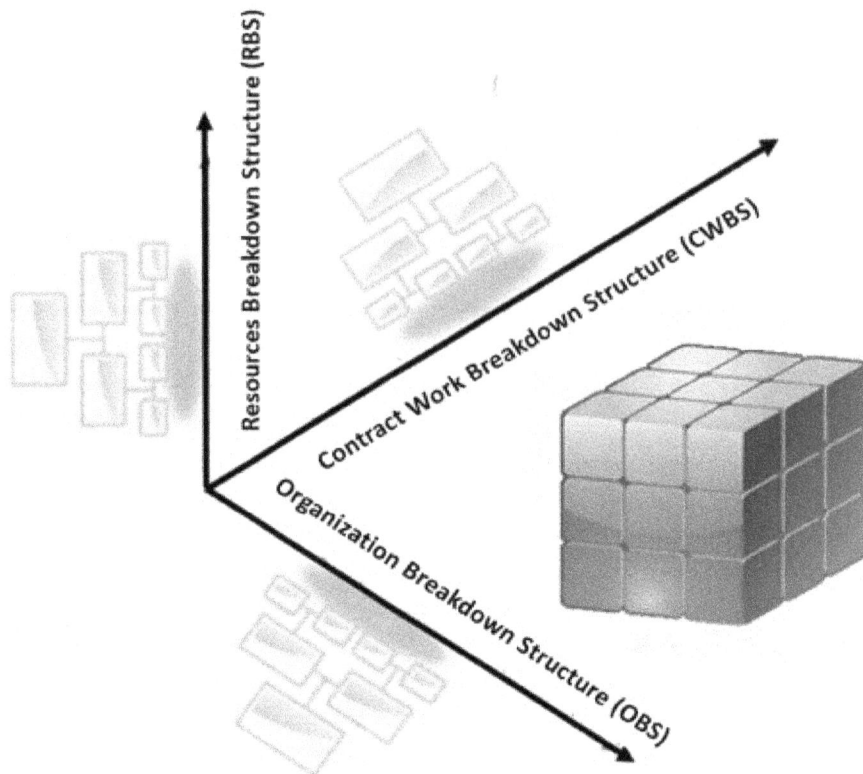

Figure 40: The Organization Breakdown Structure

An example of RBS is illustrated below (Figure 41):

COR Coding	Level 1 Title	Level 2 Title	Level 3 Title	Level 4 Title
A	General Costs			
AE		Material Related Costs		
AEA			Capital Spares	
AEB			Commissioning Spares	
AEC			Freight	
AED			Customs Charges, Fees, and Duties	
B	Bulk Material			
BE		Electrical Bulk		
BEA			Cables and Cable Accessories	
BEB			Cables Supports and Transit	
BEE			Accessories	
BJ		Instrument Bulk		
BJA			Instruments	
BJC			Cables and Cable Accessories	

COR Coding	Level 1 Title	Level 2 Title	Level 3 Title	Level 4 Title
BL		Piping Bulk		
BLA			Pipework	
BLB			Manually Operated Valves	
BLC			Supports	
BQ		Civil Works Bulk		
BQA			Concrete, Cement, Sand, and Aggregates	
BQB			Reinforcement Bars / Rods and Pre-stressing Cables	
C	Construction Overheads			
CA		Contractor's Organization		
CAA			Construction Management	
CAB			General Site Administration	
E	Equipment			
EE	Electrical Equipment			
EEE		Electrical Equipment		
EEEC			Contract Equipment (panel, relay boxes)	
ER	Miscellaneous Mechanical Equipment			
ERX		Miscellaneous Package Units		
ERXE			Potable Water Treatment Package	
K	Engineering Manpower			
KA		Engineering Management and Administration		
KAA			Management	
KAB			Contract Management	
KAC			Project Control	
KAD			Administration	
KAE			Document Control	
KAF			Data Processing (IT)	
KAG			Quality Management	
KB		Procurement		
KE		Electrical		
KJ		Instrumentation		
KL		Piping		
KO		Operation and Maintenance		
KP		Process		
KQ		Civil Engineering		
KR		Mechanical		
KS		Health, Safety, and Environment (HSE)		
KZ		Multidiscipline		
L	Direct Labor			
LE		Electrical – Direct Labor		
LJ		Instrument – Direct Labor		
LL		Piping – Direct Labor		
LQ		Civil Works – Direct Labor		
LR		Mechanical – Direct Labor		
LS		Safety – Direct Labor		
M	Indirect Labor			
MA		Foreman / Supervisor		
MB		Quality Control		
MC		Scaffolding		
MD		Cleaning		

COR Coding	Level 1 Title	Level 2 Title	Level 3 Title	Level 4 Title
ME			Transport	
MF			Rigging	
MG			Material Control	
MK			Safety	

Figure 41: Resource Breakdown Structure (RBS)

A few points about the 3-D WBS must be noted for the OBS, which in a way directly influences the CWBS. Technical matters handled with the PBS influences the organization – traces of the PBS can be found in the OBS. This is the same with the activities (ABS) matters which influences the organization – meaning project managers can find evidence of the ABS in the OBS. Engineering, procurement, and installation departments may have overlapping tasks and responsibilities, especially within engineering or installation companies.

Location is also easy to find inside OBS. As a result, crossing the WBS and the OBS codes to create the work packages is intuitive. The OBS, at the elementary (or family) level of breakdown, is based on the same primary structures than the WBS.

The second matter related to the interface sections is that People's (building-related) skills are relative to items close in proximity on the PBS and ABS breakdown structure Axis. The interfaces of a skilled engineer of a rotating machine or installation of electrical elements may be in close proximity to each other. The consequence is the lower level of the OBS is a very close match to the WBS.

The 3-D or multi-dimensional breakdown structure method is no longer viewed as a flat-file, single-dimensional model, but instead a relational or object-oriented model that enables different stakeholders in the project to see the deliverables from that project sorted and organized in a way that makes logical sense. This could potentially become unmanageable as tasks grow. The 3-D WBS method allows project-level viewing related to needs and available data. This simplifies the assignment of a group of resources to a group of the task when a single person is in charge of the group.

The work package is responsible for managing most scheduled activities and items that are close to each other on one or two of the Axis. This follows the functional skills of the responsible person or the organization following the V-cycle phase or the area of the site. In conclusion, the OBS is also a 3-D structure. It can be considered as compatible with the 3-DWBS and allow the modeling of coordinates for OBS with a compatible format with the one of the 3-D WBS.

The Cost Breakdown Structure

The CBS (Cost Breakdown Structure) is composed of:

- the ACcounting Breakdown Structure
- the CUrrency Breakdown Structure
- the Financial Value Breakdown Structure

The accounting breakdown includes a special part to hold the financial part of the risks.

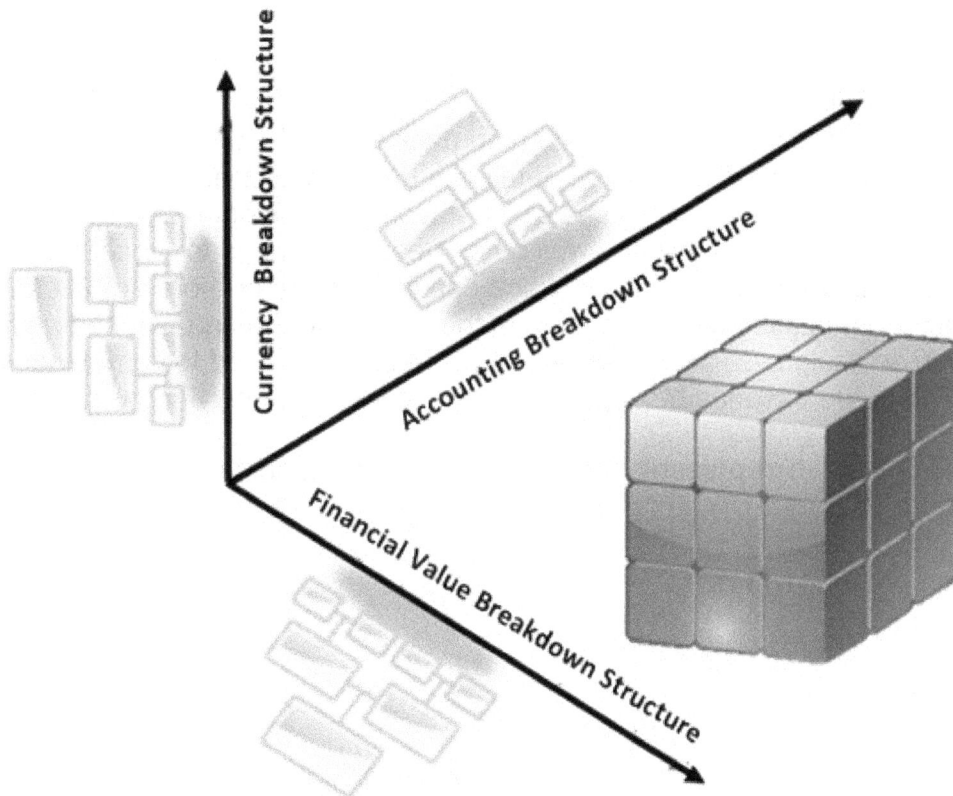

Figure 42: The Cost Breakdown Structure

The 3-D WBS has a profound influence on Breakdown structures. First, ACBS (ACounting Breakdown Structure) is influenced by the OBS and by extension by the 3-D WBS breakdown PBS/ABS/LBS. Then, CUBS (CUrrency Breakdown Structure) follows OBS and CWBS and is influenced by the 3-D WBS breakdown PBS/ABS/LBS. The FVBS (Financial Value Breakdown), is influenced by the CWBS and the 3-D WBS in itself, and especially the PBS. The financial breakdown will follow the scope of work and scope of work and relies massively on products (refer to ABS for the intellectual portion of the work) in most cases. Financial Value Breakdown Structure (FVBS) also includes disciplines coming from the influences of ABS. The CBS is also a 3-D structure. The CBS can be considered compatible with both 3-DWBS and OBS and allows the modeling of coordinates for the CBS compatible format with the OBS and the 3-DWBS.

Responsibility Assignment Matrix (RAM)

OBS and WBS are organized in a matrix. This matrix is called the Responsibility Assignment Matrix (RAM). At the crossing of the OBS and WBS there are two kinds of information:[50]

- The allocation of the resources on the schedule tasks, at the lowest levels of the tree structures
- The definition of the Work and Planning packages, with one unique individual responsible, at whatever level of detail has been developed. A Work Package consists of one or more activities which have been assigned to a specific resource or resources – and – which has been authorized to proceed or commence, while a Planning Package consists of one or more activities which have been identified and scheduled in the future, but has not yet had any specific resources assigned - and/or – has not yet been authorized to commence work on. This is the essence behind 'Rolling Wave' or 'Moving Window' planning.

A 2-D or 'flat-file' representation of the Work and Planning Package concept is shown in figure 43.

---

[50] *3-D Work Breakdown Structure Method - PM World Library. (n.d.). Retrieved from pmworldlibrary.net/wp-content/uploads/2013/04/pmwj9-apr2013-Moine-3-D-Work*

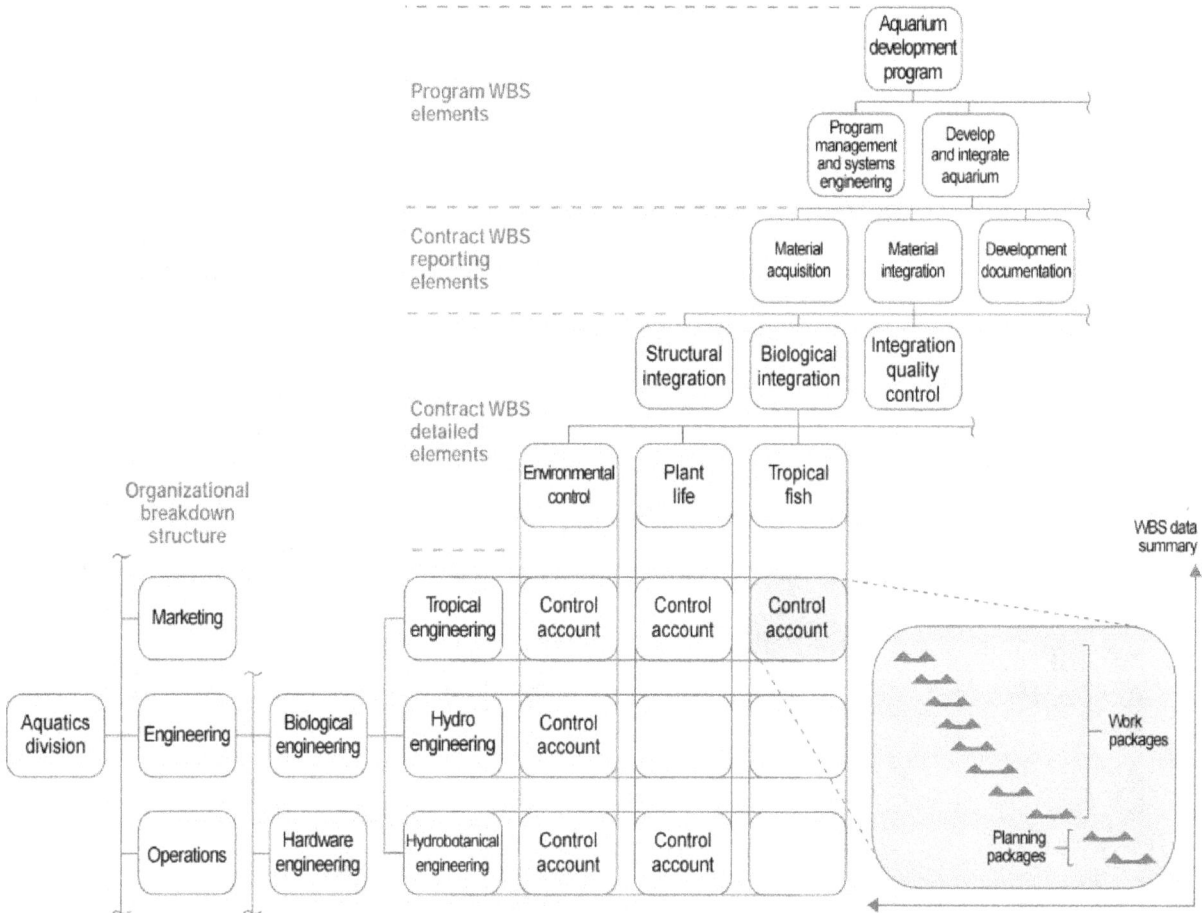

Figure 43: Assigning Responsibility Using Control Accounts or Responsibility Matrices[51]

Figure 43 illustrates a conceptual use of a 2-D model; how the WBS and OBS are matrixed in such a way that for every work package there is one and only one person (usually a project manager) responsible. These are textbook cases of what is considered 'Control Accounts' and define the responsibility of a single person – either from the owner or from the contractor's perspective. When the work package is assigned at the Owners level, that person (architect or engineer) is responsible for monitoring the progress of the prime contractor or sub-contractor. When the owner is a government agency, this is also known as the 'Control Account.' Normally it would be the architect, engineer, or in the case of a government project the Control Account Manager (CAM; or Government Contract Manager [GCM]) who authorizes the work package and determines when the work package is completed per the contract deliverables list.

When a work package has been authorized, it is then assigned to either the

[51] Best Practices in Capital Budgeting. (2009). GAO, 217. SCEA (2003), Retrieved from http://www.gao.gov/new.items/d093sp.pdf

prime contractor or one or more sub-contractors' work crew to execute. Normally it would be the trade or discipline's foreman or superintendent who would be the single person responsible for the execution of that work package in accordance with the technical specifications and contractual terms and conditions.

WBS	Project Team Members					Other Stakeholders		
Element / Activity	I.B. You	M. Jones	R. Smith	H. Baker	F. Drake	Sponsor	Client	Functional Manager
1.0.1.1 Activity A	N				R			
1.0.1.2 Activity B		R	C					
1.0.1.3 Activity C	R		S			A		G
1.0.2 Activity D			R		S			A
1.0.3.1 Activity E			R			N		
1.0.3.2 Activity F				R				
1.0.3.3 Activity G	R				S	A	A	
1.0.4 Activity H		R				C	N	

Key: R = Responsible; S = Support; C = Must be Consulted; N = Must be Notified; A = Approval; G = Phase Gate Reviewer

Figure 44: Responsibility Assignment Matrix (RAM) Sample[52]

---

[52] Responsibility Assignment Matrix Example- Guild of Project Controls Module 3.5 Creating the Control Accounts Figure 3, Retrieved from http://www.planningplanet.com/guild/gpccar/creating-control-accounts

In some organizations, a RAM is also called a 'RACI Chart' or 'RACI Table' (Responsible, Accountable, Consulted, or Informed).[53]

WBS Element / Activity	Functions							
	CEO	CFO	Business Executive	CIO	Sponsor	Operations Manager	Project Manager	PMO Manager
1.0.1.1 Activity A	A	R/A	C	C	R/A	R/A	A	C
1.0.1.2 Activity B		C	I		I	I	A	C
1.0.1.3 Activity C	I		I		I	I	A	C
1.0.2 Activity D	I		I		R/A	I	A	C
1.0.3.1 Activity E	C	I	I		R	R	A	C
1.0.3.2 Activity F	C	A	I		R	R	A	C
1.0.3.3 Activity G	A	A	I		R	R	A	C
1.0.4 Activity H	A	C	I		C	I	A	C

Key: R = Responsible; A = Accountable; C = Consulted; and I = Informed

Figure 45: Responsible, Accountable, Consulted, or Informed" (RACI) Example

[53] RACI Table Example- Guild of Project Controls Module 3.5 Creating the Control Accounts Figure 4
http://www.planningplanet.com/guild/gpccar/creating-control-accounts

The Project Cube

In the 3-D WBS method, the Work Packages (WP) are the intersection of the three 3-D structures WBS, CBS, and OBS, taking into account the responsibilities in the OBS. A Resources and costs-loaded task can be defined as the cross of all those the three 3-D structures WBS x OBS x CBS, taking into account the Resources (RBS) in the OBS ("x" = a crossing axis).

Project cube = WBS x OBS x CBS (demonstrated in Figure 46):

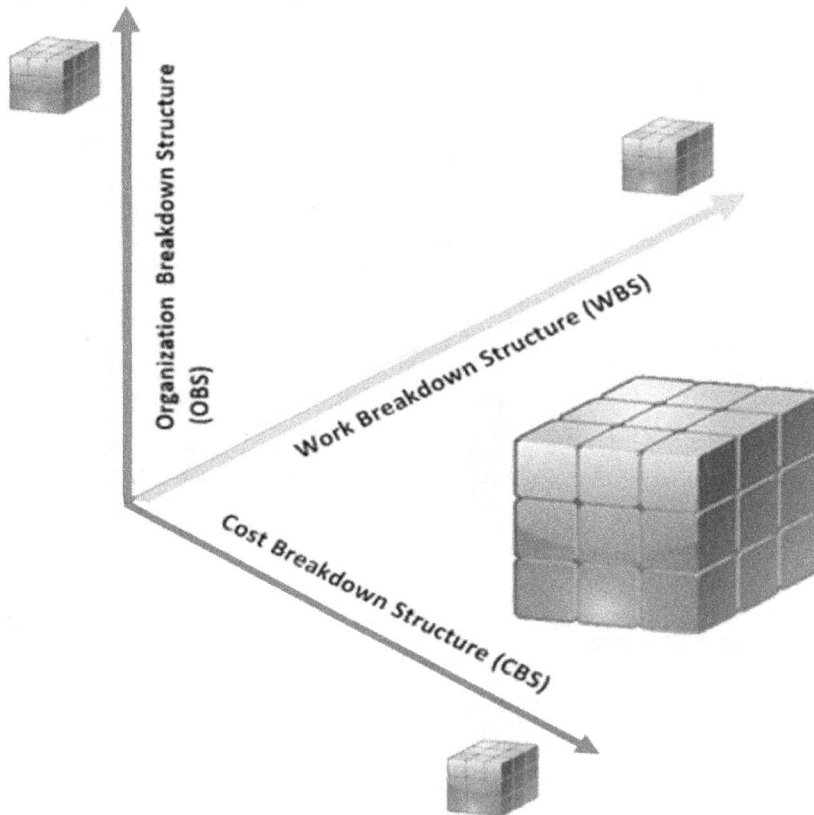

Figure 46: The Project Cube

The Figure 46 Project cube is the 'GPS' (Global Positioning System) of the project, meaning it can be view as allowing to 'locate' and define anything on a project. Following conclusions of compatible coordinates, some simple GPS coordinate can be created. Those coordinates are ideal references for BIM purposes. Coordinates can be used to unify (or determine) the 'location' of any item in the BIM project model.

Contract Work Breakdown Structure

The Contract Work Breakdown Structure (CWBS) is a tree, representing how a contract is organized for the project and is decomposed (deconstructed) following the contract or sub-contract structure of the project. The first level of this structure is close to the last level of the OBS and describes the contract allocation of the project (how many contracts, with what name). Nearly every building project is a contract; if you extend the notion to internal contracts such as engagement between services (and departments) of a company, you should be able to identify a match to the lower level of the OBS, just before RBS.

The second level of the structure and the following levels are the clauses, sub-clause, and annexes for the number of each of the contract tasks or elements listed on the first level. Compare this CWBS to the 3-D WBS structure and the LBS while locating what is or is not in each of the contracts.

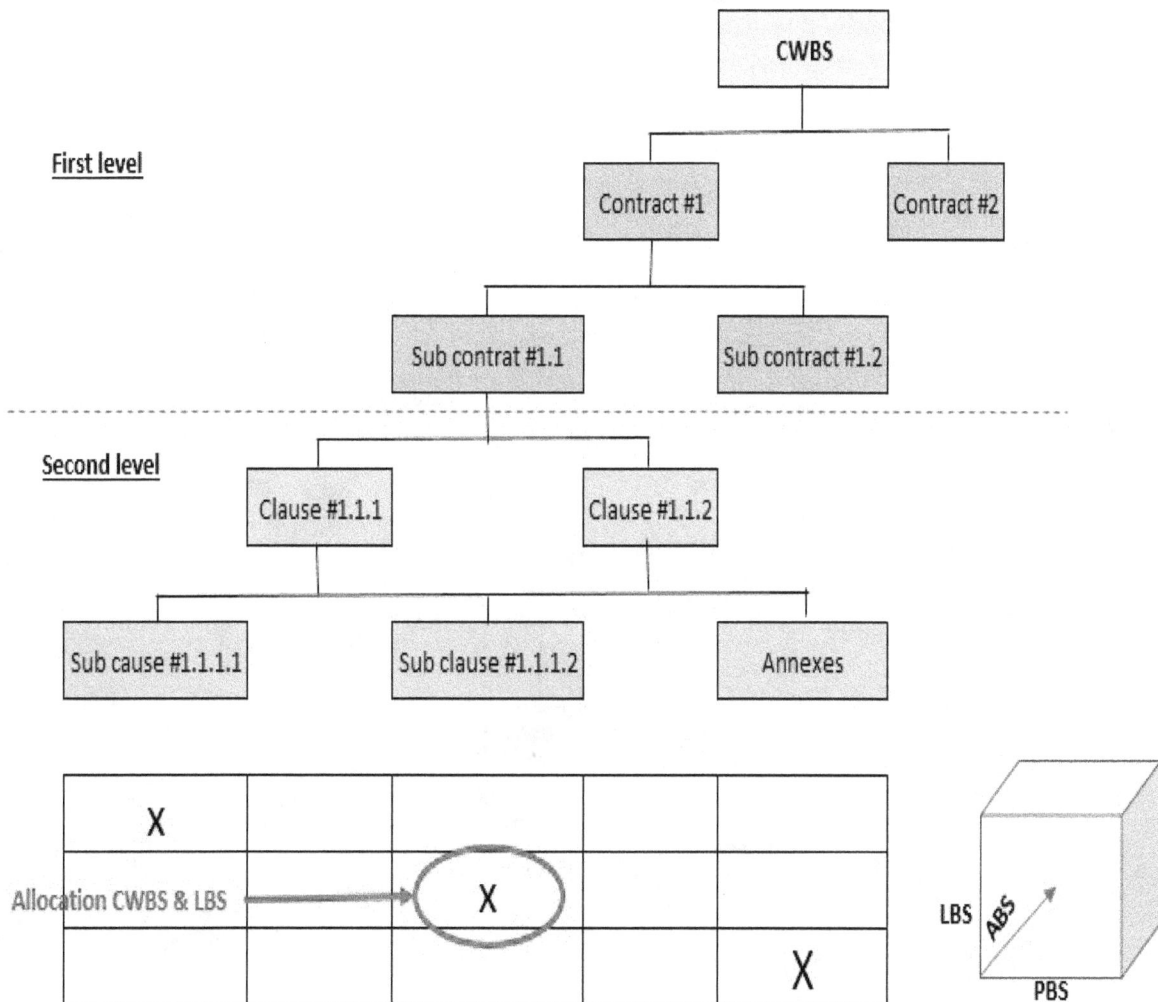

Figure 47: Crossing WBS x LBS

Deploying the full CWBS of the project allows identification of missed scope elements not included in the contract and of missed risks not allocated to a contractor. This is a precious tool – one that contract managers can easily use to avoid litigation and cost overruns. Leynaud encountered this at the end of the 1990s that was developed on a Lotus spreadsheet (software) and was limited to part of the PBS. Leynaud also used this, with success, to quickly review construction contracts' Scope of Work (SOW) to see if the elements were exhaustive and covered the full project scope. This review element was useful; today's project management and SharePoint software simplify this process.

The Contract Work Breakdown Structure has a powerful use for the BIM, even if it means additional work in the beginning. The CWBS link, with the contract, allows simplifying references to the contractual part per each project item. The Contract Work Breakdown Structure levels are defined as follows:

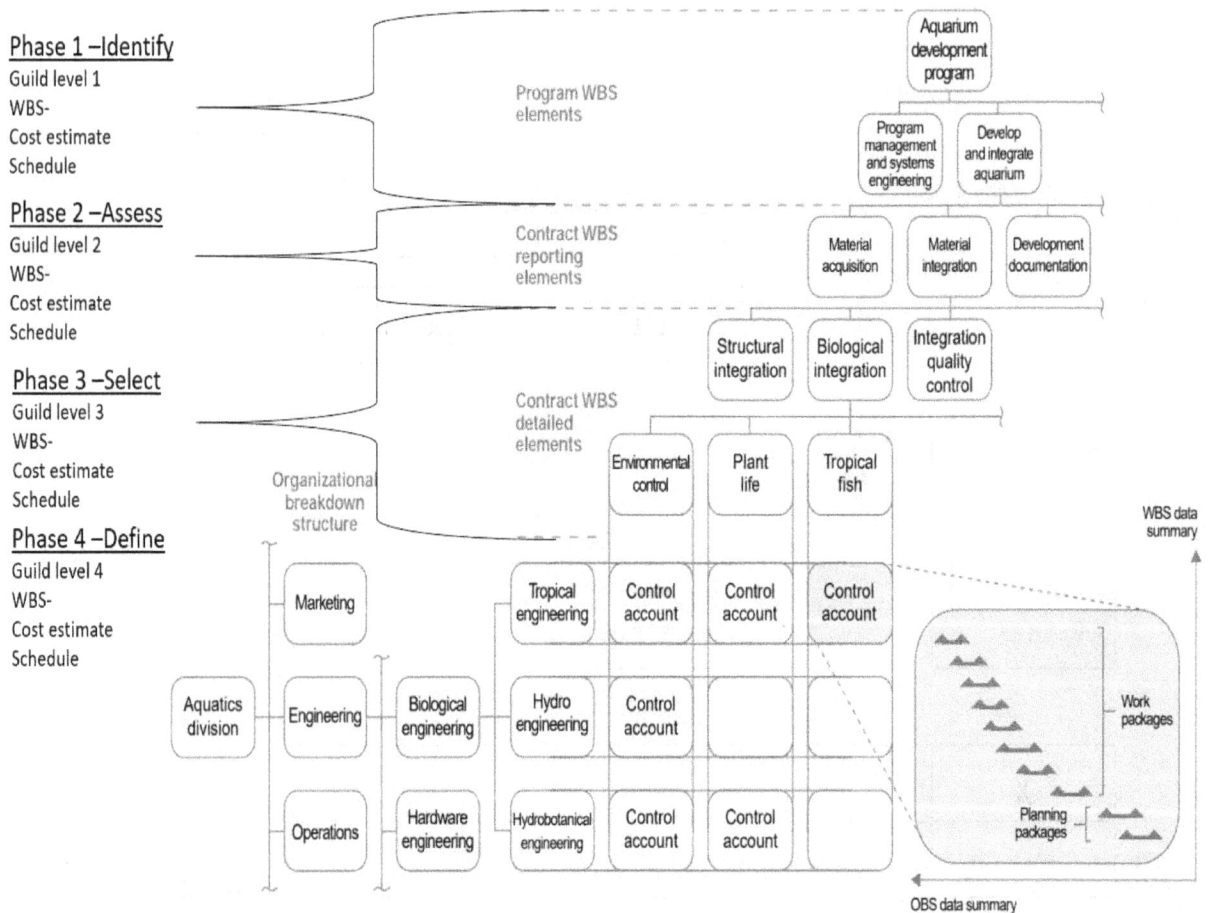

Figure 48: Illustrating the Concept of the Control Account and Work Package Activities

Integrated Project Management Around the Project Cube

All the Project Management Disciplines described in the PMBOK revolves around the Project cube, which also 'moves in time' (per a calendar schedule). The following illustrates this concept.

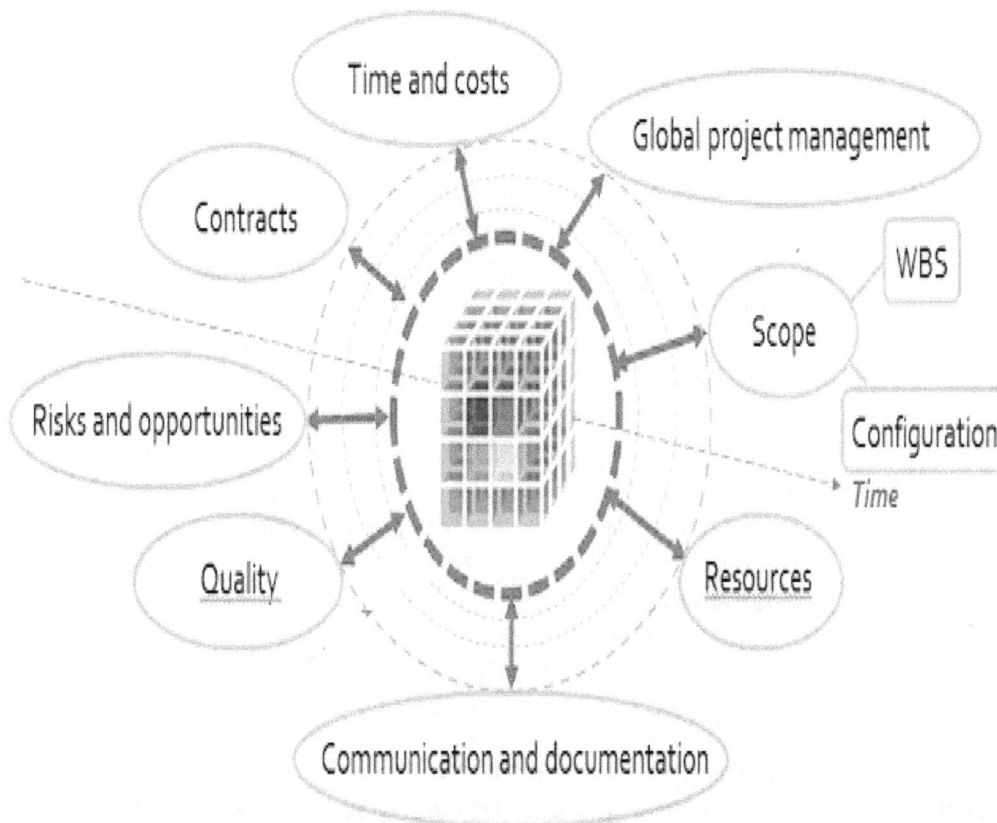

Figure 49: Integrated Project Management

Imagine integrated project management, with the projected cube at its center. The Project cube is the epicenter of project management. The project management cube could produce reports, use dashboards like EVM S-curves, time-time diagrams, workload plans, and could be linked to a planning software to produce Gantt and PERT[54] diagrams, in a bi-directional way. All the Project Management disciplines are linked to the projected cube. The following picture illustrates this concept.

---

[54] *A PERT (Program Evaluation Review Technique) chart - project management tool used to schedule, organize, and coordinate tasks within a project; a methodology developed by the US Navy (1950s) to manage the Polaris missile program.*

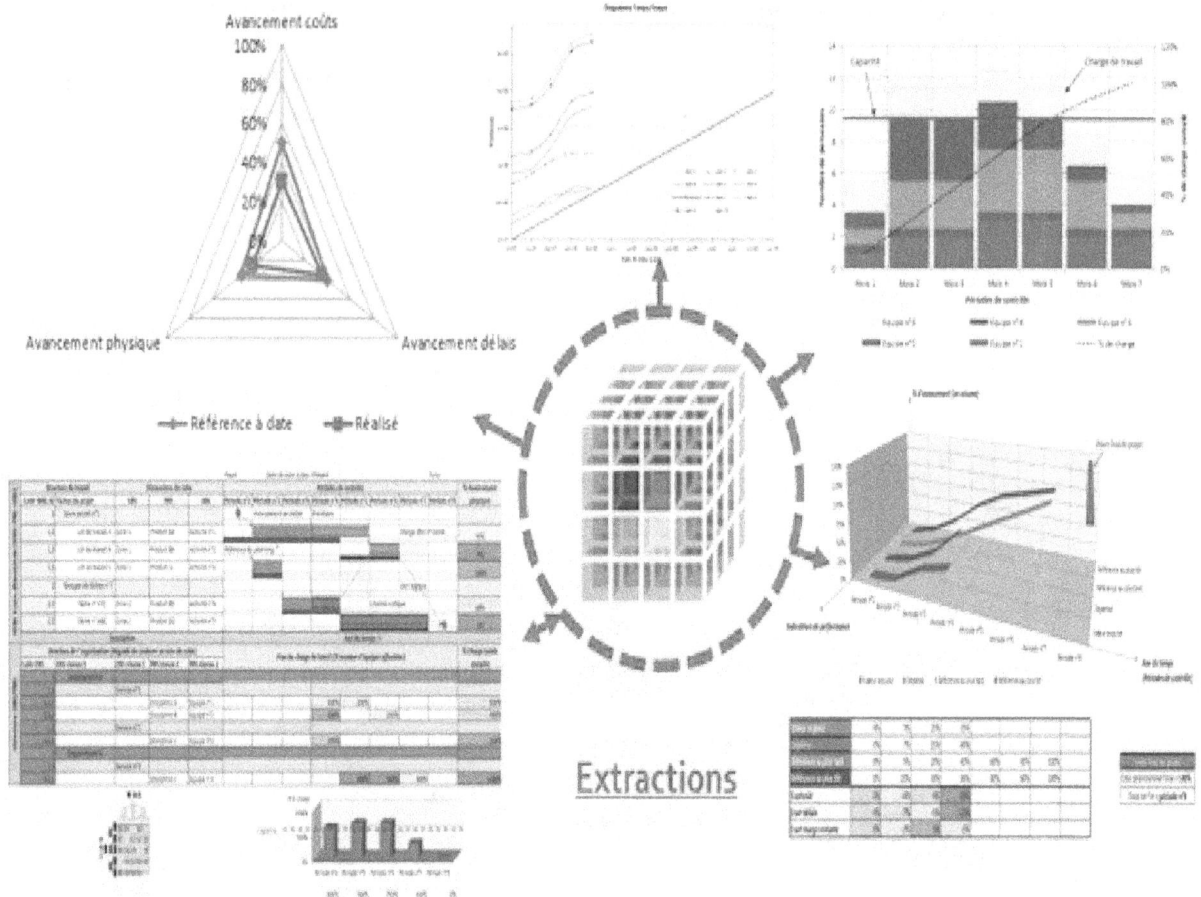

Figure 50: Project Management Planning Conceptual Software Output Model

This concept can be integrated directly into the BIM system. Once integrated by the project management and team, this concept will greatly improve communications as well as reduce communication misunderstandings, missed elements or tasks, and avoid project errors.

Chronology of the Breakdown Structures

Each tree structure must be progressively elaborated – meaning developed at increasing levels of detail. When a move from the WBS to Activities occurs, there must be sequence or chronology – one activity must occur before another one can occur. For example, Activities (ABS) linked together to form a Process, with a logical order of execution of Activities. Products (PBS), for the construction phase, must be organized as a flow diagram, which indicates the sequence of installation / construction of the Products. Even the Locations (LBS) – functional or physical – must have a chronology. Kilometric distance points or markers of a linear project can define the chronology. The primary breakdown structures of the WBS (LBS, PBS, and ABS) are represented in one dimension with a chronology – a logical chronology – in the order of the schedule. The figure below shows a tree structure with a chronology.

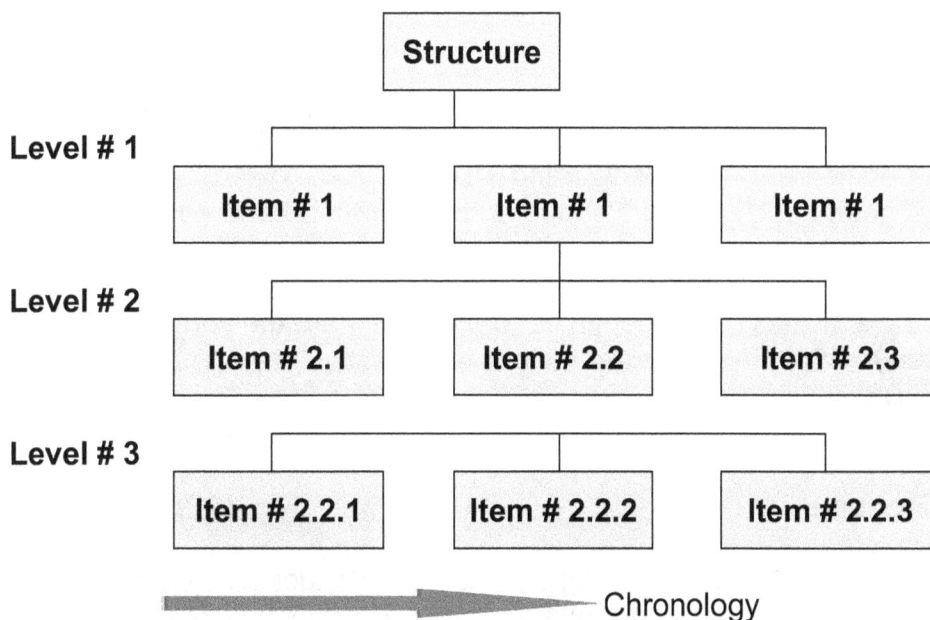

Figure 51: Primary Tree Structure of the WBS with A Chronology Sample

Instantiated Product Breakdown Structure (PBS)

The Instantiated Product Breakdown Structure (PBS) is defined as an Instantiation of products. Before being installed or constructed (ABS) for any given location (LBS), the Product (PBS) must be standardized, but to become unique, requires the coding structure to contain sufficient characters to differentiate between the same products (in the example below, piles) used in different locations. Figure 52 (following) below shows a PBS, for a civil works project.

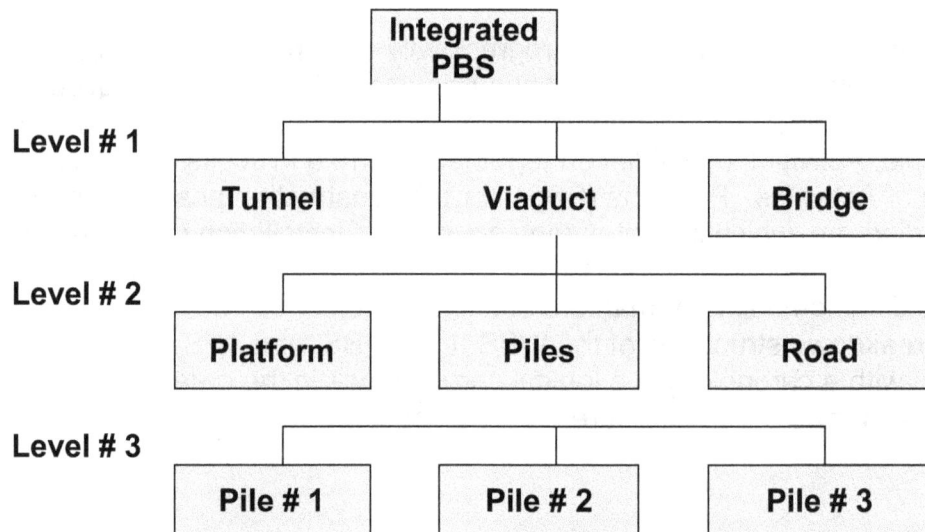

Figure 52: Product Breakdown Structure (PBS) Sample

These products must be uniquely differentiated by assigning a number, so the products become 'Pile #1,' 'Pile #2,' and 'Pile #3.' Radio Frequency Identifiers (RFID's) will be attached to each product, so there is clear identification of exactly which pile or other product goes to each location. This enables the warehouse to ensure the right product is released for installation at the correct location. It is the same family of products; the activities (ABS) deployed to produce it are the same (from a planning point of view). When Products are instantiated (PBS), they can be assigned in a Location (LBS).

Vertical Products

There are horizontal Products and vertical Products. Vertical products are common to several Zones, whereas a horizontal Product belongs to separate Zones. In a building: the elevator cabin is a vertical Product (no pun intended!) as it belongs to all the floors; whereas walls are horizontal Products, and each floor has its walls.

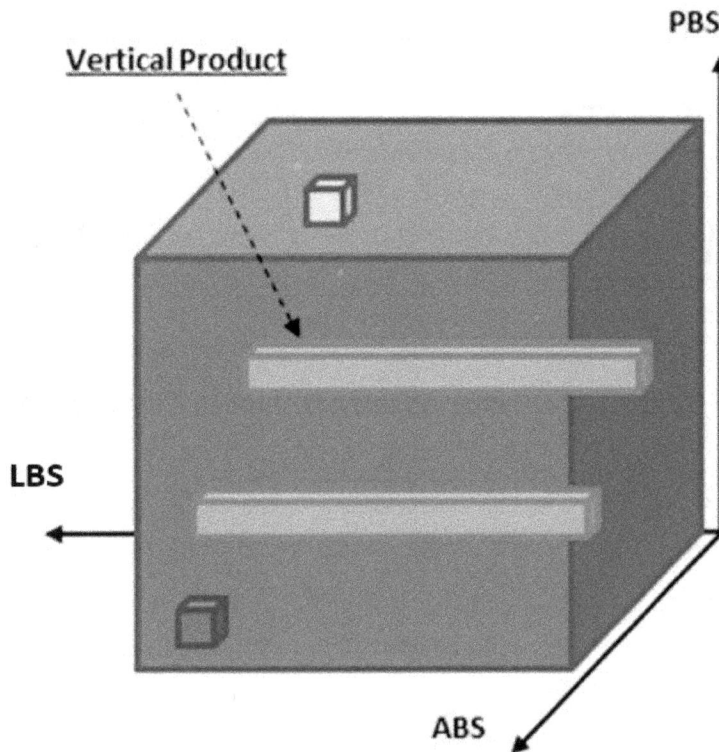

Figure 53: Vertical Products

In the WBS matrix, project managers can create a family of vertical Products (for instance two elevator cabins) by instantiating Products on the extended Product axis, and then by installing the vertical Products in a common Zone, which is vertical.

Creating the Activity Breakdown Structure

To serve the purpose for which they were intended, that is, to act as a set of instructions to be executed in the field, the Activity names in the Activity Breakdown Structure (ABS) should conform to the following 'best practices.'

Form, Pour and Strip Pier Footings, Column Lines A-1 through A-6 and B-6 through B-12

Action Verb
What to you
want me to do?

Noun
What to you want
me to do it to?

Further Instruction/Clarification
What is the scope of this activity?
Where do I start and when am I done?

Blind Flange and Hydtro-Test 16" Pipe- Spools #21 through #30 to 120 PSI for 12 hours

Action Verb
What to you
want me to do?

Noun
What to you want
me to do it to?

Further Instruction/Clarification
What is the scope of this activity?
Where do I start and when am I done?

Install and Test Work Stations, Rooms 304 and 305 using CV Test Procedure XYZ

Action Verb
What to you
want me to do?

Noun
What to you want
me to do it to?

Further Instruction/Clarification
Using what test procedure?

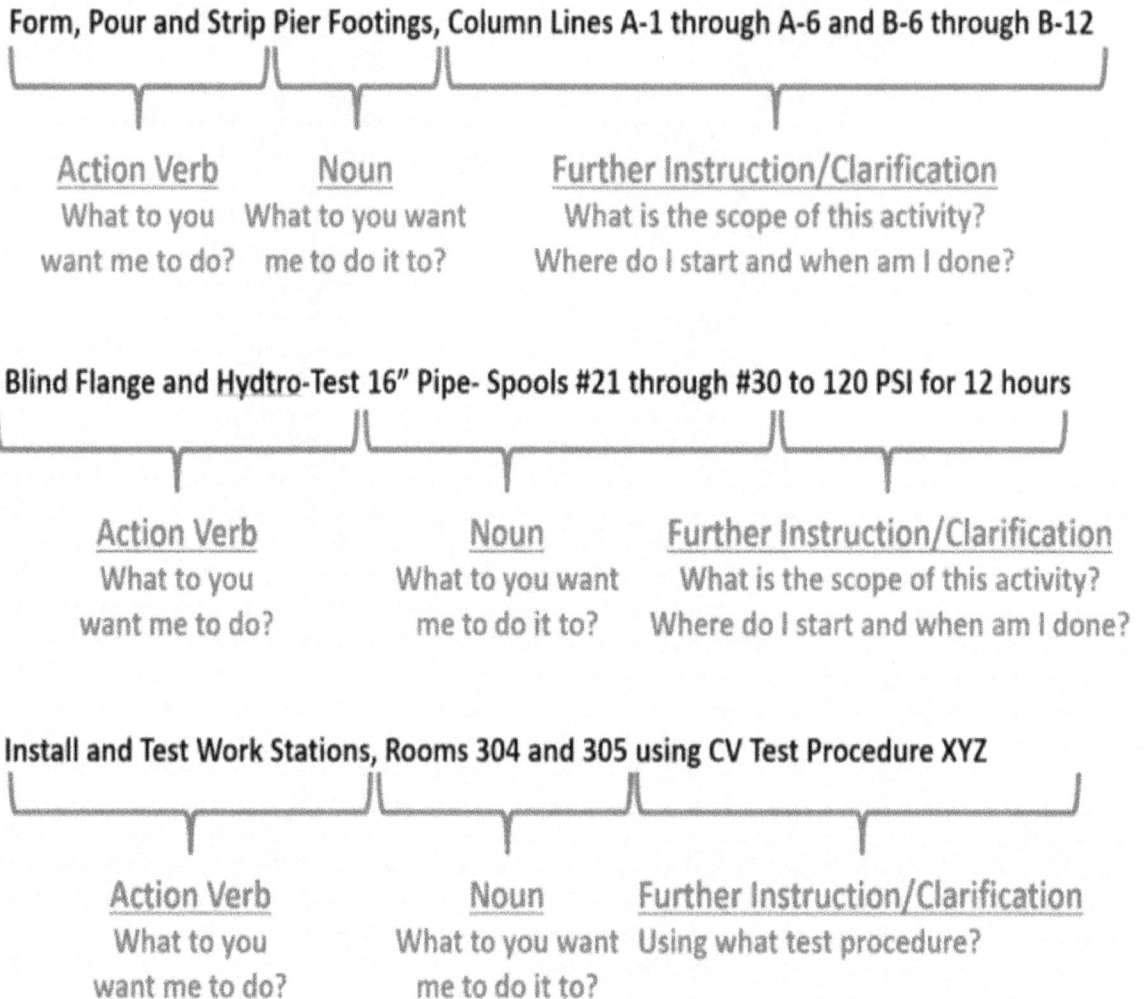

Figure 54: "Best Tested and Proven" Activity Naming Conventions

Using the examples above, the result is a 4-D model: The activity name indicates: 1) install and test (ABS), 2) workstation(s) (PBS) using action verbs, 3) which happens in a specific place, room numbers (304 and 305; LBS) using a noun, and 4) what and which task has to be performed to a specific standard found in the contract documents (CWBS) (using CV Test Procedure XYZ). This Activity Name contains references to four different sort fields.[55]

For another example, activity indicates 1) blind flange and hydro test (ABS), 2) 16" pipe spools (PBS), 3) #21 - #30 (LBS) to (CWBS), and 4) 120 PSI for 12 hours. The task is the last element of the work or planning package and is the concatenation

---

[55] *Guild of Project Controls Module 7.3 "Identify and Capture All Activities" http://www.planningplanet.com/guild/gpccar/identify-capture-schedule-activities*

between a Location, a Product, and an Activity (or any other coding structure which is appropriate or relevant). In the 3-D WBS model, each branch of the WBS is one task. For instance, in the example illustrated below, the tasks are directed by the equation: WBS = LBS x PBS x ABS. The task of this branch is 'Station New York center – Track – Installation.'

- Zone #1 = Station New York center
- Product #1.2 = Track
- Activity #1.2.2 = Installation.

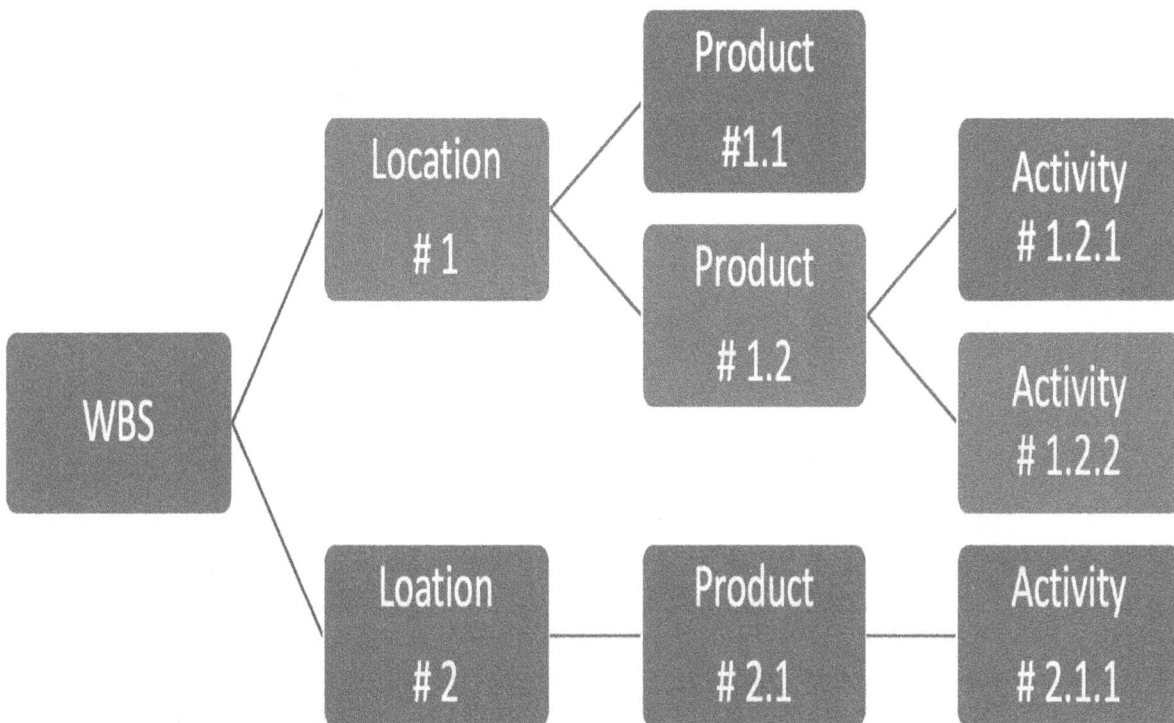

Figure 55: Concatenation between Location, Product, and Activity in a 3-D WBS Model

The Nature of Relationships in a Schedule

Adopting the 3-D WBS approach, illustrated by the figure below, logic links have three dimensions. Explained another way, there exists not only logical links between tasks of type, finish-to-start, start-to-start, or finish-to-finish but the logical links can be established between the other dimensions as well; e.g., between any two or more Locations (LBS); between any two or more Products (PBS), or between any two Activities (ABS).

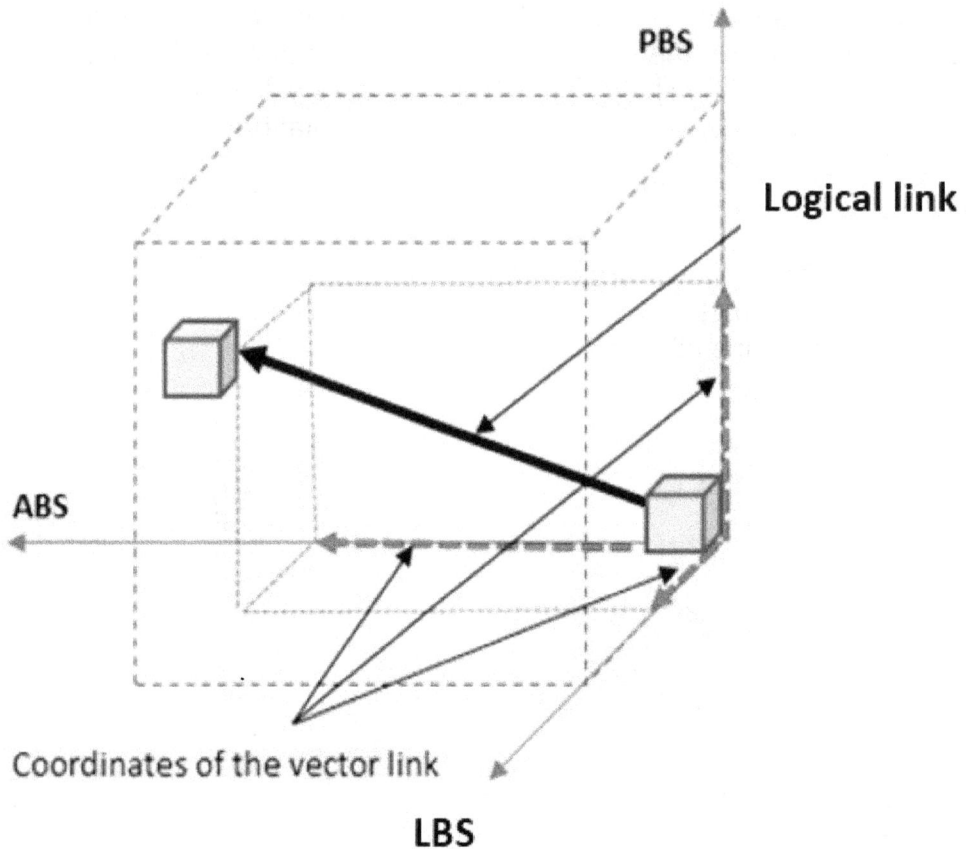

Figure 56: Logic Links Coordinates on a WBS Cube Sample

A construction project of an infrastructure of railways analyzed for links between the tasks results in: 'Zone #1 – Track-Installation' and 'Zone #2 – Track-Installation,' and are linked from finish-to-start. They are of the form 'Zone-Product-Activity,' and only the Zone differs between these two tasks, thus a link of Location nature. Tasks for the 'Building A-Transformer-Installation' is linked to the tasks for 'Building A-Cable-Installation,' with a finish-to-start link. This time, the Product differs between these two tasks, thus a logical link of a Product nature. If the tasks 'Building A – Transformer-Transportation' and 'Building A – Transformer-Installation' are linked, this incidence creates an activity that differs between these two tasks, thus a link of Activity nature.

When a schedule is created, the planner/scheduler (with the help of the project team) will define all the logical links within the method. The team will define the links of the Activities, then the Products, and finally the Locations. As a result, the logical connections of the schedule will be structured, and the quality of the schedule will be better. The logical link can also be coded with their respective OBS and CBS coordinates in the projected cube. As with other structures, this principle can be applied to CWBS and others as demonstrated in the Tesseract section and figures.

What is a 3-D Structured Schedule?

A 3-D structured schedule is a schedule completed with the 3-D WBS method, understanding that (as described above) the planner/scheduler is not limited to only three dimensions, but can add as many dimensions as are appropriate or relevant. To keep the explanations simple this section will concentrate on the 3-D model.

The elementary tree structures are crossed (intersect) to create the list of tasks, the three natures of logical links (Location, Product, and Activity) are defined, and then durations are calculated inside the three dimensions of the WBS. The result is a well-structured schedule, as illustrated in the figure below. The name of the tasks is clear, e.g., the Task name = 'Zone-Product-Activity.' "Each task has codes (attributes) identifying Zones, Products, and Activities levels #1, 2, and 3 (or more). If the schedule is well structured, then data can be easily found by sorting, filters, and groups."[56]

---

[56] Cubix Project Management - 3-D Work Breakdown Structure Method. (n.d.). Retrieved from breakdown233.rssing.com/chan-12384124/all_p1.html

	Nom de la tâche	PBS instancié	Lots	Durée	PK début	PK fin	GBS level 1	GBS level 2	PBS level 1	PBS level 2	ABS level 1	ABS level 2
	GBS level 1: Secteur n°1			120j								
	GBS level 2: Tronçon n°1			120j								
	PBS level 1: Communication			120j								
1	Études générales-Système Radio-Tronçon n°1		Lot n°1	40 jours	3000	0	Secteur n°1	Tronçon n°1	Communication	Système Radio	Études	Études générales
2	Études détaillées-Système Radio-Tronçon n°1		Lot n°1	60 jours	3000	0	Secteur n°1	Tronçon n°1	Communication	Système Radio	Études	Études détaillées
7	Études générales-Système téléphonie-Tronçon n°1		Lot n°2	40 jours	3000	0	Secteur n°1	Tronçon n°1	Communication	Système téléphonie	Études	Études générales
8	Études détaillées-Système téléphonie-Tronçon n°1		Lot n°2	60 jours	3000	0	Secteur n°1	Tronçon n°1	Communication	Système téléphonie	Études	Études détaillées
13	Approvisionnements-Emetteur radio-Tronçon n°1	Emetteur n°1	Lot n°1	120 jours	1500	1600	Secteur n°1	Tronçon n°1	Communication	Emetteur radio	Approvisionnements	Approvisionnements
14	Pré-installation-Emetteur radio-Tronçon n°1	Emetteur n°1	Lot n°1	15 jours	1500	1600	Secteur n°1	Tronçon n°1	Communication	Emetteur radio	Montage	Pré-installation
15	Montage-Emetteur radio-Tronçon n°1	Emetteur n°1	Lot n°1	30 jours	1500	1600	Secteur n°1	Tronçon n°1	Communication	Emetteur radio	Montage	Montage
16	Câblage-Emetteur radio-Tronçon n°1	Emetteur n°1	Lot n°1	10 jours	1500	1600	Secteur n°1	Tronçon n°1	Communication	Emetteur radio	Montage	Câblage
17	Test équipement-Emetteur radio-Tronçon n°1	Emetteur n°1	Lot n°1	5 jours	1500	1600	Secteur n°1	Tronçon n°1	Communication	Emetteur radio	Essais	Test équipement
28	Approvisionnements-Récepteur radio-Tronçon n°1	Récepteur n°1	Lot n°1	120 jours	1500	1600	Secteur n°1	Tronçon n°1	Communication	Récepteur radio	Approvisionnements	Approvisionnements
29	Pré-installation-Récepteur radio-Tronçon n°1	Récepteur n°1	Lot n°1	15 jours	1500	1600	Secteur n°1	Tronçon n°1	Communication	Récepteur radio	Montage	Pré-installation
30	Montage-Récepteur radio-Tronçon n°1	Récepteur n°1	Lot n°1	30 jours	1500	1600	Secteur n°1	Tronçon n°1	Communication	Récepteur radio	Montage	Montage
31	Câblage-Récepteur radio-Tronçon n°1	Récepteur n°1	Lot n°1	10 jours	1500	1600	Secteur n°1	Tronçon n°1	Communication	Récepteur radio	Montage	Câblage
32	Test équipement-Récepteur radio-Tronçon n°1	Récepteur n°1	Lot n°1	5 jours	1500	1600	Secteur n°1	Tronçon n°1	Communication	Récepteur radio	Essais	Test équipement
43	Approvisionnements-Réseaux téléphonie-Tronçon n°1	Réseaux téléphonie n°1	Lot n°2	120 jours	0	3000	Secteur n°1	Tronçon n°1	Communication	Réseaux téléphonie	Approvisionnements	Approvisionnements
44	Pré-installation-Réseaux téléphonie-Tronçon n°1	Réseaux téléphonie n°1	Lot n°2	15 jours	0	3000	Secteur n°1	Tronçon n°1	Communication	Réseaux téléphonie	Montage	Pré-installation
45	Montage-Réseaux téléphonie-Tronçon n°1	Réseaux téléphonie n°1	Lot n°2	30 jours	0	3000	Secteur n°1	Tronçon n°1	Communication	Réseaux téléphonie	Montage	Montage
46	Câblage-Réseaux téléphonie-Tronçon n°1	Réseaux téléphonie n°1	Lot n°2	10 jours	0	3000	Secteur n°1	Tronçon n°1	Communication	Réseaux téléphonie	Montage	Câblage
47	Test équipement-Réseaux téléphonie-Tronçon n°1	Réseaux téléphonie n°1	Lot n°2	5 jours	0	3000	Secteur n°1	Tronçon n°1	Communication	Réseaux téléphonie	Essais	Test équipement
58	Tests système-Système Radio-Tronçon n°1		Lot n°1	10 jours	3000	0	Secteur n°1	Tronçon n°1	Communication	Système Radio	Essais	Tests système
61	Tests système-Système téléphonie-Tronçon n°1		Lot n°4	10 jours	3000	0	Secteur n°1	Tronçon n°1	Communication	Système téléphonie	Essais	Tests système
64	Tests d'ensemble-Système global communication-Tronçon n°1			0 jour	3000	0	Secteur n°1	Tronçon n°1	Communication	Système global communication	Essais	Tests d'ensemble
	GBS level 2: Tronçon n°2			120j								
	GBS level 1: Secteur n°2			120j								

Figure 57: Task Levels in the 3-D WBS with Identified Locations, Products, and Activities on Three or More Levels

The Speed in Building a Schedule with 3-D WBS Tools

Instead of breaking up work tasks into simple and manageable elements in a top-to-bottom manner, the 3-D WBS method defines three elementary and independent tree structures: Locations, Products, and Activities.[57] The WBS method then crosses the structures (via intersections) within the WBS matrix. An analysis of the holistic view of the intersections or correspondences of the three trees provides an exhaustively detailed and scheduled list of project's tasks and integrates durations, which allows export into the planning software (e.g., Microsoft Project or Primavera P6). No data entry is necessary for planning. It saves considerable labor (man-hours), and energy (productivity). This process is the first factor of reduction of labor; the 3-D WBS method

---

[57] 3-D Work Breakdown Structure Method - Pm World Library. (n.d.). Retrieved from http://pmworldlibrary.net/wp-content/uploads/2013/04/pmwj9-apr2013-Moine-3-D-Work

brings into the equation or project management.[58]

The second element that saves time is the factorization of Products within the WBS matrix. Each elementary piece of data is entered only once, in only one place. During the generation of the schedule or the analysis of all correspondences, data is developed or multiplied, which saves consequential time. A project planner can build a schedule of ~2,000 tasks from raw data in only three days, whereas generally, it takes around 30 days to enter all the data for such a schedule. The time-savings by using the 3-D WBS method and its tools could provide a return on investment (ROI) factor of potentially 10-fold.

Previously, when a schedule was to be built, the planners used software dedicated to project planning such as Microsoft Project, Primavera P6, or another software package. Project managers then defined and built the schedule directly within the software. Project managers next structured iterations of the project within a top-down approach by breaking up the project into simple elements and manageable tasks (classical WBS) directly within the planning software. The schedule of the project was built gradually to the final result.

The 3-D WBS method proposes a different planning approach. The 3-D WBS method requires data to "… be structured before being integrated within the planning software. The development of the WBS of the project or its …"[59] tree structure is not obtained by a top-down approach or a bottom-up approach but by a mix between the elementary structures that compose the entirety of the project, including Locations, Products, and Activities. The structure of the project (WBS), the list of tasks within the project is coded and is completed using the 'WBS matrix' (prototype software). The project is defined completely within WBS matrix, and the resulting database is exported into the planning software to generate a schedule.

There is an important understanding to consider at this stage. Fast doesn't mean without deep and efficient control of the result by the planner. It is essential to understand by using the 3-D WBS methodology; there is a tendency to create more work than needed. Once the planning is completed, project managers should codify every task with its CWBS coding standards. By doing so, task verification is created and included in the scope of work of the project, is an option to be exercised by the client, or is a variation or change order (modification).

The Standard or Classical WBS Does Not Exist

The WBS is a cross between LBS (Locations), PBS, and ABS according to the 3-D WBS method. The task is the concatenation of three tree structures (the 3-D): WBS = LBS x PBS x ABS. In a project, physical Locations are specifics to the project. On the construction site, locations of the products are dependent upon the site, whereas PBS

---

[58] *3-D Work Breakdown Structure Method - PM World Library. (n.d.). Retrieved from pmworldlibrary.net/wp-content/uploads/2013/04/pmwj9-apr2013-Moine-3-D-Work*

[59] *Cubix Project Management - 3-D Work Breakdown Structure Method. (n.d.). Retrieved from breakdown233.rssing.com/chan-12384124/all_p1.html*

and Processes (ABS, Actions) can be standard for a family of the project. A PBS and ABS can be standardized for a product line, but not the WBS, because a standard WBS does not exist. Project managers and planners should strive towards building a standard schedule to avoid wasting time. So essentially a standard WBS does not exist. A standard schedule does not exist, for a product line (a project family in an industry); but a standard PBS (seen as standard "Pure" PBS combinate with standard FBS) and a standard ABS (Activity, not a task) does exist.

The WBS is an intersection between LBS (Locations), PBS and ABS according to the 3D WBS method. The task is the concatenation of three tree structures (the 3D): WBS = LBS x PBS x ABS. In a project, physical Locations are specific to the project. On the construction site, locations of the products are dependent upon the site, whereas PBS and Processes (ABS, Actions) can be standardized for a family of the project. A PBS and ABS can be standardized for a product line, but not the WBS, because a standard WBS does not exist. Project managers and planners should not try to build a standard schedule – mostly to avoid wasting time.

Note the myth of standard WBS as the one of standard PBS is very persistent, even today. How often have we heard, "who are you to say to people that this is not existing for most of the project industry?" The authors believe this myth is the consequential belief of financial, computers, and consultants deploying SAP or Oracle Application on large scales. These subject matter experts may not have known enough to understand the project concept while starting to deploy that system.

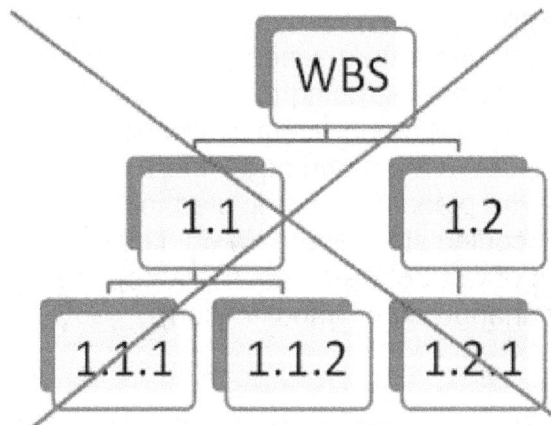

Figure 58: Standard WBS does not exist

Why do these specialists believe standard PBS and WBS was the Holy Grail? Because those Enterprise Resource Planning (ERP) projects originated from the manufacturing industry. Mass manufacturing is the king of pure PBS and mass industry is the king of nomenclature. In a factory, product nomenclature is detailed, standard, and fully integrated into the ERP. The specialists and subject matter expert consultants adapting the ERP project to the industry is generating a lower number of the items by product or unique items for construction, for example, instigating the possibility of the standard to simplify a job or task. This way of viewing WBS and PBS is still causing concerns addressed by adding more code into the ERP to use the projected cube and its composition of items within the 3-D WBS, the 3-D CBS, and the 3-D OBS. The results are requirements for more than one code for 3-DWBS, for CBS and OBS to use the outcome of the ERP to link it with the BIM model.

3-D Work Breakdown Structures for IT Projects

What is important in Information Technology is the number of separate, achievable applications necessary to generate an entire software application. It is necessary to complete a specific number of work tasks for coding to adopt a software to, in turn, perform an action on a specific material, different environment, e.g., a target machine of different type: an OS (operating system), on computer screens, within flows of communication, and/or via the computing power of the machine. One can characterize these types of achievable separate applications by 'types of target machines.'

If the differences between target machines are critical, as well as the efforts to arrive at the result (or stepped result), the adaptation to environmental targets can be regarded as a sub-project. The 'Types of target machines' can be Functional, Physical, or Environmental. Samples are noted below:

Type of Target Machine – Functional

- a waiter or a customer point of sale (POS) application
- a real-time distributed application: a module turns on the petrol pump, the exchange of the station with petrol meter, or interface with the bank for payment processing
- pieces of an application of distributed calculation being carried out on parallel machines which treat each one part of the total treatment with a supervisory machine
- a deployed software on a mobile object, e.g., a plane comprising several treatment units which dialogue between the external units and a central calculator

Type of Target Machine – Physical

When one wishes to test the application on different material architectures, examples would be:

- an application which turns on PC, Tablet, mobile device, or smart-phone;
- a website with a posting and menus planned specifically for shelf and smart-phone.

Type of Target Machine – Environmental

To test on different OSs, e.g., applications on Linux, Windows, MAC, or Unix use the lower levels of the decision-tree structures of Zones as types of target machines. This Environment or Zones can be physical, which gives the name of this tree structure, the Geographical Breakdown Structure (GBS). The concept of geographical location has a parallel to material architectures. The concept 'of functionalities' prevails in the logic structure of an Information Technology project. The concept is at the top of a decision-tree structure of a 3-D WBS. Activities are deployed on modules (a family of functions) assigned to functional Zones. Each functional Zone understands a set of functionalities.

In the two other demonstrated decision-tree structures of the 3-D WBS (e.g., the Products (Product Breakdown Structure; PBS) and the Activities (Activity Breakdown Structure; ABS)), are the higher levels of these decision tree structures abstract concepts (functional systems and macro-Activities). The lower levels of these decision tree structures are concrete concepts (components, equipment, works, and precise (Activities). The following figure illustrates the decision-tree structure of the Zones for an IT project.

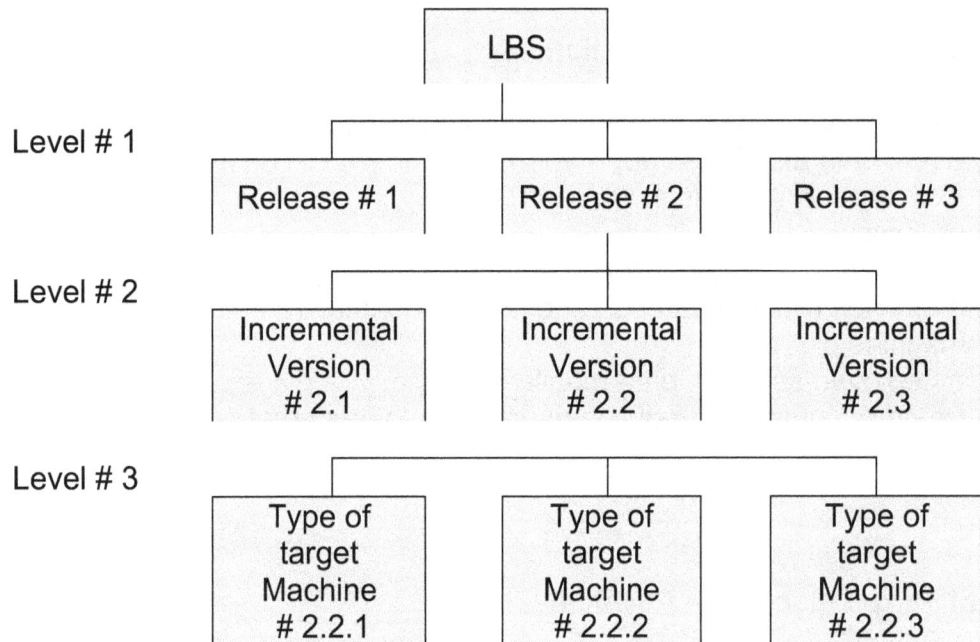

Figure 59: Locations for an IT Project

The version of the software is specified (an evolution of the functionalities of a module (Product)). According to 3-D WBS, a version can be seen as an instantiated Product – since two different versions from the same module are carried out starting from the same Activities. More generally, if the project is industrial … of infrastructure type, Product development, or Information Technology … Locations are of a Physical-functional nature (Sylvain Le Muet Delays, 2014).

3-D WBS Applied to EPCM Projects

EPCM Projects and Extended Product Breakdown Structure

Engineers for an Engineering, Procurement, and Construction Management (EPMC)[60] project should orient the schedule to Products when contracts are lump-sum contracts paid by results, deliverables, or products (e.g., 'Work Results' - CSI's Master Format or OmniClass Table 23). An engineer wants to manage the contractors from a master schedule so they will know 'What' the contractors do – more 'Products,' and less 'How' they do the work (Activities; ABS). The Engineer should know 'How' (ABS); the contractors perform the work because that data is included in their schedules, but not in the master schedule of the Engineer. A Product oriented schedule means the PBS must be in more detail than the ABS (in the WBS).

A Product Breakdown Structure is the integration of functional or process systems at its higher levels and 'Pure' Products (refer to the 3-D WBS 'V' lifecycle section) that are (most of the time) on the last levels of the breakdown structure (except for spare parts and specific projects delivery).

'What' does one need to manage? A Product Breakdown Structure is a kind of object – concrete – that is not abstract. So, for an EPMC project:

- Engineering phase, PBS is mainly oriented in Systems
- Procurement phase (consultations to delivery on site) PBS is an oriented system and drills down to Pure Products by using supply contracts; on the contractor's level (point of view), PBS of the procurement phase can also be viewed as supply-contracts oriented (contracts have FBS/Pure PBS coordinates)
- Construction phase, PBS is Pure Products oriented
- Pre-commissioning phase, PBS is Pure Products oriented then slowly evolves into a structured System
- Commissioning phase, PBS is Systems oriented

The PBS changes nature in different phases of the project. Figure 60 below illustrates the nature of PBS during the phases of the project.[61] Those considerations underline the necessity of a PBS that combine both a System- and Pure-product approach.

---

[60] *Engineering, Procurement, and Construction Management (EPCM) is a common form of contracting arrangement for large projects within an infrastructure, including industries such as mining, natural resources, and energy.*
[61] *Ccs/tms320f28335: Unwanted EPWM Interference. - C2000 32 ... (n.d.). Retrieved from e2e.ti.com/support/microcontrollers/c2000/f/171/t/627174*

SBS, Systems

Engineering

Contracts
(from consultation to
delivery on site)
Procurement

PBS, Products
Construction

SYS, Systems
Commissioning

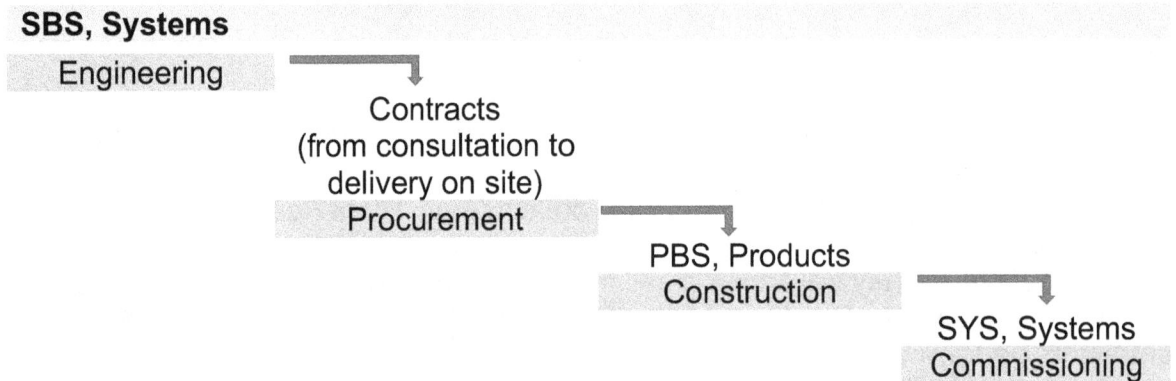

Figure 60: Extended PBS During Different Phases of the Project

Product Breakdown Structure in Work Breakdown Structure Matrix

Activities (ABS) are deployed on Products (PBS), and the Products are assigned 'somewhere' (LBS), in a Location (functional or physical/geographical). These three decision-tree structures are the three main dimensions of the WBS. The term PBS equals PBS (Pure products) and functional systems, including Systems extended by Pure Products. The PBS can also include special items like Contracts and can be used for construction projects. Systems are analyzed, the contracts are approved with contractors in the procurement phase, the products are erected or constructed within the construction phase, and then Systems are tested in the commissioning phase.

The products are not managed directly by the engineer after the purchase order; the Contracts are managed, but not the Products at this stage. The PBS means 'What' shall be managed, the 'What' depends at what point at which of the project phases. Hence, the simplified WBS matrix can be presented as illustrated below.

Location	Location #1	Location #2	Location #3	Product#1.A	Product#1.B	Extented products level #1	Extented products level #2	Engineering Activity #1 Sub-activity #1.1	Sub-activity #1.2	Procurement Activity #2 Sub-activity #2.1	Sub-activity #2.2	Construction Activity #3 Sub-activity #3.1	Sub-activity #3.2	Sub-activity #3.3	Tests Activity #4 Sub-activity #4.1	Sub-activity #4.2	Sub-activity #4.3
Instantiated Product	X					System #1	Sub system #1	1	2								
	X					System #2	Sub system #2	1	2								
	X					Services Contract	Contract #1			1							
	X					Product Contract	Contract #2			1							
	X					Product Contract	Contract #3			1							
		X	X			Product A	Product #1					1	2	3			
						Product A	Product #2					1	2	3			
	X					System #1	Sub system #1								1	2	3
	X					System #2	Sub system #2								1	2	3

Figure 61: Extended PBS Simplified WBS Matrix

Analyzing cross-references of a WBS matrix enables a list of tasks scheduled with task codes generated by an algorithm using a Visual Basic for Applications (VBA) into a Microsoft Excel spreadsheet. The result is imported into the planning software to generate a schedule. Activities, Products, and Locations are logical links that are automatically created based on the order number in the WBS matrix.

Managing Claims with 3-D WBS or Managing Claims with Project Cube model and CWBS structure

Every structure of the 3-D WBS (ABS, PBS, LBS), and complementary structures of the projected cube (OBS and CBS and their composing structure) and CWBS are useful tools to manage claims. Consider these two general types of reasons for claims that are …

1) … directly and entitled by application of contract clauses, such as variations and/or

2) … motivated by imprecisions or a contract omission / not covered by clauses

The scope defined in any single contract between the owner and contractor is defined by the Contractual Work Breakdown Structure (CWBS). Then project managers can subtract remaining portions (or project cube) by crossing the remaining portion of the CWBS and the projected cube. The results are what is *not* covered by a contract on the project. For any work not yet or not intended to be subcontracted out (e.g., owner supplied equipment or services), that work should be identified by using the term 'Not Contracted Portion' (NCP). The NCP should be monitored closely; its evolution is key to Contracts administration of the project. This NCP portion can be increased or reduced, which is why it should be closely analyzed and monitored. The main causes of evolution are any of the following:

- Normal increase (or decrease) of the NCP – there is more (or less) to do, but it is recognized and managed without a contract, clause, or modifications
- Abnormal increase (or decrease) of the NCP enabling a split after analyzing it in:
    - Additions (or reduction of) work that *can* be claimed under one of the contracts by one of the parties (including insurances) (Type A)
    - Additions (or reduction of) work that cannot be claimed under one of the contracts (such as misses, work to be redone, adding unexpected costs…) by any party (Type B)

The abnormal increase (or decrease) portion is discussed in this chapter and opens an understanding for some compensations of the increase/decrease for the concerned party(is). The 3-D WBS method helps to monitor the work portion claimed by the parties involved in the project and provides, once implemented, a powerful tool to eliminate oversights within the contract project.

Type A. In this case, there is no contractual or judicial fight about the reason and the nature of the claim, no contest of the right to claim, but only discussions about amounts, durations, and delays (if any). What is useful for claims directly entitled by the application of the contract clauses is the object of the claim can be fully identified by making a subtraction between two states of the NCP (previous and actual). The projected cube must be updated per the extension or reduction of scope, so in the case of a claim, it is easy to identify – once every breakdown in place.

There are advantages provided by the 3-D WBS method, notably the precise definition of the added (or reduced) work, services, or other items subject to claims. If the projected cube is well-defined, the claim's administration can be improved, and teamwork facilitated; all parties will know exactly what is subject to claim. The 3-D WBS can be used to communicate the content of the claim and, to go further, can later be used to manage the entire claim because everything is included (cost, delays, scope). See the conclusion of this section for more details about the advantages.

Type B. This case is a difficult claim that can lead to disputes up to arbitration or into judicial lawsuits. In some claims involving additional (or reduction of) work, the 3-D WBS method can demonstrate the effectiveness of the case documentation. Documentation can be achieved by using the comparison of NCP state and demonstrating a precise definition of what is part of the additional (or reduction of) work. The 3-D WBS method can be used as documentation of what was not included in the original contract scope.

Conclusion

Using a 3-D WBS method on a project allows management of overall detailed contract configurations. This project process is comparable to the use of the technical configuration management systems managing the evolutions of designs today (with the need for external management). The NCP identifies and clearly identifies that portion of the work not yet contracted and is not intended to be contracted (e.g., owner-supplied equipment or services) between the contract parties. Management of the modification of the NCP will improve claim management on the overall level. The updated and extensive documentation of the NCP will reduce the question of whether it is or not a claim issue with facts and documentation within the 3-D WPS. By closely managing the NCP, sharing this management between parties provides complimentary relations and communications.

Imagine adding an NCP chapter to the configuration management committee (or team) of the project. These additional committee-team members, mainly composed of contract professional of each party, handle the contractual portions based on the global 3-D WBS model. This results in total concordance with the changes examined and decided in the configuration committee, centering on the technical issues.

3-D Work Breakdown Structures and International Standards

OmniClass and 3-D WBS

OmniClass[62] is a strategy for classifying the entire 'built environment'; it is a classification system for the construction industry as a standard for organizing all construction (project) information. OmniClass consists of 15 tables, each representing a different facet of construction information. The content of the OmniClass tables can be viewed on the OmniClass website.

"The 3-D WBS is based on three main dimensions: Locations (LBS), Products (PBS), and Activity (ABS)."[63,64] The fourth dimension is the Organization (OBS) extended by the Resources (RBS), and the fifth dimension is the Costs Breakdown Structure (CBS). Each table of an OmniClass classification can be seen as a parallel axis of the three main Axis of the WBS cube, as illustrated below:

- Location Breakdown Structure (LBS) can be modeled by: 'Spaces by function' (table 13), 'Spaces by forms' (table 14), and 'Elements' (table 21)
- Product Breakdown Structure (PBS) can be modeled by the table 11, 'Construction entities by function' (table 11), 'Construction entities by forms' (table 12), 'Products' (table 23), and 'Information' (table 36)
- Activity Breakdown Structure (ABS) can be modeled by: 'Works Results' (table 22), 'Phases' (table 31), and 'Services' (table 32)
- Organization Breakdown Structure (OBS, extended by the RBS, fourth dimension) can be modeled by 'Disciplines' (table 33), and 'Organizational roles' (table 34)
- Resource Breakdown Structure (RBS) can be modeled by 'Tools' (table 35)

Properties of tasks can be modeled by a Materials (table 41) and a Properties (table 49). Thus, the OmniClass and the 3-D WBS models are compatible.

---

[62] Introduction and User's Guide - OmniClass. (n.d.). Retrieved from omniclass.org/tables/OmniClass_Main_Intro_2006-03-28.pdf
[63] Emerald AACE 2017 – Weekly Blog – Page 7. (2017, Sep. 17). Retrieved from http://emeraldaace2017.com/page/7/
[64] Chambers, M. D. (2013, Jun. 1) Inside CSI: Using CSI Formats Effectively. Retrieved from https://www.constructionspecifier.com/using-csi-formats-effectively/

UniClass 2 and 3-D WBS

The corresponding structures between the standard UniClass 2 and the 3-D WBS trees are noted below in Figure 62.

No Table	Description UniClass 2	Dimension 3-D WBS
Co	Complexes	PBS
En	Entities	ZBS
Ac	Activities	ABS
Sp	Spaces	ZBS
EF	Entities by Form	PBS
Ee	Elements	PBS
Ss	Systems	PBS
Pr	Products	PBS
ZZ	CAD	Properties
PP	Project Phases	ABS

Figure 62: UniClass and 3-D WBS

ISO 12006 and 3-D WBS

The corresponding structures between the standard ISO 12006 and 3-D WBS trees are noted below in Figure 63.

Description = ISO 12006	Dimension of 3-D WBS
Construction Entity	PBS
Construction Complex	PBS
Spaces	ZBS
Construction Entity Part (?)	PBS
Element	PBS
Work Result	ABS
Management Process	ABS
Work Process	ABS
Construction Entity Life-Cycle Stage	ABS
Project Stage	ABS
Construction Product	PBS
Construction Aides	PBS
Construction Agents	OBS
Construction Information	Characteristics
Property / Characteristic	Characteristics

Figure 63: ISO 12006 vs. 3-D WBS

NorSok Standard Z-014 and 3-D WBS

The Norsk Sokkels Konkuranseposisjon (Norsok) standards were developed by the Norwegian petroleum industry to ensure adequate safety, value added, and cost-effectiveness for the petroleum industry development and planning operations. The Norsok standard describes a system for coding of cost and weight estimates and as-built/experience data. The system is comprised of three sets of complementary sub-coding systems labeled as PBS, SAB, and COR:

- Physical Breakdown Structure (PBS): This hierarchical structure defines the Physical/Functional components of Projects during any phase of development. The PBS provides a coding structure, enabling any Oil and Gas Production and processing facility configuration scheme to be coded.
- Standard Activity Breakdown (SAB): This hierarchical structure provides a timescale attribute to describe when during – the project lifetime – expenditures and activities occur.
- Code of Resource (COR): This hierarchical structure classifies all project resources and categorizes resources according to primary, secondary, and tertiary levels of resources.

The PBS of NorSok can be compared to the PBS of 3-D WBS. The SAB of NorSok can be compared to the ABS of 3-D WBS. The COR of NorSok can be compared to the OBS/RBS of 3-D WBS. The 3-D WBS method can be based on NorSok Standard Z-014, but zones must be added. Thus, the NorSok Standard Z-014 and the 3-D WBS method are compatible.

KKS Classification and 3-D WBS

The Kraftwerk-Kennzeichen System (KKS) is a standard code for power generation plants. It has three different codes compatible with the 3-D WBS model:

- Process-related identification are Products (Systems/Pure Products) in the 3-D WBS method
- Point of installation identification that is Locations in the 3-D WBS method
- Location identification is Locations in the 3-D WBS method

Serial number of breakdown level	0	1	2	3
Process-related identification	Total Plant	System Code	Equipment Unit Code	Component Code
Point of Installation Identification	Total Plant	Installation Unit Code	Installation Space Code	
Location Identification	Total Plant	Structure Code	Room Code	

Figure 64: *The KKS Method*

3-D WBS and 4-D BIM

The 3-D WBS method takes its meaning from the vertical column of the index system of the BIM. The 3-D WBS can act as the missing link of the global coordinate system. The future of project scheduling is the Building Information Modeling (BIM), or 4-D BIM schedules, in which units are built in 3-D, connected with Gantt schedules, and coordinated with 3-D drawings of the plant. Research is currently being developed through OmniClass and NorSok – two international standards coding systems for projects – useful for the construction of a 4-D BIM schedule. A standard WBS codification is required for these tools. The 3-D WBS method offers true multi-dimensional schedules since the elementary structures of the schedule are linked.

The challenge of the industrial building of the future is to be precise. The standard codification of tasks for BIM codification of tasks will enable the exchange of data between the 3-D, 4-D, 5-D, 6-D, and 7-D BIM software. Schedules done with the 3-D WBS method can have a standardized WBS, because the interactions of the PBS and ABS are standardized for a Product line (e.g., nuclear power plant or a sewage treatment plant). Only the Locations change between projects of the same Product line. Note that standard schedules do not exist, because the Locations in each project are different. The 3-D WBS model provides a practical answer to 4-D BIM because it integrates the third dimension – the Locations. Schedules structured with 3-D WBS method are perfect for BIM applications because the foundation is the standard.

Take a piano, for example. Put your fingers on the piano keys so between the first and second finger there are 1.5 notes, and between the second and third finger there is one note, the result is a major chord. In between the first and second finger, there is one note, and between the second and third finger there are 1.5 notes, you get a minor chord. That is the method, and the piano is the tool. The tool needs a method that requires a standard.

The tools for the 3-D WBS method are Primavera P6, Spider Project, MS Project, Costing tools, or the 4-D BIM. The standard is OmniClass, UniClass2, ISO12006, NorSok Z-014, KKS, and internal standards (crossing PBS x ABS).

The Value Breakdown Structure

Features & Benefits

The Value Breakdown Structure (VBS)[65] solves the question of why use the 3-D WBS modeling method (Stephen A. Devaux, Analytic Project Management, 2014). Every project and program is an investment and is undertaken to generate greater value and benefits to the sponsor / customer / investor than the cost of the resources invested. The relative success or failure of the project can be represented as expected project profit, e.g., the difference between the total cost of the resources invested and the value that the project is expected to generate.

---

[65] *The Value Breakdown Structure (VBS): What, How and Why ... (n.d.). Retrieved from https://totalprojectcontrol.wordpress.com/2015/04/03/the-value-breakdown-structure-vbs-what-how-and-why/*

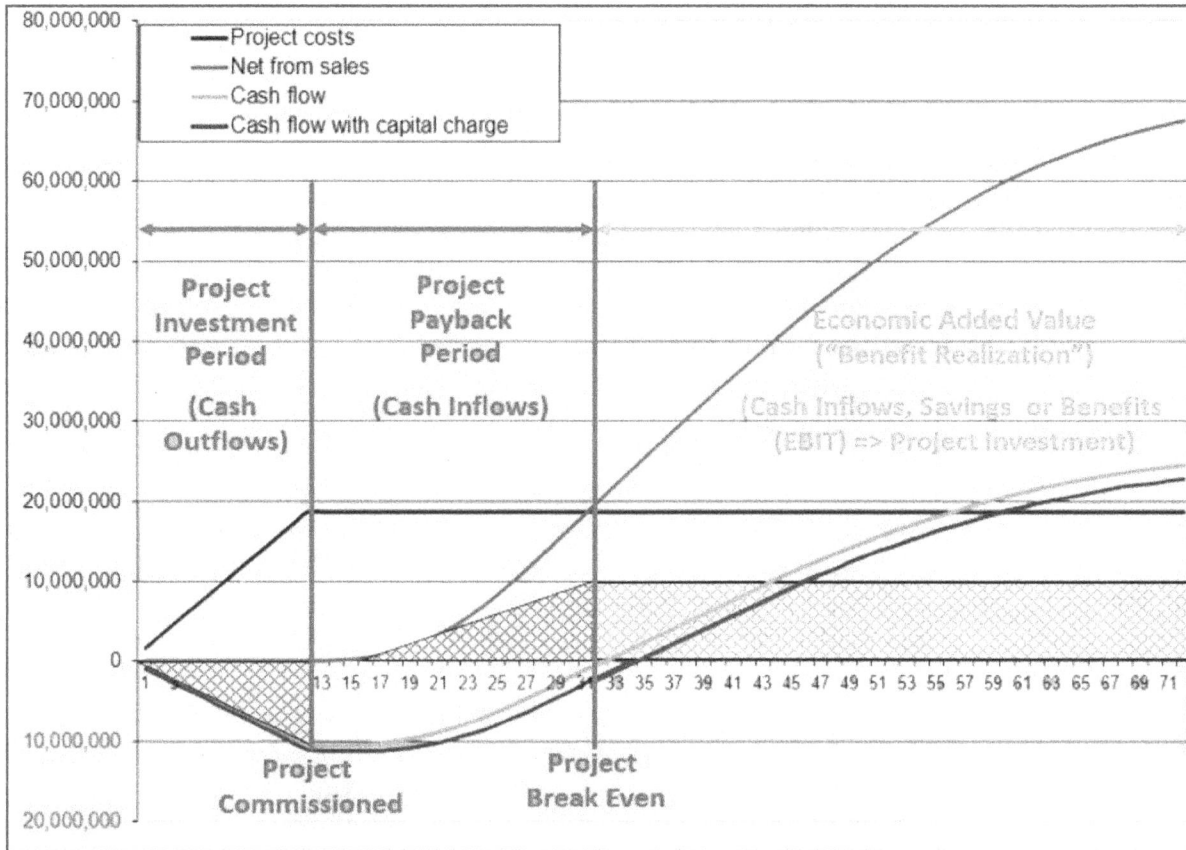

Figure 65: Economic Added Value (EVA) Illustrated using Payback Analysis

The value-added stipulation illustrates a serious misunderstanding in project metrics: the conflation of the unfortunately misnamed 'earned value' with the project's 'business' or 'investment' value. Earned value is always based on resource usage: the total resource budget or the budget for labor or specific material. However, this has nothing to do with the value the project is expected to generate. Indeed, no intelligent sponsor would ever invest $1M in a project the product of which he values at exactly $1M – even the least project risk and shortest project duration would dictate that the sponsor would only invest $1M if he expects it create more than $1M in value. Sometimes an expected value may be much greater than $1M – an enabler project, for instance, such as a new platform on which many valuable systems may be loaded, may create value and opportunity worth many multiples of the platform creations project budget. That budget would be the basis for the project's earned value.

Value, in the form of Return on Investment (ROI) or Net Present Value (NPV; or any other name), is the reason for every program and project.[66] Profits are carefully analyzed and tracked on all investments. On projects alone (where the project team

---

[66] *Net Present Value: NPV is described as the present value (PV) of all the cash flows (inflows being positive cash and outflows being expenditures), which means the NPV can be considered a formula for revenues … minus costs. If NPV is positive - that results in the value of revenues (cash inflows) greater than the costs (cash outflows).*

can make decisions that greatly impact value), this driving investment metric is never estimated. Investment measures are tracked and conveyed to the project team as a precision metric for decision-making.

The project's value is created by the scope: mostly the Product scope, but occasionally with some value added by the project scope (e.g., improved organizational skills with a new manufacturing technology). The resource budget is loaded into the elements of the work breakdown structure and summed to the top to create both the budget and the earned value baseline for each summary element and the whole project.

Value behaves differently from cost; tracking value is just as important. "Whereas cost is always additive (the sum of the dollar costs of five detail activities is always equal to the dollar cost of their parent summary activity), the value is not. The value of the two activities may be less or more than the sum of each, e.g., they may either duplicate some of the other's value or complement (increase) each other's value."[67] Mandatory activities/work packages/projects have a value equal to that of the entire project or program. If an airplane valued at $1M, but the left wing was omitted, the entire airplane has 'zero' value – unless and until that wing is added – making the wing a value-added of $1M. The right wing has the same value! However, the value of the two (mandatory) wings does not sum to $2M. The total value is relative to the $1M value of the whole project (completed).

Optional activities have a value equal to the difference between the total expected project value and what the project would be worth if all other work was completed – except that optional work (activity/work package/project within a project/program). The Value Breakdown Structure (VBS) may be identical in format to the WBS, but it will be loaded with different data (dollars related to value instead of actual cost) and not necessarily be additive to the branches. It provides the following benefits:

- Prioritization of work based on the classification of mandatory vs. optional work
- Prioritization of work based on the classification of different optional work based on its relative value
- Recognition of project value accumulation on terms other than the earned value (e.g., cost)
- Recognition of accrued (e.g., salvageable) project value if considering project truncation
- Quantification of value impact if there is a scope reduction

Identification of work whose value-added is less than its true cost is particularly important whenever there is a change in the schedule such that new optional work migrates to the critical path and acquires critical path-drag and drag-cost (true cost = resource cost plus drag-cost; Devaux, 2014).[68]

---

[67] The Value Breakdown Structure (VBS): What, How and Why? (2005, Apr. 3), Retrieved from
https://totalprojectcontrol.wordpress.com/2015/04/03/the-value-breakdown-structure-vbs-what-how-and-why/
[68] Devaux, S. A. (2014). President, Analytic Project Management, Instructor, Consultant, and Author. Managing Projects as
Investments.[(c)] Contributed and printed with permission, at: https://amzn.to/2VfMgCe

Return of Experiences

Subway Project

The very first time one of the authors had an opportunity to use the 3-D WMS model was in 2001. There was a request for a contract bid (request for bid; RFB) for a subway project, which encompassed a level 3 WBS and defined the level(s) compatible with the AACEI standard. This assignment was a challenge because of the restricted time period of only one week for the research, planning, and delivery of the bid to the client. The only way to face this major challenge was to organize the work in a very standardize and efficient way.

The idea was to define the GBS of the project with stations and sub-stations. Not a very difficult job as the bid listed those elements, with the exception of some unique elements about the depot and the Central Command Center (CCC). It was necessaryy to redefine those two zones later, because of mutual exclusivity of the depot and CCC zones. The problem was solved by defining the CCC as a zone in itself at the higher level of the breakdown and by switching the depot zone into the rail portions and utility buildings. This allows a split between the inter-station and the station portions.

Another problem encountered for the GBS elements was the necessity to isolate the station portion, the technical rooms, and the platform. Those noted elements will be handled between members of the contractor consortium. The first levels of the GBS are influenced by the OBS, especially to properly organize any contract job. The lower levels are usable for the general planning as a consequence of the share of the work between the stakeholders of the project involved at the building site.

The second thing to handle was defining the ABS which served every member of the consortium. It would be fortunate to have a baseline (or template) already set up for the ABS, as well as for the PBS. A tailored baseline for the ABS would provide a roadmap for consortiums tasks, as well as the interface work by others. An ABS would not be developed at the same level for each branch, because of the purpose and supporting OBS items relative to the overall project. For example, the installation tasking was split into two types, electrical and mechanical. The electrical installation was split into three parts, including the cable laying and connections. Mechanical installation was not split as it concerned the vast majority of the time for a single material. The logical conclusion is the first levels of ABS details were influenced by and relative to the PBS.

To overcome potential conflicts between systems and products entities, the proposal for two codes, one for the Systems (FBS) and one for the physical and virtual products (PBS) would be accommodated by ensuring the PBS structure was created in separate units within the 3-D WBS. A strict product breakdown (PBS) was the most logical way to split the installation work, while the system breakdown (FBS) was necessary to split testing and integration work. The first level of the PBS is primarily influenced by the GBS breakdown, a logical progression, as products are located somewhere, physical (as well as virtual), and are supported by physical products.

Using these processes and procedures, the planning and contract development team can document the sequential installation work draft within two days, then have another two days to finesse the details, plan the testing, and validate the sequence of the construction project. During the second set of two days, the first set of operations plans were quality assured to pinpoint any overlooked elements.

Another point of using 3-D WBS was the lower levels of each of the breakdown structure (ABS, PBS, GBS) were structurally influenced by the other breakdown structure (ABS, PBS, GBS); higher levels of the PBS are structurally influenced by the GBS, and lower levels are structurally influenced by the ABS. Higher levels of the ABS are structurally influenced by the PBS, while the lower level is structurally influenced by the PBS. Structural influences between different levels of each breakdown showcase the strength and power of the 3-D breakdown model which is conceptually self-sustaining. Those structural breakdown influences and the self-sustaining property is verified in a 3-D model described and for other breakdown structures such as CBS and CWBS.

Constructing a contract bid draft, and then drawing conclusions from the effort of this operational experience, resulted in practical observations. Initially, three breakdowns were enough to define the WBS with an ABS, a GBS, and an additive combination of the PBS/FBS. Each of the breakdowns of the WBS 3-D influenced other breakdowns in its higher level and the remaining breakdown in its lower ones. All of those influences were exclusive, meaning each of the breakdowns was only present for once each within the three layers (main, higher level, and lower level). Deeper breakdowns are influenced by the OBS – especially in the share of work and the interfaces. The definition of level 3 is the result of the three breakdowns crossing each other at intersections, with three levels of details (at least) for each of the structure.

This process for creating contract bids, the structure, and the definition updated and coordinated within AACEI standards, enabled the metro system subway planning project to be completed within two weeks for a satisfactory client contract bid.

3-D Planning of the Lusail LRT Project

Moine, was responsible for a 40-day planning mission to plan the construction of the light subway of Lusail (Qatar, Doha), a town in the planning stages that didn't exist yet, for a large VINCI project (2009). The scope of the project of Lusail LRT (Light Railway Transit System)[69] was composed of four subway lines (30 kilometers; crisscrossing each other), including eight underground stations, 25 air stations, a workshop, and a viaduct. The project was planned in several phases of design and construction in a geographically located desert. The complexity of this kind of project involved avoiding obstacles. This complexity was a paradoxical conundrum since the obstacles were as yet unknown … they did not yet exist.

Moine structured the project using the 3-D WBS method. Each unique

---

[69] Cubix Project Management - 3-D Work Breakdown Structure Method. (2013, Jan. 22). Retrieved from
http://breakdown233.rssing.com/chan-12384124/all_p1.html

geographical Location(s), the Product(s), and the Activity(is) was identified and then combined within the WBS matrix. This manner of planning was not conventional. This method and manner was a unique way of project planning at the time, so there was a need to explain it to the members of the VINCI project team who were not yet familiar with the methodology.

Figure 66: LRT of Lusail

During this project planning stage, Moine described the cube under the construction phase. The project involved building Products somewhere. In other words, the 3-D WBS illustrated the intersections between the Locations, the Products, and the Activities. Moine identified vertical and horizontal Products within the plan. For example, the heating system in the apartment building is a horizontal Product, whereas the elevator, which crosses all the floors of the building, is a vertical Product. That elevator applied to the track within the matrix crosses all the geographical Zones. The track is a vertical Product.

Since the prototype software for the WBS Matrix merged from the elementary breakdown structures of this project, the project planner could add more features, then obtain detailed data from the subject matter experts of the team, resulting in a Gantt diagram of 3,000 tasks (within Microsoft's Project), coupled automatically with a time-location diagram (Time Location System [TILOS] software), and completed the project planning in 30 days. The project plan was provided to a local project planner, and the objectives and project planning were completed 10 days in advance of the contract deliverables date.

What is unique about the 3-D WBS method is that project planners can create and build upon the schedule without touching the planning software. A project planner can build the 3-D WBS within the prototype software 'WBS matrix' Structure of the project. When the 3-D WBS planning matrix is completed, the user and planning software can automatically generate a schedule in seconds.

This Process introduces a vital time-saver for the creation of the building schedule. It is also why the 3-D WBS methodology is so effective and productive. The schedules that are structured and created in 3-D WBS are more functional and practical than the traditional planning method because the schedules structured in 3-D are symmetrical.

3-D Planning of the Construction of Trams for Tours

When Moine worked with the project coordinator of the first tramway line in the city of Tours (2010), the project coordinator was very familiar with the details of the project. The project coordinator had the whole scope of the project – but they were in his head. Teaming together and using the 3-D WBS methodology, 80% of the project planning schedule was completed in one week, which is phenomenal in the industry. The planning was completed using MS Project schedule, coupled to a time-location diagram, and carried out in TILOS for 1,500 tasks.

The project manager and coordinator team used the WBS Matrix prototype to structure the project. The team included Locations, Products, and Activities, then cross-matched them within the WBS matrix, to deduce from the data the final list of the structured tasks to be scheduled. All that was left was for the planning to be completed was to import the data into the planning software to create the project schedule.

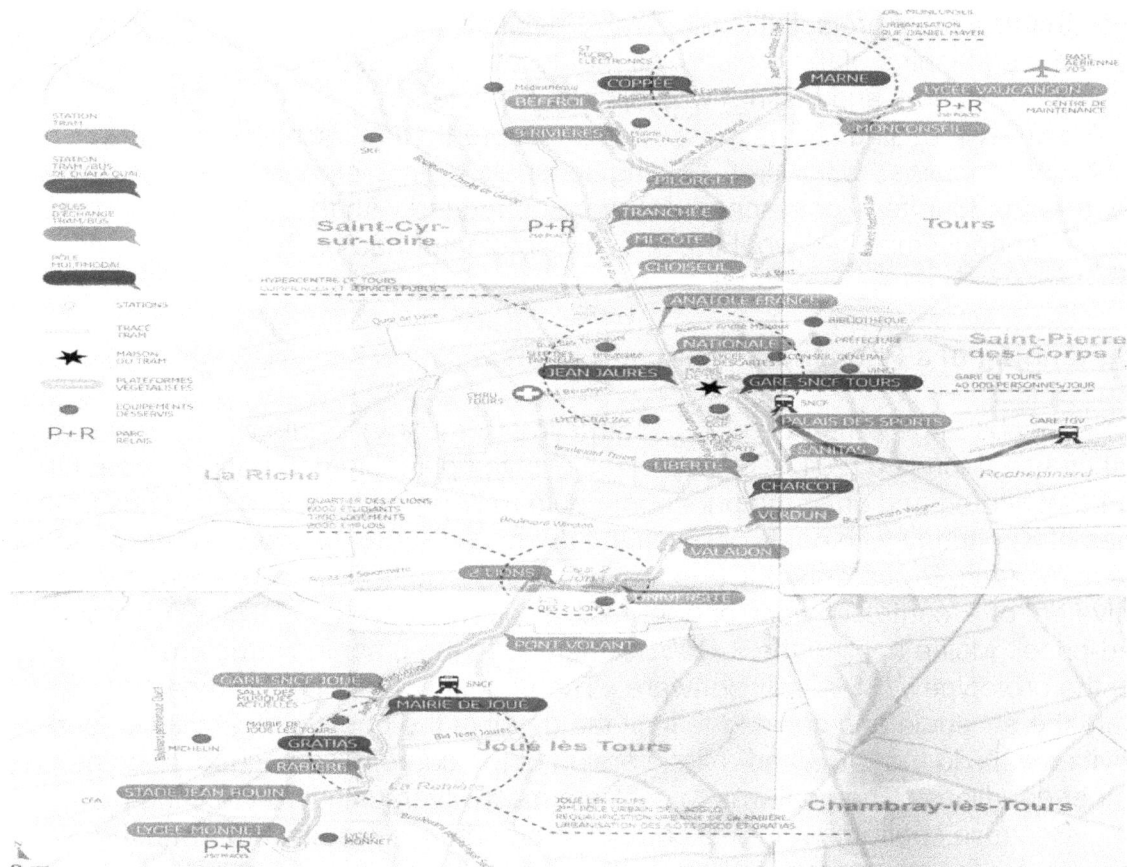

Figure 67: The Tramway Line of the Town of Tours

The project coordinator understood the finer the details in the planning better than the holistic control of the project in operational phases of the project. The tramway line was designed in small sectional units of 200 meters for Locations. The planning of a linear-work timeline is characteristic of a 3-D WBS structured schedule.[70] There were between five to six phases of work identified as 'Track Installation' on the completed line, referring to 'teams' which worked in parallel to each other, and within approximately 30 Locations. The mistake was avoided in planning six individual tasks 'Track Installation' corresponding with the six phases of work. Instead, more tasks were created for the 'Track Installation' than there were Locations (~30 tasks). These tasks were logically linked between together by logical links Finish-to-Start of the type Locations; since the 3-D model indicates a Finish-to-Start logical link can be of three natures: Location, Product, or Activity. By the end, on the time-location schedule, the six phases of work were apparent but broken down into about 30 elementary tasks, illustrated within a Gantt diagram. In the building phase, the project control result for track installation would be more precise.

---

[70] *Cubix Project Management - 3-D Work Breakdown Structure Method. (2013, Jan. 22). Retrieved from breakdown233.rssing.com/chan-12384124/all_p1.html*

In this kind of project, it is the 'Track Installation,' which outlined the conditions for 100% of the planning of the project. All that followed (infrastructure completions, systems installation, and testing) was directly impacted by any delay of the 'Track Installation.' Preceding issues must be fixed before the next scheduled 'Track Installation' combined with a free-floating schedule to limit impacts and mitigate risks. After three or four iterations, schedules were generated with the help of WBS matrix, and the schedule matched what the project coordinator had his head.

3-D Planning of a Phosphate Treatment Plant

Jacobs Engineering Group (Construction Company) required a Project Planner in Casablanca, Morocco (2012). The project involved planning a phosphate treatment plant that filtered and dried the phosphate pulp transported to future pipelines from the mines of Khouribga with goals of obtaining dry phosphate for export.[71] This project was an Engineering, Procurement, Construction, Management (EPCM) project; the equivalent of a 'control of work' project. The contract's characteristics were mostly fixed-price. Moine applied the 3-D WBS method to the planning structure of the project with the prototype WBS Matrix software. The project manager was limited in time to create the schedule and decided to limit the detail of the Locations, Products, and Activities to build the WBS and a first version of the coordination schedule of the project to meet deadlines. The goal was to create a macro- versus micro-planning plan.

Because contracts with a fixed price are related to results, e.g., with the Products, for the macro level of Zone given, the goal was to detail the Products more than the Activities, which seemed logical. For project engineers, the objective of the contract (Products) is to save time and man-hours. The project engineer must have a method to see the overall contractors' work (Activities, more important for details), but less of the Products (less important for details), and how each contractor performs. The choice was to detail Products more, related to engineering knowledge of the project, so the project engineer could pinpoint where delays could potentially occur and update data.

The project concept was of 'extended Products.' The Project Manager manages the phases of the project. For the design, the Engineering project manager manages the functional systems and sub-systems, but the Procurement or Functional Contracts Manager manages the contracts in the procurement phase. In the construction phase, equipment is installed somewhere, so Product Installation, Testing, and Commissioning are managed in the construction phase. The significant changes of the objects managed on the Product axis obliged the planners to produce matrices of logical links between each phase, to define which contract (Procurement phase) provided what equipment in the construction phase, regarding schedule logical links, and the detailed design and the procurement phase.

On a factory project, Geographical locations are useful in the construction phase,

---

[71] *Cubix Project Management - 3-D Work Breakdown Structure Method. (2013, Jan. 22). Retrieved from breakdown233.rssing.com/chan-12384124/all_p1.html*

are integrated into planning, and must be accompanied by a diagram that defines each Location. It is a drawing accompanying the schedule; the goal is to locate precisely each of the area of work to be done when reading the schedule.

A project planner can spend the crucial time to fill the WBS matrix (Prototype software) – as much as up to two weeks – while an expert in the process could complete a WBS matrix in two days. Within this project, the planners were inputting data to define the whole of the Locations, the Products, and the Activities, e.g., to define the WBS. Once all the data was input into the WBS matrix, the generated schedule PRIMAVERA P6 was provided on one day and contained 1,200 tasks.

3-D Planning of an Installation of Nuclear Power Plant Piping

Moine offered his subject matter expertise as a planning consultant on an installation project for piping within a nuclear power plant (Flamanville, France; 2012).[72] In the beginning, the project seemed complex. The power station was compiled of as many as 15 buildings, 150 locations, and 2,300 rooms. Imagine the complexity of the tasks: 15 x 150 x 2,300 x 2 x 10, possibly resulting in over a million individual tasks! This construction project would create a huge schedule and task planning that could have been feasibly unmanageable.

The complexity of this type of project is the water, and other pipes pass through multiple locations: on the first floor, then the second, then they return to the basement, and then back to the first floor. Supports and pipes were required to be installed requiring an understanding of each pipe as it belonged to an isometric line within a functional system. To install a pipe, as well as installing the supports, each required about 10 activities (actions), including boarding (layout and support), welding (joining), and quality control (to quality assurance and safety standards).

The goal when planning this construction schedule was to answer the question: "What is the tiled progress within the planning schedule for the factory? More specifically, regarding activity and concerning the installations of the supports and the pipes?" From data already established within the MS Excel spreadsheet (the tree structure of the locations), the 3-D WBS methodology could be used. The 3-D WBS method partnered the data with the prototype software 'WBS matrix,' generated a schedule of quality Primavera P6 of 1,700 tasks – in only three hours.

It was not a simple question of just planning the isometrics in the construction phase (contrary to tests), but geographical locations had to also be considered. The planners limited the scope to two levels for the Locations in the WBS, defined the two products installed, e.g., supports and pipes, then deployed activities on these products. The rooms were modeled like steps on the schedule's task, making it possible to measure physical progress (similar to Gantt chart updates and maintenance activities) to chart milestones. Logical sequences were next modeled regarding Locations, Products, and Activities. The 3-D WBS method indicated there existed three natures of

---

[72] *Planning Description: Cubix Project Management - 3-D Work Breakdown Structure Method. (2013, Jan. 22). Retrieved from breakdown233.rssing.com/chan-12384124/all_p1.html*

logical relationship links. This method of structuring the project made it possible to answer the essential question: "What is the progress is at this point in time?"

Using this process, within a few hours, about 80% of the schedule had been generated. There were some small items to be tweaked, adjustments to the schedule durations, and various finishes for the remaining 20% of the detailed items. This demonstrated that, with the 3-D WBS method and the prototype software 'WBS matrix,' project planners can create schedules five times faster and better than the standardized method. The 3-D WBS method and the prototype software 'WBS matrix' became a revolutionary idea in the world of construction project planning.

3-D Construction Planning for the French Ministry of Defense Ballard Building

Another planning mission was the project 'Ballard,' for Bouygues Bâtiment Company, in Paris, France (2012). This new Pentagon of the Ministry for Defense is the most emblematic project of building in France. Moine had only six months to complete the planning schedule for 10 buildings. The consultant project planner was limited to an average of 1,200 tasks per building's schedule to remain reasonable and to have manageable schedules.

Figure 68: Construction of the Ballard Ministry, for Bouygues Bâtiment, Paris, France

Moine worked with a subject matter expert (SME) within the building and planning industry and applied the 3-D WBS methodology to generate the schedules. The Project Planner (Moine) and the SME used the prototype software VBA Excel 'WBS Matrix' were able to finalize 10 schedules with Primavera P6 in only one month with deliverables provided to the client five months sooner than the requested deadline. The Project planner and SME were able to add more data to the software to fill in the details of a building comparative to other variables within 'WBS matrix,' and within 15 minutes, the schedule of 1,200 tasks was generated using the Primavera P6! The 3-D WBS method made the process possible to generate the schedules at extraordinary speed. There remained important definitions to finalize schedules completely, but 20% of the remainders were basic work, which can take up the duration of the entire project. Most important … the client was satisfied with the speed and the planning process.

Advantages and Benefits of the 3-D WBS

Time and Effort Savings

For project tasks to be identified, the factorization of the Activities (How?), Products (What?) and Locations (Where?) are determined. The data input of corresponding factorized 'WBS matrix (prototype software) data makes it possible to automatically develop the whole project's tasks. Time saved compared to manual construction of a WBS can be considered as soon as the number of tasks is identified. In the WBS matrix tools and 3-D WBS method, it is possible to build a schedule of 4,000 tasks in as little as four days, whereas a traditional approach could require weeks to possibly months of research, analysis, and work. The time saving is generally 10 times the labor required for manual planning. Using a 'Fragnet' library (or templates) for baseline tasks to plug into a more complex project, helps to expedite the creation of schedules for similar projects.

Detection of Possible Synergies

The principle of factorization, for the 'three dimensions' of the tasks, also supports a rationalization of the planning of the tasks by identifying the Activities, the Products, and the Reference Locations that build the tasks, to better compare the tasks between them, and to consider unique synergies (e.g., common resources) between the tasks. These possible synergies can make it possible to improve creativity and to optimize the realization of the tasks. This is known as 'resource leveling' or 'resource optimization' and is particularly useful on projects such as offshore oil platforms, where the total headcount is limited or constrained so that the mix of trades on any given shift or day is likely to change.

Coherences of Durations and Costs and Better Interface Management

The comparison of tasks makes the project management easier by factorization based on the use of three dimensions: Activities, Products, and Locations. This allows monitoring over a project's duration, including costs, by pointing to statistical discrepancies during any task durations. This also allows user-entered cost data for activities and products. This enables quality assurance via coherence checking. The 3-D WBS makes it possible to locate precisely interfaces, assign in and out coordinates and then classify them in term of complexity. This allows better management and greatly simplifies communication.

A Better Understanding of Projects

The 3-D model poses simple mathematical and/or data-based explanations of concepts that enable stakeholders to visualize the project deliverables at any given point in the project's life span. The 3-D WBS model[73] demonstrates three natures of logical links, e.g., Location, Product, and Activity. These links make it possible to build the project schedule methodically, realistically, and practically. The concept of work and tasks of the project is better defined and understood because the 3-D WBS model posits that, 'to work, it is to do (Activity), something (Product), somewhere (Location).' The concept of the levels of the schedule is now understandable. In Figure 69, a schedule of level two corresponds to two levels of detail of the Activities. If the ABS has two levels of detail, then the schedule is a level-two schedule. The following graphic describes a level-two schedule.

---

[73] *3-D Work Breakdown Structure Method - Pm World Library. (n.d.). Retrieved from pmworldlibrary.net/wp-content/uploads/2013/04/pmwj9-apr2013-Moine-3-D-Work*

Phase 1 –Identify
Guild level 1
WBS-
Cost estimate
Schedule

Phase 2 –Assess
Guild level 2
WBS-
Cost estimate
Schedule

Phase 3 –Select
Guild level 3
WBS-
Cost estimate
Schedule

Phase 4 –Define
Guild level 4
WBS-
Cost estimate
Schedule

Program WBS elements

Contract WBS reporting elements

Contract WBS detailed elements

Organizational breakdown structure

Aquarium development program

Program management and systems engineering

Develop and integrate aquarium

Material acquisition

Material integration

Development documentation

Structural integration

Biological integration

Integration quality control

Environmental control

Plant life

Tropical fish

Marketing

Tropical engineering

Control account

Control account

Control account

Aquatics division

Engineering

Biological engineering

Hydro engineering

Control account

Operations

Hardware engineering

Hydrobotanical engineering

Control account

Control account

WBS data summary

Work packages

Planning packages

OBS data summary

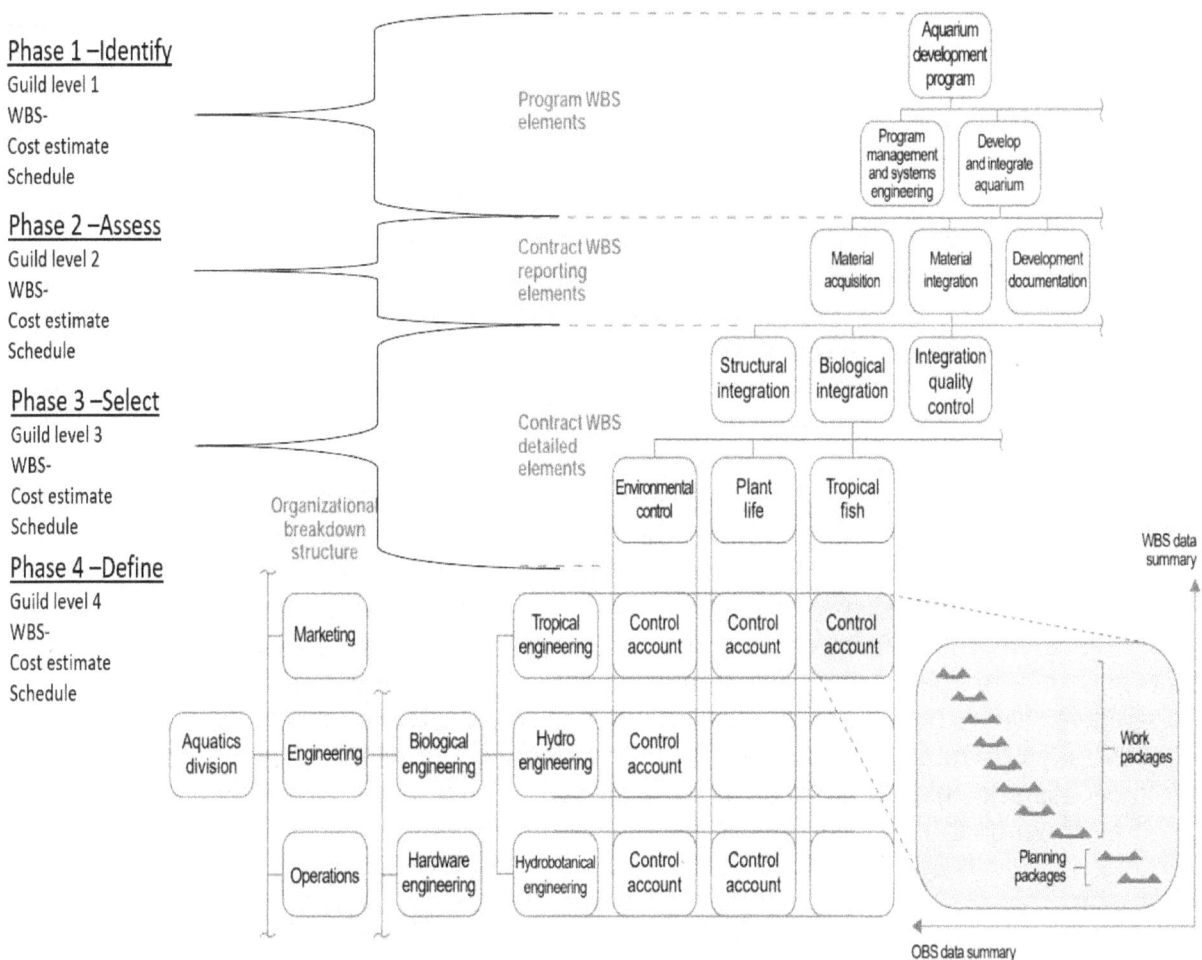

Figure 69 - 3-D WBS Defining Various Levels

Integrated Project Management and Better Structuring of Projects

The 3-D WBS makes it possible to connect all the disciplines (theme sets) of project management described in the PMBOK from PMI. The 3-D WBS model also makes it possible to produce dashboards and multi-disciplinary reports for the decision makers. The WBS of the project is no longer built by decomposition (sometimes referred to as 'backward chaining') – starting from the top of the tree structure of work (approach top-down), but instead by crossing (development) of the three elementary breakdown structures, namely the breakdown structures of Locations, Products and Activities, which constitute the 3-D WBS. Similar to the traditional approach, these tree structures are mutually exclusive and collectively exhaustive. In the 3-D WBS method, the rationalization references Locations, Products, and Activities thus employs unique Location names, Product names, Activity names; by crossing them (intersection), to preserve understanding, and identification in the definition of the tasks. There also exists a systematic algorithm of the creation of the WBS (method). Whatever the project: Activities are deployed on Products, which are possibly instantiated (specified) before being assigned at Zones. This rationalizes the manner of obtaining the complete list of the tasks of the project.

The reasoning for 'Top-Down' Versus 'Bottom-Up.'

"One does not reason anymore on the last levels of the breakdown structures."[74] The 3-D project management implies one affects anymore systematically of the elementary resources on elementary tasks of schedule, which is unmanageable and complicated when the number of data is important to manage, but one places oneself on the level which one wishes, according to the need and of the information one has, to assign for example groups of resources to groups of tasks, with a single person in charge by group."[75] This method makes it possible to manage complicated tasks but making the tasks simpler and more practical. The approach 'top-down' is more natural since it leaves the simplest (of the concept) to go towards more complex (the concrete detail). The bigger and more complex the project, the more the 3-D WBS model brings added value in the reduction of planning, man-hours, and overhead cost savings.

The 3-D WBS makes it possible to comprehend, in a rational and structured way, any project, whether it is industrial, infrastructures, product development, or information technology. The solid structuring of methodology allows a high level of coherence, exhaustiveness to details, and automation. The 3-D WBS method ensures practical effectiveness (results and time-saving) and inefficiency (savings of resources and net profits). It is possible – thanks to the 3-D model – to have real-time vital information, directed towards the person who needs that information.

Capitalization of the Discipline Data and the Processes

The 3-D WBS model posits that a standard or a standard schedule that does not exist because the Locations are different for each project. For example, a project carried out in Paris, or New York inevitably does not have the same geographical parameters. On the other hand, for a line of a unique type of manufactured "product or a kind of project, the Products and the deployed Activities are standard, as well as the generic logical links between these two tree structures (within a Zone)."[76] It is possible to have useful models during the creation of a new project. This saves time during the structuring and the planning of a project and makes it possible to homogenize and standardize the projects between them, regarding deployed Products and the process of realization.

---

[74] *3-D Work Breakdown Structure Method - Pm World Library. (n.d.). Retrieved from pmworldlibrary.net/wp-content/uploads/2013/04/pmwj9-apr2013-Moine-3-D-Work*
[75] *3-D Work Breakdown Structure Method - Pmworldjournal.net. (n.d.). Retrieved from pmworldjournal.net/wp-content/uploads/2013/04/pmwj9-apr2013-Moine-3-D-Wor*
[76] *3-D Work Breakdown Structure Method - Pmworldjournal.net. (n.d.). Retrieved from pmworldjournal.net/wp-content/uploads/2013/04/pmwj9-apr2013-Moine-3-D-Wor*

The Tesseract

The 5W-2H method and Project Management

The 3-D WBS method answers the fundamental questions of who, what, when, where, why, and who and for what and how much. The 5W-2H stands for **W**ho, **W**hat, **W**hen, **W**hy, **W**here (5-W's), and **H**ow are we doing Products and for **H**ow Much (For W*hat*)? The answers put the relationship into reality for all of the following questions.

WHAT are we doing? We create Product (PBS, Product Breakdown Structure), like Information Technology modules, civil works components, functional systems, equipment, and deliverables. This attribute defines what the project is going to create or produce. This filtering and sorting would most likely be based on OmniClass Table 22 or NorSok Z-014 Activity Breakdown Structure (ABS) but could be based on other coding structures – depending on how any specific stakeholders need or want to see the deliverables from their organized project.

HOW are we doing Products? We deploy Activities (ABS, Activity Breakdown Structure) on Products to produce them, similar to the design, procurement, and installation. This is the interface where 3-D BIM (Building Information Modeling) becomes a factor. The 2-D BIM design is animated to become 3-D BIM, showing step-by-step how the components, using activity-based management, are to be created in sequence. This will also provide the quantities (Bill of Materials [BoM] or Bill of Quantities [BoQ]) which go into calculating the durations (WHEN) and the costs (How Much).

WHERE are the Products assigned? Products are assigned to a Location (LBS, Location Breakdown Structure), like a release, a wave of the prototype, a processing unit, and geographical area. This filtering and organization of the deliverables based on the coding structures have been designed to show project managers wherein the project any specific object (e.g., equipment or permanent material) will be located. Using OmniClass, this would most likely be Table 21, Elements, or for NorSok Z-014, it would be Physical Breakdown Structure (PBS).

WHO is doing the work? Resources (RBS, Resource Breakdown Structure) belong to an organization (OBS, Organization Breakdown Structure) that performs the work. This is the classic Organization Breakdown Structure (OBS). If OmniClass was adopted, then it would be Table 33- Disciplines or Table 34- Organizational Roles. Using NorSok Z-014, this would be the Code of Resources (COR) coding structure.

WHEN is the work done? Tasks (the intersections or crossing between ZBS,

PBS, and ABS) are scheduled in time. The HOW uses the standardized coding structure (e.g., OmniClass or NorSok Z-014) that enables the 3-D database to communicate with the 4-D BIM CPM Scheduling database which, using the standard forward pass/backward pass calculations, shows us WHEN each activity is scheduled to start and finish.

WHY is the work done? We perform the project to obtain the Project / Product Value (ROI/NPV) required. This attribute enables a look at the project deliverables regarding why they are being created. What purpose are they intended to serve? Referencing OmniClass, this would most likely be:

- Table 11 - Construction Entities by Function
- Table 13 - Spaces by Function

HOW MUCH is the cost of the project? Resources (RBS) are assigned to tasks to calculate the cost of the project. The HOW using the standardized coding structure (e.g., OmniClass or NorSok Z-014) enables the 3-D database to communicate with the 5-D BIM Cost Estimating database. By telling us how many resources we need (people, machines, equipment) and knowing the duration from the 4-D BIM schedule, the 5-D BIM cost estimating software can calculate the cost of each component even down to the activity level. (Activity-based Costing)

FOR WHAT is the work done? Products (PBS) are created with the physical-functional characteristics required, and the quality level required. This attribute enables a look at the project deliverables for their use. Referencing OmniClass, this would most likely be:

- Table 12 - Construction Entities by Form
- Table 14 - Spaces by Form
- NorSok Z-014 - does not offer this option, although it could easily be inferred by the Component or PBS sort.

Russian Nesting Doll

The challenge is to get people to stop thinking in the traditional two-dimensional model advocated by PMI et al. and start to think in multi-dimensions. The understanding is – using a relational or object-oriented database – the project can be 'sliced and diced' in easier-to-understand portions. A view of portions placed at the top of the hierarchy can change as can the order of the other sort of possibilities. This provides a nearly infinite way to view project parameters and details. The best way to illustrate this concept is to think of each field as being a Russian Nesting Doll and that while we can start with the Project being the highest level, we can choose, which of are the levels at the top, while also enabling a view of subsequent priorities.

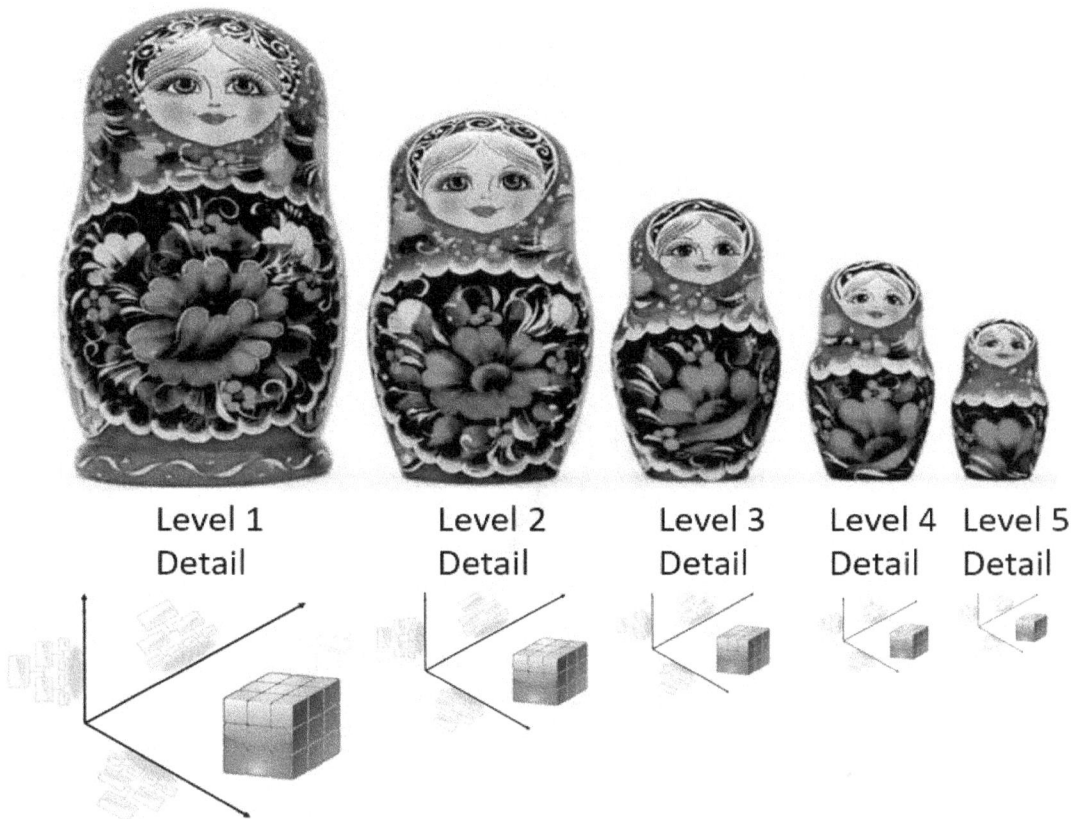

Figure 70: Russian Nesting Doll Illustrating the concept of the "project cube."

In Figure 70 above, we can see that applying the Russian Nesting Doll analogy results in greater levels of detail or granularity of understanding of the three dimensions chosen – that must always remain the same.[77] Using the same sorts shown in this figure, Conceptual Explanation of the 3-D Model above, we have filtered the data based on the ABS, PBS, and LBS. Drilling down identifies more refinement regarding the Activities, Products, and Locations, to focus on finer details. Drilling down results in the capability to view each cube as a smaller clone of the next highest level.

From a practical perspective, most projects are defined by OWNERS in the contract documents at Levels 3 or preferably 4, while most CONTRACTORS plan and execute the work at Levels 4 or 5. Note these are general rules and that specific conditions may justify varying levels of detail provided by owners and/or contractors.

---

[77] *Adapted from Legomenon Russian Matryoshka Nesting Dolls. Retrieved from: https://legomenon.com/russian-matryoshka-nesting-dolls-meaning.html*

Star Tetrahedron Project

As in Garrett Lisi's theory of everything, as many as eight dimensions can realistically be envisioned for a project, particularly in tetrahedrons.[78] In Figure 71 below, in blue, the Scope dimensions of the 3-D WBS: PBS (what?), ABS (How?), LBS (Where?), and configuration management (For what?). In red, the Value dimensions of the 3-D WBS: OBS/RBS (Who?), CBS (How much?), Time (When?), and Value of the Project/Product (Why?). For clarity, the dimensions are reduced to a point.

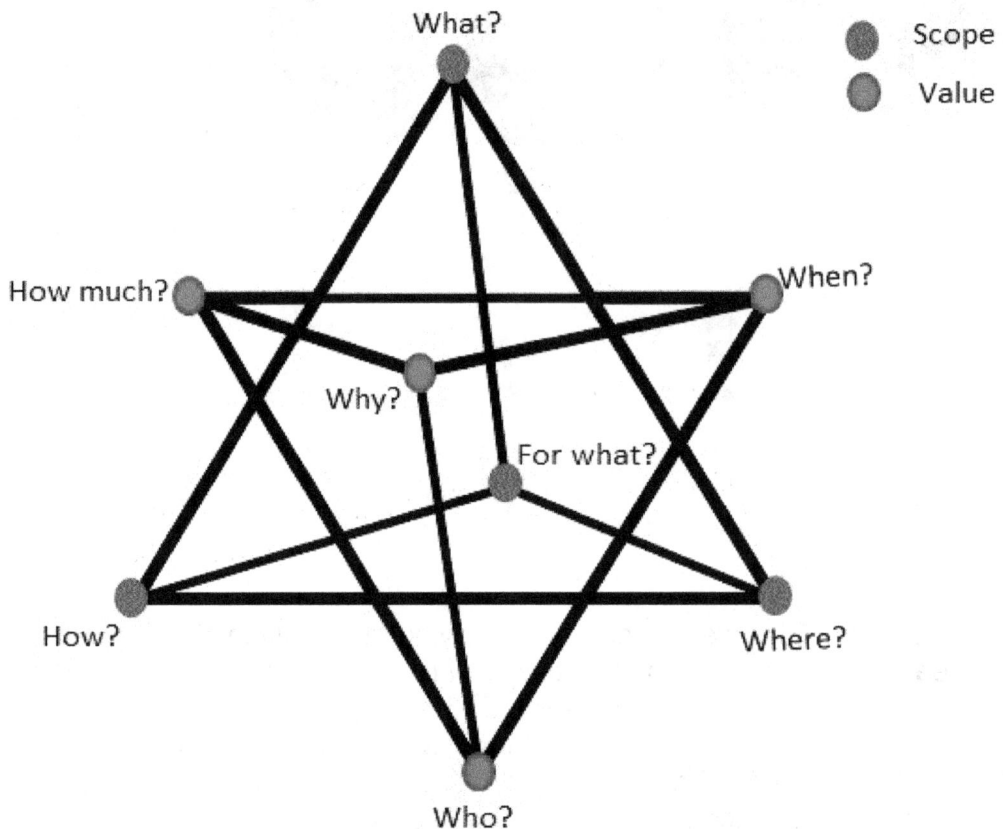

Figure 71: Adaptation of Lisi's 8-Dimensional Model

[78] W18_GW_8 Dimensions of WBS – Kristal Aace (2014, Jun. 28). Retrieved from
https://kristalaace2014.wordpress.com/2014/06/28/w18_gw_-8-dimensions-of-wbs/

Project Break Down as Fractals

In the fractal method, the basic structure repeats, not only at the macro level (the universe for instance) but also at the micro- and sub-micron levels. For a project it is the same, the star tetrahedron of the project repeats up to the micro level, as tasks. It is also the same for a project portfolio. Eventually, a project environment looks like a constellation of fractal points or stars. When you structure a program, a project, a task, or a project portfolio, always ask the same questions: why, what, how, where, who, when, how much, for what? Whatever the level, it is the same, like fractals (Figure 72 following).

Figure 72: Constellation of Planning Points.

Multi-Dimensional WBS Process of Projects Structuration

When structuring a project with Multi-Dimensional WBS method, solve the following questions, in this order (as shown in figure 73, below):

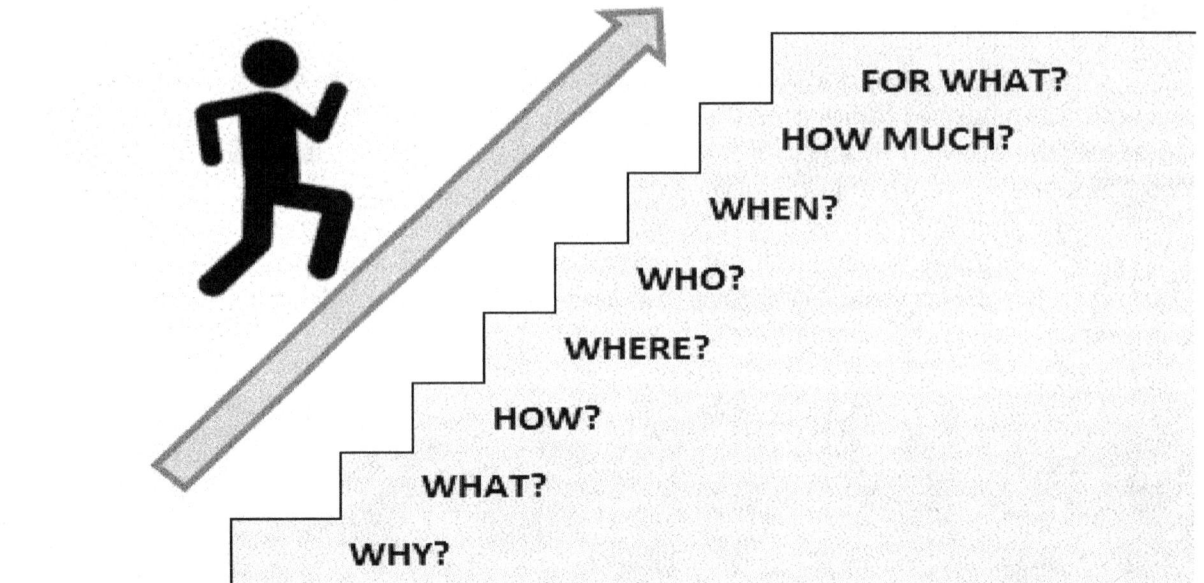

Figure 73: Logical Order of Questions in Project Planning in the 3-D WBS Method

Project System Synoptic

In Figure 74 below, we find the three main dimensions of the Project cube: WBS x OBS x CBS, the time, and the questions why (input) and for what (output) ... so the results are eight dimensions (8-D) to describe one project.

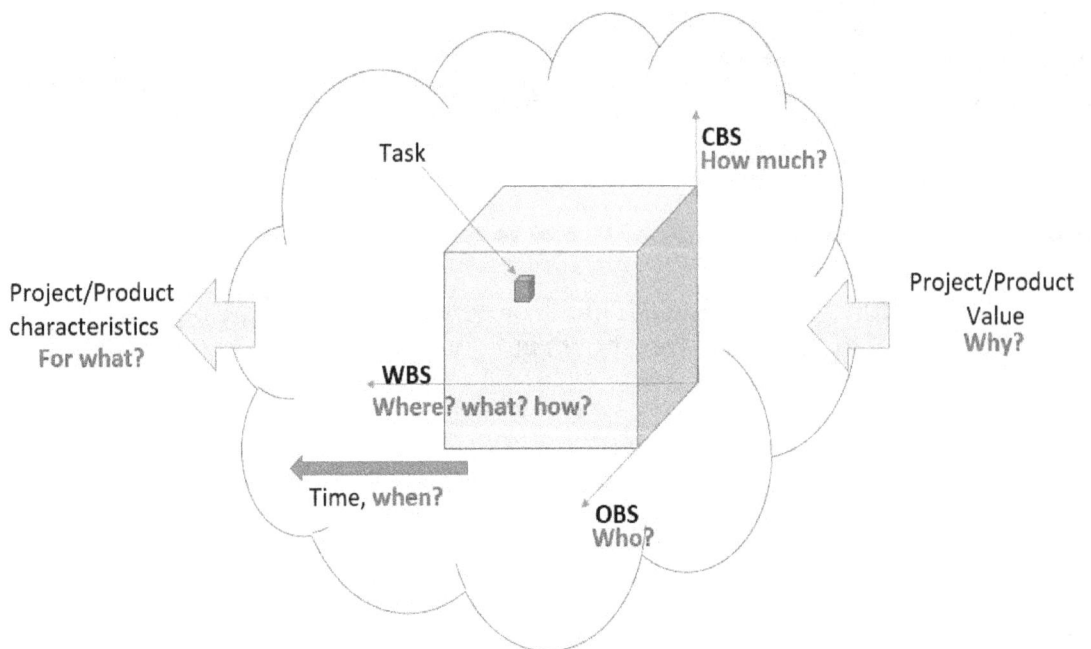

Figure 74: The Project system

The above (Figure 74) and below (Figure 75) pictures represent a Tesseract (hypercube) with its four dimensions: WBS, OBS, CBS, and (the) Time.

Figure 75: The Tesseract

Construction Specifications Institute/ISO OmniClass, with their 15 tables, is likely to be the dominant set of standardized coding structures – at least for the building and construction industry (environment). If there is no agreement to adopt standardized coding structures within the industry, then time and money will be wasted trying to write macros to translate existing cost, estimating, and scheduling databases into OmniClass Tables.

The Theoretical Tesseract Unfolded

Another modeling view is presented in Figure 76 and Figure 77. The described theoretical Tesseract is unfolded, allowing the view of the Tesseract from a contractor and stakeholders' perspectives, as discussed in the next sections.

WHY?

WHERE?

HOW MUCH?

WHAT?

FOR WHAT?

HOW?

WHEN?

WHO?

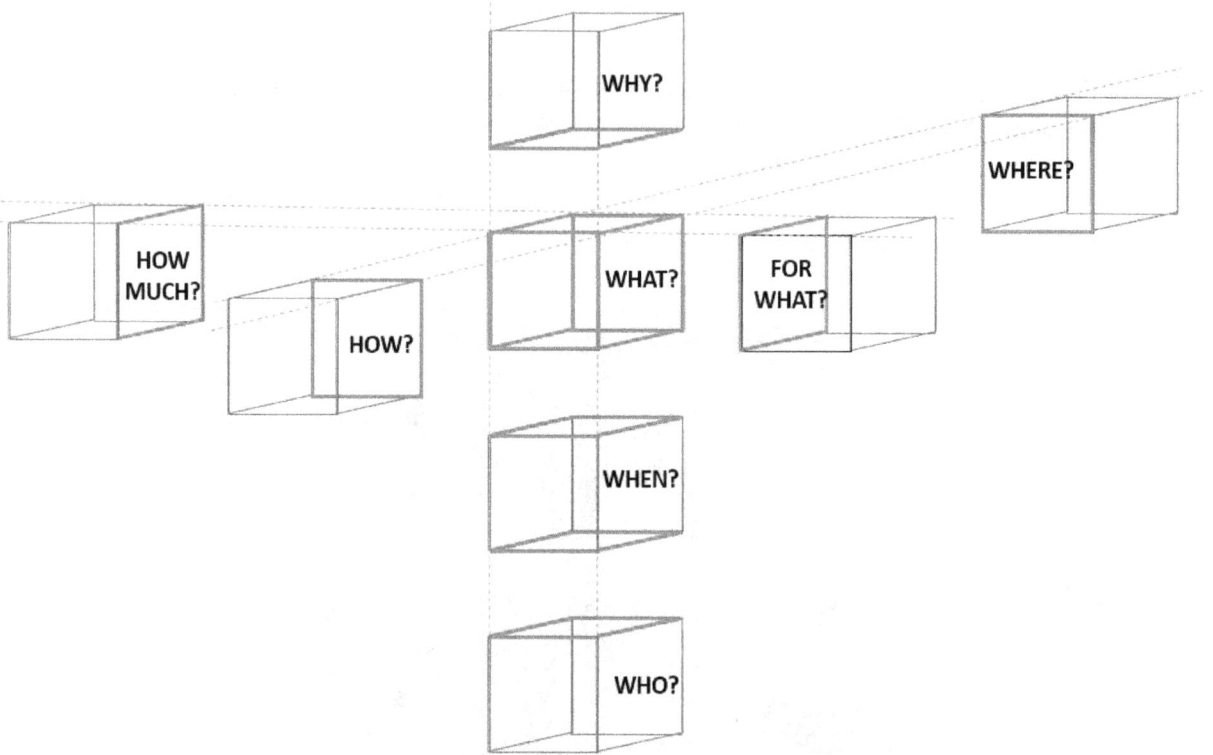

Figure 76: The Theoretical Tesseract unfolded

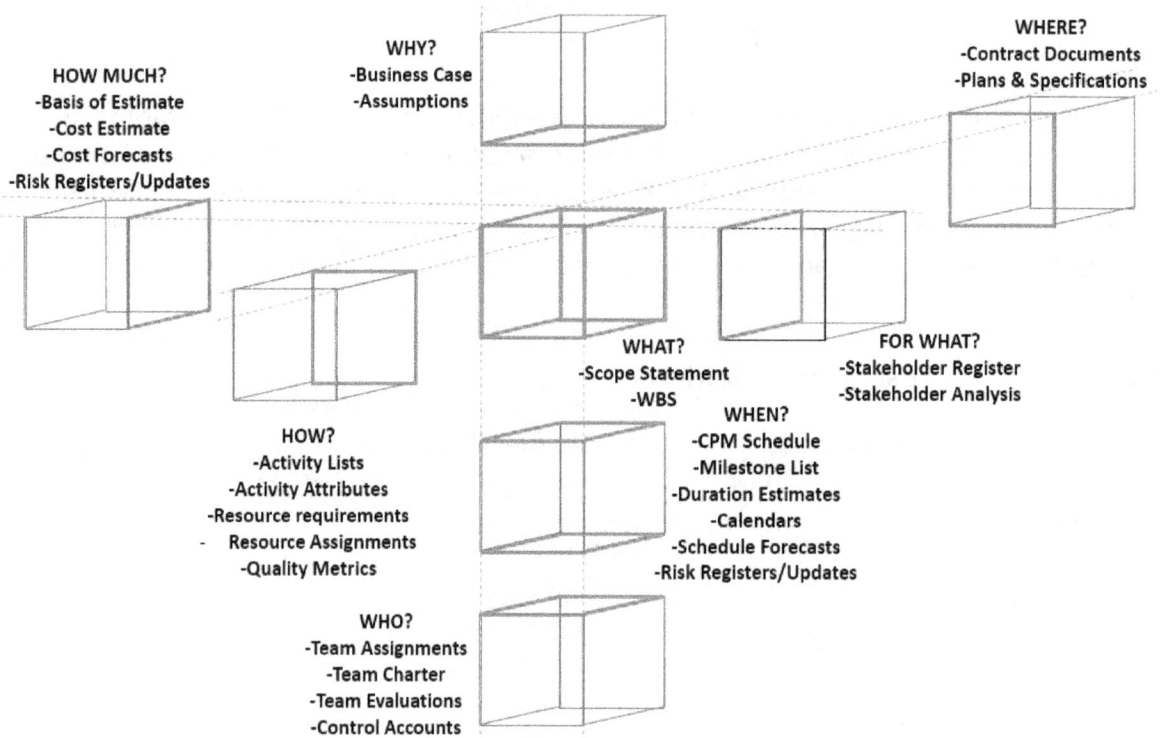

HOW MUCH?
-Basis of Estimate
-Cost Estimate
-Cost Forecasts
-Risk Registers/Updates

WHY?
-Business Case
-Assumptions

WHERE?
-Contract Documents
-Plans & Specifications

WHAT?
-Scope Statement
-WBS

FOR WHAT?
-Stakeholder Register
-Stakeholder Analysis

HOW?
-Activity Lists
-Activity Attributes
-Resource requirements
- Resource Assignments
-Quality Metrics

WHEN?
-CPM Schedule
-Milestone List
-Duration Estimates
-Calendars
-Schedule Forecasts
-Risk Registers/Updates

WHO?
-Team Assignments
-Team Charter
-Team Evaluations
-Control Accounts

Figure 77: Another View of the Tesseract Unfolded

Mapping an ERP's Chart of Accounts to Building Information Modeling Software

Using OmniClass Coding Structures and Activity and Multi-Dimensional Project Breakdown Structure Based Costing/Management – a Contractor's Perspective

As the world of construction is automated through the use of the Building Information Modeling (BIM), particularly during the early design phases, the opportunity to find errors or omissions is high and the costs to correct are low. Those responsible to execute projects – the owners and contractors project managers, cost estimators, schedulers, document controllers, project controllers et al. – have not yet caught up with architectural and engineering counterparts to ensure consistent work complementary "to and supportive of the use of BIM and related evolving technological advances, specifically, the use of Enterprise Resource Planning (ERP) systems."[79, 80] "The inherent problem with 'flat file' or single dimension WBS/CBS structures is not all stakeholders need to see the project deliverables in the same way. This led to the evolution of multi-dimensional, relational, or object-oriented-database coding structures."[81]

The idea or concept of multi-dimensional Work Breakdown Structures (WBS) or Cost Breakdown Structures (CBS) is not new. After World War II, building construction specifications began to expand, as more advanced materials and choices became available. The Construction Specifications Institute (CSI) was founded in 1948 and addressed the organization of specifications using a numbering system similar to the Dewey Decimal System (DDS) used by libraries.[82] The purpose or objective of the numbering system was to ensure a specification appeared once and only once in any set of contract documents, thus eliminating redundancy or conflicting information in the contract documents, and in turn, reducing claims and disputes.

In 1963, CSI published a format for construction specifications, with 16 major divisions of work. These 16 divisions were built around work packages normally and customarily sub-contracted by prime contractors to specialty sub-contractors (e.g., site work, concrete, HVAC, electrical) or prime contractors would supply their own workforces (e.g., general building, masonry, finishes, doors, and windows).

---

[79] *Introduction - PMWorldLibrary.net. (n.d.). Retrieved from pmworldlibrary.net/wp-content/uploads/2018/04/pmwj69-Apr2018-Giammalvo-E*

[80] *Giammalvo, P. D. Mapping ERP "Chart of Accounts" to Building Information Modeling Software Using OmniClass Coding Structures and Activity Based Costing/Management - A Contractor's perspective. (2019). PM World Journal, VII, 4 Retrieved from https://pmworldjournal.net/article/mapping-erp-chart-of-accounts-to-building-information-modeling-software/*

[81] Giammalvom, P.D. (2018, Apr.) *Mapping ERP Chart of Accounts to BIM. OmniClass coding & Activity Based Costing. PM World Journal. VII, IV. www.pmworldjournal.net*

[82] *Construction Specifications Institute History (n.d.) Retrieved from acsi.org/?option=com_content&view=article&id=52&Itemid=59%20en.wikipedia.org%2Fwiki%2FConstruction_Specifications_Institute*

The need for standardized terms to sort or view work and associated costs was reaffirmed by the Norwegian government, who initiated a project to standardize the cost coding structures coming from production shared with contractors drilling for oil in the North Sea (1992). The standardized Cost Coding structure, known a 'NorSok Z-014,' is still in use after 26+ years, undergoing only two revisions.[83]

In the early- to mid-1970s, around the same period that MasterFormat was evolving within CSI, the U.S. General Services Administration (GSA), in conjunction with the USA-based American Institute of Architects (AIA), commissioned Hanscomb Associates, Inc., to create a standardized construction cost-coding structure, originally named 'Master costs.' The GSA and AIA renamed this structured methodology UniFormat, which enabled capture and summation of costs by building components.[84] ASTM International began developing a standard for classifying building elements (1989), based on UniFormat, and renamed to UniFormat II."[85]

When CSI's MasterFormat and ASTM's UniFormat were combined, this provided a two-dimensional (2-D) sort capability used to view project deliverables.[86] The OmniClass Construction Classification System (known as OmniClass or OCCS originated around 2000 as a product of the Construction Specifications Institute. The OCCS incorporates other extant systems currently in use as the basis of many of the original CSI Tables – MasterFormat™ for work results, UniFormat for elements, and Electronic Product Information Cooperation (EPIC) for structured products.[87]

The OmniClass Construction Classification System (OmniClass or OCCS) is a means of organizing and retrieving information specifically designed for the construction industry. OmniClass is useful for applications for BIM, including organizing reports and object libraries to providing a way to scroll up or drill down through data to get the information for reporting functions. OmniClass draws from other extant systems in use to form the basis of its Tables "wherever possible – MasterFormat™ for work results, UniFormat™ for elements, and EPIC (Electronic Product Information Cooperation) for products."[88]

OmniClass was designed to provide a standardized basis for classifying information created and used by the North American architectural, engineering and construction (AEC) industry, throughout the full facility life cycle from conception to demolition or reuse and encompassing all the different types of construction that make up the built environment. OmniClass is intended to be the means for organizing, sorting, and retrieving information and deriving relational computer applications. OmniClass consists of 15 hierarchical tables, each of which represents a different facet of construction information. Each table can be used independently to classify information or entries, or it can be combined with entries on other tables to classify

---

[83] NorSok Standard Z-014, Rev. 1. SCCS (2002 version) Retrieved from https://www.standard.no/pagefiles/951/z-014.pdf

[84] American Society for Testing and Materials (ASTM). Retrieved from https://en.wikipedia.org/wiki/ASTM_International

[85] Charette, R. P. Building Design Management with ASTM E1557 UniFormat II Retrieved from: http://uniformat.com/index.php/using-uniformat-ii/building-design-management#astme1557

[86] Pm World Journal Volume Vii, Issue 4 April 2018 Archives ... (n.d.). Retrieved from pmworldjournal.net/issue/pm-world-journal-volume-vii-issue-4-april-2018/

[87] About OmniClass, OmniClass™ A Strategy for Classifying the Built Environment. (n.d.). Retrieved from http://omniclass.org/about/

[88] Zaid, M. (2017, Dec. 25) OmniClass Definition - Precast Concrete. Retrieved from http://esolution-pt.com/show-blog-details/omniclass-definition-2017-12-25

more complex subjects. This is the basis for the use of multi-dimensional Work and Cost Breakdown Structures.

OmniClass provides a basic structure of information about construction grouped into three primary categories composing the process model: construction resources, construction processes, and construction results. These are then divided into 15 suggested Tables for organizing construction information. The OmniClass Tables correspond to this arrangement of information:

- *Tables 11-22 to organize construction results*
- *Tables 23, 33, 34, and 35, and to a lesser extent 36 and 41, to organize construction resources, and*
- *Tables 31 and 32 to classify construction processes, including the phases of construction entity life cycles*

The framework for object-oriented information implements the basic approach of ISO 12006-2 but uses entries on these tables as defining points (or characteristics) for object-oriented information organization. The 'object-oriented' approach describes the characteristics of things without imparting a grouping preference or hierarchical order.[89]

In the object-oriented approach, the object is central, acting as a basis for characteristics or properties that describe the object. The described object can then be grouped with similar objects using a classification arrangement like OmniClass. The framework established by ISO/PAS 12006-3 enables computers to store and relate data in an object-oriented manner, while OmniClass Tables provides humans with data viewpoints to establish relationships between objects.

Having provided a brief overview of the history and evolution of multi-dimensional (relational or object-oriented) coding structures, this sets the stage to provide answers to the following question: Is there a way to map the coding structures from the OmniClass Tables to today's ERP systems, specifically to the Cost of Goods Sold and Revenue Recognition sections? The hypothesis proposes using Activity Based Costing at a minimum of Level 3 and preferably Level 4 of the CPM schedule, that it is not only possible but relatively easy to accomplish this objective.[90]

The definitions will help readers understand the terminologies used in the later explanations and descriptions.

Enterprise resource planning (ERP)[91] "… a process by which a company (often a manufacturer) manages and integrates important parts of its business. An ERP management information system integrates areas such as planning, purchasing,

---

[89] Zaid, M. (2017, Dec. 25) OmniClass Definition - Precast Concrete. Retrieved from http://esolution-pt.com/show-blog-details/omniclass-definition-2017-12-25

[90] Guild of Project Controls Compendium and Reference (CaR) On different levels of CPM schedule, refer to GPCCaR Module 7.1 Figure 8 (Membership access only) Retrieved from planningplanet.com/guild/gpccar/introduction-to-managing-planning-and-scheduling

[91] Kenton, W. (2019, Feb. 6). Enterprise Resource Planning (ERP). Retrieved from https://www.investopedia.com/terms/e/erp.asp

inventory, sales, marketing, finance, and human resources."[92]

Direct Cost[93] An expense traced directly to (or identified with) a specific cost center or cost objects, e.g., department, process, product or Activity. Direct costs (e.g., labor, material, fuel or power) vary with the rate of output, but are uniform for each unit of production, and is usually under control and responsibility of a department manager. Most costs are fixed in the short run and variable in the long run. Also called direct expense, on cost, variable cost, or variable expense, and grouped under variable costs.

Indirect Costs[94] Overhead not directly associated (e.g., office expenses, telephone expenses, R&D) with the production of goods or services. In project management, there are two types, Project Indirect (Overhead) Costs and Home-Office Overhead Costs.

Activity-Based Management (ABM)[95] Approach to management that maximizes value-adding activities while minimizing or eliminating non-value-adding activities. The ABM's objective is to improve the efficiencies and effectiveness of an organization in securing its markets. It draws on activity-based costing (ABC) as its major source of information and focuses on: (1) reducing costs, (2) creating performance measures, (3) improving cash flow and quality and, (4) producing enhanced value products.

Activity Based Costing (ABC)[96] Cost accounting approach is concerned with matching costs with activities (cost drivers) that cause costs. It is a method of absorption-costing and replaces the labor-based costing system. ABC states: (1) products consume activities, (2) the activities (not products) that consume resources, (3) activities are cost drivers, and (4) activities are not necessarily based on the volume of production. Instead of allocating costs to cost centers (e.g., finance manufacturing, marketing), ABC allocates direct and indirect costs to activities such as order processing, resolving customer complaints, setting up a machine, or constructing a building. A sub-set of activity-based management (ABM), ABC enables management to understand better: 1) how and where a firm makes a profit, 2) indicates where money is being spent, and 3) which areas have the greatest potential for cost reduction.[97]

---

[92] Introduction - Pmworldlibrary.net. (n.d.). Retrieved from pmworldlibrary.net/wp-content/uploads/2018/04/pmwj69-Apr2018-Giammalvo-E

[93] Direct Cost. Business Dictionary. (nd). Retrieved from http://www.businessdictionary.com/definition/direct-cost.html

[94] Indirect Cost. Business Dictionary. (nd). Retrieved from http://www.businessdictionary.com/definition/indirect-overhead-cost.html

[95] Activity Based Management. Business Dictionary. (nd). Retrieved from http://www.businessdictionary.com/definition/activity-based-management-ABM.html

[96] Activity Based Costing. Business Dictionary. (nd). Retrieved from http://www.businessdictionary.com/definition/activity-based-costing-ABC.html

[97] ABC was developed by Robert Kaplan and Robin Cooper of Harvard University (late 1980s). Most of the basis for APPLIED ABM/ABC is based on the published work of Mr. Gary Cokins (https://www.linkedin.com/in/garycokins/)

Generally Accepted Accounting Principles (GAAP)[98] Authoritative rules, practices, and conventions providing broad guidelines and detailed procedures for preparing financial statements, tax returns, and handling accounting concerns. Generally accepted accounting principles provide objective standards for judging and comparing financial data and its presentation and limits directors' from presenting unrealistic financial data through creative accounting. An auditor must certify the provisions of GAAP are followed in reporting an organization's financial data to be accepted by investors, lenders, and tax authorities.[99]

A 'Contractor' (or Sub-Contractor) organization A business entity that 'initiates, plans, executes, controls and closes' projects where the project itself is a Profit Center, e.g., a contractor or sub-contractor is in the business of assuming the risk of being able to 'initiate, plan, execute, control and close' the project in exchange for a known or committed cost, as an organization's primary business objective.

An 'Owner' organization A business, governmental agency, or other entity that 'initiates, plans, executes, controls and closes' projects where the project itself is a Cost or Investment Center, e.g., for the 'Owner,' the project is an Expense, and the value of undertaking any project derives not from the project, but the Product the project was undertaken to create. Usually, this 'product' takes the form of some type of Asset. (Financial, Human, Physical, Informational, or an Intangible).

Problem Definition

There are two generally accepted standardized sets of coding structures. One coding structure has been tested and proven globally to work for the accounting sector. The second structure has been tested and proven to work for the building environment or the architectural, engineering, and construction (AEC) sectors using 4-D BIM. The second structure uses the OmniClass coding to enable data exchange to the CPM scheduling software, and 5-D BIM, using the OmniClass coding structure to feed data into the Cost Estimating software packages.

So the question is – how to get these two standard sets of codes to be able to exchange data for cost, resource, and scheduling? Using Activity-Based Management and Activity Based Costing seems to be the simplest and most logical approach to enable data exchanges in both directions - between the 3-D, 4-D, and 5-D BIM ERP software systems as demonstrated in Figure 78).

---

[98] *GAAP Standards Business Dictionary. (nd). Retrieved from http://www.businessdictionary.com/definition/generally-accepted-accounting-principles-GAAP.html*
[99] *Most developed countries (Canada, India, Japan, UK, US, etc.) have a GAAP (which may differ in minor or major details).*

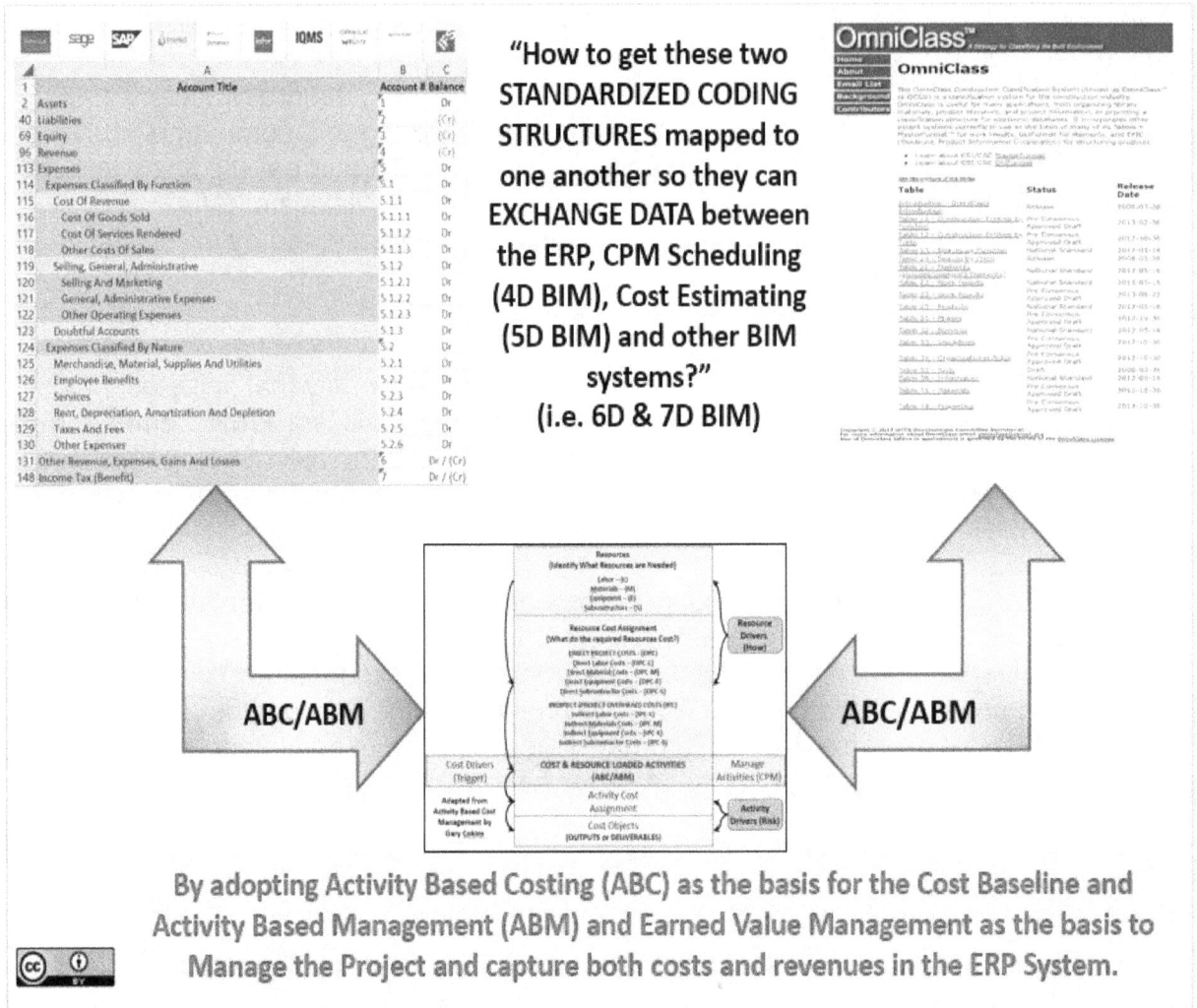

Figure 78: Graphical Illustration of the Problem

Defining Activity-Based Management

"Activity-Based Management is an alternate way to filter, sort, organize and show cost data that makes sense to stakeholders responsible for initiating, planning, executing, controlling, and closing projects. It is exactly the same cost and resource data found in most accounting software, but through the use of specific activity coding structures, enables a view of data presented in a practical manner to decision-makers about how the project is managed, or once the project has started, what changes or course corrections are needed to finish the project "on time, within budget, and in substantial conformance to the contractual requirements defined by the Contractual Work Breakdown Structure (CWBS)."[100]

---

[100] *Introduction - Pmworldlibrary.net. (n.d.). Retrieved from pmworldlibrary.net/wp-content/uploads/2018/04/pmwj69-Apr2018-Giammalvo-E*

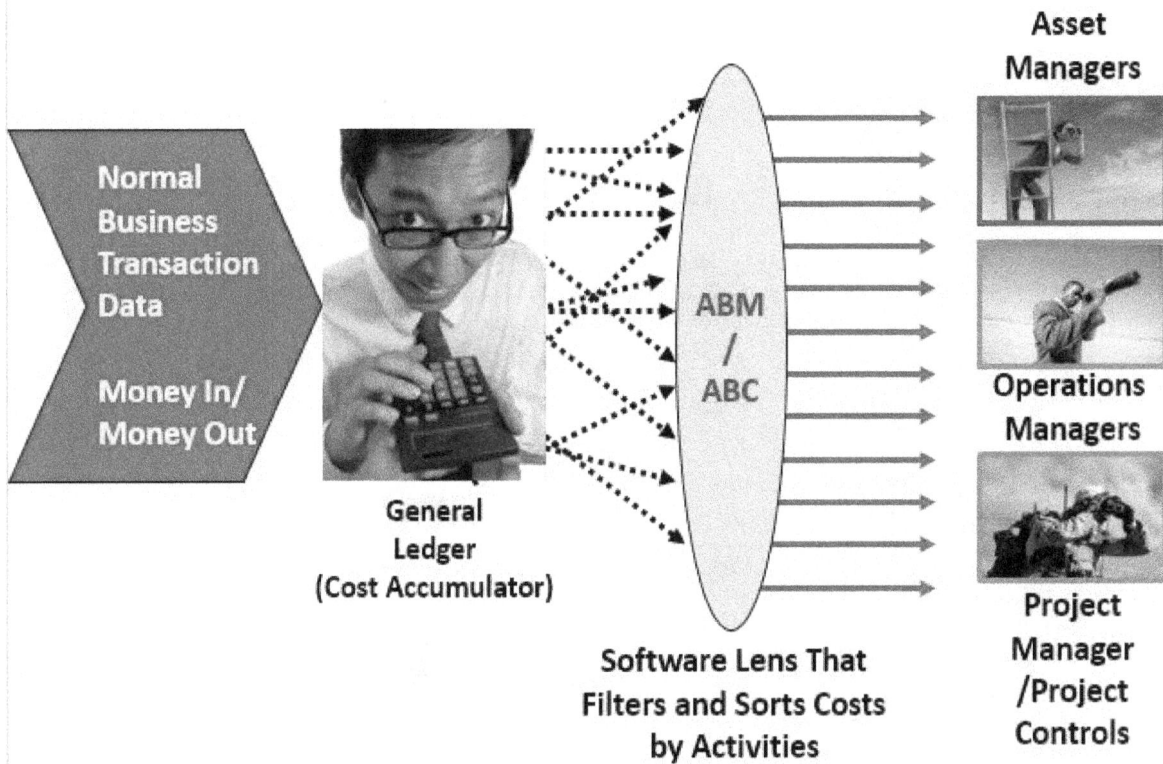

Adapted from Activity Based Cost Management by Gary Cokins

Figure 79: Graphical Illustration of the ABM/ABC System works

Figure 79 above demonstrates that Activity-Based Management is not a separate accounting system. All ABM requires are additional fields and associated coding structures to enable filter and sort of cost data that enables project managers to make sound project-related business decisions. As an example, in Figure 80 (below), we can see in Scenario 1, General Ledger shows this project is in financial trouble. The planned costs to date were $41K, and the actual charged costs to date are $51.8K, with a $10.3K cost overrun. Data shows the project is in financial trouble (25% over budget), but the project manager cannot see a vital detail from Scenario 1. The report shows 'Salaries' with a $6K over-run, making up ~60% of the problem, but the project manager does not know Whose salaries. Scenario 2 shows the same values. The planned costs to date were $41K, and the actual charged costs to date are $51.8K with a $10.3K cost overrun. Sorting the cost information as the project managers versus the accountants, the project team and other key stakeholders can switch to the Activity-Based Management view to view and use this data to make informed and rational decisions to address the problem.[101]

---

[101] *Implementing Activity-Based Costing" (nd). Institute of Management Accountants. Retrieved from https://www.imanet.org/insights-and-trends/strategic-cost-management/implementing-activity-based-costing?ssopc=1*

From the General Ledger...

Chart of Accounts View   ①

Telecom Implementation

COA CATEGORY	PLANNED	ACTUALS	VARIANCE
Salaries	$18,000	$24,000	$(6,000)
Equipment	20,000	20,000	-0-
Travel Expense	2,000	4,400	(2,400)
Supplies	1,000	2,400	(1,400)
Rent	500	1,000	(500)
TOTAL	$41,500	$51,800	$(10,300)

We know the bad news (we are bleeding to death financially) but what it doesn't tell us is WHERE we are bleeding...

... to the ABC/ABM Database Sort...

Activity Based View (WBS/CBS)   ②

Telecom Implementation

ACTIVITIES	PLANNED	ACTUALS	VARIANCE
Survey Site	$5,000	$4,800	$200
Prepare Site Design	5,000	7,500	$(2,500)
Deliver Equipment	2,000	3,500	(1,500)
Install Antennae	6,000	6,000	-0-
Install Feeder Lines	12,000	15,000	(3,000)
Test Antennae Line System	1,500	1,500	-0-
Install BTS Cabinet	2,000	2,000	-0-
Install Power System	2,000	2,000	-0-
Commission BTS	1,000	1,000	-0-
Connect Transmission	1,000	2,500	(1,500)
Integrate BTS	1,000	1,500	(500)
Produce Site Folder	2,000	2,000	-0-
Conduct Site Assessment	1,000	2,500	(1,500)
TOTAL	$41,500	$51,800	$(10,300)

... by moving to an ACTIVITY based Accounting System, we can identify sources of problems related to COST... (WHERE we are losing (or making) money)

Figure 80: Illustrating the differences between General Ledger and Activity-Based Management Views

In the ABC database sort view, installing the Feeder Lines – cost over-run of $3K is evident – and Preparing the Site Design has a cost over-run of $2.5K and represents those activities project managers should focus on to find out why the salaries or other expenses are so much higher than the original estimate. This illustrates the bad and good news. Project managers can also see from this data set; the company is making money on Surveying the Site.

Explanation of the GAAP Accounting Chart of Account Titles & Codes

In Figure 81 (following), the typical titles and coding structures, known as the Chart of Accounts is demonstrated.[102,103]

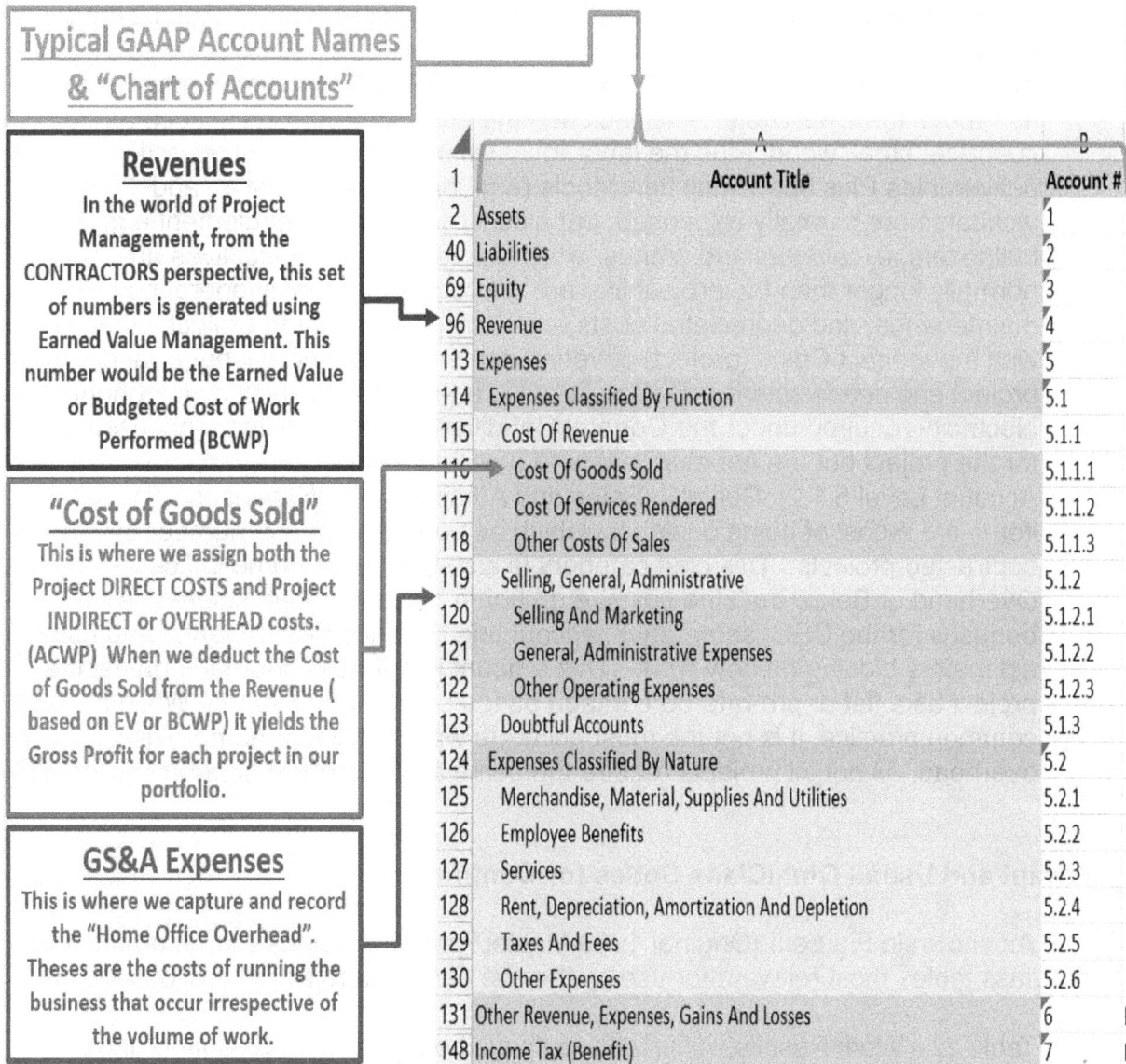

Typical GAAP Account Names & "Chart of Accounts"

Revenues

In the world of Project Management, from the CONTRACTORS perspective, this set of numbers is generated using Earned Value Management. This number would be the Earned Value or Budgeted Cost of Work Performed (BCWP)

"Cost of Goods Sold"

This is where we assign both the Project DIRECT COSTS and Project INDIRECT or OVERHEAD costs. (ACWP) When we deduct the Cost of Goods Sold from the Revenue (based on EV or BCWP) it yields the Gross Profit for each project in our portfolio.

GS&A Expenses

This is where we capture and record the "Home Office Overhead". Theses are the costs of running the business that occur irrespective of the volume of work.

	Account Title	Account #
1		
2	Assets	1
40	Liabilities	2
69	Equity	3
96	Revenue	4
113	Expenses	5
114	Expenses Classified By Function	5.1
115	Cost Of Revenue	5.1.1
116	Cost Of Goods Sold	5.1.1.1
117	Cost Of Services Rendered	5.1.1.2
118	Other Costs Of Sales	5.1.1.3
119	Selling, General, Administrative	5.1.2
120	Selling And Marketing	5.1.2.1
121	General, Administrative Expenses	5.1.2.2
122	Other Operating Expenses	5.1.2.3
123	Doubtful Accounts	5.1.3
124	Expenses Classified By Nature	5.2
125	Merchandise, Material, Supplies And Utilities	5.2.1
126	Employee Benefits	5.2.2
127	Services	5.2.3
128	Rent, Depreciation, Amortization And Depletion	5.2.4
129	Taxes And Fees	5.2.5
130	Other Expenses	5.2.6
131	Other Revenue, Expenses, Gains And Losses	6
148	Income Tax (Benefit)	7

Figure 81: GAAP "Chart of Accounts" Showing Project Related Accounts

---

[102] GAAP, Ltd. Retrieved from https://www.ifrs-gaap.com/basic-gaap-chart-accounts
[103] Adapted from "What is GAAP" (n.d.) Retrieved from https://www.accounting.com/resources/gaap/

In the context of project management, at least from the perspective of the Contractor, the three major Sections that projects impact are:

1) Account Level 4: Revenues: From a Project perspective, Revenues, called Earned Value or Budgeted Cost of Work Performed (BCWP), are recognized on a project once work is physically completed. From an Accounting perspective, the Revenue is not recognized until the work has been billed and the client has paid the bill. This results in time lags between the time the work has physically been completed and when accounting recognizes the Earned Value or BCWP as Revenue to be reconciled.

2) Account Level 5.1.1.1: Cost of Goods Sold (COGS). Sometimes referred to as 'Above the Line' costs. This includes the project Direct Costs, such as concrete, steel, wood, Plus the labor to install or fabricate required activity deliverables Plus both small hand-tools (e.g., drills, electric saws, and jackhammers normally Expensed, but also large pieces of equipment e.g., bulldozers, excavators and cranes, which, because their useful lives are normally longer than the project life, are depreciated and only operating, maintenance, and depreciated costs are charged against the project, along with the Indirect Costs (project) covering items, e.g., project manager and project engineer's salaries, Safety, QA/QC, on-site trailers, trucks, telephone, electricity required under the General Condition. These are items necessary for the project but are not chargeable to any single activity.

3) Account Level 5.1.2: General, Sales and Administration Expenses. These items are a cost of doing business, which accrues despite the number of contracted projects. This cost category is also known as Home Office Overhead or Below the Line costs, e.g., home office facilities, salaries, and bonuses for the CEO, secretaries, accounting / finance departments, and cost estimators bidding on new work. This amount is normally charged against the project as a flat or pro-rata percentage based on monetary value. While a common practice, it is not the most accurate way to allocate home-office overhead, as not all projects require the same administrative support.

Relevant and Useful OmniClass Codes for Contractors

As shown in Figure 5 (Original 1963 MasterFormat Divisions), there are four OmniClass tables most relevant for use by the site Contractors and Sub-Contractors:

1) Table 22 - Work Results. This table defines the Deliverables required under or by the contract documents. This is normally known as the Contractual Work Breakdown Structure and defines what the Contractor must deliver or create to have completed the project. While the WBS defines What needs to be done, it is the next level deeper, the Cost and Resource Loaded CPM schedule, which tells us How (what is the sequence of activities or the workflow) as well as When the work will be done, which is established by

early, late start, and finish dates, calculated by a forward and backwards pass.

2)   Table 23 - Products.[104] This table contains almost 7,000 Products used in the construction process. These products can be broken down into a more refined set of codes:

     a. Products are 'commercial off the shelf' (COTS) items you can purchase at any hardware store, e.g., paints, lumber, insulation, plumbing pipes, electrical wire.

     b. Fabricated Products are a somewhat unique class of product. These are NOT COTS) but items designed specifically for a single project, and fabricated either likely fabricated off-site, e.g., laminated panels, structural beams, cabinetry, digesters, switchgear, and pre-fabricated structures like pre-engineered buildings or communications or power transmission towers

     c. Consumable products. Consumables are usually COTS and can be expensed either as Direct Costs (if remaining with the project when completed) or Indirect Costs if consumed for General Conditions activities. Examples of direct consumables are nails, screws / fasteners, caulking / sealing compounds, joint tape, fittings, elbows, and couplers. Examples of Indirect Consumable costs are paper for the office-photocopy machine, gloves, and personal safety equipment, and the office coffee-maker. These are a separate class not usually charged to any activity, but purchased, consumed, and replenished when they run low. When performing cost estimates, these items are usually budgeted using a percentage of total cost or another factored estimating model.

     d. Fixtures are a unique class of product used in construction because, in many contracts, the actual fixture (e.g., lights or bathroom) are not specified, but the contractor has to provide an Allowance the owner uses to select specific lighting or bathroom fixtures at the installation time.

     e. Bulk Products. These are primarily covered in Materials Table 41 (see Figure 82), such as Loam or Topsoil, which are purchased by the truckload and may be allocated for later purchase.

---

[104] *OmniClass Construction Classification System (OmniClass) (n.d.) Retrieved from http://www.omniclass.org/*

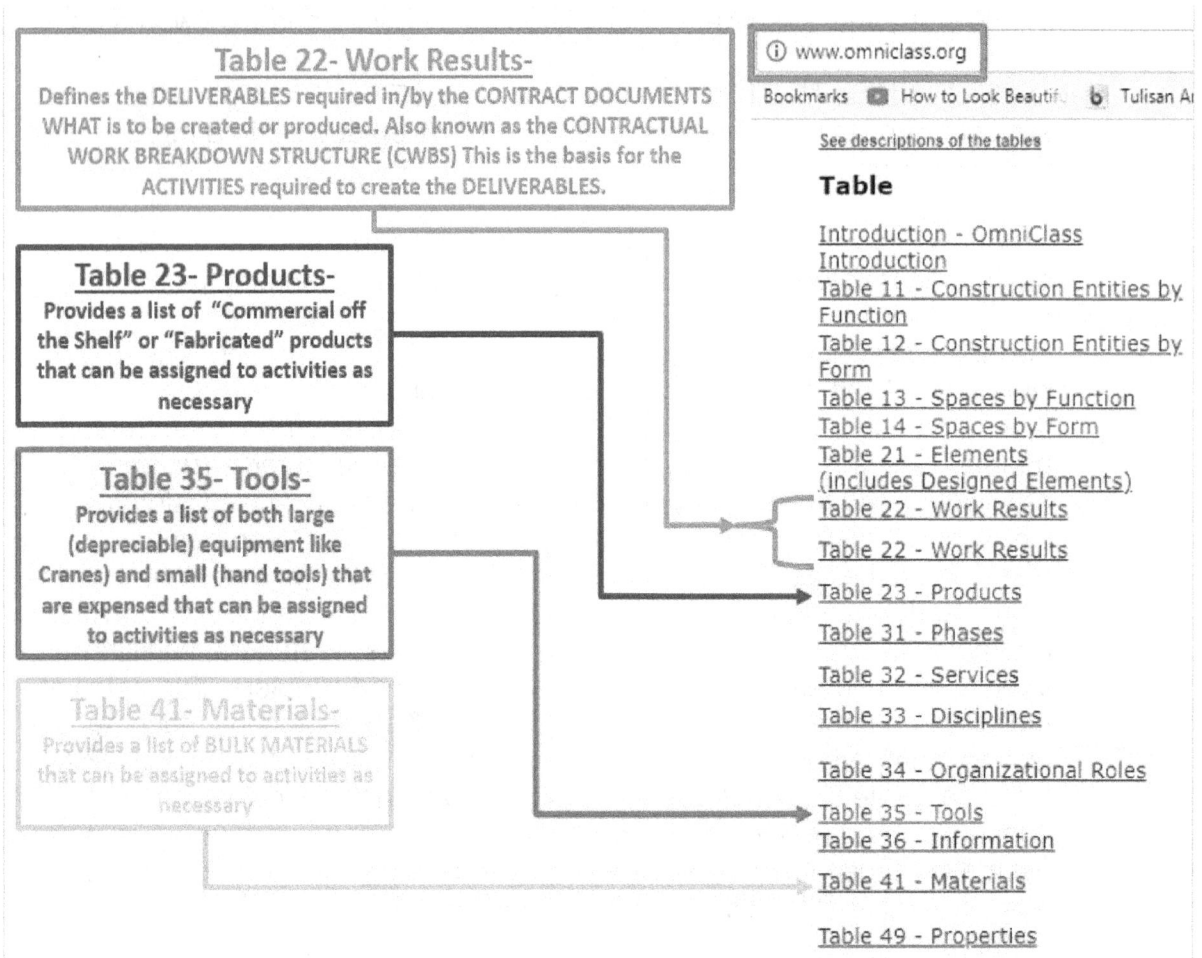

Table 22- Work Results-
Defines the DELIVERABLES required in/by the CONTRACT DOCUMENTS WHAT is to be created or produced. Also known as the CONTRACTUAL WORK BREAKDOWN STRUCTURE (CWBS) This is the basis for the ACTIVITIES required to create the DELIVERABLES.

Table 23- Products-
Provides a list of "Commercial off the Shelf" or "Fabricated" products that can be assigned to activities as necessary

Table 35- Tools-
Provides a list of both large (depreciable) equipment like Cranes) and small (hand tools) that are expensed that can be assigned to activities as necessary

Table 41- Materials-
Provides a list of BULK MATERIALS that can be assigned to activities as necessary

ⓘ www.omniclass.org

Bookmarks How to Look Beautif. b Tulisan Ar

See descriptions of the tables

Table

Introduction - OmniClass Introduction
Table 11 - Construction Entities by Function
Table 12 - Construction Entities by Form
Table 13 - Spaces by Function
Table 14 - Spaces by Form
Table 21 - Elements (includes Designed Elements)
Table 22 - Work Results

Table 22 - Work Results

Table 23 - Products

Table 31 - Phases

Table 32 - Services

Table 33 - Disciplines

Table 34 - Organizational Roles

Table 35 - Tools
Table 36 - Information

Table 41 - Materials

Table 49 - Properties

Figure 82: The 15 OmniClass Tables and the four used by Contractor's and Sub-Contractors

3) Table 35 - Tools. While this table may appear to be self-explanatory, there are two types of tools to consider:

a. Expensed Tools - drills, electric jackhammers, circular saws, grinders, and hand tools normally charged to the project and considered to have no residual value at the end of the project. The cost of tools is normally included in the cost of the standard crews who will be using them. Any tool Leased or Rented, regardless of size, is either a Direct or Indirect Expense.

b. Depreciated Tools - tools' whose useful life extends beyond any single project and are company owned (not leased or rented), e.g., cranes, bulldozers, excavators, and welding machines. As the depreciation expense can have a major impact for any company who owns their own heavy equipment, it is best to carry the depreciation as a below-the-line-cost and have an internal lease or rental rate to the projects that include the depreciation expense.

4) Table 41- Materials. A list of bulk materials normally purchased by the truck-load, or by the trailer, tank, or rail-car volumes. These may be used if a contractor has set up their concrete batch plant or asphalt plant rather than being used for most construction sites.

What does the Matrix between the WBS and CBS look like?

The matrix formed when we match the WBS, and the CBS looks no different than when we combine the WBS and the OBS to form the Work Packages or Control Accounts. The WBS (Table 22) is listed on the Y-Axis, and the Table 23, Products, Table 35, Tools and Table 41, Materials are shown on the X-Axis, resulting in a matrix that looks like what is shown in Figure 83.

Table 22 – Work Results	Table 23 – Products		Table 35 – Tools		Table 41 – Materials		Cost Estimating Database Labor
Activity ID #1000	OmniClass Code – P		OmniClass Code – T		OmniClass Code – M		RS Means Standard Crews
Activity ID #2000	OmniClass Code – P		OmniClass Code – T		OmniClass Code – M		OmniClass Code – P
Activity ID #3000							OmniClass Code – P
Activity ID #4000							
Activity ID #5000							
Activity ID #6000							
Activity ID #7000							
Activity ID #8000							
Activity ID #9000							
Activity ID #nnnn							

Figure 83: Conceptual Illustration showing the relationship between Activities from Table 22 and Costs from Tables

23, 35 and 41 PLUS Labor coming from the Cost Estimating Database (Commercial or In-House)

Just as with the Work Package or Control Account process, the intersection between the Activities and the Products, Tools, and Materials give us a Partially cost-loaded Activity, which is essential for use in Earned Value (see Guild of Project Controls Module 3.5.[105] What about the Labor component? To find that information, review an in-house or commercial cost estimating database, which has adopted CSI Uniformat (OmniClass Table 21) and CSI MasterFormat (OmniClass Table 22) as the cost-estimating, coding structure.

To see a more realistic explanation of this process, view the example to 'Form, Pour and Strip" 4 25' long, 5 KIP Cast in Place Concrete Beams, one on each of the North, East, South, and West walls.' This is an example of a composite estimate easily applied to any repetitive process. To explain what we are looking at in Figure 84; this data was taken from the 2018 RS Means 'Facilities Construction Costs' (pp. 99 and 1,400).[106]

#	Crew C-14A ①	Contractors Bare Costs		Including Contractors OH & P		Contractors Crew Cost Per Labor Hour	
		Hourly ③	Daily ④	Hourly ⑥	Daily ⑦	Bare Costs ⑨	Billing Rate Including OH & P
1	Carpenter Foreman	$52.70	$421.60	$85.55	$684.40	$50.54	$81.64
16	Carpenters	$50.70	$6,489.60	$82.30	$10,534.40		⑫
4	Rodmen	$54.65	$1,748.80	$87.30	$2,793.60		
2	Laborers	$39.85	$637.60	$64.70	$1,035.20		
1	Cement Finisher	$47.55	$380.40	$75.20	$601.60		
1	Equipment Operator	$53.75	$430.00	$84.80	$678.40		
1	Gas Engine Vibrator		$25.60		$28.16	⑩	⑬
1	Concrete Pump (Small)		$881.60		$969.76	$4.54	$4.99
200	Total Daily Labor Hours		$11,015.20		$17,325.52	$55.08	$86.63

② ⑤ ⑧ ⑪ ⑭

RS Means Facilities Construction Costs 2018- Page 1400

Figure 84: RS Means Table is showing how the costs of Standardized Crews are calculated.

---

[105] *Guild of Project Controls Compendium and Reference (CaR). (Membership required for access). Retrieved from www.planningplanet.com/guild/gpccar/creating-control-accounts*

[106] *Adams, B. (2019). Facilities Construction Costs with RSMeans Data: 2019 (Means Facilities Construction Cost Data) Annual Edition. Retrieved from https://amzn.to/2VkRfSf*

Standard Crew, Equipment, and Labor Calculation

---

1. The Labor component of the activity is based on Standardized Crews, using Crew C-14A = five Construction Workers and one Foreman, and two pieces of equipment – one Expensed and one Depreciable (cell 2-B; identifier '1').

2. The total crew members (25 people) X 8 hours per day = 200-person-hours (cells A2:A6; identifier '2')

3. Column 3 provides the base pay hourly rate for a single worker.

4. Column 4 shows an extended value calculated by multiplying the # of each trade person X 8-hour day X the hourly rate for that trade providing a Daily cost of each.

5. Cell 4-11 (identifier '5') sums the total Bare Costs for Labor and Equipment

6. In Column '6', the Marked-Up Hourly rate from Column 4 covers costs of both Project and Home Office Overhead and adds a Profit

7. Column '7' contains the Marked-Up hourly rate shown in Column '6' for each tradesperson X 8-hours a day, identifying the daily fee the contractor should charge to cover the project and home-office overhead and to make a profit on direct or indirect labor

8. Row 8 (item cell 'F-11') shows the sum of both Labor and Equipment includes Mark-Ups for the daily Billing Rate for the crew the Contractor would use when creating the cost estimate

9. Item 9 (item cell 'G2') is calculated by taking 200 total labor-hours shown in Item 2 and divide it into the Total Daily Bare Cost shown in the # 5 cell to obtain the Bare Cost of this crew at $50.54 per hour

10. Item 10 shows the total Bare Costs of Only the equipment ($25.60 + $881.60) divided by 200 crew hours (2) which provides a Bare Cost for the equipment of $4.54 (per hour)

11. Item 11 (cell 'G-11') provides the sum of both labor and equipment Bare Costs (hourly) worked noted in Column 7 (item 9; cell 'G-2')

12. Taking the 200 total labor hours shown in item 2 and divide it into the Total Daily Marked Up Costs shown in item 8, the sum indicates Marked-Up Billing Rate of this crew at $81.64 (hourly)

Standard Crew, Equipment, and Labor Calculation

---

13. Item 13 shows the total Marked Up Costs of Only the equipment ($28.16 + $969.76) divided by 200 crew hours (2) which indicates Marked-Up Cost for the equipment of $4.99 (hourly)

14. The value shown under item 14 is the Marked-Up Cost of both Labor and Equipment per crew hour worked

With single-digit Earnings Before Interest and Taxes (EBIT) profit margins for most contractors, capturing this information provides a competitive advantage as companies can use today's productivity as the basis to bid tomorrows work. In the event of a claim or dispute, these records showing both per unit and per hour costs become indispensable when preparing for arbitration or litigation.

How to Integrate Labor, Materials & Equipment into each Activity

An understanding of the development of the Standardized Coding Structures is vital for discussion of real examples. In the following table, the structures of development are identified with activities noted in Figure 85.

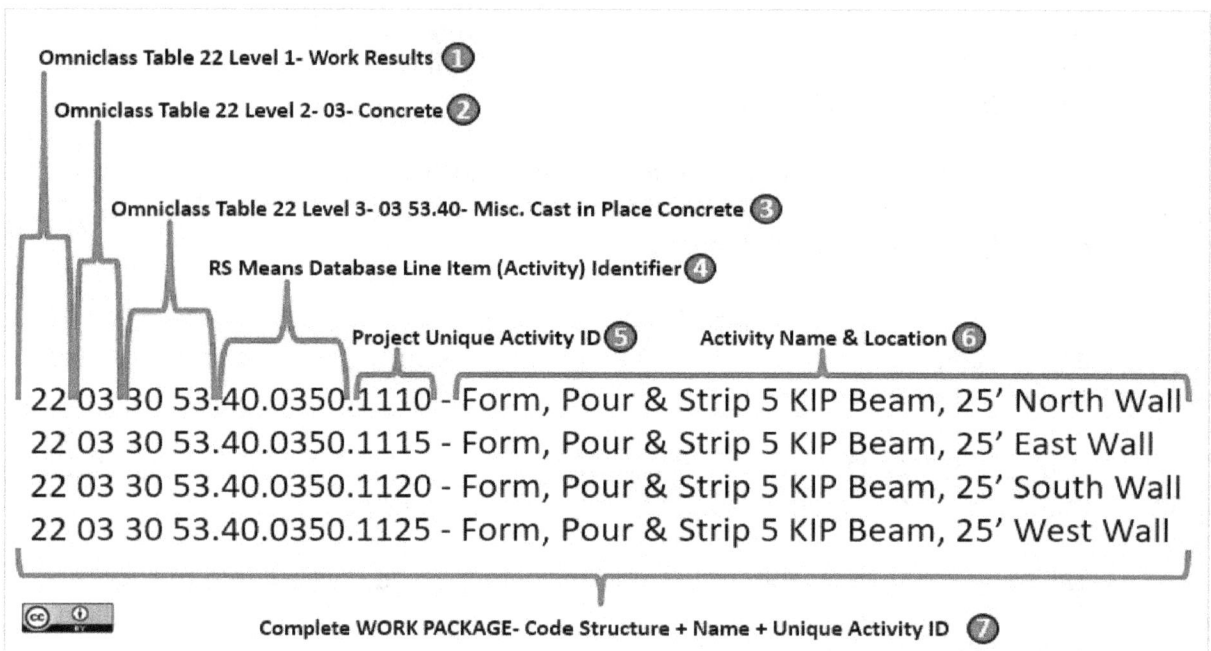

Omniclass Table 22 Level 1- Work Results ①

Omniclass Table 22 Level 2- 03- Concrete ②

Omniclass Table 22 Level 3- 03 53.40- Misc. Cast in Place Concrete ③

RS Means Database Line Item (Activity) Identifier ④

Project Unique Activity ID ⑤   Activity Name & Location ⑥

22 03 30 53.40.0350.1110 - Form, Pour & Strip 5 KIP Beam, 25' North Wall
22 03 30 53.40.0350.1115 - Form, Pour & Strip 5 KIP Beam, 25' East Wall
22 03 30 53.40.0350.1120 - Form, Pour & Strip 5 KIP Beam, 25' South Wall
22 03 30 53.40.0350.1125 - Form, Pour & Strip 5 KIP Beam, 25' West Wall

Complete WORK PACKAGE- Code Structure + Name + Unique Activity ID ⑦

Figure 85: Explanation of the Combined/Integrated OmniClass Table 22 with the RS Means Database Codes

---

Standardized Coding Structures

1. OmniClass Table 22 which is Work Results; a basis for Standardized WBS.

2. Level 1 of OmniClass Table 22 WBS; 03 is always Concrete.

3. Level 2 of OmniClass Table 22 WBS; 03 30 is always Cast in Place Concrete

4. Level 3 of the OmniClass Table22 WBS; 03 30 53 is always Miscellaneous Cast in Place Concrete

5. Level 4 of the WBS marks the End of OmniClass Table 22 and indicates where the commercial or in-house coding structure takes over going into greater detail. Level 4 is unique to RS Means; Level 4 - 03 30 53.40 is always Concrete in Place

6. Level 5 of the WBS 03 30; 53.40.350 is always Form Pour & Strip 5 KIP Beams, 25". By adding in a Unique Activity ID, planners can go one level deeper, Level 6 where a differentiator is noted between the identical beams for each of the four walls - N, S, E, and W.

7. Indicates a complete Work Package consisting of four identical activities, located in different parts of the structure.

If we take the same breakdown structure shown below and add identification numbers to the example, the following illustrates the results (Figure 86): To explain what is shown in Figure 86, below is a brief explanation of each column and number used in the cost estimate.[107]

---

[107] Adams, B. (2019). Facilities Construction Costs with RSMeans Data: 2019 (Means Facilities Construction Cost Data) Annual Edition. Retrieved from https://amzn.to/2VkRfSf, p. 99.

03 Concrete ①									
03 30 Cast in Place Concrete ②									
03 30 53 Miscellaneous Cast in Place Concrete ③									
03 30 53.40 Concrete in Place ④									
0.0010 0.0020 0.0050	Including Forms (4 uses), reinforcing steel, concrete placement and finishing, unless otherwise indicated.	Crew Type	Daily Output per Unit	Labor Hours per Unit	Unit of Measure	Material Costs	Labor Costs	Equip-ment Costs	Total Costs per Unit	Total Price/Unit Including OH&P
0.0300	Beams- 5 kip per lineal foot, 10' long spans	C14-A	15.62	12.8	Cubic Yard (CY)	$340.00	$645.00	$58.00	$1,043	$1,475
0.0350	Beams- 5 kip per lineal foot, 25' long spans	"	18.55	10.78	CY	$355.00	$545.00	$49.00	$949	$1,325
⑤		⑥	⑦	⑧	⑨	⑩	⑪	⑫	⑬	⑭

Source- RS Means Facilities Construction Costs 2018- Page 99

Figure 86 RS Means Table showing how to Calculate the Cost of each of the Four Activities.

RS Means Facilities Construction Costs

1.   Level 1 of OmniClass Table 22 WBS; 03 is always Concrete.

2.   Level 2 of OmniClass Table 22 WBS; 03 30 is always Cast in Place Concrete

3.   Level 3 of the OmniClass Table22 WBS; 03 30 53 is always Miscellaneous Cast in Place Concrete

4.   Level 4 showing the OmniClass Table 22 Codes plus the RS Means Line Items; 03 30 53.40 is always Concrete in Place

5.   Level 5 showing the combination of OmniClass Table 22 PLUS the RS Means Line Item; 03 30 53.40.350 is always Form Pour & Strip 5 KIP Beams, 25". By adding in a Unique Activity Identity, one level deeper is possible, Level 6 to differentiate identical beams for each of four walls - N, S, E, and W

6.   Standardized Crew C-14A (see Figure 84 to see details of this Crew)

RS Means Facilities Construction Costs

---

7. Daily Output (average) that Crew C-14A produces for this type of activity per Cubic Yard of Concrete

8. Average number of crew-hours per cubic yard of concrete for this activity (Productivity)

9. Unit of Measure - Cubic Yards of Concrete in place including forming, placement of reinforcing steel, placing, and finishing of concrete and forms stripping

10. Direct Material Costs per Unit of Measure (CY)

11. Direct Labor Costs per Unit of Measure (CY)

12. Direct Equipment Costs per Unit of Measure (CY)

13. Summation of the Direct Material, Labor and Equipment Costs

14. Marked-Up costs of the Direct Costs for Material, Labor and Equipment, including Project and Home Office Indirect (Overhead) costs and Profit.

What does Cost Data look like using Activity-Based Costing?

When the information is added to the Cost Estimating Database (in this example, using the cost data from RS Means as shown in Figure 87 into the Activity Based Costing (ABC) format, this is what it looks like:[108,109]

---

[108] Cokins, G. (1996). Activity-Based Cost Management Making It Work: A Manager's Guide to Implementing and Sustaining an Effective ABC System, Retrieved from https://amzn.to/2tCPh3N

[109] 2019 Facilities Construction Costs (ISBN# 978-1946872562). (2019). Retrieved from https://www.rsmeans.com/products/books/cost-books/facilities-construction-costs-book.aspx, p. 99.

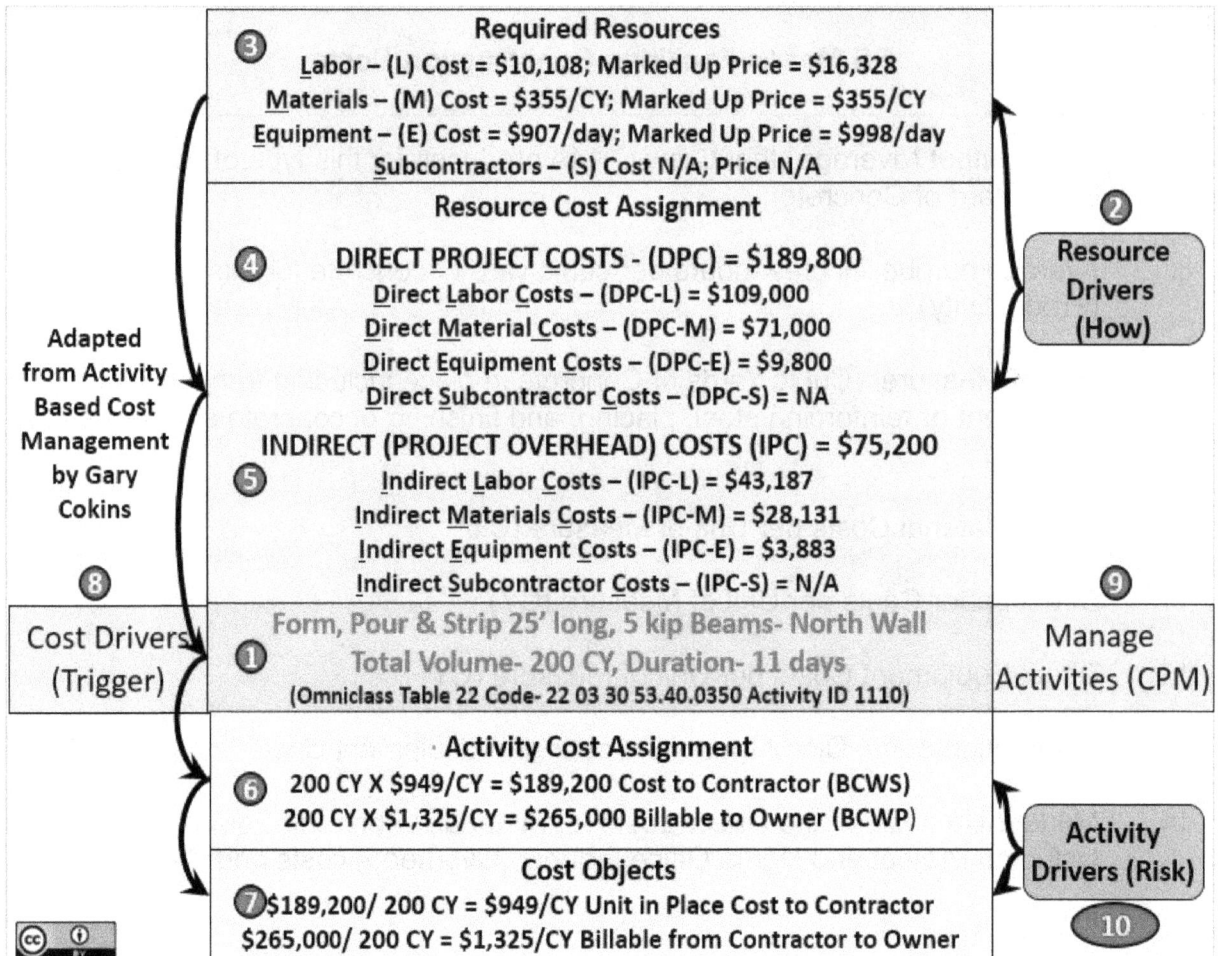

Required Resources
③ Labor – (L) Cost = $10,108; Marked Up Price = $16,328
Materials – (M) Cost = $355/CY; Marked Up Price = $355/CY
Equipment – (E) Cost = $907/day; Marked Up Price = $998/day
Subcontractors – (S) Cost N/A; Price N/A

Resource Cost Assignment
② **Resource Drivers (How)**

④ **DIRECT PROJECT COSTS - (DPC) = $189,800**
Direct Labor Costs – (DPC-L) = $109,000
Direct Material Costs – (DPC-M) = $71,000
Direct Equipment Costs – (DPC-E) = $9,800
Direct Subcontractor Costs – (DPC-S) = NA

Adapted from Activity Based Cost Management by Gary Cokins

INDIRECT (PROJECT OVERHEAD) COSTS (IPC) = $75,200
⑤ Indirect Labor Costs – (IPC-L) = $43,187
Indirect Materials Costs – (IPC-M) = $28,131
Indirect Equipment Costs – (IPC-E) = $3,883
Indirect Subcontractor Costs – (IPC-S) = N/A

⑧ **Cost Drivers (Trigger)**

① Form, Pour & Strip 25' long, 5 kip Beams- North Wall
Total Volume- 200 CY, Duration- 11 days
(Omniclass Table 22 Code- 22 03 30 53.40.0350 Activity ID 1110)

⑨ **Manage Activities (CPM)**

Activity Cost Assignment
⑥ 200 CY X $949/CY = $189,200 Cost to Contractor (BCWS)
200 CY X $1,325/CY = $265,000 Billable to Owner (BCWP)

Activity Drivers (Risk)

Cost Objects
⑦ $189,200/ 200 CY = $949/CY Unit in Place Cost to Contractor
$265,000/ 200 CY = $1,325/CY Billable from Contractor to Owner

⑩

Figure 87: Adapting the Information from the Cost Estimating Database into Activity Based Costing Format

---

Cost Estimating Database Adapted into Activity Based Costing Format

1. Activity Name and Unique ID – Everything starts with Activity Based Costing (ABC) and ultimately, Activity Based Management (ABM). In the example, the activity from the Bill of Materials (BoM) or Bill of Quantities (BoQ) requires 200 Cubic Yards (CY) of concrete. Dividing the 200 CY by the Productivity of 18.55 CY per day for Crew C-14A indicates this activity will take 10.78 days, rounded to 11 days duration. This is an Average or P50 value (no risk contingency or buffer built in).[110,111]

---

[110] *Guild of Project Controls Compendium and Reference Module 7. Retrieved from*
http://www.planningplanet.com/guild/gpccar/introduction-to-managing-planning-andscheduling
[111] *Guild of Project Controls Compendium and Reference Module 8. Retrieved from*
http://www.planningplanet.com/guild/gpccar/introduction-to-managingcost-estimating-budgeting

---

Cost Estimating Database Adapted into Activity Based Costing Format

2. Resource Drivers - Resources to execute activity and how it will be done

3. Labor, (Crew C-14A), Materials (From either OmniClass Table 23 or 41) and Equipment (From OmniClass Table 35)

4. Breaks cost into detailed categories, whether Direct, Project, or Home Office (Indirect/Overhead) costs; details are necessary for ERP systems to categorize costs using GAAP Chart of Accounts for tax accounting and financial reporting

5. Breaks cost into more detailed categories, whether Direct, Project, or Home Office (Indirect/Overhead) costs; details are necessary for ERP systems to categorize costs using GAAP Chart of Accounts for tax accounting and financial reporting

6. By multiplying the estimated quantities from the BoM/BoQ X the Direct costs yield the Contractors Costs, the resulting number provided to the Project Manager is what is expected to meet or beat. When using Earned Value Management, performance against this target is measured by Schedule Variance (SV), Cost Variance (CV), Cost Performance Index (CPI) moreover, Schedule Performance Index (SPI)[112]

7. Once work starts, by capturing then dividing the Actual Units In Place into the Actual Costs Of Work Performed (Actual Units/ACWP) provides the Contractor updates to the cost estimating database, using current productivity and cost data as a basis on which to bid future contract work

8. Trigger to each activity is either the start or completion of a predecessor activity (for contractor's perspective), depending on identified logic

9. One of the most important tenets of project management from the Contractor's perspective is 'You cannot manage a project by managing the money.' To effectively manage a project, manage the Workflow (the activities) and using ABC/ABM, the 'money will follow the work' (both cost and revenue)

---

[112] *Guild of Project Controls Compendium and Reference Module 9. Retrieved from http://www.planningplanet.com/guild/gpccar/introduction-to-managingcost-estimating-budgeting*

Connecting the Dots on Capturing and Exchanging Cost and Revenue Data

The purpose of this book is to explain and demonstrate how the Standardized Codes of Accounts from OmniClass could be mapped to the Standardized Chart of Accounts recommended by GAAP.   Figures 10 and 11 were created to illustrate how the mapping is completed using Activity Based Costing (ABC), and Activity Based Management (ABM) as the Integrator or 'go-between.'

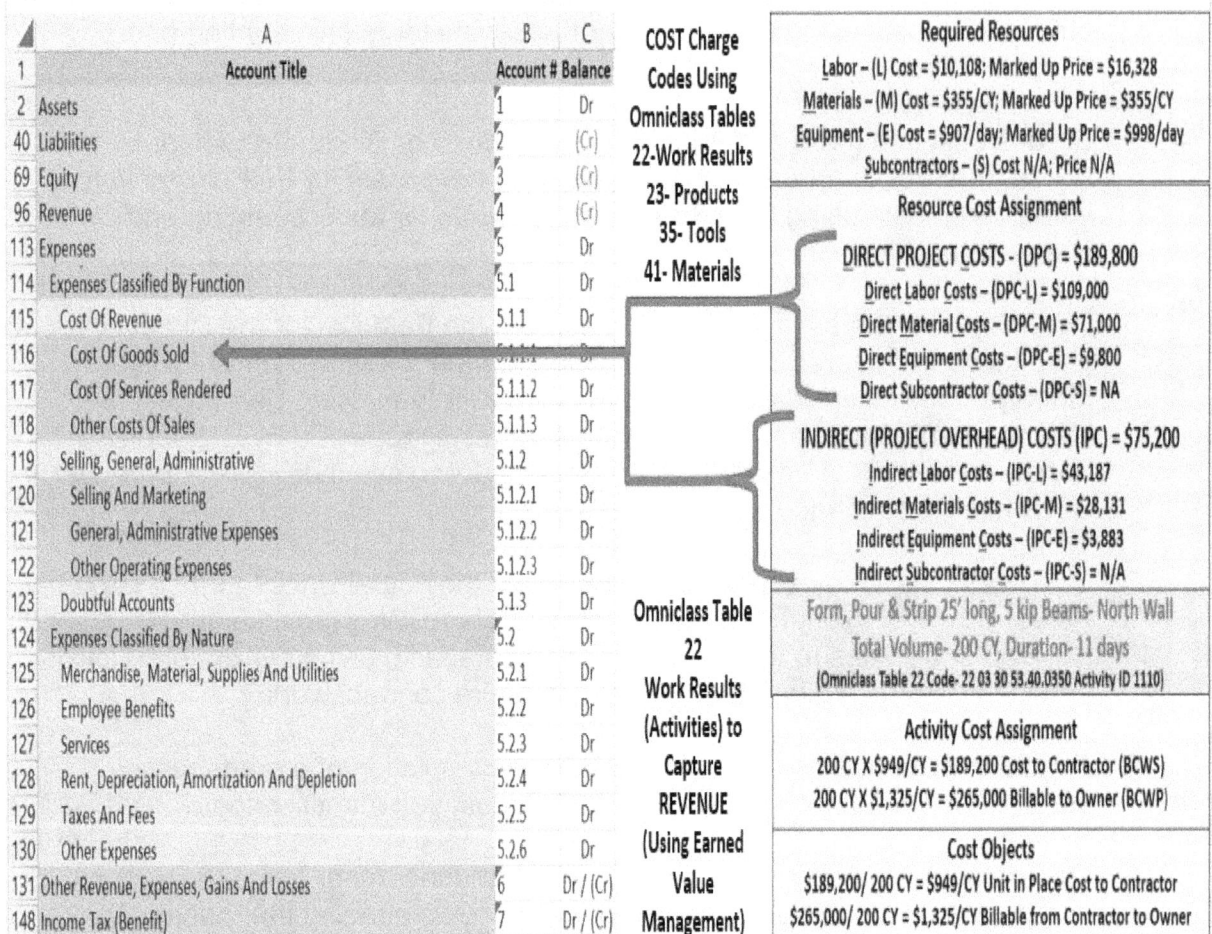

	A Account Title	B Account #	C Balance	
1	Account Title	Account #	Balance	COST Charge Codes Using Omniclass Tables
2	Assets	1	Dr	
40	Liabilities	2	(Cr)	
69	Equity	3	(Cr)	22-Work Results
96	Revenue	4	(Cr)	23- Products
113	Expenses	5	Dr	35- Tools
114	Expenses Classified By Function	5.1	Dr	41- Materials
115	Cost Of Revenue	5.1.1	Dr	
116	Cost Of Goods Sold	5.1.1.1	Dr	
117	Cost Of Services Rendered	5.1.1.2	Dr	
118	Other Costs Of Sales	5.1.1.3	Dr	
119	Selling, General, Administrative	5.1.2	Dr	
120	Selling And Marketing	5.1.2.1	Dr	
121	General, Administrative Expenses	5.1.2.2	Dr	
122	Other Operating Expenses	5.1.2.3	Dr	
123	Doubtful Accounts	5.1.3	Dr	Omniclass Table 22
124	Expenses Classified By Nature	5.2	Dr	Work Results
125	Merchandise, Material, Supplies And Utilities	5.2.1	Dr	(Activities) to
126	Employee Benefits	5.2.2	Dr	Capture
127	Services	5.2.3	Dr	REVENUE
128	Rent, Depreciation, Amortization And Depletion	5.2.4	Dr	(Using Earned
129	Taxes And Fees	5.2.5	Dr	Value
130	Other Expenses	5.2.6	Dr	Management)
131	Other Revenue, Expenses, Gains And Losses	6	Dr / (Cr)	
148	Income Tax (Benefit)	7	Dr / (Cr)	

Required Resources
Labor – (L) Cost = $10,108; Marked Up Price = $16,328
Materials – (M) Cost = $355/CY; Marked Up Price = $355/CY
Equipment – (E) Cost = $907/day; Marked Up Price = $998/day
Subcontractors – (S) Cost N/A; Price N/A

Resource Cost Assignment
DIRECT PROJECT COSTS - (DPC) = $189,800
Direct Labor Costs – (DPC-L) = $109,000
Direct Material Costs – (DPC-M) = $71,000
Direct Equipment Costs – (DPC-E) = $9,800
Direct Subcontractor Costs – (DPC-S) = NA

INDIRECT (PROJECT OVERHEAD) COSTS (IPC) = $75,200
Indirect Labor Costs – (IPC-L) = $43,187
Indirect Materials Costs – (IPC-M) = $28,131
Indirect Equipment Costs – (IPC-E) = $3,883
Indirect Subcontractor Costs – (IPC-S) = N/A

Form, Pour & Strip 25' long, 5 kip Beams- North Wall
Total Volume- 200 CY, Duration- 11 days
(Omniclass Table 22 Code- 22 03 30 53.40.0350 Activity ID 1110)

Activity Cost Assignment
200 CY X $949/CY = $189,200 Cost to Contractor (BCWS)
200 CY X $1,325/CY = $265,000 Billable to Owner (BCWP)

Cost Objects
$189,200/ 200 CY = $949/CY Unit in Place Cost to Contractor
$265,000/ 200 CY = $1,325/CY Billable from Contractor to Owner

http://whatis.techtarget.com/definition/GAAP-generally-accepted-accounting-principles

Adapted from Activity Based Cost Management by Gary Cokins Using Data from RS Means Facilities Cost 2018

Figure 88: Illustrating how using ABC/ABM can tie the OmniClass Coding Structure to the GAAP Coding Structure

Figure 88 shows clearly how, using ABC/ABM based on the OmniClass Tables 22 - Work Results, and matrixed against Tables 23, Products, Table 35, Equipment, and Table 41, how Materials can aggregate, and how categorizing the data costs can enable transfer of data to the GAAP coding structure.[113]   Figure 88 illustrates the Project Direct and Indirect Costs; values would be exported into the Cost of Goods Sold (CoGS) accounts for each project. Nearly all projects are required to carry a percentage of Home Office Overhead costs. To accommodate this overhead requirement, consistent with ABC/ABM, one or more activities called 'Home Office Overhead' should be created and those costs loaded into the project. Overhead Cost should not be entered on a pro-rata or percentage basis, but as a separate stand-alone activity (or activities). By isolating the Home Office Overhead from the Project Direct/Indirect costs, this action enables the contractor to manage the Home Office Overhead costs as aggressively as they manage the project Direct and Indirect Project Costs.

The data from the Home Office Overhead costs would not be expensed under the heading of Cost of Goods Sold, but instead under the heading of the below-the-line costs – General, Sales, and Administrative costs. For example, the Cost Estimators/Quantity Surveyors responsible for preparing a bid are normally based in the home office. If a bid is submitted and the project is won, then their time preparing that bid would be appropriately charged against the project as a Cost of Goods Sold (GAAP 5.1.1.1).[114] However, for all the projects bid and lost, the time spent preparing those bids would be charged against GAAP 5.1.2.1 Selling and Marketing expense. On the Revenue side, Figure 89 illustrates how the data generated by using Earned Value Management, once billed to the client and paid for, will accrue to GAAP account 4.1.1.1, by renaming Products as Projects.

---

[113] *Adapted from "Implementing Activity Based Costing" (n.d.) IMA and Gary Cokins* https://goo.gl/t39BzG *and from "What is GAAP"
        (n.d.) http://www.accounting.com/resources/gaap/*
[114] *What is GAAP? (nd). Retrieved from https://www.accounting.com/resources/gaap/*

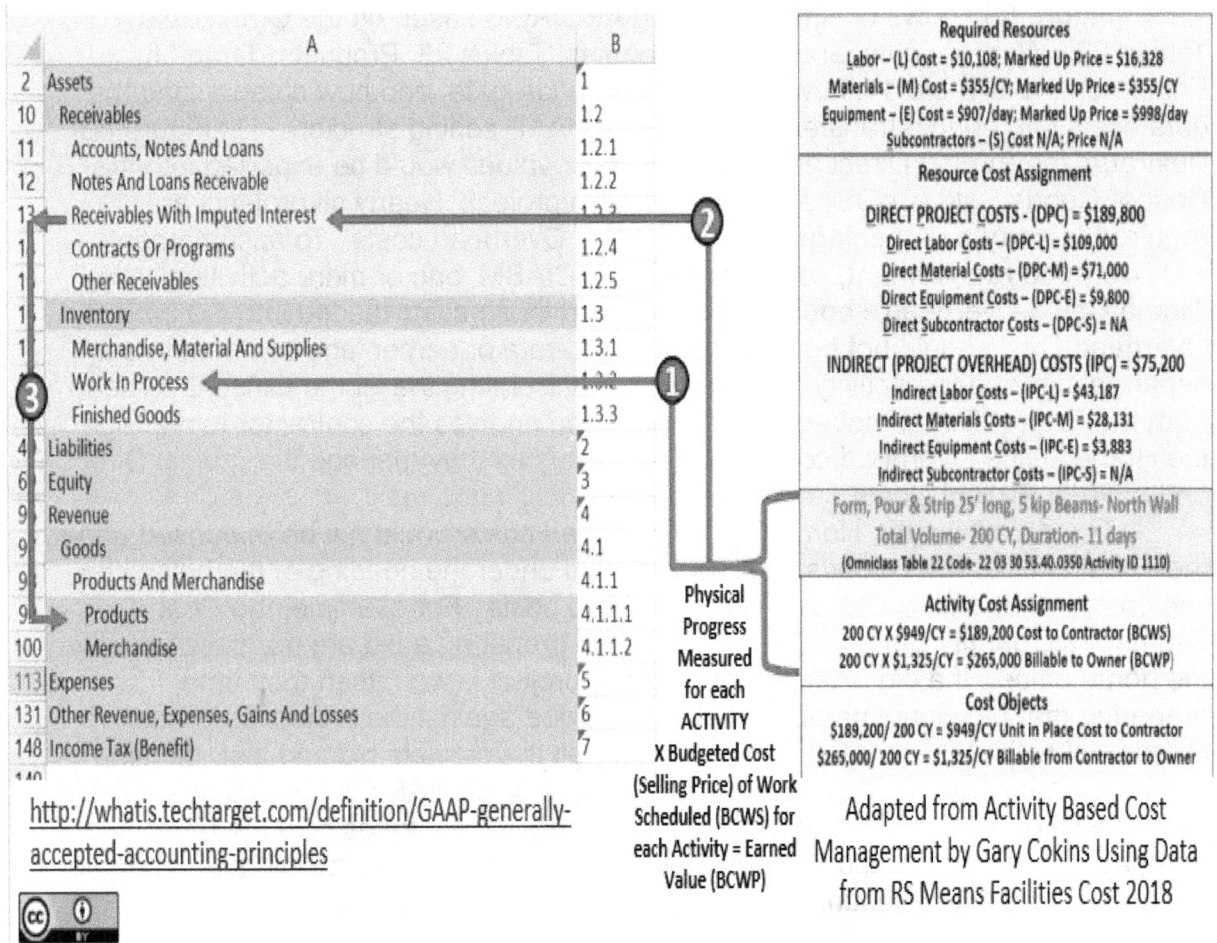

Figure 89: Showing how Revenue Generated using Earned Value Management flows into ERP Software

There are three steps in using Activity Based Management combined with Earned Value to capture real-time status on any project for data entry into the ERP Accounting Module.[115]

1) Work Physically Completed, but not yet been Billed, is recorded as Work in Progress (GAAP Chart of Accounts #1.3.2); at the end of the month or other agreed to dates, the accumulated Earned Value (BCWP) is transferred from Work in Progress to Accounts Payable[116]

2) Once the accumulated Earned Value (BCWP) of the work in place has been billed to the client, the data is then moved from Work in Progress to Accounts Receivable (GAAP #1.2.3)

---

[115] Cokins, G. (1996). *Activity-Based Cost Management Making It Work: A Manager's Guide to Implementing and Sustaining an Effective ABC System*, Retrieved from https://amzn.to/2tCPh3N

[116] *Guild of Project Controls Compendium and Reference Module 9.3.3.1. Retrieved from http://www.planningplanet.com/guild/gpccar/introduction-to-managingcost-estimating-budgeting*

3)   As soon as the invoice (based on the accumulated Earned Value from each activity) has been paid by the client, the payment is recorded as revenue against each project (GAAP 4.1.1.1)[117]

If advanced payments or earnest money is paid by the contract owner to the building contractor upon signing the contract (a common practice in the Middle East and Asia), that deposit would be recorded as a pre-paid account receivable (negative balance for that account) and be offset either with the first actual progress billing based on physical progress (EVM) or amortized over more than one billing. Consistent with earned value as being a pay-for-performance model, advance payments are not a best-practice. Earned value is based on prompt payment for work done in substantial conformance to the technical requirements and in fulfillment of the contractual terms and conditions - the 'shall' clauses in the contract.

Conclusion, Recommendations, and Follow-Up Actions

In the introduction of this book, the goal was to answer the question: Is there a way to map the coding structures from the OmniClass Tables to today's ERP systems, specifically to the Cost of Goods Sold and Revenue Recognition sections? The hypothesis was that, by using Activity Based Costing at a minimum of Level 3 and preferably Level 4 of the CPM schedule, it is possible and relatively easy to accomplish this objective.

Based on the demonstrations and explanations showing What to do and How to do it, the use of Activity Based Costing combined with Activity-Based Management serves as a relatively simple, yet reliable, way to enable data exchanges between Activities from Table 22, has been cost- and resource-loaded using Tables 23, 35, and 41 combined with data from an in-house or commercial database, through the Activities to be allocated into the appropriate General Ledger accounts. On the flip side, the Actual Costs for Labor, Materials, and Equipment, flow from the ERP system back into the Cost Estimating System, ensuring the most recent cost and productivity information when a bid is submitted.

As a disclaimer, while this system has been used by the author for over 40 years and has proven to work, based on his first-hand experiences as a general contractor where his own money is on the line if the project succeeds or fails, past performance is no guarantee of future results. For those wishing to adopt/adapt this system for their organization, the author highly recommends a pilot project (following Lean Six Sigma ERP implementation stages) rather than trying to roll it out across the entire organization before testing to see if the system works with specific ERP-based Cost Estimating and CPM Scheduling software packages. Customization may be required to get systems to accurately, reliably, and precisely exchange data.

For more detailed information on how to use this system, the Author urges

---

[117] *Guild of Project Controls Compendium and Reference Module 9.3. Retrieved from*
        http://www.planningplanet.com/guild/gpccar/introduction-to-managingcost-estimating-budgeting

readers to subscribe to the Guild of Project Controls Compendium and Reference (GPCCaR).[118] Access is free of charge; however, it does require the creation of a user profile (no cost; ~15 minutes of effort).

The 3-D WBS Matrix

The 3-D WBS matrix for the above application is presented below in Figure 90.

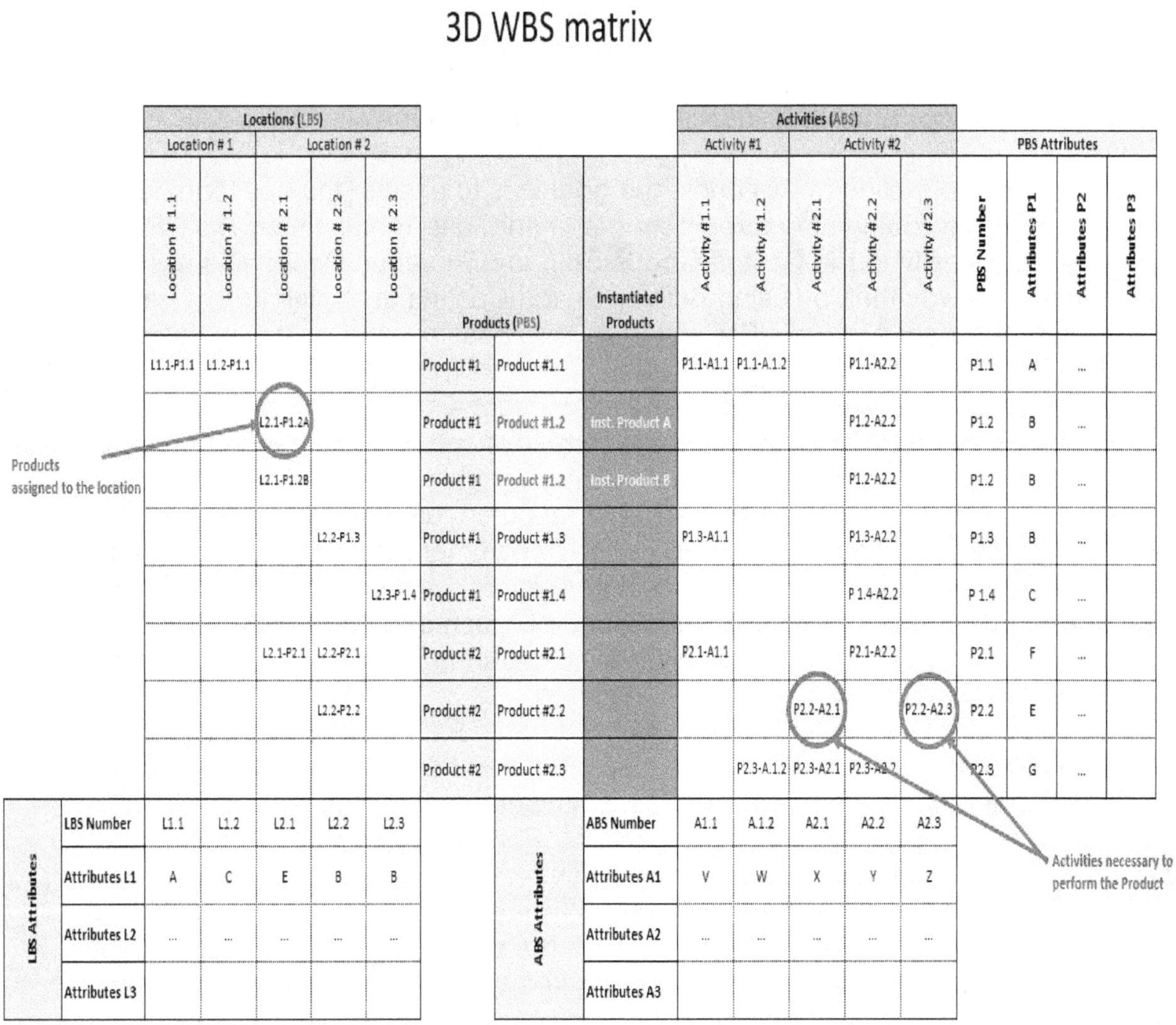

Figure 90: The 3-D WBS Matrix

---

[118] Guild of Project Controls Compendium and Reference (GPCCaR) Retrieved from http://www.planningplanet.com/guild/GPCCAR-modules

Products are deployed on Activities and Activities are assigned to Locations. An algorithm extracts the list of tasks.

5-D WBS Matrix

Products can be divided into three categories:

- Product
- Tools
- Material

The 5D WBS matrix below integrates these three categories to create the complete WBS code in Figure 91.

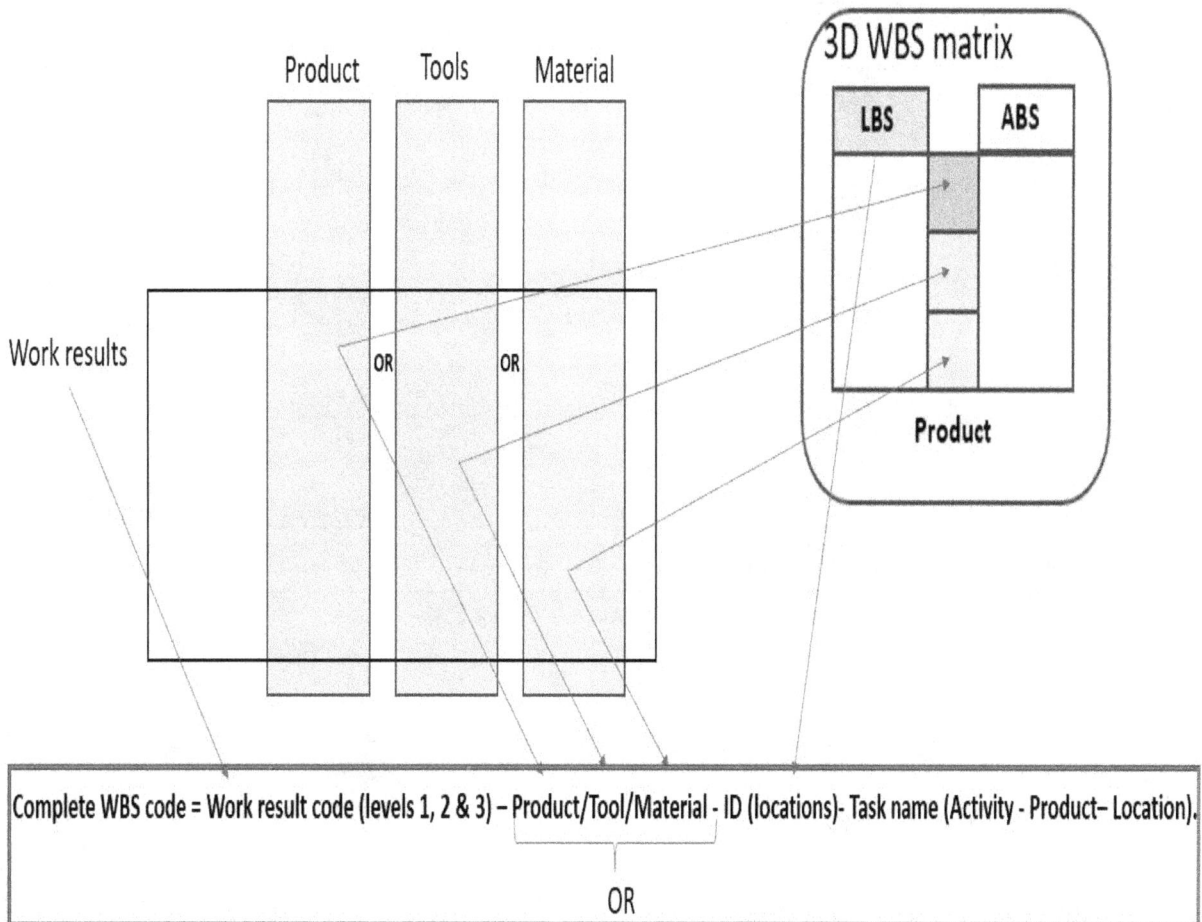

Figure 91: 5D WBS matrix

6-D Matrix: WBS x CBS

The 5D WBS matrix is crossed with the CBS to obtain the complete WBS and CBS code, as shown below in Figure 92.

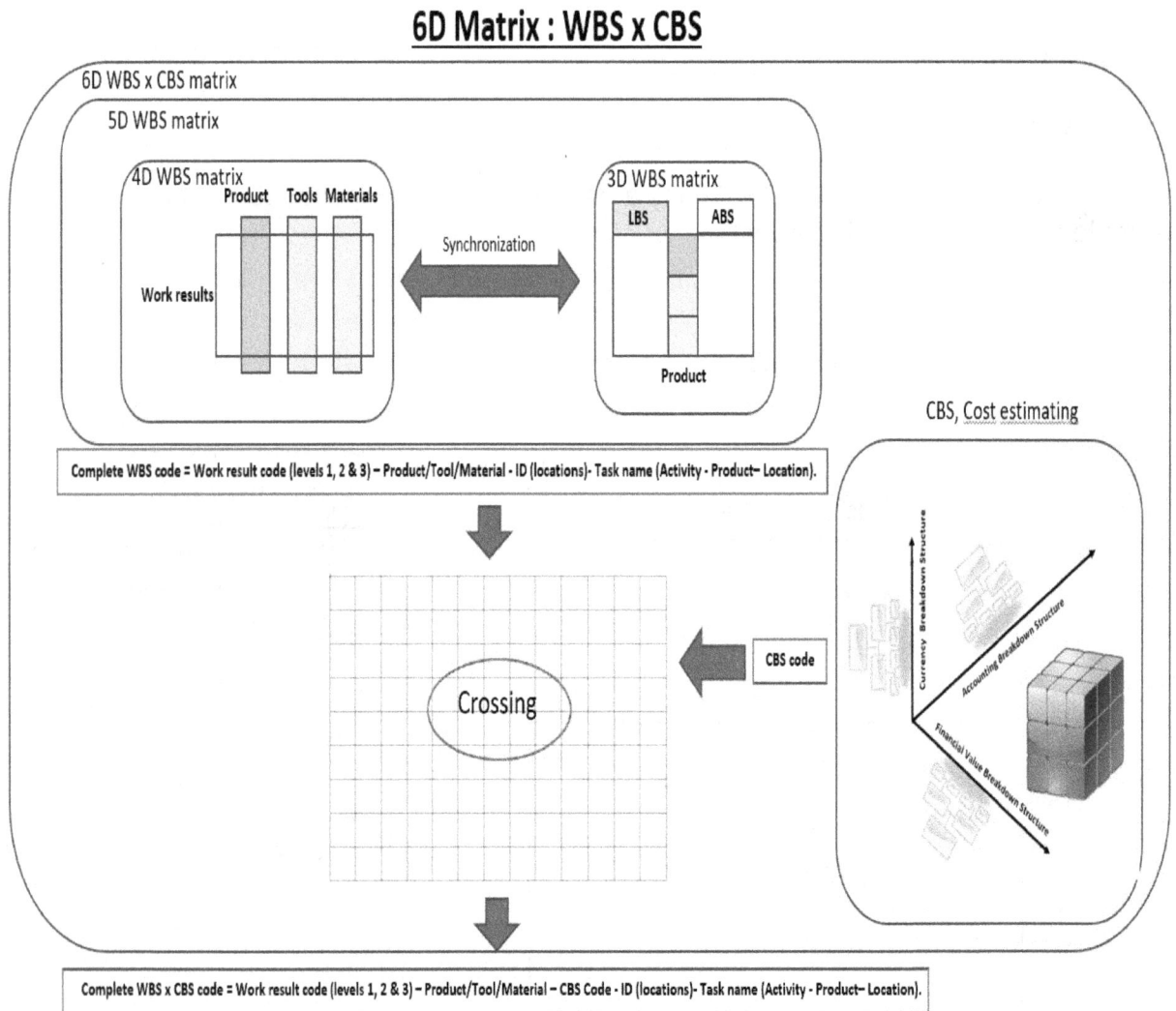

Figure 92: 6D Matrix: WBS x CBS

7-D Matrix: WBS x CBS x OBS

The complete WBS x CBS x OBS code is obtained by the crossing between the 6D matrix and the OBS, as shown below in Figure 93.

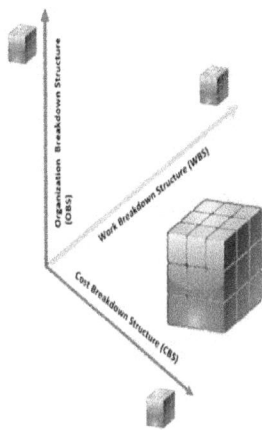

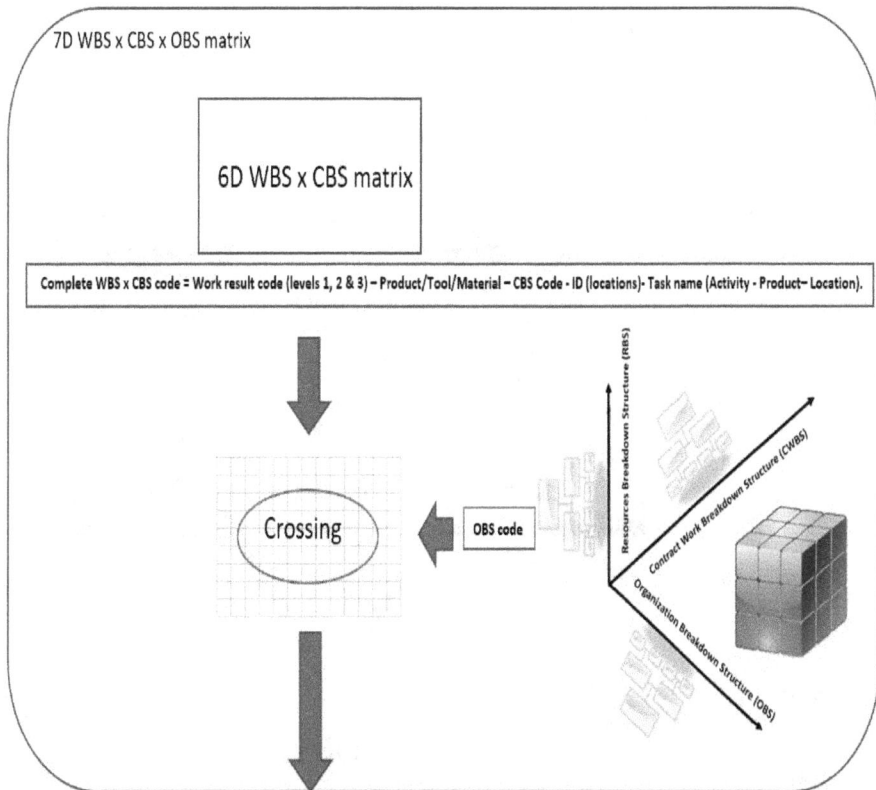

Figure 93: 7D matrix – WBS x CBS x OBS

8-D Matrix: WBS x CBS x OBS x Performance (6D BIM) – Star Tetrahedron

If the Performance is integrated, the picture documents the results, as noted below in Figure 94.

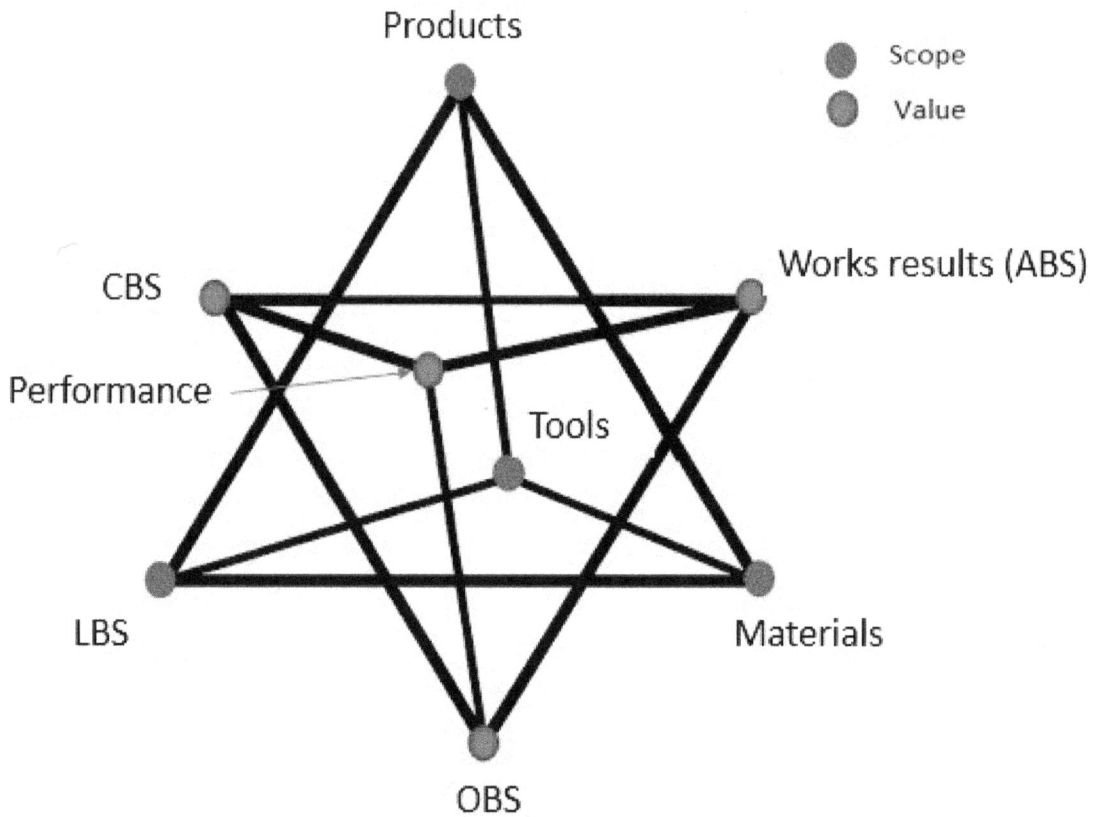

Figure 94: Star Tetrahedron

The Tesseract unfolded in a Contractor perspective

Another presentation of this modeling is presented below in Figure 95. It is constructed with the theoretical Tesseract unfolded.

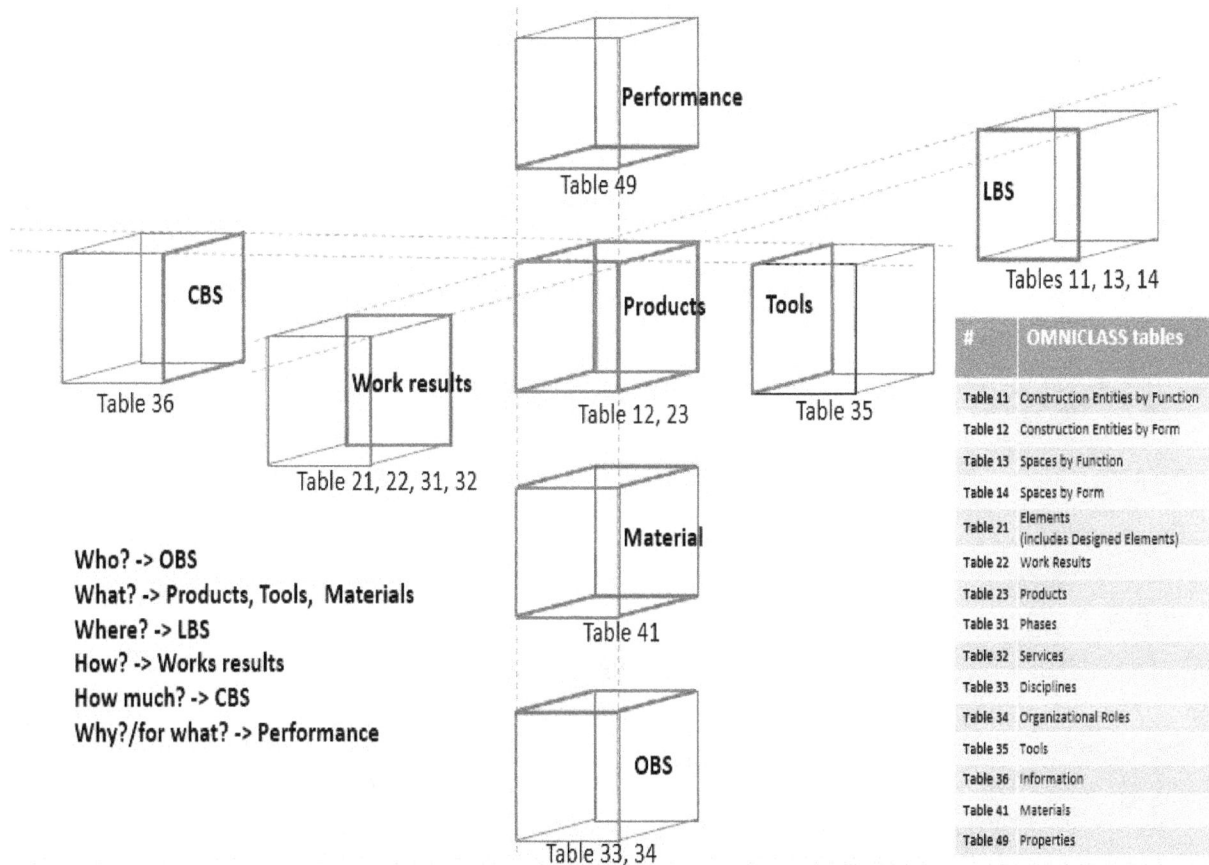

Who? -> OBS
What? -> Products, Tools, Materials
Where? -> LBS
How? -> Works results
How much? -> CBS
Why?/for what? -> Performance

#	OMNICLASS tables
Table 11	Construction Entities by Function
Table 12	Construction Entities by Form
Table 13	Spaces by Function
Table 14	Spaces by Form
Table 21	Elements (includes Designed Elements)
Table 22	Work Results
Table 23	Products
Table 31	Phases
Table 32	Services
Table 33	Disciplines
Table 34	Organizational Roles
Table 35	Tools
Table 36	Information
Table 41	Materials
Table 49	Properties

Figure 95: Tesseract unfolded in a Contractor perspective

Multi-Dimensional Project Breakdown Structure - A Stakeholder's Perspective

The evolution from two dimensional or flat-file databases of project breakdown structures towards relational or object-oriented project breakdown structures continues in the industry. As Virtual Reality (VR) technology becomes closely integrated with the design and construction processes, the authors predict movement towards using the databases to create complex Tesseract models. The VR is still in the creative stages, so following Steven Covey's advice to "… begin with the end in mind," this is what this book is about.

Section Organization

This section is organized around the Knowledge Areas developed by the Association for the Advancement of Cost Engineering (AACE) in their body of knowledge, the 'Total Cost Management Framework,' and adopted and refined by the Guild of Project Controls in their 'Compendium and Reference' document (GPCCAR). These two models are consistent with the approach the Project Management Institute is taking with revisions to the PMBOK Guide 6th Edition (2017).

- Integration – How each of the multi-dimensional tree structures can or should be able to work together, with an objective to support Virtual Reality (VR), Augmented Reality (AR), and Systems Dynamics (SD) models through the use of 2D Building Information Modeling (BIM), 3-D BIM, 4-D BIM, and 5-D BIM (and higher D levels).
- Creating and Managing Databases – As the primary interfaces between 3-D, 4-D, and 5-D BIM revolve around the productivity and cost-estimating databases, the 4-D, and 5-D BIM need to generate the Cost and Resource Loaded CPM Schedule.
- Stakeholder Management – No project can succeed unless the needs, wants, and expectations have been identified and the project designed to address and satisfy the same.
- Scope Management – Scope Management and scope definition are codified by the WBS structure and defined in the WBS Dictionary as the Work Breakdown Structure (WBS). The WBS, at any point in the asset or project lifespan, should represent 100% of the scope defined by stakeholders. In databases used by project managers, the WBS forms the Y-axis. The WBS, when deconstructed to the lower levels, provides an Activity Breakdown Structure (ABS), which in turn provides steps to accomplish to produce deliverables. An ABS does not give a sequence or duration – only actions for completion.
- Risk & Opportunity Management (ROM) - As ROM can be a weakness in both asset and project management, instead of leaving it until the end, the authors

included it right after Scope Management. If the WBS represents 100% of the scope, and WBS is used as the basis for the Risk/Opportunity Analysis, the probability of missing any risk or opportunity event is reduced and produces a Risk Breakdown Structure (RIBS).

- Contract Management – Contract management is one of the first decisions from the Risk/Opportunity analysis – the make-or-buy decision – does the company do it 'in-house' or sub-contract. The result of this process produces the Contract Work Breakdown Structure (CWBS). For any given project there potentially will be more than one, as is it not just the prime contractor, but the subs and subs to the subs who also will have CWBS.

- Resource Management – Once the 'make or buy' decision has been made, the owner knows what resources for which they are responsible for producing their WBS deliverables. The contractor, via the contract documents, knows what WBS elements for which they are responsible. Contractors can estimate what resources will be needed. Execution of this process yields the Resource Breakdown Structure (RBS).

- Schedule Management – Schedule creation requires three facts:
  - ✓ What is the Scope of Work for which the owner and contractor are responsible? (WBS)
  - ✓ What are the Risks inherent to this project? (RIBS)
  - ✓ What Resources are available and what are their costs and productivity? (RBS)

  The Schedule Management Processes combines the Activity Breakdown Structure produced by decomposing the WBS down to level 4, 5, or 6 (or from a 3-D BIM), sequencing those activities (from a 4-D BIM or from those doing the work) with the outputs from the Cost and Productivity databases, which generate the durations, costs, and resources assigned to each activity. When a schedule is discussed, it means a full cost and resource-loaded schedule (plan) which is designated as the CPM. When the CPM is fully cost- and resource-loaded and has been accepted by the management-decision team, the CPM then becomes the Performance Measurement Baseline or PMB.

- Cost Management – Cost and Schedule management are iterative, and timing is vital for scheduling (e.g., summer or winter; rainy or dry season?). The costs of the resources, including labor, materials, and equipment are vital pieces of knowledge. This database of information is known as the Cost Breakdown Structure or CBS.

- Progress Management and Reporting – Progress Management processes capture the physical progress in the field compared against the project plan, the actual costs of that progress, and calculations compared against the Performance Measurement Baseline (PMB) which is the full cost- and resource-loaded CPM schedule (CPM) submitted to and accepted by the owner.

- Managing Change - Every project will experience contract changes (Modifications; MODS) and needs a database to capture and track changes and will need to measure / assess the impact of changes against the approved Performance Measurement Baseline (PMB). The objective is a recovery or rebaseline plan.

- Managing Claims – Projects will result in disputes or claims, so it is important to include an analysis of what that database would look like in both two and three dimensions. This database is known as the Claims Breakdown Structure (CLBS).

The Different Needs of the Stakeholders

Developing multi-dimensional models for use in Virtual Reality (VR), Augmented Reality (AR), or Systems Dynamics (SD) requires a quick review of basic geometry to understand the theory and concepts. A hypercube is a 3-D projection of an 8-cell shape when animating a simple rotation about a plane which bisects the figure from front-left to back-right and top to bottom.[119] The construction of a hypercube can be imagined in the following way (demonstrated in Figure 96, following).

- 1-dimensional: Two points A and B can be connected to a line, giving a new line segment AB.
- 2-dimensional: Two parallel line segments AB and CD can be connected to become a square, with the corners marked as ABCD.
- 3-dimensional: Two parallel squares ABCD and EFGH can be connected to become a cube, with the corners marked as ABCDEFGH.
- 4-dimensional: Two parallel cubes ABCDEFGH and IJKLMNOP can be connected to become a hypercube, with the corners marked as" ABCDEFGHIJKLMNO

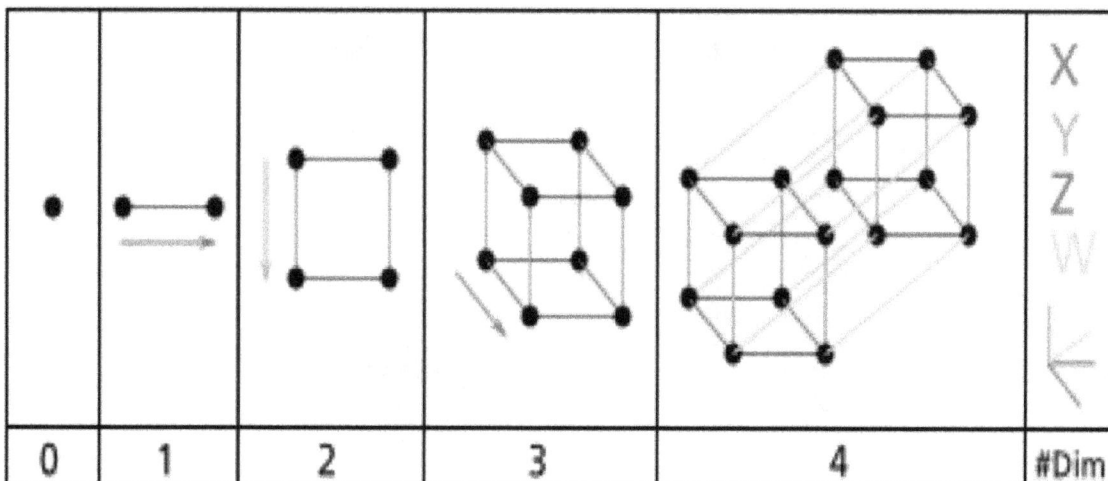

Figure 96: A diagram showing how to create a tesseract from a point

---

[119] For an interactive model of a "hypercube" or tesseract, visit: https://www.thingiverse.com/thing:1197328

As we can see from Figure 97 below, the traditional flat file, or two-dimensional breakdown structure, allows the creation of a matrix. The classic example of this is the creation of Control Accounts or Planning/Work Packages by intersecting the Work Breakdown Structure with the Organizational Breakdown Structure.

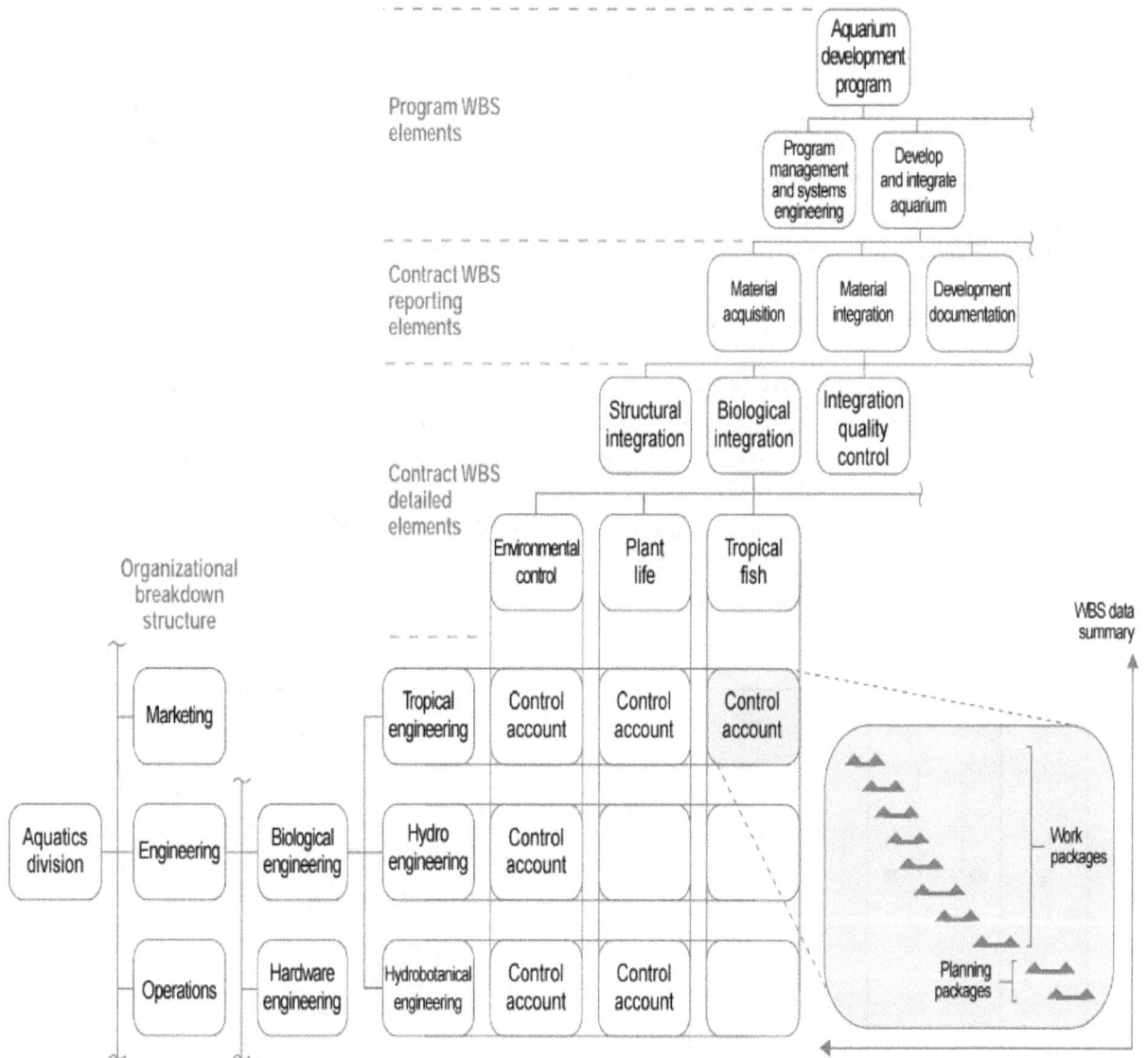

Figure 97: Typical 2D model- OBS x WBS Matrix = Control Accounts (SCEA, 2003)

Keeping the Russian Nesting Doll analogy in mind, the level of detail shown can range from Level 1, Program WBS, down to Level 3 or 4, Control Accounts, and even further deconstructed down to the Planning and Work Packages (activities) shown at

Level 4 or Level 5.[120] The proposition is to add another dimension to the flat file, creating a Cube from the Square (Figure 96 a diagram showing how to create a tesseract from a point). Like the Russian Nesting dolls, each 3-D cube varies in size from Level 1, Program or Project WBS cube down to Level 4 or 5 which contain the Planning or Work Packages. Deconstructing the scope into more detail, each cube will remain a discrete subset of the larger cube above. The summation of the entire scope is contained in a lower level, or 'child' cubes exactly equals 100% of the scope of the 'mother' or higher-level cube. As the 3-Dimensional geometric model of the project is created, apply non-Euclidean geometry to define or explain the relationships between any two or more cubes using mathematical formulas. Using the data from these databases to create a 'hypercube' or tesseract model using Virtual Reality software to analyze the dynamic relationships between the cubes is where the future lies for construction and project planning.

The following terms are used throughout this section and to fully understand and appreciate what is being shared, it is vital these definitions be reviewed before moving ahead: [121]

- "Flat-File Databases: Data is stored in one or more readable files, usually text format

- Hierarchical Databases: Data is stored in tables with parent/child relationships with a hierarchical structure; this is the most common type used for WBS, OBS, or Risk/Resource Breakdown Structures

- Network Databases: These databases are similar to the hierarchical model but allow flexibility; e.g., a child table can be related to more than one parent table

- Relational Databases: "In the relational database model, data is stored in a relational or object-oriented database, more commonly known as tables. Tables, records (sometimes known as tuples[122]), and fields (sometimes known as attributes) are the basic components as shown in Figure 98. Each piece of data, e.g., last name or a telephone number, is stored in a table field; each record holds a complete set of field data for a particular table. In the example, the table maintains customer shipping address data. Last_Name and other column headings are fields. A record, or row, in the table, comprises the set of field data in context: all the address data required to ship an order to a specific customer. Each record can be identified by, and accessed through, a unique identifier – a

---

[120] *GAO Cost Estimating and Assessment Guide: Best Practices for Developing and Managing Capital Program Costs (2009, Mar.). US Government Accountability Office: Applied Research and Methods, p. 217. Retrieved from http://www.gao.gov/new.items/d093sp.pdf*

[121] *Learn It: The Power of the Database. (n.d.). Retrieved from https://whatis.techtarget.com/reference/Learn-IT-The-Power-of-the-Database*

[122] *A tuple is a sequence of immutable Python objects. Tuples are sequences, like lists. The differences between tuples and lists are the tuples cannot be changed, unlike lists; tuples use parentheses, whereas lists use square brackets. Creating a tuple is as simple as creating different comma-separated values; Retrieved from https://en.wikipedia.org/wiki/Tuple*

primary key. In the Customer_Shipping table, the Customer_ID field could serve as a primary key because each record has a unique value for that field's data."[123],[124]

Field Names	Typical Database Components							
	ID	First	Last	Apt	Address	City	ST	Zip
Records	101	John	Smith	147	123 1st Street	Chicago	IL	60635
	102	Jane	Doe	13 C	234 2nd Street	Chicago	IL	60647
	103	June	Doe	14 A	243 2nd Street	Chicago	IL	60647
	104	George	Smith	N/A	345 3rd Street	Chicago	IL	60625

Figure 98: Data for the Example Above - Customer_Shipping

- Object-Oriented Databases: OOD was developed (the late 1980s to early 1990s) to deal with data types for which the relational model was not well-suited. Medical and multi-media data required a more flexible system for data representation and manipulation. This model was adopted for use in BIM. In this type of database, each object (e.g., a brand XYZ water pump, 500 GPM capacity) would be stored in an object library, and each object would come with already embedded, standardized-coding structures (likely OmniClass) in the object. In addition to the coding structure, there may be additional data such as sales price, operating- or life-cycle costs, delivery lead times, and cost or time to install. Some data (e.g., delivery lead times to a specific location or installation costs) would need to be adjusted using the contractor's database of costs and durations for each unique location.
- Object-Relational Databases: A hybrid model that combines features of relational- and object-oriented models.[125]

Introduction and Integration Management

To organize the explanation with a format most recognizable, knowledge areas defined by PMI in their PMBOK Guide 2015; AACE in their Total Cost Management Framework, 2nd Edition, and the Guild of Project Controls Compendium and Reference were used. This enables observation of how to use the three-dimensional approach based on 12 applications or the following knowledge areas, such as in Figure 99:

---

[123] *Learn It: The Power of the Database. (n.d.). Retrieved from https://whatis.techtarget.com/reference/Learn-IT-The-Power-of-the-Database*

[124] *Learn It: The Power of the Database. (n.d.). Retrieved from https://whatis.techtarget.com/reference/Learn-IT-The-Power-of-the-Database*

[125] *Learn It: The Power of the Database. (n.d.). Retrieved from https://whatis.techtarget.com/reference/Learn-IT-The-Power-of-the-Database*

Knowledge Areas

1.	Integration
2.	Creating and Managing Databases
3.	Stakeholder Management
4.	Scope Management
5.	Risk and Opportunity Management
6.	Contract Management
7.	Resource Management
8.	Schedule Management
9.	Cost Management
10.	Progress Management and Reporting
11.	Managing Change
12.	Managing Claims

Figure 99 - Knowledge Areas from PMBOK, AACE, and GFCCR Total Cost Management

This sequence was chosen as it roughly represents the sequence that Project Managers would be expected to follow starting with creating the databases necessary to provide the productivity, cost and resource information that the 3-D BIM and VR software needs to turn the 2D and 3-D BIM design into 4-D BIM (schedule) and 5-D BIM (cost) Models. As the BIM software evolves, data would be added for 6-D BIM (Sustainability Modeling) and 7-D BIM (Facilities Operation and Management). To refer to the 3-D WBS Method part is to recognize the relationships of the tree structures within the Project.

Creating and Managing Project Management Databases

The primary database used by 4-D BIM (CPM Scheduling) is usually a relational database similar to RS Means[126] and the Guild of Project Controls Module 11.3 Designing the Project Database (planningplanet.com/guild/gpccar/designing-the-project-database). Whether created in-house or commercial-off-the-shelf, the information contained in the database should be pretty much the same. What is important to notice is RS Means has adopted CSI's MasterFormat as the coding structure of choice. Items 1, 2 3, 4, and 5 are important, as those explain how the coding structure works from Level 1 down to Level 5. CSI's MasterFormat is almost identical to OmniClass Table 22; Figure 100 shows what the Activity Level cube would look like in OmniClass. [127]

---

[126] *RS Means Facility Cost Data (2016) abebooks.com/RSMeans-Facilities-Construction-Cost-Data-2016/18438043904/bd*
[127] *Guild of Project Controls Compendium and Reference Module 11,3. Designing the Project Database. (nd). Retrieved from http://www.planningplanet.com/guild/gpccar/introduction-to-managingcost-estimating-budgeting*

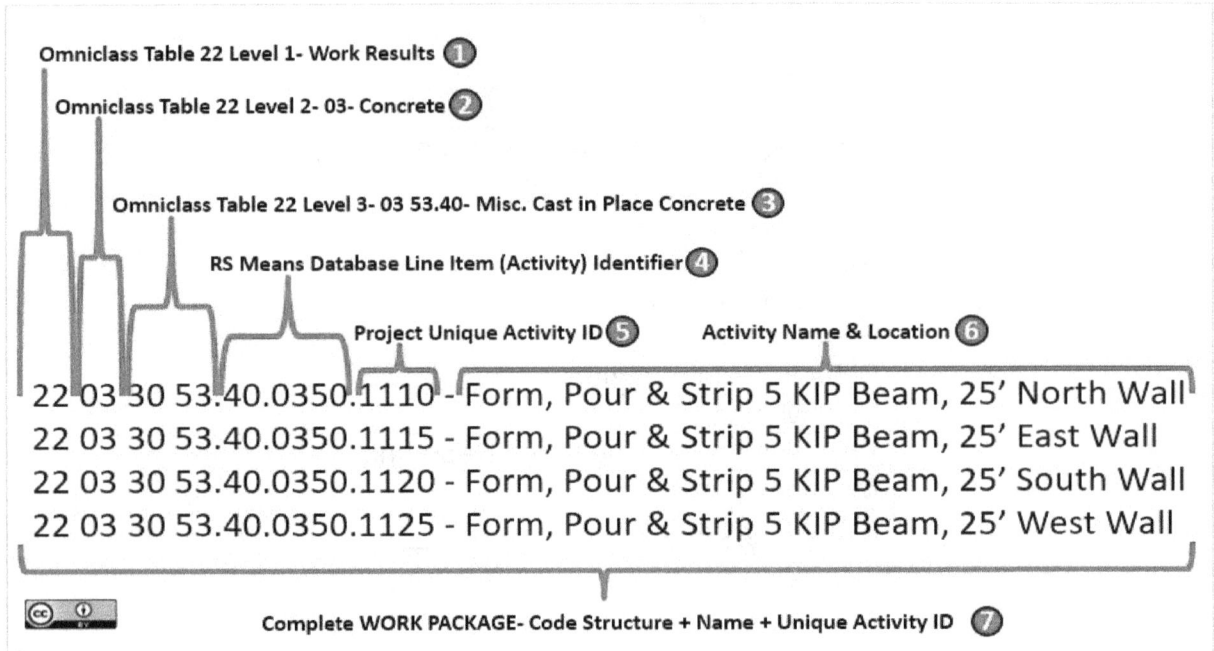

Omniclass Table 22 Level 1- Work Results ①

Omniclass Table 22 Level 2- 03- Concrete ②

Omniclass Table 22 Level 3- 03 53.40- Misc. Cast in Place Concrete ③

RS Means Database Line Item (Activity) Identifier ④

Project Unique Activity ID ⑤   Activity Name & Location ⑥

22 03 30 53.40.0350.1110 - Form, Pour & Strip 5 KIP Beam, 25' North Wall
22 03 30 53.40.0350.1115 - Form, Pour & Strip 5 KIP Beam, 25' East Wall
22 03 30 53.40.0350.1120 - Form, Pour & Strip 5 KIP Beam, 25' South Wall
22 03 30 53.40.0350.1125 - Form, Pour & Strip 5 KIP Beam, 25' West Wall

Complete WORK PACKAGE- Code Structure + Name + Unique Activity ID ⑦

Figure 100: R.S Means Database Coding Structure Explained

The example illustrates the levels of detail most Contractors would normally develop and maintain for contract bids, estimates, projects, and databases, which is why these coding structures are critical to maintaining for Vertical Integration capabilities. This enables the owners to roll-up to the contractor's detailed cost estimates for their own use down to Level 3 minimum or more ideally, Level 4. This enables owners to develop their own budgets to compare against the building contractors proposed costs of the entire project.

Means-Database, Coding-Structure Elements

---

1. 03 is CSI's Level 1 WBS. Using CSI's MasterFormat or OmniClass Table 22, Division 03 covers all concrete work.

2. 03 30 is CSI/OmniClass Level 2, e.g., 03 30 is only concrete which is cast in place.

3. 03 30 53 is CSI/OmniClass Level 3, e.g., 03 30 53 covers miscellaneous cast in place concrete; the minimum level of detail Owners should be providing to Contractors in the contract documents.

Means-Database, Coding-Structure Elements

4. 03 30 53.40 is the CSI/OmniClass heading that covers Miscellaneous Beam Concrete in Place; ideal or recommended Level of Detail Owners should be providing to Contractors in the contract documents.

5. 03 30 53.40.0350 is the Activity level of detail the contractor develops from contract documents provided by the Owner. If there were more than ONE of these same activities (e.g., several different places in the project which required the "Forming (0.0010); Installing Rebar (0.0020) and Placing and Finishing Concrete (0.0050) 25' Span Beams, then the contractor would add another level of code.) If there are three Places in the project, then 03 30 53.40.0350.1000 would be the coding structure the contractor could use to identify the first location, 03 30 53.40.0350.2000 for the second location and 03 30 53.40.0350.3000 for the third and final location

With the coding structure is explained, explore what a well-established time, cost, and productivity database might look like (Figure 101). [128,129,130]

03 30 Cast in Place Concrete ①											
03 30 53 Miscellaneous Cast in Place Concrete ②											
03 30 53.40 Concrete in Place ③		⑦	⑧	⑨	⑩	⑪	⑫	⑬	⑭	⑮
0.0010 / 0.0020 / 0.0050	Including Forms (4 uses) ④ reinforcing steel, concrete placement and finishing, unless otherwise indicated.	Crew Type	Daily Output per Unit	Labor Hours per Unit	Unit of Measure	Material Costs	Labor Costs	Equipment Costs	Total Costs per Unit	Total Price/Unit Including OH&P
0.0300	Beams- 5 kip per lineal foot, 10' long spans ⑤	C14-A	15.62	12.8	Cubic Yard (CY)	$315.00	$490.00	$48.50	$853.50	$1,225.00
0.0350	Beams- 5 kip per lineal foot, 25' long spans ⑥	"	18.55	10.78	CY	$325.00	$415.00	$40.50	$780.50	$1.100.00

Figure 101: Case Study Using Commercial Database Information

[128] *Guild of Project Controls Compendium and Reference. Introduction to Managing Cost Estimating & Budgeting. Module 8.1. Retrieved from http://www.planningplanet.com/guild/gpccar/introduction-to-managingcost-estimating-budgeting*
[129] *Guild of Project Controls Compendium and Reference. Introduction to Managing Project Databases, Module 11.1. Retrieved from http://www.planningplanet.com/guild/gpccar/introduction-to-managingcost-estimating-budgeting*
[130] *Giammalvo, Paul D (2015); Course materials adapted from / contributed to under Creative Commons License BY v 4.0; Adapted from R.S. Means 2008 Facility Cost Estimating Database. Available at: https://amzn.to/2BTOUq6*

Case Study Using Commercial Database Information

1. 03 30 - Cast in Place Concrete is CSI MasterFormat/OmniClass Table 22 2nd Level WBS Structure. (Level 1 is 03 is Concrete, and Level 2 is 03 30 is Cast in Place Concrete)

2. 03 30 53 – Misc. Cast in Place Concrete is CSI MasterFormat/OmniClass Table 22 3rd Level WBS (Level 1, 03 is Concrete, Level 2, 03 30 is Cast in Place Concrete)

3. 03 30 53.40 - Concrete in Place is CSI MasterFormat/OmniClass Table 22 Level 4 WBS; from this level down becomes not only a WBS but a Cost Breakdown Structure (CBS) and a Productivity Breakdown Structure (PBS). One coding structure serves three purposes. Level 3 of the WBS is the minimum level of detail an owner should be providing to a contractor, assuming the owner wants to minimize claims and disputes and obtain highly competitive bids.

4. 03 30 53.40.0010, 03 30 53.40.0020, and 03 30 53.40.0050 - an Activity consisting of Forming (0.0010), Installing Rebar (0.0020), and Placing and Finishing Concrete (0.0050)

5. Two types of Activity 03 30 53.40.0300 – one based on 10' (foot) long spans" and the second 03 30 53.40.0350 based on 25' (foot) long spans; depending on the number of scenarios, other cos, and productivity calculations can be created for combinations.

6. Using Activity 03 30 53.40.0350 to form, reinforce, place concrete, and strip 25' long, 5-kip (5,000 lbs.) beams. Notice the piece of information missing from this is the Quantity Take Off (QTO) or Bill of Materials (BOM). When using BIM, use these coding structures. If BIM is not used, quantity take-offs will need manual methods.

7. Identifies the crew composition to calculate productivity and costs. For this example, use Crew C-14A. See below for details that make up Crew C-14A.

8. Daily average output Crew C-14A can produce – a (P50) value not adjusted for risks. This is important data the Planner/Scheduler uses to calculate the Duration, and the Cost Estimator needs to know to estimate the Costs.

9. The number of Crew Labor Hours per Cubic Yard (CY) of beam concrete; a useful piece of data for project control professionals, but especially planners / schedulers, as many projects are not tracked based on money, but on man-

Case Study Using Commercial Database Information

hours expended or earned vs. planned man-hours (covered in Module 9 - Managing Progress).

10. Unit of Measure. In this case, it is Cubic Yards (CY), but it could have been Cubic Meters (M3) or any other fast and reliable way to measure physical progress.

11. Field to enter Material Costs. As material costs tend to be location specific, the professional cost estimate needs to update and adjust these values for different locations.

12. Labor Costs - As with Material costs, labor costs are variable and need to be checked and validated by the cost estimator/project controller for each location and trade.

13. Equipment Costs - Tend to be less variable than material or labor costs, but also need to be updated at least semi-annually (preferably quarterly). Equipment productivity tends to be relatively stable and predictable.

14. Total Costs is the sum of 11, 12, and 13

15. Marked Up Costs (Contractors Selling Price) is shown in this column and ranges from about 44% to 47% to cover Project Overhead, Home Office Overhead, and all the other items shown above in Figure 101; R.S. means 2008 Facility Cost Estimating Database Back Cover Showing Labor Rate Markups

16. Crew C-14A can produce on average, 18.55 Cubic Yards (CY) per day for this activity. Different activities will have different productivity rates.

17. On average, it takes 10.782 labor hours per Cubic Yard (CY) in place for this activity. Different activities will have different productivity rates.

18. Material Costs for this activity is $315.00 per Cubic Yard of Concrete in place

19. Labor Costs for this activity is $415.00 per Cubic Yard of Concrete in place

20. Equipment Costs for this activity is $40.50 per Cubic Yard of Concrete in place

21. Total Costs per Cubic Yard of Concrete in Place is $780.50

22. Fair Market Value or Contractors Selling Price for each Cubic Yard of Concrete

Case Study Using Commercial Database Information

in Place is $1,100, including markup for OH&P of ~47% (16% Home Office Overhead + 16% for Project Overhead + 15% for Contractors Gross Profit = 47%)

What this means is once the Standardized the Records and Fields are established, data becomes relatively easy to enter and update for the actual costs and productivity to fit local conditions. Knowing the base composition of each crew, it is easy to adjust the crew composition to fit local practices, labor laws or union agreements.[131]

#	Crew C-14A ①	Contractors Bare Costs		Including Subcontractors OH & P		Contractors Cost Per Labor Hour	
		Hourly	Daily	Hourly	Daily	Bare Costs	Billing Rate Including OH & P
1	Carpenter Foreman	$40.10	$320.80	$66.40	$531.20	$38.36	$63.65
16	Carpenters	$38.10	$304.80	$63.10	$504.80		
4	Rodmen	$43.00	$344.00	$73.55	$588.40		
2	Laborers	$30.25	$242.00	$50.10	$400.80		
1	Cement Finisher	$37.00	$296.00	$58.00	$464.00		
1	Equipment Operator	$39.85	$318.80	$62.90	$503.20		
1	Gas Engine Vibrator		$24.80		$27.28		
1	Concrete Pump (Small)		$728.20		$810.02	$3.77	$4.14
200	Total Daily Labor Hours ②	③ $8,425.40		④ $13,558.70		⑤ $42.13	⑥ $67.79

Figure 102: Case Study Demonstrating Crew Composition Details

Case Study Demonstration Crew Composition Details
(RS Means Facilites Construction Costs 2018 – p. 1,400)

1.   Crew C-14A consists of eight Labor and Equipment items; one carpenter foreman plus 16 carpenters, four rodmen, two laborers, and one equipment operator.

2.   This crew of 25 people equals 25 man-days of labor and assuming they are

---

[131] Source: Guild of Project Controls Module 11.3 Designing the Project Database
http://www.planningplanet.com/guild/gpccar/designing-the-project-database and Giammalvo, Paul D (2015) Course Materials Adapted from R.S. Means 2008 Facility Cost Estimating Database. Contributed Under Creative Commons License BY v 4.0

Case Study Demonstration Crew Composition Details
(RS Means Facilites Construction Costs 2018 – p. 1,400)

working an 8-hour day = 200-man hours of labor per crew working daily

3.   The bare Cost of this crew is $8,425.40 daily (bare costs = wages + fringe benefits for labor and depreciated costs of the equipment)

4.   What the Prime Contractor has to charge for this crew to work one day

5.   Cost of the supervision/tools provided by the prime contractor to the subcontractor

6.   Additional amount the Prime Contractor has to add to cover Overhead and Profit (O&P) on Foreman and Concrete pump the prime contractor provided. Thus the Prime Contractor would have to take the $13,558.70 and add the OH&P of $67.79 for the Foreman and Pump for a total of $13,626.79 per 8-hour working day.

Having established, and kept current, a Project Controls Database when we have created a schedule – either manually or done by the 4-D BIM software – then we have to draw from this database to create a Resource Pool, Resource Assignments, or Resource Dictionary in order to justify costs, budgets, and durations. The project manager/project team can review Activity Based Costing (ABC) and Activity Based Management (ABM), the 2-D data sorting used by these databases is the Activity Breakdown Structure (ABS) on the Y-axis and the Cost Breakdown Structure (CBS) on the Z-axis. To make this particular 'cube' work from the perspective of creating a 3-D S-Curve, use the Schedule Breakdown Structure (CPM) created by the 3-D BIM software, as the Z-axis or 3rd dimension.

Note the CPM Schedule is a combination of the ABS with the logic and sequencing produced by the 4-D BIM software and the Activity Durations calculated by multiplying the Quantities from 3-D BIM X Productivity (using Units/day or Hours/Unit in Place). This shows the conversion from the 2D database above into the 3-D cube in Figure 103 below.

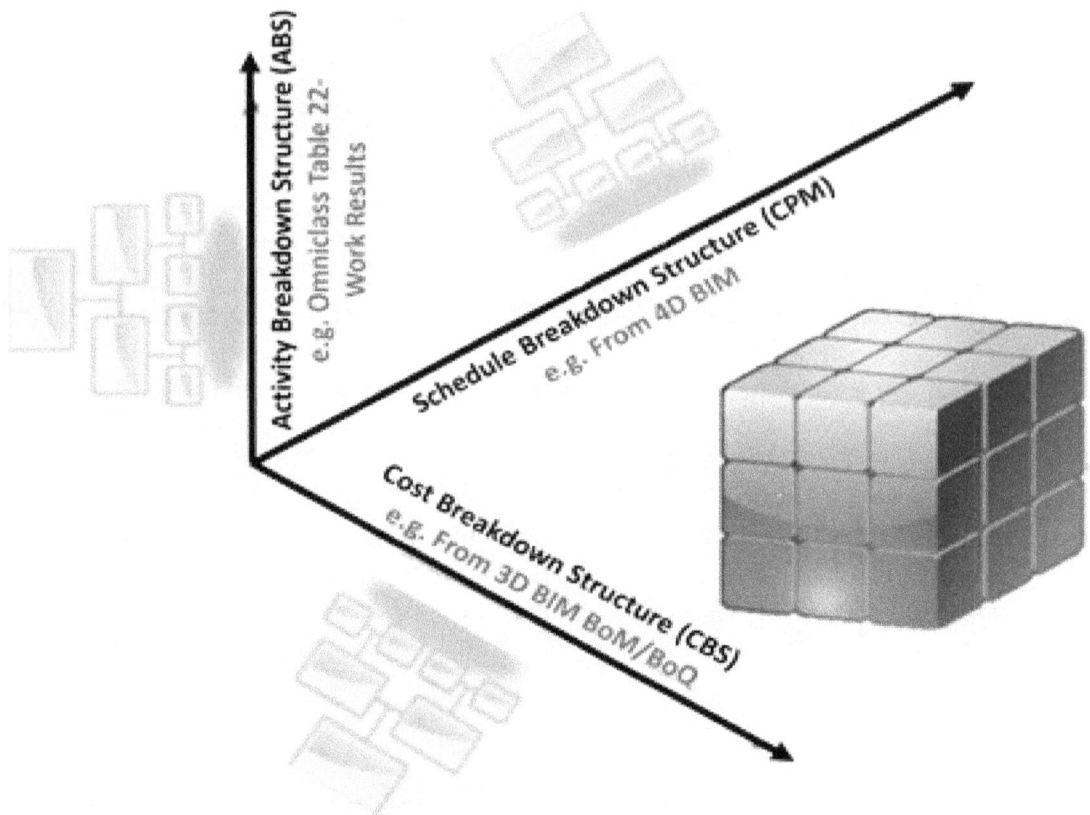

Figure 103: Cost Loaded CPM Schedule using ABS X CBS X CPM combinations

When looking at this cube, understand that while this would be a common way to combine the data to produce a 3-D model of value to the project manager/project team, other combinations are possible. Depending upon the needs of any stakeholder, it is possible to create additional dimensions – or vectors could be added – creating a tesseract perspective.

Stakeholder Management

Key Definitions for this Section - The following terms are used throughout this section and to fully understand and appreciate what is being shared, it is important that these definitions be reviewed before proceeding further. When used in this book, the term 'stakeholders' fall into six categories:

Beneficiaries - Usually the customer client or product end-user the project was undertaken to deliver; those entities who benefit from the product of the project.

Negative Beneficiaries - Those stakeholders who will either be negatively impacted temporarily while the project is executed (e.g., people who have to detour while new water pipes are being installed in their neighborhood) or permanently (e.g., someone who lost their home to a new roadway being built).

Implementers - Those leading or serving on the project team, including owner's staff, contractor's staff along with subcontractor and vendors – anyone who provides support to the execution of the project.

Decision makers - The most obvious are the Asset Managers who act as sponsors for a Capital Expense (CAPEX) funded project or Operations Managers who act as sponsors for Operations Expense (OPEX) funded projects. Other examples would be the local building or electrical inspectors.

Financiers - This includes the banks, shareholders, bondholders, or those in the finance or accounting department.

Regulators - Any governmental or quasi-governmental agencies, including non-government organizations (NGOs). Prime examples are the Environmental Protection Agencies or Boards of Health; any governmental agency that publishes rules or regulations with which the project must comply .

Defining Stakeholder Needs, Wants, and Expectations

As we can see from Figure 104, definitions for Building Information Modeling[132] regarding the Scope of Work should be defined using 2D and 3-D BIM software. The 3-D BIM software provides the project management/control professionals with:

- Technical Specifications (quality assurance and acceptance of deliverables)
- Bills of Materials/Bills of Quantities (types of materials / how much are needed)
- Sequence or Logic of the work (what is done first, second, third ...)

Put into context, being able to meet or exceed stakeholder expectations regarding the time the section below on scheduling will provide a more detailed explanation, and in terms of meeting or exceeding stakeholder expectations regarding cost or budget, see the section on costs for more specific examples. A typical 3-D model would have Roles and Responsibilities (RAM or RACI) on the Y-axis and viewed over time; project managers could use the CPM schedule (CPM) on the X-axis for which project sponsors and key stakeholder decision-makers are looking for from the project

---

[132] *Origins of BIM. Bimpanzee Blog (ND) http://www.bimpanzee.com/about-building-information-modeling--bim-.html*

manager/project control team. For the Z axis, show the roles and responsibilities by WBS, which gives the Control Accounts. For the Z-axis choose the Discipline Breakdown Structure (DBS).

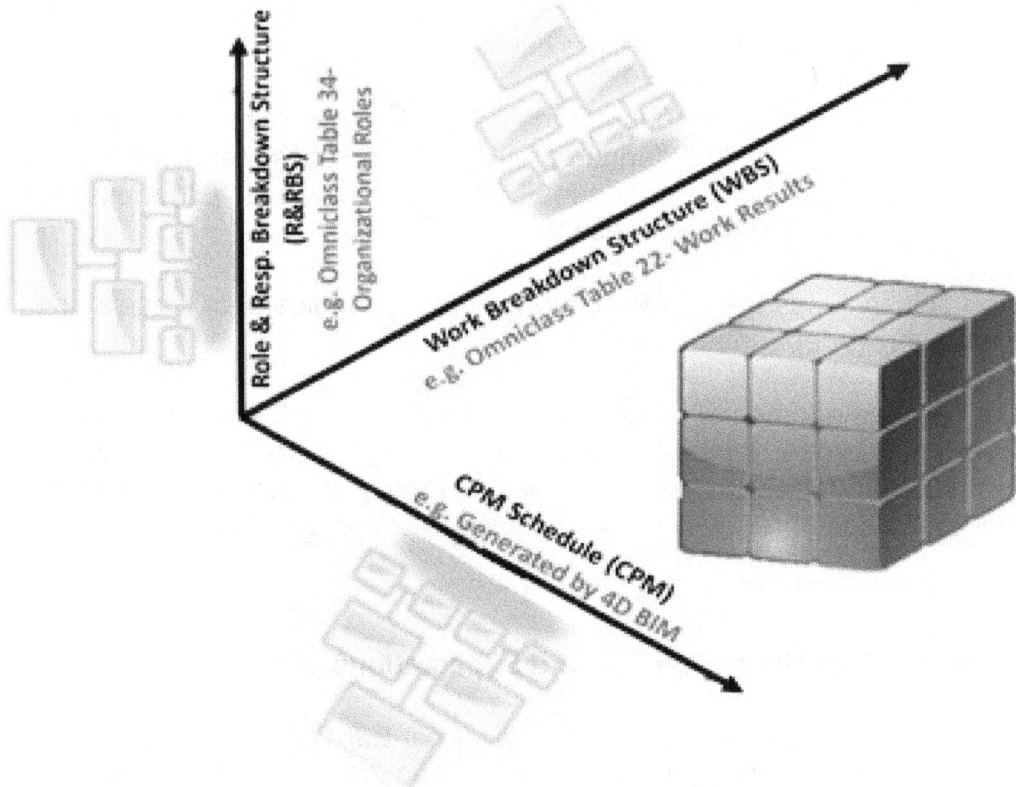

Figure 104: Control Account Cube created by combining the R&RBS X CPM X WBS

Scope Management

The following terms are used throughout this section and to fully understand and appreciate what is being shared, it is important that these definitions be reviewed before proceeding further: [133]

---

[133] *Wideman, M. (2017) Wideman's Comparative Glossary of Project Management Terms*
    maxwideman.com/pmglossary/PMG_W00.htm

- Work Breakdown Structure (WBS)[134] - A task-oriented detailed breakdown, which defines the work packages and tasks at a level above that defined in the networks and schedules; initiates development of the Organizational Breakdown Structure (OBS), and the Cost Breakdown Structure (CBS); provides foundation for determining Earned Value and activity networks.
- Work Breakdown Structure Dictionary (WBSD)[135]- Describes each element in the WBS including a Statement of Work (SOW); describes the work content of the WBS element, and a Basis of Estimate (BOE); describes how the budget of the element was developed; more information about each WBS element may include the responsible organization, contract number, and more. The WBS Dictionary often results in the project or contract Statement of Work (SOW).
- Work Breakdown Structure Related to CPM Schedule - the Work Breakdown Structure (WBS) and the CPM Schedule are directly related; when using the Phase Gate Approach, the WBS and the CPM Schedule evolve simultaneously; it is not necessarily a Top-Down or Bottom-Up approach, but a process which evolves (traditionally) concurrently using a progressive elaboration, as shown in Figure 105 below.[136]

---

[134] Wideman, M. (2017) Wideman's Comparative Glossary of Project Management Terms
    maxwideman.com/pmglossary/PMG_W00.htm
[135] Wideman, M. (2017) Wideman's Comparative Glossary of Project Management Terms
    maxwideman.com/pmglossary/PMG_W00.htm
[136] Adapted from Lewis, James, Project Managers Desk Reference, p. 91.

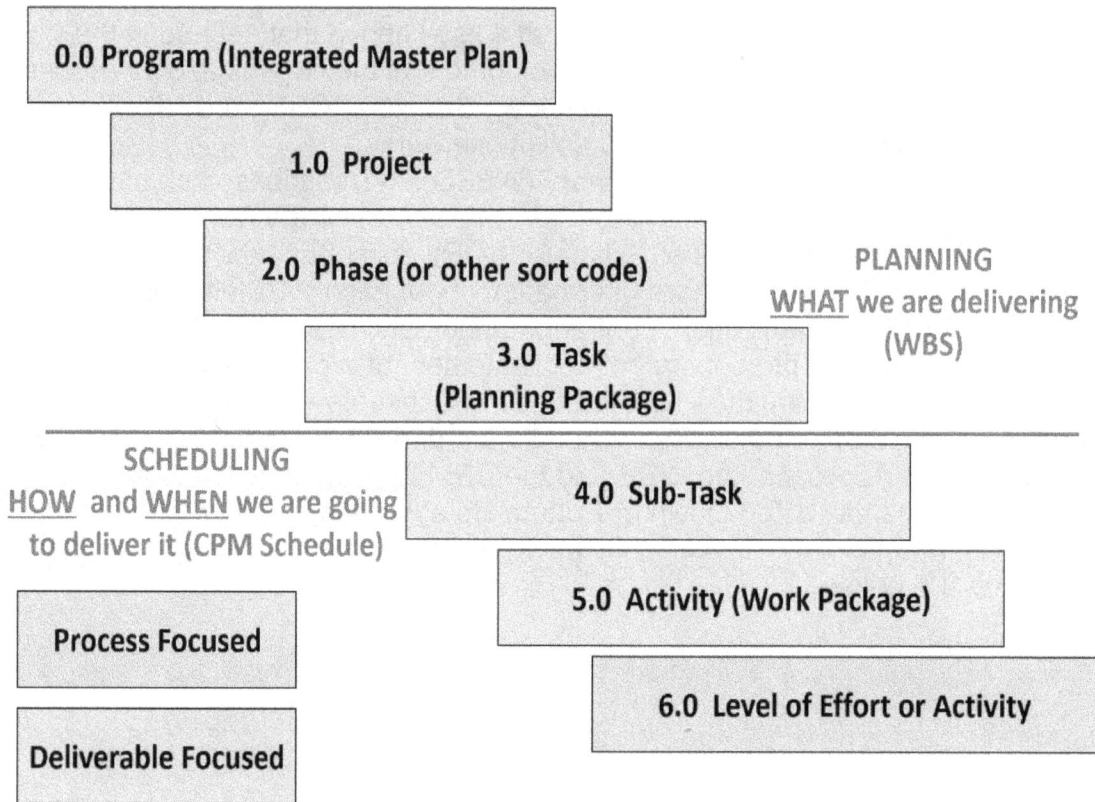

Figure 105: Combined WBS and Schedule Level Names

At any given phase of the project lifespan (or life-cycle) the level of Scope is defining What we need or want in the project and How and When we are going to produce each deliverable should be documented. Similar to the Russian Doll analogy, each phase gate will produce more and more detail – both in terms of the deliverables – as well as how and when those deliverables are going to be created.

Work Breakdown Structure – Explanation

Figure 106 below, shows an example of a WBS based on OmniClass Table 22 - Work Results showing the OmniClass Table 31 Phases.

Table 22 — Work Results

OmniClass Number	Level 1 Title	Level 2 Title	Level 3 Title	Level 4 Title
	Phase 1 or "IDENTIFY" Phase	Phase 2 or "ASSESS" Phase	Phase 3 or "SELECT" Phase	Phase 4 or "Define" Phase

Numbers and Titles

OmniClass Number	Level 1 Title	Level 2 Title	Level 3 Title	Level 4 Title
22-01 00 00	General Requirements			
22-01 30 00	Phase 1 / Identify Level 1- WBS Schedule Cost Estimate	Administrative Requirements		
22-01 31 00		Project Management and Coordination		
22-01 31 13			Project Coordination	
22-01 31 14		Phase 2 / Assess Level 2- WBS Schedule Cost Estimate	Facility Services Coordination	
22-01 31 16			Multiple Contract Coordination	
22-01 31 19			Project Meetings	
22-01 31 19 13				Preconstruction Meetings
22-01 31 19 16				Site Mobilization Meetings
22-01 31 19 23				Progress Meetings
22-01 31 19 33				Preinstallation Meetings
22-01 31 23			Project Web Site	
22-01 31 26			Electronic Communication Protocols	
22-01 32 00		Construction Progress Documentation		
22-01 32 13			Scheduling of Work	
22-01 32 16			Construction Progress Schedule	
22-01 32 16 13				Network Analysis Schedules
22-01 32 19			Submittals Schedule	
22-01 32 23			Survey and Layout Data	
22-01 32 26			Construction Progress Reporting	
22-01 32 29			Periodic Work Observation	
22-01 32 33			Phase 3 / Select Level 3- WBS Schedule Cost Estimate	Phase 4 / Define Level 4- WBS Schedule Cost Estimate
22-01 32 36				
22-01 32 43				
22-01 35 00		Special Procedures		
22-01 35 13				
22-01 35 13 13				

Figure 106: OmniClass Table 22 Work Results in Two Dimensions - By Phase (Table 31) x Work Results

As illustrated by the Russian Nesting Dolls theory, each Phase of the Project Life Span evolves, for application of progressive elaboration, producing more details regarding what the stakeholders need or want the project to produce or create. This is known as scope definition. (e.g., "Deliverables" or "Work Results"). Starting with OmniClass Table 22 which in the 2D format shows Phases on the X-axis and required Deliverables on the Y-axis, project managers can decide what is needed on the Z axis. This data could be any of the other tables, depending on what or how the stakeholders need to see the information. For illustration purposes, taking the 2D model above, and adding Products as the third dimension, the result is a 3-D model that looks like Figure 107:

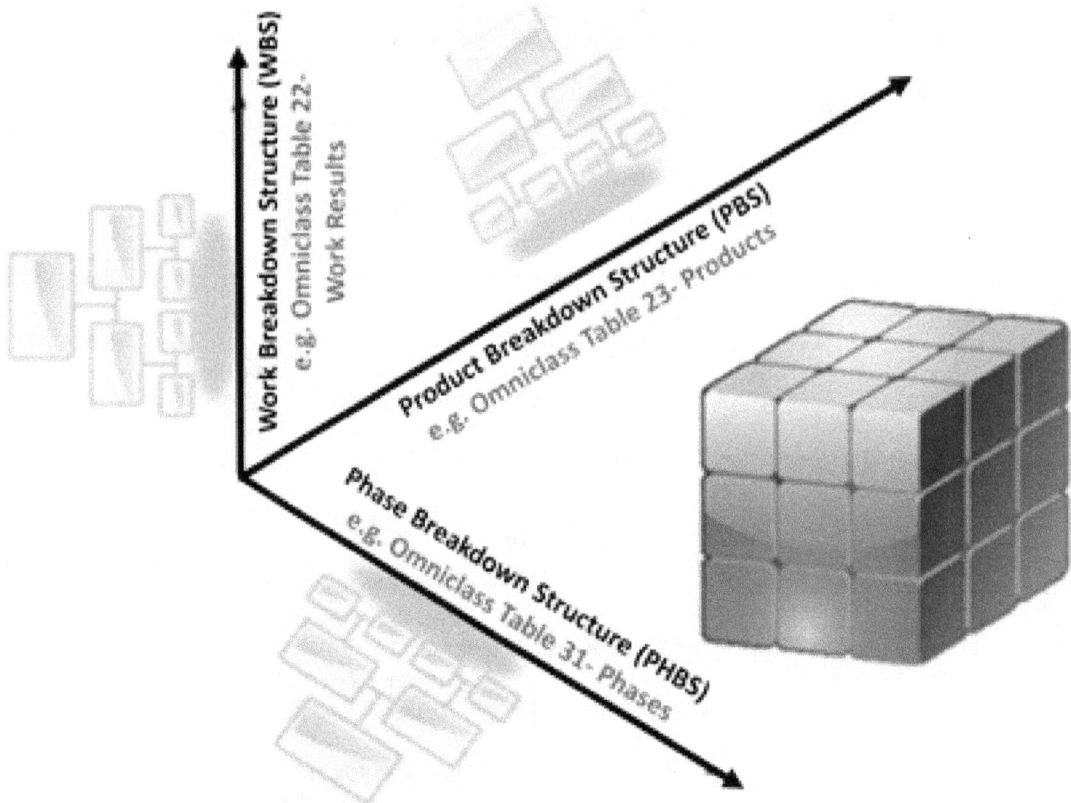

Figure 107: Illustrating the 3-D model of WBS X PHBS X PBS

The example in Figure 107 was developed creating a matrix of Work Results X Phases. In the example in this book, we want to define the scope of work (the 3-D WBS) by creating a 3-D matrix defined by Activity Breakdown Structure (ABS) X Product Breakdown Structure (PBS) X Location Breakdown Structure (LBS). Remember that, unlike using the traditional WBS approach, project managers can now define the WBS as being any combination of a minimum of three perspectives. Another way to look at the data using the example in Figure 108 is to concatenate the Activity Breakdown Structure (ABS) X Location Breakdown Structure (LBS) X Product Breakdown Structure (PBS).

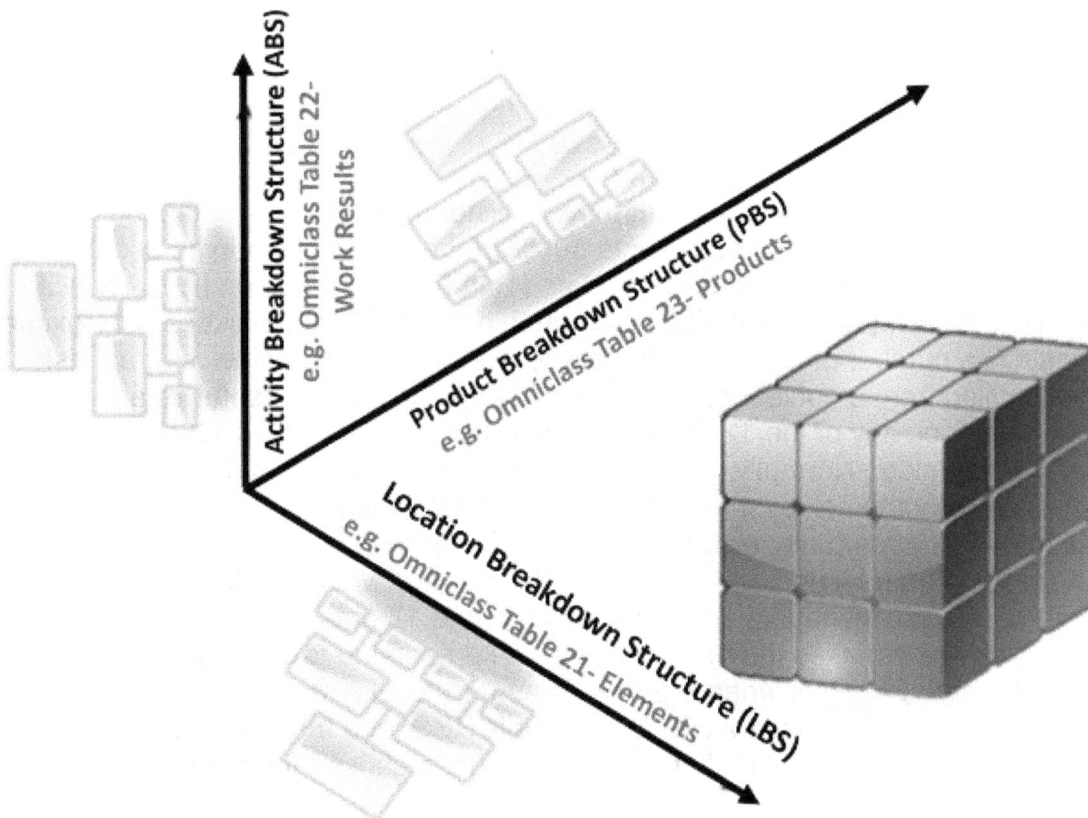

Figure 108: Illustrating the 3-D model of ABS X LBS X PBS

Risk and Opportunity Management

Key Definitions for this Section - The following terms are used throughout this section and to fully understand and appreciate what is being shared, it is important that these definitions be reviewed before proceeding further:

- Risk - A probability or threat of damage, injury, liability, loss, or any other negative occurrence caused by external or internal vulnerabilities (physical, legal, etc.) that may be avoided through preemptive action.
- Opportunity – A circumstantial set of exploitable events with an uncertain or certain outcome, requiring commitments of resources, and/or involving exposure to unique or otherwise risk(s).
- Risks and Opportunities are not necessarily two heads of the same coin, but two distinct and separate constructs; while similar in process, risks and opportunities do not necessarily have correlation or causal relationship to the other; not every risk has an alter ego of opportunity nor does every opportunity necessarily have unique or significant risks.

- Risk/Opportunity Register - A database of risks and risk attributes (e.g., lessons learned documentation or library) used as a basis to characterize, sort, filter, and prioritize tasks for future risks or opportunities for management decision-making based on quantifiable values.

When creating a Risk or Opportunity Register (in an Access database or an Excel spreadsheet), the WBS represents 100% of the scope of work, so use the WBS coding structures on the Y-axis, (identified as (1) in Figure 109 below).[137] A typical Risk/Opportunity Database, identified as item 2 in Figure 108, consists of approximately 12 fields. (The number of fields varies, but the example shown below is a real risk register coming from a nuclear plant and is fairly robust.) To be useful as a management tool, any of the 12 fields are sortable. Select the field which illustrates the third or X dimension. Normally, we Rank Order risks by EMV (item 3). To calculate EMV first quantify the risk by monetizing it. To monetize the risk, multiply the Cost Impact if the risk/opportunity event does occur (Column G) by the probability the event will happen (Column H) and that yields the (3) Expected Monetary Value or EMV (Column I). Project managers can choose any of the 12 data fields as being a valid Z axis; the one which makes the most sense when presenting to management would be to use EMV (item 3). Thus when creating three (or more) dimensional model, following the model below, the Y-axis is WBS, the X-axis is RBS, and the Z-axis is EMV. Any of the other 11 fields (or a combination) could have been chosen for more than 3 dimensions.

---

[137] Guild of Project Controls, Module 4.1 Introduction to Managing Risk and Opportunity
http://www.planningplanet.com/guild/gpccar/introduction-to-managing-risk-and-opportunity Figure 7

② Risk Breakdown Structure (RBS) Database Fields

A	B	C	D	E	F	G	H	I	J	K	L
WBS Element	Risk/ Opportunity Event	Risk/ Opportunity Trigger	Type of Risk/Opportunity	Risk/ Opportunity Owner	Internal or External Risk /Opportunity	Quantitative Risk/ Opportunity Analysis (Impact)	Quantitative Risk/ Opportunity Analysis (Probability)	Quantitative Risk/ Opportunity Analsysis / Expected Monetary Value (EMV)	EMV Ranking	Strategic Risk/Opportunity Responses	Tactical Risk/Opportunity Response
①								**③**			
From WBS	Actual Risk or Opportunity Event	Is there an "Early Warning" Sign?	Phase 1- Focus on Business Risks/Opportunities? Phase 2- Focus on Technical Risks/Opportunities? Phase 3- Focus on Procurement Risks/Opportunities Phase 4- Focus on Constructability Risks/Opportunities? Phase 5- Focus on Safety, Health, Environmental Risks/Opportunities	Name of Individual Responsible to Track, Report and Manage Risk/ Opportunity Event	Is the Risk/Opportunity INTERNAL (we have control over) or EXTERNAL (we have little or no control over)	Estimated Monetary Impact If the Risk Event Occurs	Estimated Probability of the Risk Event Occuring	Monetary Impact X Probability of the Event Occuring (G X H = I)	Ranked Ordered by EMV (Sorted from Highest EMV to Lowest EMV)	RISK Deflect? Mitigate? Transfer? Accept? OPPORTUNITY Exploit? Share? Enhance? Ignore?	Immediate Response if the Risk Event or Opportunity Does Happen

Figure 109: 'Best in Class' Risk Management Database Showing Field Names and Descriptions

So what should the other two (or more) axis be? Knowing the WBS, done correctly, will define 100% of the project scope at any point in time, wouldn't it make sense to create the 2-D square using Expected Monetary Value (EMV) on the X-axis and WBS (Column A) as the Y axis? Assuming the goal is a 3-D model only then choose the third dimension or axis? How about the Schedule? (CPM from 4-D BIM) Alternatively, Cost? (CBS from 5-D BIM) Alternatively, Quality? From 3-D BIM Technical Specifications? Alternatively, how about instead of limiting ourselves to using only three dimensions, we create a tesseract model using six dimensions? What the WBS X EMV X CPM approach would look like in three dimensions would be (see Figure 110):

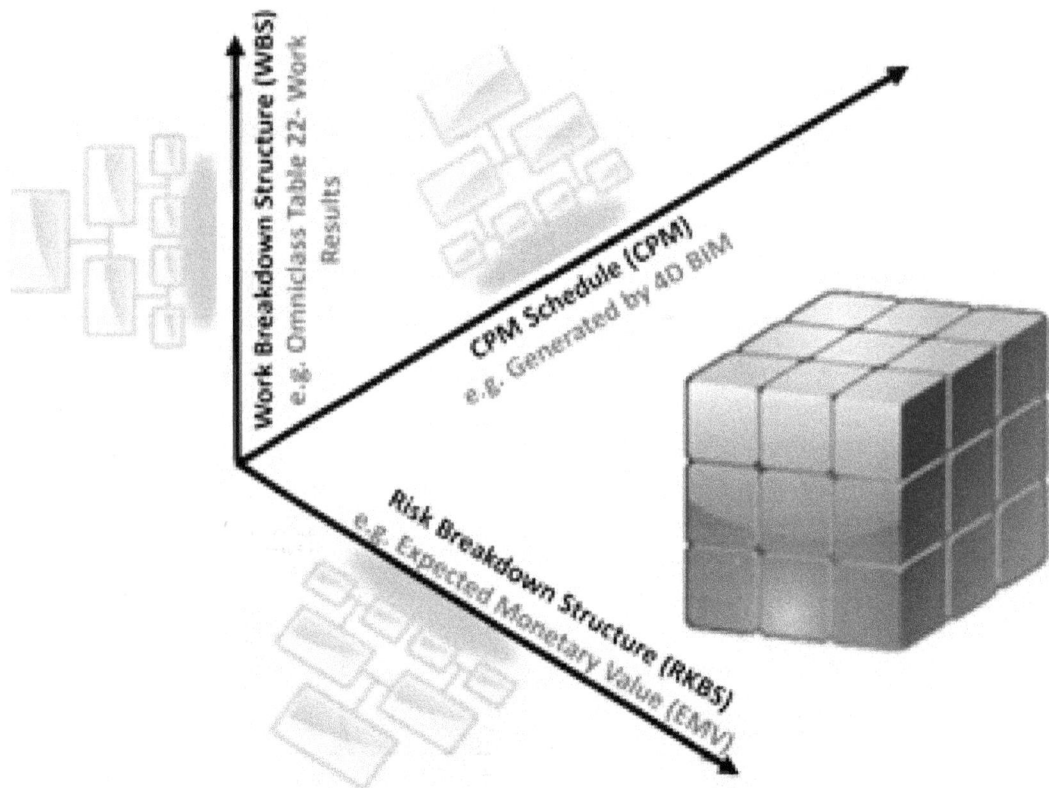

Figure 110: What a Risk Cube using WBS X EMV X CPM Cube Looks Like

This example explains why the need to move from a three-dimensional model to a tesseract-based model. Why should we be limited to looking only at the risk or opportunity regarding WBS X EMV X CPM? Why not be able to add dimensions, that using Virtual Reality, we could see what is known as the secondary impacts? If something happens to negatively impact the schedule, what will that mean regarding costs (EMV X CPM X WBS X CBS)? What will the impact be on quality (EMV X CPM X WBS X CBS X QBS)? Are there tradeoffs between time, cost, and quality to reach an optimized solution? This kind of modeling cannot be done unless a model is created using Systems Dynamics software. The challenge is going to be how to turn the Systems Dynamics model into something illustrated and understand using Virtual Reality? Using these three (or more) dimensions, and looking back at the Russian Nesting Doll analogy, the 3-D Cube defining the triangulation between the CPM, WBS, and RBS could be anywhere from the Program or Project Level down to a single activity or string of activities. The ideas will be explored in greater detail in the final section.

Contract Management – Explanation

Contract Work Breakdown Structure (CWBS) is the work sub-set for the entire program or project for which the owner has determined should be broken out into one or more prime or general contracts. Each prime or general contractor normally sub-divides and sub-contracts to specialty contractors who are subject matter experts in site work, electrical, plumbing, and HVAC. The Russian Doll analogy indicates each level of detail becomes more refined. Because the coding structure is hierarchical, it rolls up or rolls down to the reporting or management level. This is 'vertical traceability' or 'vertical integrity' – meaning nothing is lost as the project manager concatenates the scope of work.

To ensure no work packages have been over-looked, over-lapped, or is duplicated by other contractors, project managers should ensure against 'vertical traceability' or 'vertical integrity' using appropriate coding structures, so nothing is lost in the process. There is only one code which describes each deliverable. When the traditional two-dimensional matrix is applied, the result is a structure that looks like the following.

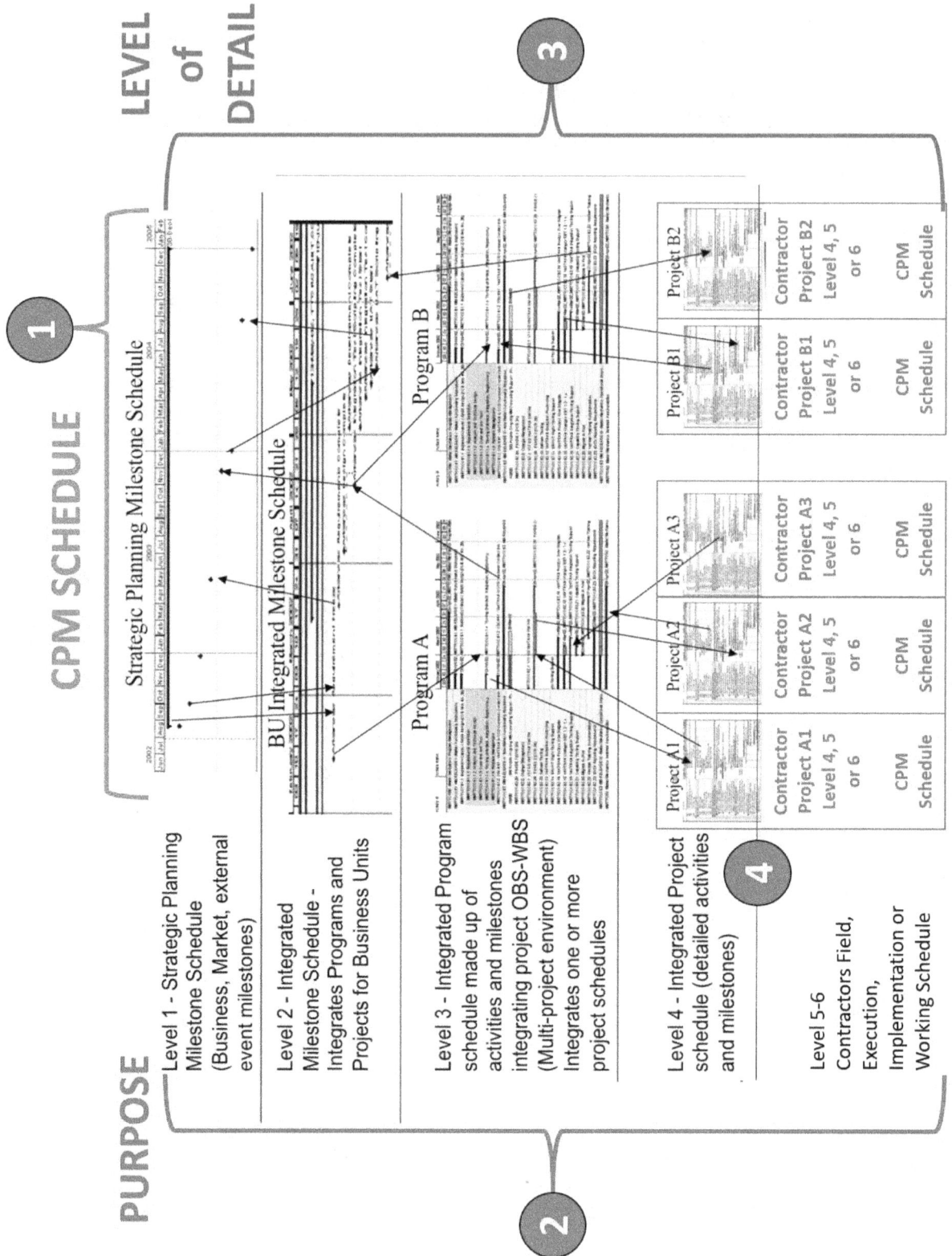

Figure 111: Vertical Traceability 2-Dimensional Model Organized by either the Purpose (WPBS) or Level of Detail (WBS) X Time or (CPM Schedule)

As shown in Figure 110 above, the X-axis would normally be Activities over time, which is shown by 1) CPM schedule (CPM), then for the Y dimension, 2) the Purpose of the schedule (WPBS), or 3) the Level of Detail, normally defined by the WBS.[138] It is at Level 4) of the WBS where the interface between the Contractor and Owner normally takes place regarding both WBS and Schedules. This is where the contractor reports progress to the owner – normally the level at which the contractor bills for work completed. Level 4 is rolled up for reporting by the owner's project manager to higher levels of management, while Level 4 and lower are used primarily by the contractor to plan and execute the work.

What is the proposed third dimension turning the Contract Work Breakdown Structure (CWBS) from a square to a cube? Referencing OmniClass tables, Table 33 in Figure 8, enables tagging an object with the names of the Disciplines (defined as the practice areas and specialties of participants) that conduct processes and procedures during the life-cycle of a construction entity.[139] Table 34 enables identification of the Organizational Roles, which are functional positions of the participants (individuals and groups conducting processes and procedures during the life cycle of a construction entity).

Applying professional judgment, create the 3-D CWBS cube of work defined by the formula = CPM X WBS X DBS. Using this combination, look at each cube to define What work (WBS) is to be completed, When (CPM), and by Which Contractor/ Subcontractor. Simultaneously, identify Who is responsible for the installation of Objects (components) shown in Figure 112, resulting in the Discipline Breakdown Structure (DBS). This is critical if the sequence consists of more than one sub-contractor or vendor.

---

[138] *Guild of Project Controls Module 7.9 Validate Horizontal and Vertical Traceability, Figure 4*
http://www.planningplanet.com/guild/gpccar/validate-horizontal-and-vertical-integration
[139] *About OmniClass. (n.d.). Retrieved from http://www.omniclass.org/about/*

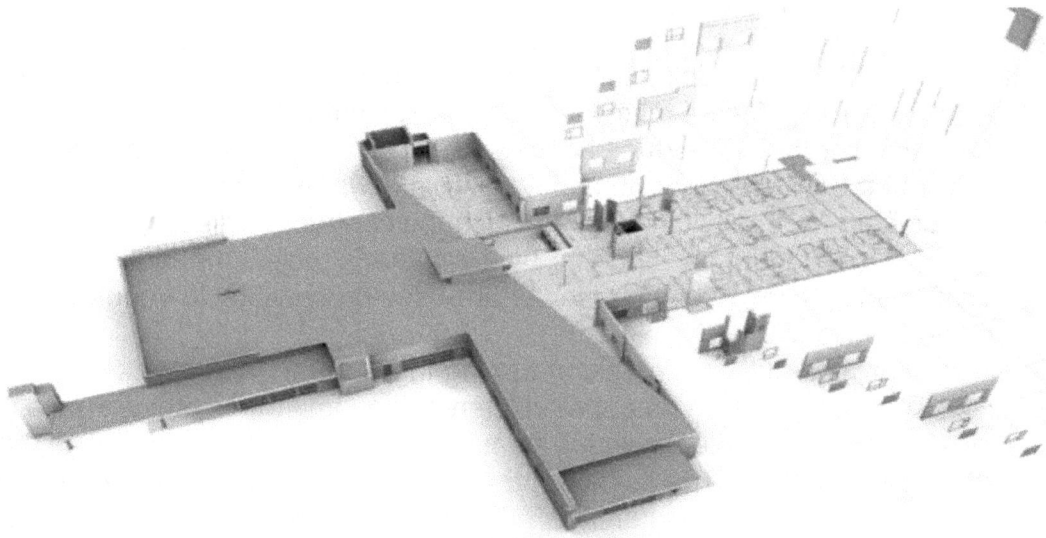

Figure 112: Progression from 2D BIM to 3-D BIM to 4-D BIM to CPM to DBS

As we can see from Figure 112 above,[140] the progression moves from 2-D to 3-D to 4-D BIM; the sequencing of the installation of each component is developed by the 4-D software and converted from a schematic view to the classic CPM schedule view as demonstrated in Figure 113.

---

[140] *CAD/CAM Services (n.d.) https://www.cadcam.org/2d-to-3-D-to-bim-conversion*

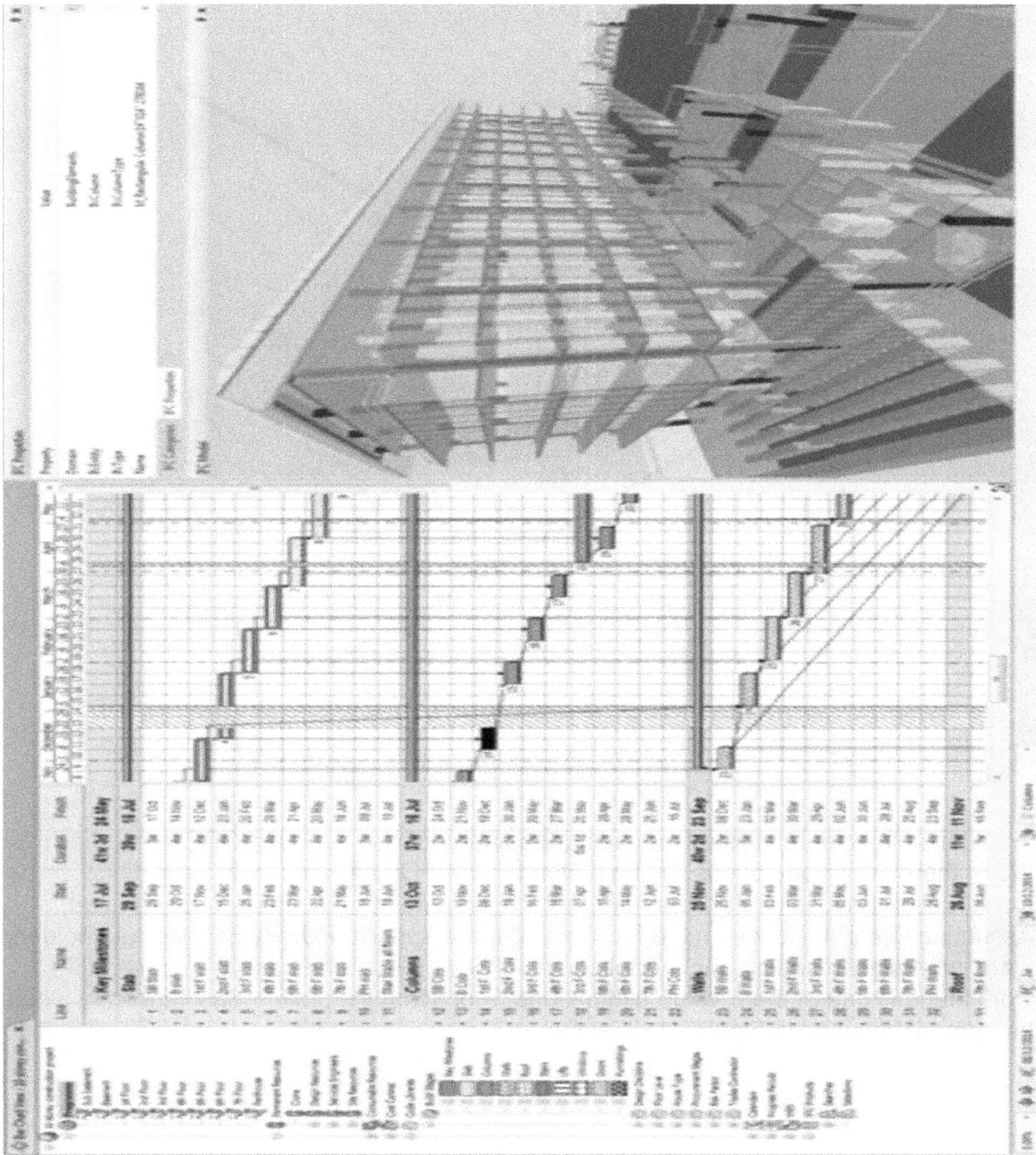

Figure 113: Progression from 3-D to 4-D BIM

Figure 114 shows what the three-dimensional cube would look like when using the WBS X CPM X DBS approach.

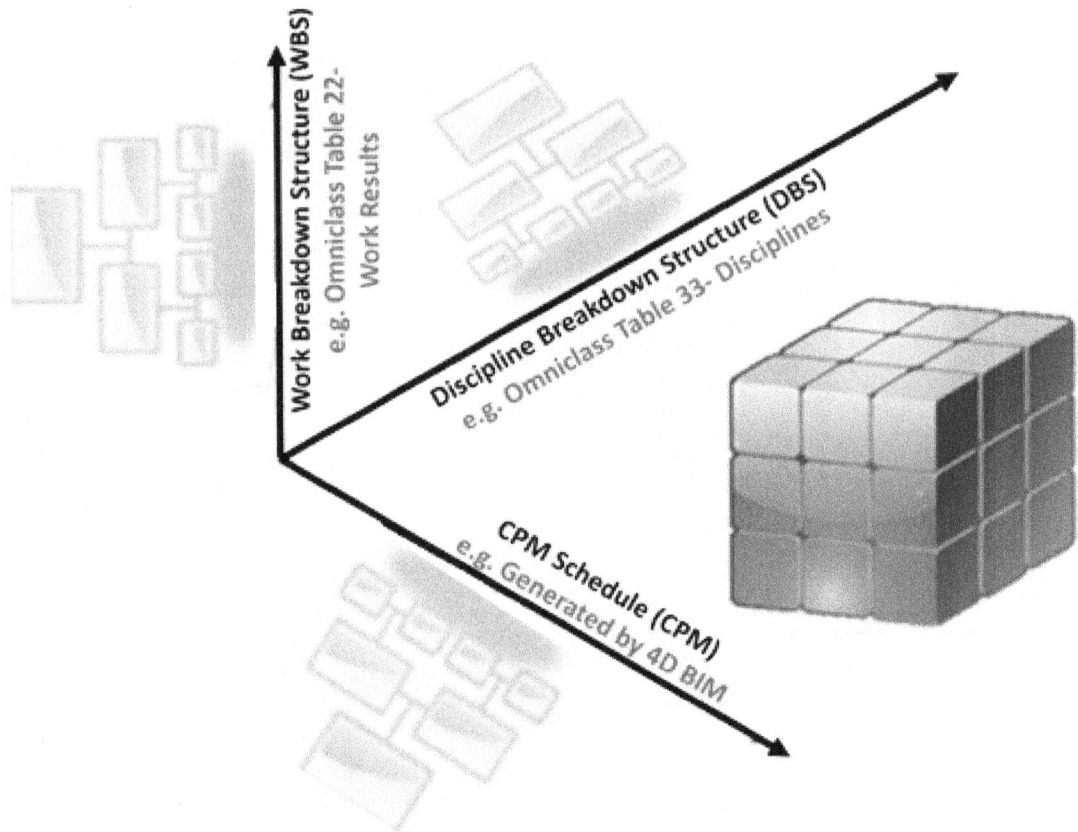

Figure 114: Contract Work Breakdown Structure defined by CPM X WBS X DBS

If stakeholders insisted on seeing the cube defined by PURPOSE instead of WBS, there are three options. Using a standardized OmniClass, then Table 11- Construction Entities by Function OR Table 13- Spaces by Function could be used. Assuming OmniClass does not offer a table for the specific PURPOSE the stakeholders were interested in seeing, the model could be viewed from the basis of Garrett Lisi's work found in one of the 8 Value dimensions, "For What Purpose." The Tesseract would be demonstrated as in Figure 115, below.

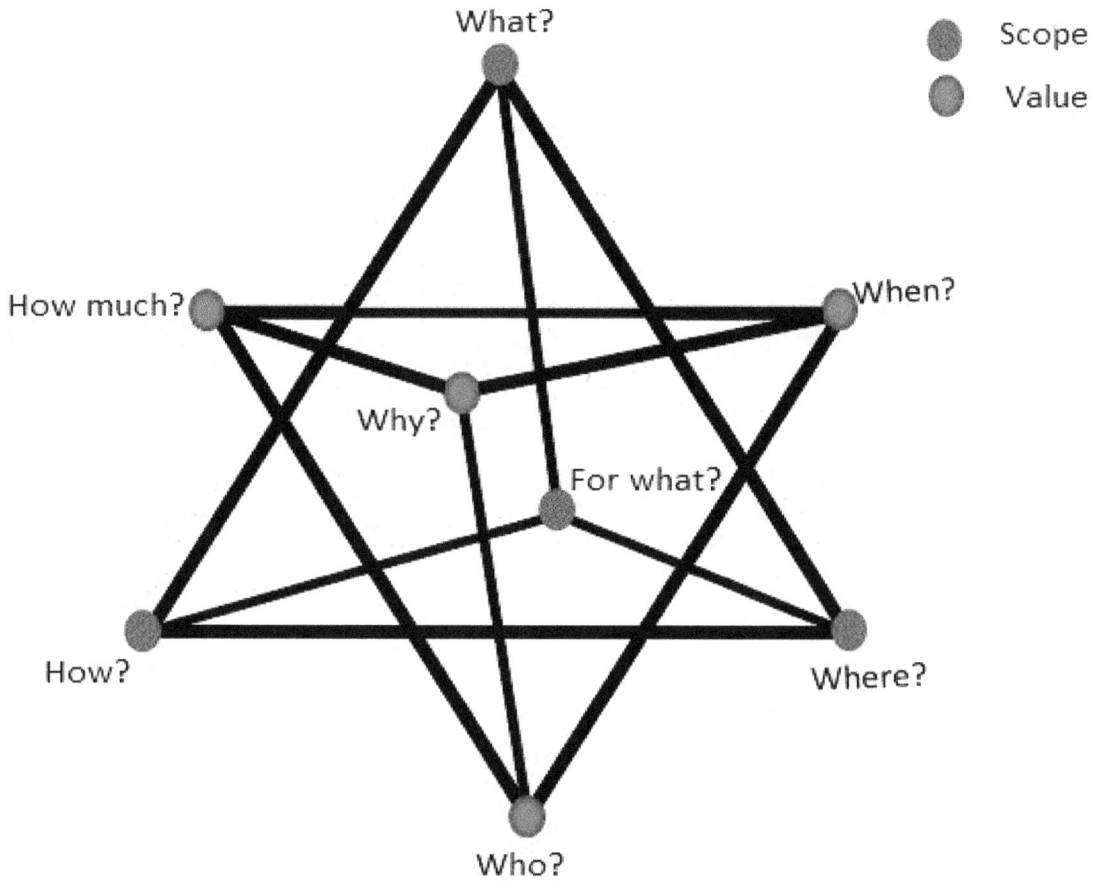

Figure 115: Garret Lisi's model

It would make sense to turn the 2-D model into a minimum of three dimensions and use CPM as one axis, the WBS as the second axis, for the third axis, and use "For What" – meaning the purpose? By using EITHER the WPBS or the WBS as the basis to roll up or roll down the data provides "Vertical Integrity" or "Vertical Traceability," which is the mark of a well-constructed WBS or CPM schedule. The 3-D cube for the Contractual Work Breakdown Structure would look like this (Figure 116).

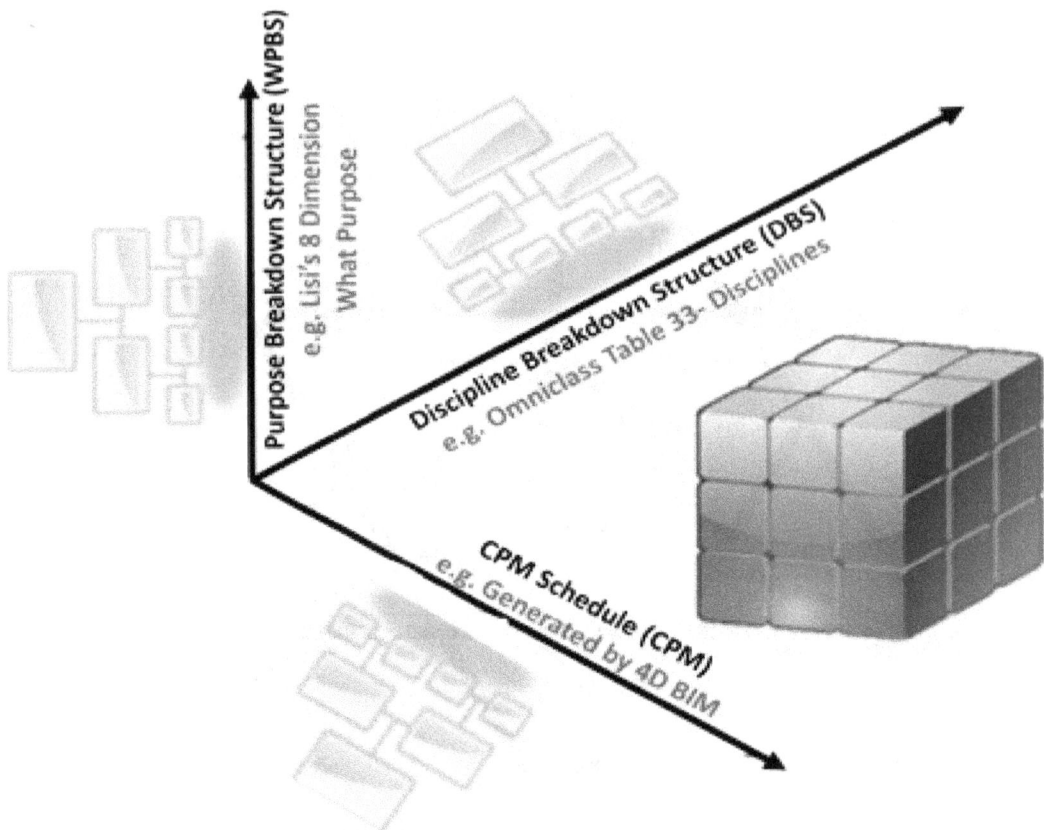

Figure 116: Contract Work Breakdown Structure defined by WPBS X CPM X DBS

Cost Estimating

Glenn Butts, Senior Cost Estimator for NASA published research showed how/why projects consistently run over budget, and those leading causes are poor or incomplete costs.[141] Of these items, the most relevant and important factor in adopting standardized WBS and coding structures, as well as viewing coding structures in multiple dimensions or perspectives. To mitigate the omission of probable scope, the best-tested and proven practices to adopt standardized Work Breakdown Structures are that …

1)   Produces multiple sorting or viewing capability
2)   Uses historically low-escalation factors
3)   Uses base-year money
4)   Ensures enough time to prepare credible estimates
5)   Avoids the use of unqualified or marginally qualified cost estimators

---

[141] Butts, G. (2009, Mar. 4). *Mega Projects Estimates - A History of Denial.* Retrieved from http://www.build-project-management-competency.com/wp-content/uploads/2010/09/Glenn.Butts-Mega-Projects-Estimates.pdf

6)   Avoids rewarding failure and/or punishing honesty
7)   Avoids omitting probable risks
8)   Avoids unrealistic/overly optimistic assumptions

Budgeting Management

Cost vs. Price. Cost is what the Owner or end user pays for products or services. Price is what a Contractor will charge an owner to supply and install goods or services. Selling Price includes the direct costs of Materials, Labor, and Equipment plus the Overhead associated with supplying and installing goods or services (e.g., tAxis, fuel, electricity, insurance) as well as the Project Overhead (e.g., project manager, safety manager salaries) plus the contractors Home Office Overhead plus any Contingency, and last, the most important piece, the Profit Margin.

Cost Estimating and Budgeting Management Examples

Figure 117 (following) illustrated a real-cost estimate developed by the U.S. Park Services and used as a baseline on USA-based projects, regardless of which state. The reason for using this database template is because it is not a theoretical approach, but an approach which has been tested and proven to work for over 20 years. The model illustrates how a multi-dimensional Cost Breakdown Structure is created using UniFormat, MasterFormat, and Activity Based Costing.

United States Department of the Interior
National Park Service
Class A Construction Cost Estimate

PROJECT COST SUMMARY

Project: Oso Comida Trailhead Improvements:
Park: Bear Arbor NRA
Park Alpha: BEAR
PMIS Number: XXXXXX

Estimate By: YIB
Date: 01/12/11
Reviewed By: BBB
Date: 01/17/11

Bid Item No.		Bid Item Description	Total Material Cost	Total Labor Cost	Total Equipment Cost	Total Direct Construction Costs	Design Contingency 2.00%	General Conditions 3.00%	General Contractor Overhead 8.50%	General Contractor Profit 10.00%	Contracting Method Adjustment 15.00%	Inflation Escalation APR 3.00% / Month 32	Bid Item Total
Bid Item:	1	Replace Pit Toilets with New Comfort Station							TOTAL VALUE OF GOVERNMENT FURNISHED PROPERTY (if any):				48,000.00
	A10	Foundations	30,028	33,082	7,293	70,403							
	A20	Basement Construction	-	-	-	-							
	B10	Superstructure	15,622	13,198	460	29,280							
	B20	Exterior Enclosure	35,992	29,477	-	65,469							
	B30	Roofing	18,471	8,706	-	27,177							
	C10	Interior Construction	25,573	9,308	-	34,881							
	C30	Interior Finishes	4,476	13,424	-	17,900							
	D20	Plumbing Systems	26,655	16,121	-	42,776							
	D30	HVAC	1,269	1,170	-	2,439							
	D50	Electrical	8,753	9,366	-	18,119							
	F20	Selective Building Demolition	463	1,990	3,862	6,315							
	G10	Site Preparation	2,188	4,362	6,952	13,502							
	G20	Site Improvements	8,900	7,300	-	16,200							
	G30	Site Mechanical	86,213	32,582	44,542	163,337							
	G40	Site Electrical	5,000	-	-	5,000							
	XX	Standard General Conditions	31,900	101,200	18,610	151,710							
Total - Bid Item	1	Replace Pit Toilets with New Comfort Station	301,503	281,286	81,719	664,508	12,370	18,926	55,233	64,980	122,403	92,813	1,031,234
Bid Item:	2	Construct New Parking Lot & Site Utilities							TOTAL VALUE OF GOVERNMENT FURNISHED PROPERTY (if any):				-
	G10	Site Preparation	2,500	11,711	19,776	33,987							
	G20	Site Improvements	143,581	36,335	43,670	223,586							
	G30	Site Mechanical	12,153	14,232	4,241	30,626							
	XX	Standard General Conditions	12,925	8,350	6,500	27,775							
			-	-	-	-							
Total - Bid Item	2	Construct New Parking Lot & Site Utilities	171,159	70,628	74,187	315,974	6,319	9,668	28,217	33,196	59,006	44,742	497,123
Bid Item:	3	Picnic Area & Trailhead Improvements							TOTAL VALUE OF GOVERNMENT FURNISHED PROPERTY (if any):				-
	G10	Site Preparation	-	11,860	4,845	16,705							
	G20	Site Improvements	59,448	25,960	12,270	97,678							
	G30	Site Mechanical	2,125	2,275	330	4,730							
	XX	Standard General Conditions	5,775	7,550	2,500	15,825							
			-	-	-	-							
Total - Bid Item	3	Picnic Area & Trailhead Improvements	67,348	47,645	19,945	134,938	2,699	4,129	12,050	14,177	25,199	19,107	212,299
		Total Bid Items 1-3	540,010	399,559	175,851	1,115,420	21,388	32,724	95,500	112,353	206,608	156,662	1,740,656

Figure 117: Real Cost Estimating Database Table Showing Fields and Rows (To see full version of this graphic go HERE https://www.nps.gov/dscw/upload/CostEstimatingHandbook_2-3-11_111417_AF.pdf and scroll down to Appendix 3,page 3 of 38)

Fields and Rows in a Real Cost Estimating Database

1) Key Field - the key Field is Bid Item (Cell B2). This is the Activity Breakdown Structure (ABS) defined by the Owner in the contract bid documents. The Bid Item (Activity Name) is 'Replace Pit Toilets with New Comfort Stations.'

2) This item represents sub-components which comprise of, or when added up, equals each Bid Item. This secondary sort is based on CSI's Uniformat or the OmniClass equivalent, Table 21 Elements. This data is provided by Owner to the Contractor. In figures 87 and 119, the contractor broke this down a level deeper based on MasterFormat or the OmniClass equivalent, Table 22 Work Results.

3) Resource Breakdown Structure for Materials (RBSM). What the contractor estimates the materials' cost for this Activity.

4) Resource Breakdown Structure for Labor (RBSL) What the contractor estimates the labor will cost for this Activity.

5) Resource Breakdown Structure for Equipment (RBSM). What the contractor

Fields and Rows in a Real Cost Estimating Database

estimates the labor will cost for this Project.

6) Resource Breakdown Structure Total Cost (RBSTC). What the contractor estimates for the Materials (RBSM) + Labor (RBSL) + Equipment (RBSE) = Resource Breakdown Structure Total Costs (RBSTC)

7) Represents percentages a contractor would typically use to adjust Costs to cover design errors and omissions.

8) Is the percentage the contractor adds to cover the general conditions required in the contract, which includes the site supervision, safety, security, envionmental, testing and related QA/QC responsibilities.

9) This percentage covers the contractors home office overhead (CEO, secretaries, accounting and business development
   a. Represents the contractors target or planned profit margin (Note for a contractor, the profit margin serves as the "management reserve".
   b. Is the percentage the contractor adds to cover unusually difficult or challenging work envionments, where the "normal and customary" practices don't apply. Working at remote sites is a common example
   c. This percentage is added to cover the contractors expectations for inflation and/or currency fluctuations
   d. This represents the contractor's Bid (Selling) Price for Activity 1, 'Replace Pit Toilets with New Comfort Stations.'

Understanding what the cost-estimating database table consists of will assist in the decision on how to turn this 2-D model into a 3-D model and forms the basis to create a tesseract and a multi-dimensional view of the costs.

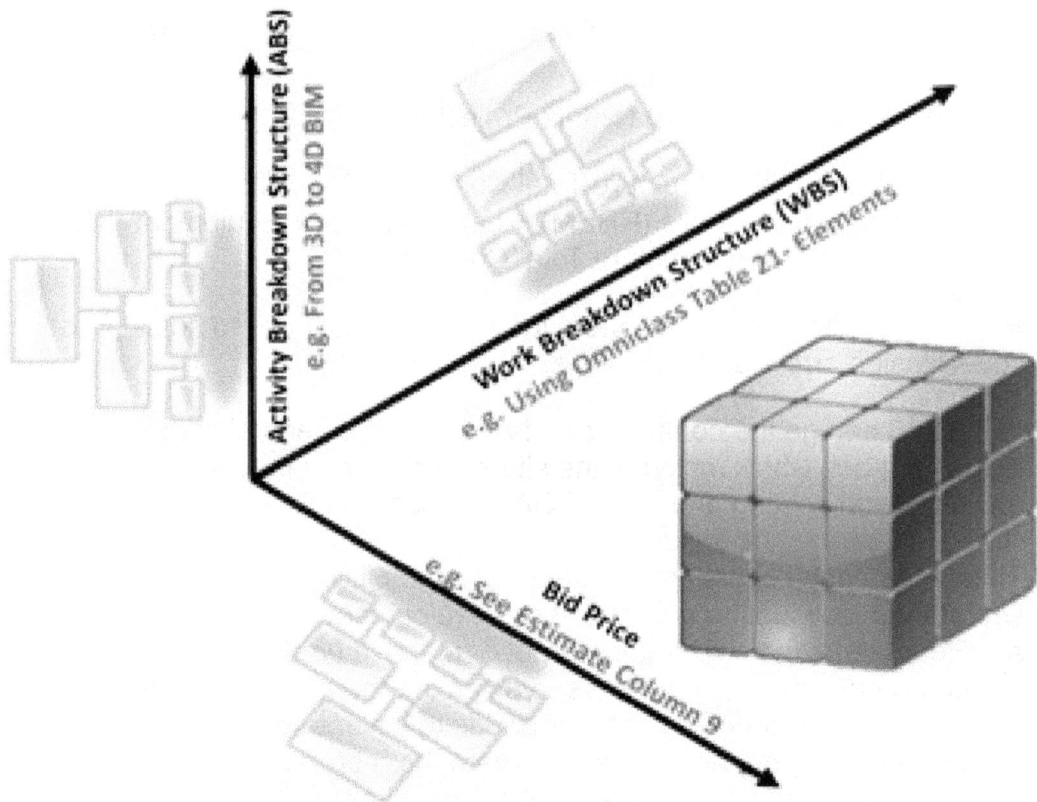

Figure 118: Cost Estimating Database Filtered and Sorted by ABS X BP X WBS

To add another dimension or level of detail is to take the "General Conditions" costs of $15,825 (see Figure 118 above under the heading of "General Conditions") and demonstrate how it was summarized for the entire project rather than for just a single Bid Item. [142,143]

---

[142] *Cost Estimating Requirements Handbook National Park Service 2011*
        https://www.nps.gov/dscw/upload/CostEstimatingHandbook_2-3-11_111417_AF.pdf
[143] *To see full version of this graphic go HERE https://www.nps.gov/dscw/upload/CostEstimatingHandbook_2-3-11_111417_AF.pdf*
        and scroll down to Appendix 3, page 22 of 38

Summary Item: XX   General Conditions   Total Cost: $151,710

Uniformat II WBS Code	Description	Quantity	Unit	MATERIAL		LABOR		EQUIPMENT		TOTALS	
				Material Cost/Unit	Total Material Cost	Labor Cost/Unit	Total Labor Cost	Equipment Cost/Unit	Total Equipment Cost	Total Cost/Unit	Total Cost
01 31	Project Management & Coordination										
01.31.13	Project Superintendent	20	Weeks	$ -	$0	$ 2,500.00	$50,000	$ -	$0	$ 2,500.00	$50,000
01.31.13	Project Manager - Half Time	18	Weeks	$ -	$0	$ 750.00	$13,500	$ -	$0	$ 750.00	$13,500
01.31.13	General Pupose Laborer - Part Time	15	Weeks	$ -	$0	$ 1,500.00	$22,500	$ -	$0	$ 1,500.00	$22,500
01.31.13	Builders Risk Insurance	1	LS	$ 3,500.00	$3,500	$ -	$0	$ -	$0	$ 3,500.00	$3,500
01.31.13	General Liability Insurance	1	LS	$ 2,000.00	$2,000	$ -	$0	$ -	$0	$ 2,000.00	$2,000
01.31.13	Payment & Performance Bond 1.5%	1	Unit	$ 15,000.00	$15,000	$ -	$0	$ -	$0	$ 15,000.00	$15,000
01.31.xx	Labor down time due to payroll interviews	1	LS	$ -	$0	$ 3,500.00	$3,500	$ -	$0	$ 3,500.00	$3,500
01.31.xx	Certified Payrol Costs	0	Unit	$ -	$0	$ 500.00	$0	$ -	$0	$ 500.00	$0
SUBTOTAL	Project Management & Coordination	1000	SF	$ 20.50	$20,500	$ 89.50	$89,500	$ -	$0	$ 110.00	$110,000

Figure 119: Going down another dimension or level of detail from ABS to WBS Level 3 using Uniformat to WBS Level 4 using MasterFormat Codes.

The Key Field is 'Bid Item.' This is the Activity Breakdown Structure (ABS) defined by the Owner in the bid documents. The "Bid Item" (Activity Name) is "Project Management and Coordination." This is a secondary filter for sorting data is based on CSI's Uniformat or the OmniClass equivalent, Table 21 Elements. This data represents the sub-components which comprise or when added up, equals each Bid Item. This data is provided by the owner to the contractor. In this graphic, the contractor has broken this down one level deeper based on MasterFormat or the OmniClass equivalent, Table 22 Work Results. In the previous example, the value of $10,575 is the portion of the total costs of $15,825 allocated to the activity 'Project Management and Coordination.' To show how we would add this 4th dimension, see Figure 120. Moving beyond the 3rd Dimension creates tesseract models and using eigenvectors and eigenvalues to analyze the relationships.

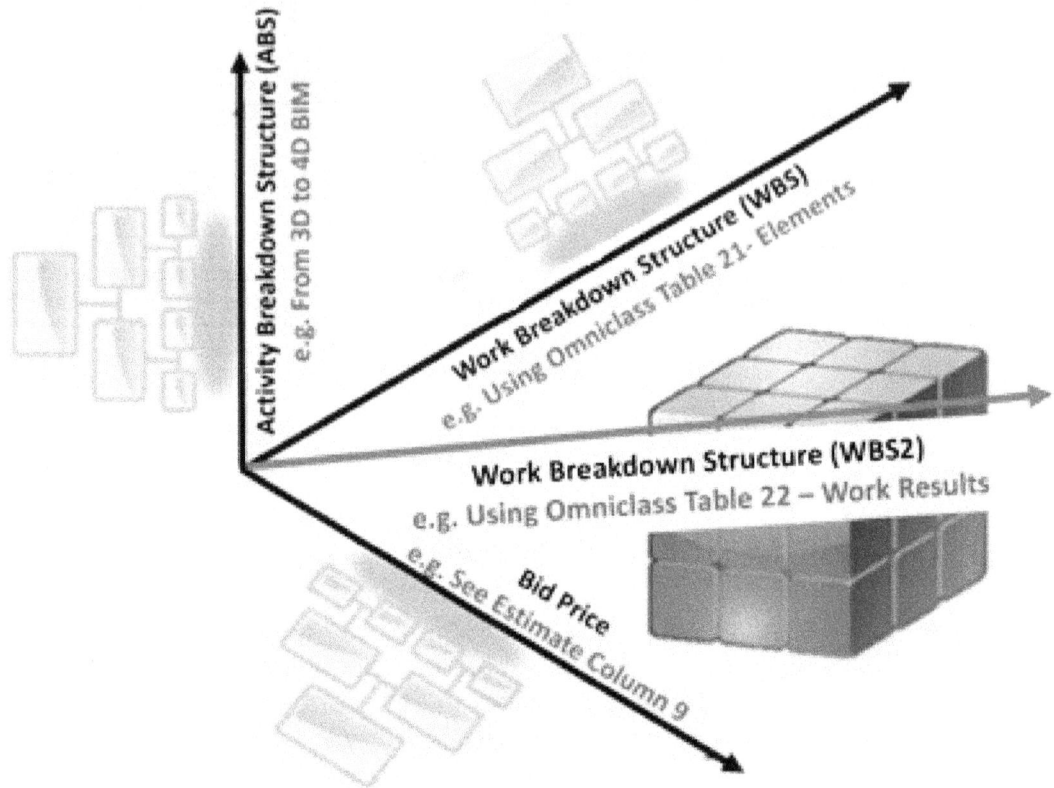

Figure 120: Conceptual layout of ABS X WBS1 X WBS2 X BP

Schedule Development and Management – Introduction, Explanation, and Examples

The "Schedule Breakdown Structure" (or CPM) is a fully costed and resource-loaded database that can be dynamically modeled using the forward pass/backward pass calculations to show when each activity is planned to start and finish. The CPM also shows if an activity is on a critical path (a delay in the activity delays the project completion by that amount of time) or if and how much float or slack time has for any activity, not on a critical path. The Schedule Breakdown Structure consists of a concatenation of the following components:

- Activities (ABS)
- + Costs (CBS) (BoM/BoQ from 3-D X Unit Cost Database)
- + Sequence (4-D BIM)
- + Logic (4-D BIM)
- + Duration (BoM/BoQ from 3-D X Productivity Database)
- + Resources (RBS) (Materials, Equipment, and People)
- <u>+ Risk Contingency</u>

  equals
- = Cost and Resource Loaded CPM Schedule (CPM)

Once the cost and resources are developed and loaded the database, there are two ways project managers and/or the project team can look at that data:

- As an "S Curve" (Cumulative costs over time – Budgeted Cost of Work Schedule [BCWS] or Planned Value [PV])
- As a Resource Histogram

This is what a typical CPM Schedule looks like as a Database - (example shown is from MS Project, but nearly all similar software programs provide similar results.) [144]

---

[144] Guild of Project Controls, Module 10.1 Managing Databases Figure 2- http://www.planningplanet.com/guild/gpccar/introduction-to-managing-project-databases

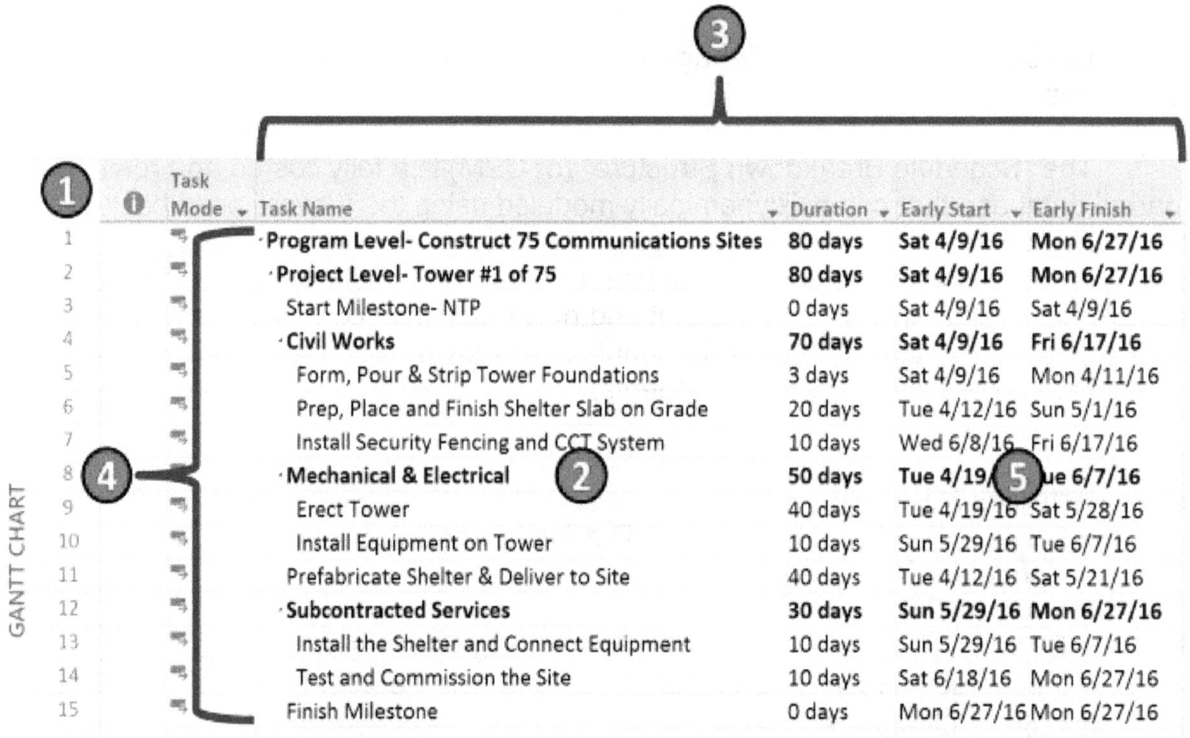

Figure 121: *Database Example from CPM Schedule Software*

CPM Schedule Software Database

1. The "Key Field" is the Activity Number - there can be one with that single unique identifier.

2. A single row which serves as the Default Activity Coding Structure. There is only one activity per row. This is the Activity Coding Structure (ABS). The ABS alone without logic, durations, costs or resources is nothing more than a single dimensional list that can be selected from by a planner/scheduler to show How the work is to be executed. When using 3-D and 4-D BIM, this sequencing will be automated in sequencing (not manually), moving from 3-D to 4-D BIM software.

3. These are examples of Fields or Attributes associated with each Row and are alpha-numeric fields containing data for the duration, calculated start / finish dates, float / slack values, logic, and resource assignments. There could be more than 100 pre-defined fields in scheduling packages (e.g., Microsoft Project or Primavera's P6), but there are more than 100 user definable fields. As with the Risks example, if using a 3-D model, planners must either concatenate several fields together (Labor, Material, and Equipment

CPM Schedule Software Database

Resources) or document those fields individually.

4. *This table contains the Activity data*

5. *Examples of Values (some entered manually, e.g., Duration, Costs, and Resource Assignments) and others are calculated (e.g., early and late finish dates, float values).*

Once the cost and resource are developed and loaded into the database, there are two ways project managers/project team can look at the data:

- As an "S Curve" (Cumulative costs over time- BCWS or PV
- As a Resource Histogram

As we have already explored how to set up and use the Resource Histograms (see Future 132) in 3-D, let's explore how to do the same for the "S Curve" as well. Figure 122 below shows the Activity Breakdown Structure (ABS) on the Y-axis, while on the Z-Axis including the full-cost and resource-loaded CPM schedule. Starting with those two parameters, project planners can include data on the X-axis to make the S Curve a better communication tool for management and other stakeholders.

The Performance Measurement Baseline (PMB) consists of the ABS X CPM X BCWS early-date X BCWS late-date curve. This legal documentation, once accepted by the Owner, becomes a baseline from which to measure and assess project progress, identify when to make payments to the contractors/vendors, identify delays and setbacks, and in the event of disputes or claims, helps to apportion responsibility for which entity caused delays or additional costs. [145]

---

[145] *Guild of Project Controls, Module 9.3 Managing Project Progress, Fig 2- http://www.planningplanet.com/guild/gpccar/introduction-to-managing-project-progress*

CPM

ABS

		W	W1	W2	W3	W4	W5	W6	W7	W8	W9
	Act A Value $840		$280	$280	$280				TIME NOW or DATA DATE		
			Activity A (Early Dates)								
			0% physical % Complete								
				$280	$280	$280					
				Activity A (Late Dates)							
				0% Physical % Complete							
	Act B Value $1000			$200	$200	$200	$200	$200			
				Activity B (Early Dates)							
				0% Physically Complete							
						$200	$200	$200	$200	$200	
						Activity B (Late Dates)					
						0% Physically Complete					
	Act C Value $960				$160	$160	$160	$160	$160	$160	
					Activity C (Early Dates)						
					0% Physically Complete						
						$160	$160	$160	$160	$160	$160
						Activity C (Late Dates)					
						0% Physically Complete					

		W1	W2	W3	W4	W5	W6	W7	W8	W9
1	/PERIOD PLANNED	$280	$480	$640	$360	$360	$360	$160	$160	$0
2	CUMULATIVE TOTAL PLANNED (BCWS or PV- Early Dates)	$280	$760	$1,400	$1,760	$2,120	$2,480	$2,640	$2,800	$2,800
3	/PERIOD PLANNED	$0	$0	$280	$640	$640	$360	$360	$360	$160
4	CUMULATIVE TOTAL PLANNED (BCWS or PV- Late Dates)	$0	$0	$280	$920	$1,560	$1,920	$2,280	$2,640	$2,800
5	/PERIOD EARNED (BCWP or EV)									
6	CUMULATIVE EARNED (BCWP or EV									
7	ACTUAL COSTS INCURRED TO DO THE WORK/PERIOD (ACWP)									
8	ACTUAL COSTS INCURRED TO DO THE WORK CUMULATIVE (ACWP)							TIME NOW or DATA DATE		

Time Now or Data Date

BCWSearly
&
BCWSlate

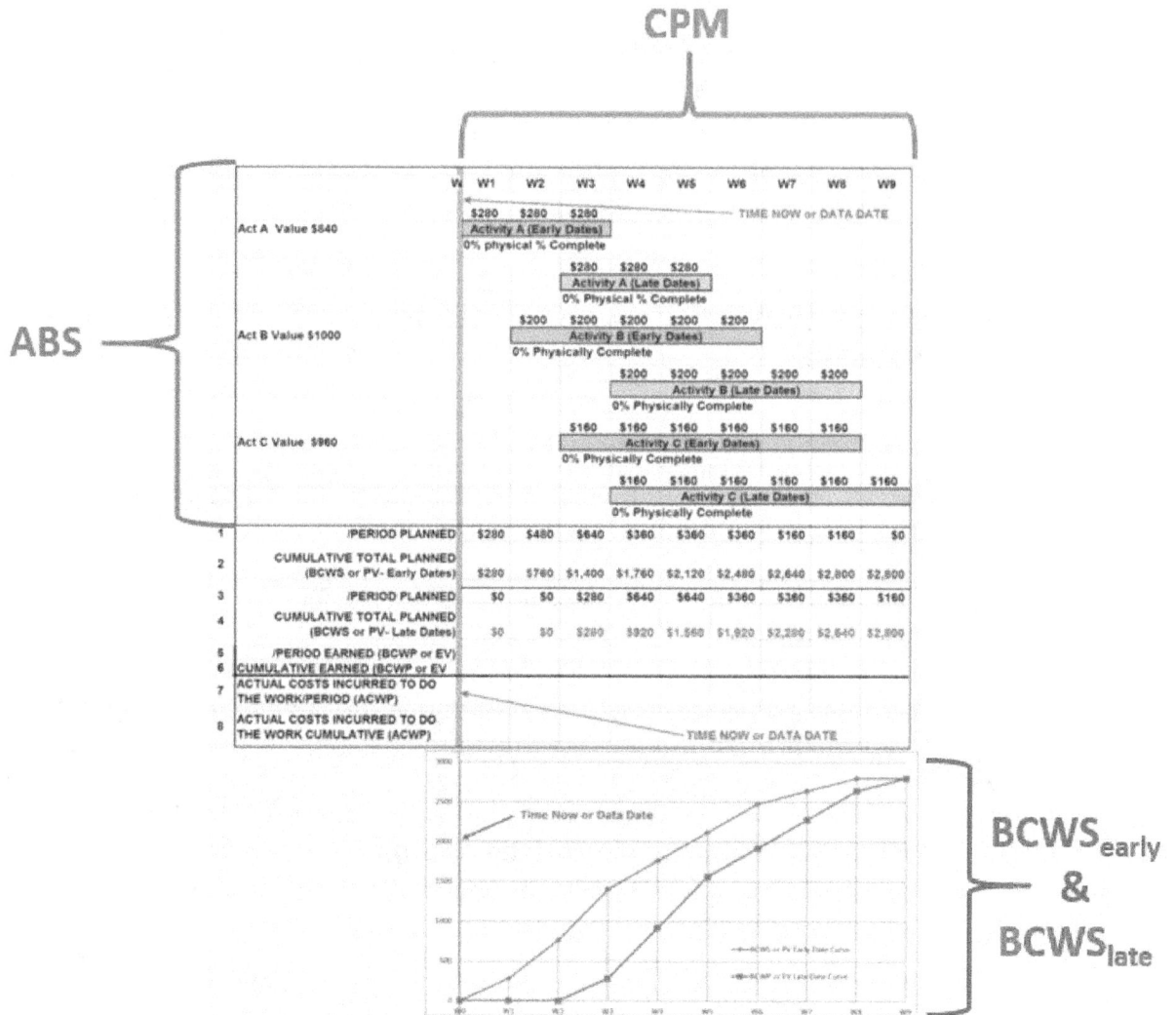

Figure 122: Standard 2D view is showing the ABS on the Y-axis and the CPM on the X-axis.

Moving from a 2-D to 3-D view, instead of generating two drawings to show the early- and late-date S curves (Cumulative BCWS$_{Early}$ and BCWS$_{Late}$ curves), we could present the graphic in three dimensions, as in Figure 123.

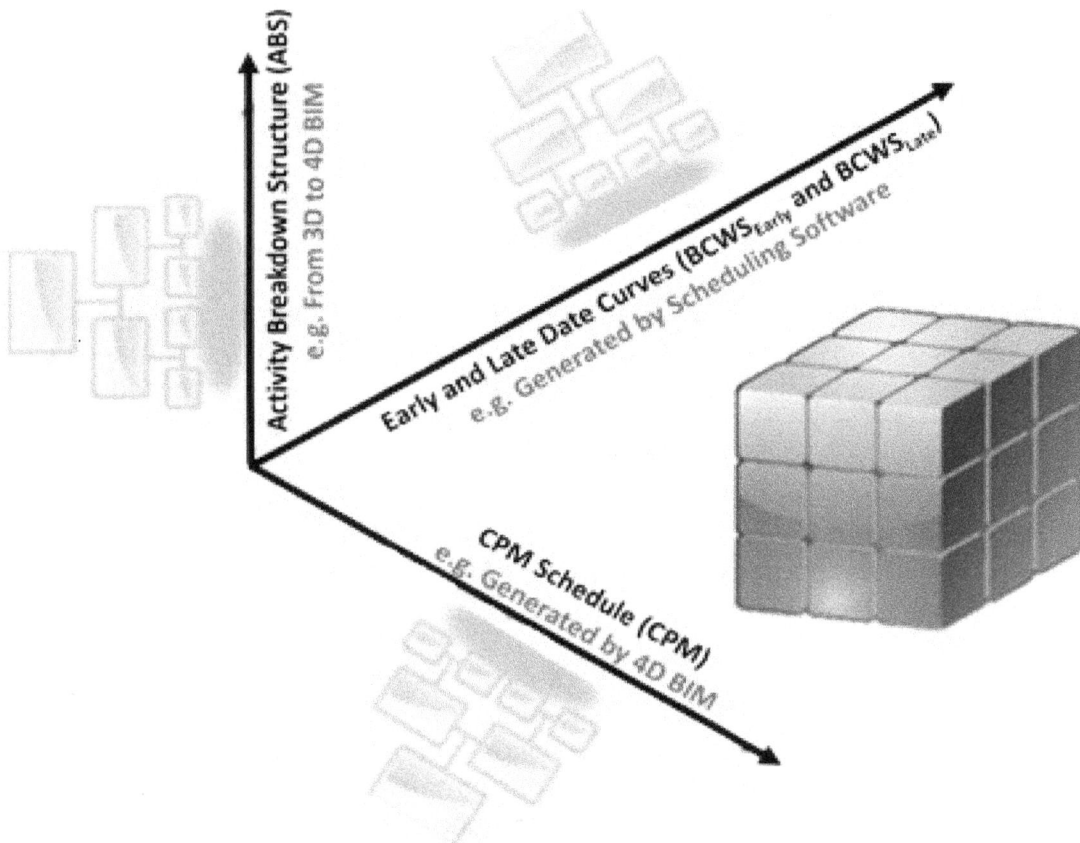

Figure 123: showing the ABS X CPM X BCWS Early and Late Date Curves

This example is only one of the hundreds of different possibilities of 3-D models generated from a full-cost and resource-loaded schedule. Imagine how much more can be accomplished for analysis and virtual exploration if more dimensions were added and simulations run using Systems Dynamics software or Virtual Reality software?

Progress Management and Reporting – Explanation

The following definitions will assist in understanding the following section's content.

- Performance Measurement Baseline (PMB) - full-cost and resource-loaded CPM schedule formally submitted by the Contractor to the Owner (or for internal projects, from the project manager to the project sponsors) that has been approved, from which progress is measured, and payment made to contractors and vendors.

- Budgeted Cost of Work Scheduled (BCWS or PV) - the cumulative value of each activity over time, plotted from a project start date to planned finish date. This is ideally shown as TWO curves: a BCWS S-curve showing the early-date cumulative values and a BCWS S-curve showing the late-date S-curve.
- Budgeted Cost of Work Performed (BCWP or EV) - the percentage of physical work completed and Owner-accepted (approved) from each activity X the BCWS for each activity. These values are summed and plotted against the BCWS early- and BCWS late-date curves. Ideally, the BCWP plot falls between the two BCWS curves.
- Actual Cost of Work Performed (ACWP or AC) - accrued costs of the work in place as of a specific cutoff date. It is important the date of the actual costs recorded matches the date the physical progress has been recorded. Otherwise, the calculations for dashboard reports will not be accurate or reliable.
- Schedule Variance (SV) = BCWP-BCWS or EV-PV
- Cost Variance (CV) = BCWP-ACWP or EV-AC
- Schedule Performance Index (SPI) = BCWP/BCWS or EV/PV
- Cost Performance Index (CPI) = BCWP/ACWP or EV/AC

Building on results from cost and resource loaded into the CPM Schedule in the previous section, once the planning has been approved and accepted, the cost and resource loaded CPM Schedule becomes a legal document, used as the basis for progress measurement, payments for work performed and in the event of delays or disputes, as the basis for evaluating, assessing and apportioning blame or responsibility for those delays.

Figure 124 shows an updated Progress Report, with not only the early- and late-date curves, but now with project progress, two additional pieces of information are displayed, which is the Actual Cost of Work Performed (ACWP or AC) and the Budgeted Cost of Work Performed (BCWP or EV).

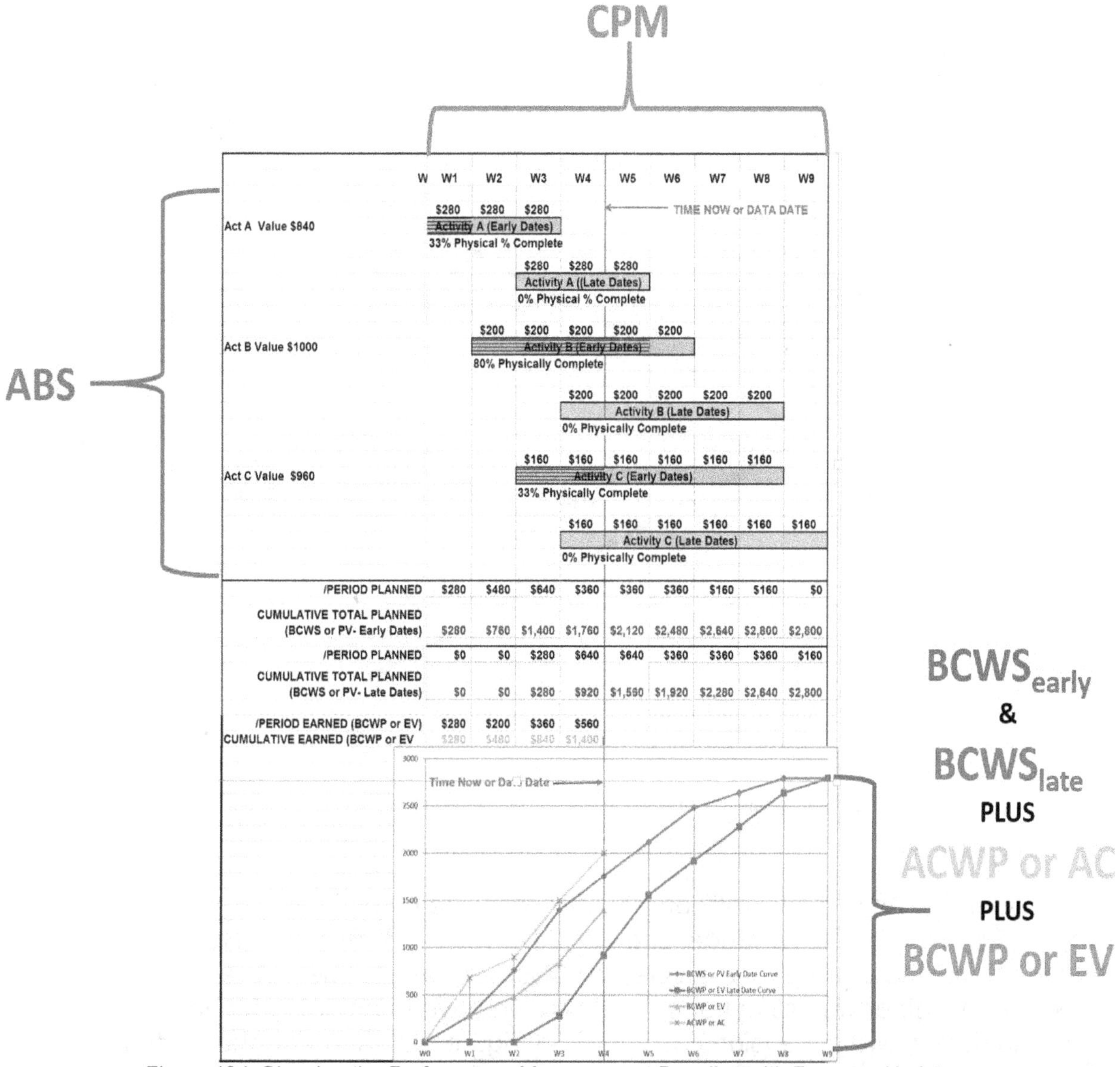

CPM

	W	W1	W2	W3	W4	W5	W6	W7	W8	W9

Act A Value $840
$280 $280 $280
Activity A (Early Dates)
33% Physical % Complete

$280 $280 $280
Activity A ((Late Dates)
0% Physical % Complete

Act B Value $1000
$200 $200 $200 $200 $200
Activity B (Early Dates)
80% Physically Complete

$200 $200 $200 $200 $200
Activity B (Late Dates)
0% Physically Complete

Act C Value $960
$160 $160 $160 $160 $160 $160
Activity C (Early Dates)
33% Physically Complete

$160 $160 $160 $160 $160 $160
Activity C (Late Dates)
0% Physically Complete

ABS

TIME NOW or DATA DATE

	W	W1	W2	W3	W4	W5	W6	W7	W8	W9
/PERIOD PLANNED		$280	$480	$640	$360	$360	$360	$160	$160	$0
CUMULATIVE TOTAL PLANNED (BCWS or PV- Early Dates)		$280	$760	$1,400	$1,760	$2,120	$2,480	$2,640	$2,800	$2,800
/PERIOD PLANNED		$0	$0	$280	$640	$640	$360	$360	$360	$160
CUMULATIVE TOTAL PLANNED (BCWS or PV- Late Dates)		$0	$0	$280	$920	$1,560	$1,920	$2,280	$2,640	$2,800
/PERIOD EARNED (BCWP or EV)		$280	$200	$360	$560					
CUMULATIVE EARNED (BCWP or EV		$280	$480	$840	$1,400					

Time Now or Data Date

BCWS or PV Early Date Curve
BCWP or EV Late Date Curve
BCWP or EV
ACWP or AC

BCWSearly
&
BCWSlate
PLUS
ACWP or AC
PLUS
BCWP or EV

Figure 124: Showing the Performance Measurement Baseline with Progress Updates

Building on the three-dimensional model created one the Baselined schedule, the 3-D model is demonstrated in Figure 125 below, including the CPM on the X-axis, the ABS on the Y-axis, and the BCWP early- and late-date curves on the Z axis. To document the full progress in multiple dimensions, add a 4th dimension, which is the Actual Cost of Work Performed (ACWP or AC) and the Budgeted Cost of Work Performed (BCWP or EV).

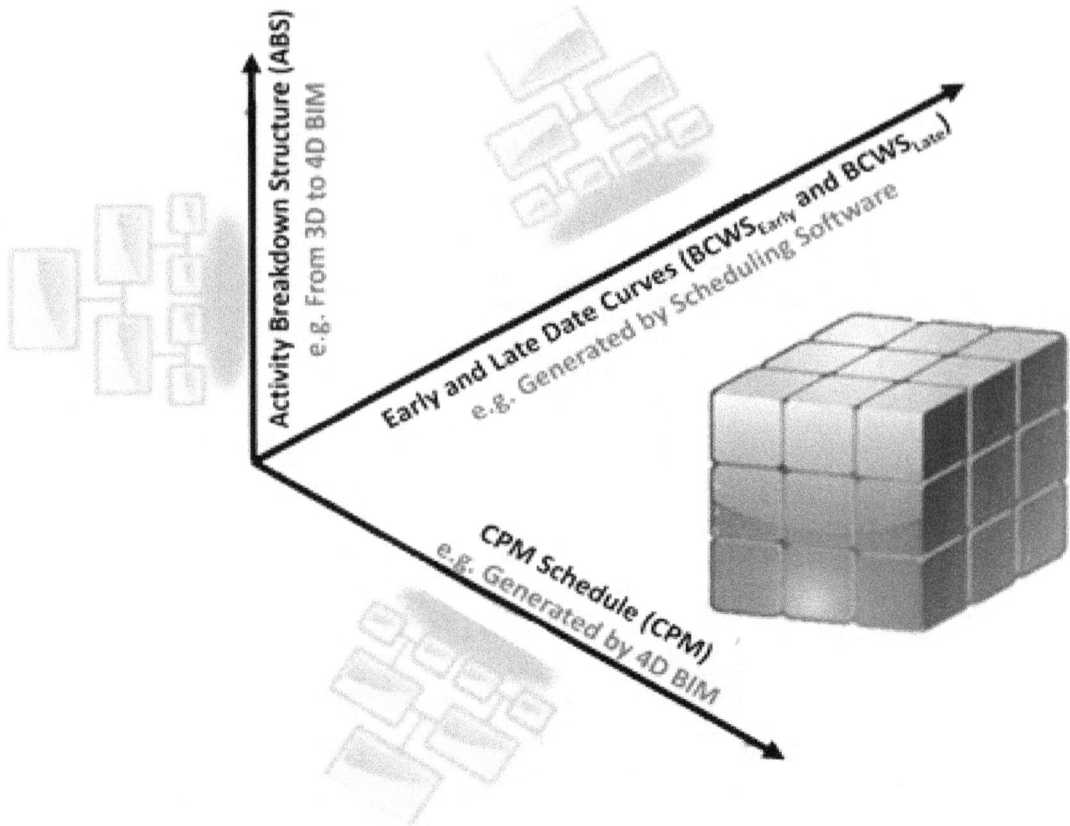

Figure 125: showing the ABS X CPM X BCWS Early and Late Date Curves

After adding in the BCWP and ACWP data, the result is an (at minimum) a 4-D model. (See Figure 126 4D Model showing ABS X CPM X BCWS X BCWP X ACWP below). While the concept of a 4-D remains somewhat of a theoretical construct, the question is whether we are better off to do as we have been doing for years and simply show the data in two dimensions as shown in Figure 123, showing the Performance Measurement Baseline with Progress Updates? Or, is there an advantage if we can 'visualize' the dynamics of the flow of money using Systems Dynamics or Virtual Reality software? Or, is this something that – while technically possible – adds no significant value to help us make a sound or better management decisions about our projects? These are the questions yet to be answered, but are going to have to be as the use of Systems Dynamics, Virtual Reality and Augmented Reality become more commonplace.

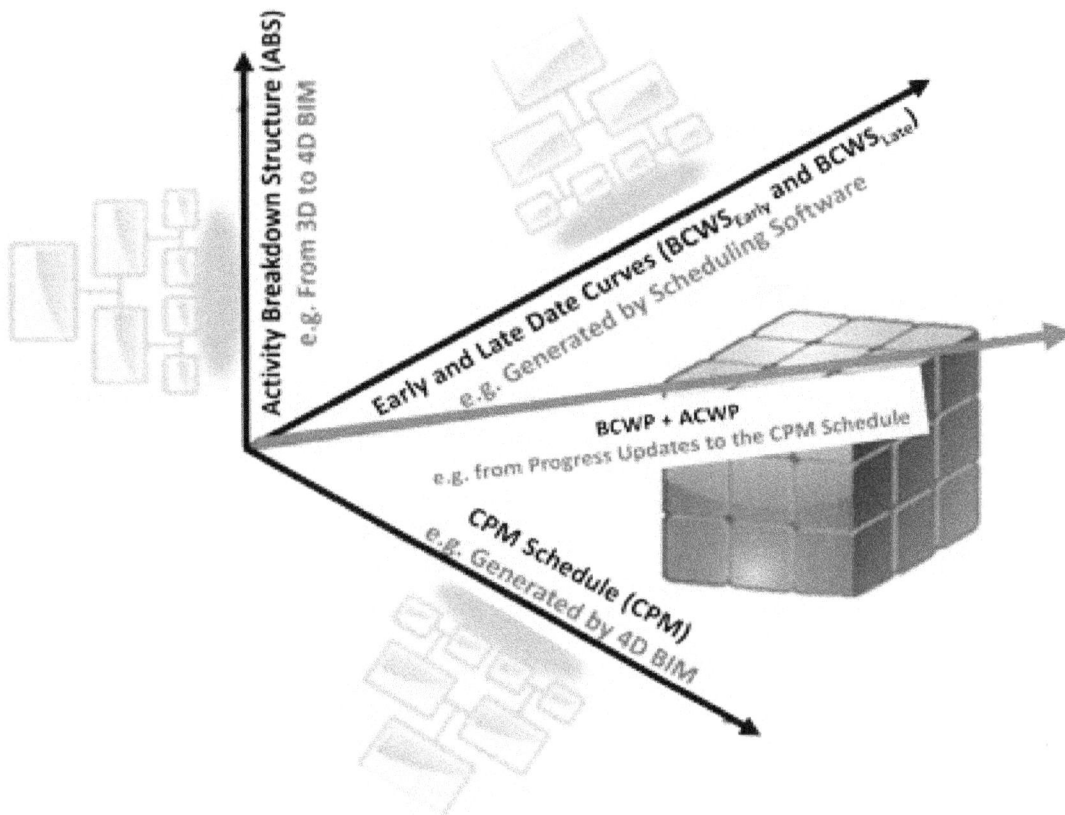

Figure 126: 4D Model showing ABS X CPM X BCWS X BCWP X ACWP

Managing Change – Explanation

A Change Order (modification or MOD) is a modification to the contract regarding time and cost both the owner and contractor have agreed to in writing. This allows the cost- and resource-loaded schedule to be changed by adding each approved change order to the project schedule.

A Cumulative Impact recognizes that whenever there are a series of change orders, the impact to the project is more than just the summation of the costs (regarding time and money) of each change order. There is a premium to this number, which accounts for the inefficiencies and disruptions to the already established workflow which has to be added to the summation of the impacts of all change orders.

Figure 127 is an example of a NASA change order with information fields normally expected in a well-designed change management database created for use by an owner's organization. There are five major fields for sorting. The Owners would want to see the impact changes orders have on both Time and Cost, and the Owner's 2D model would use the sequence of change orders, in chronological order, on the Y-axis and the CPM schedule on the X-axis.

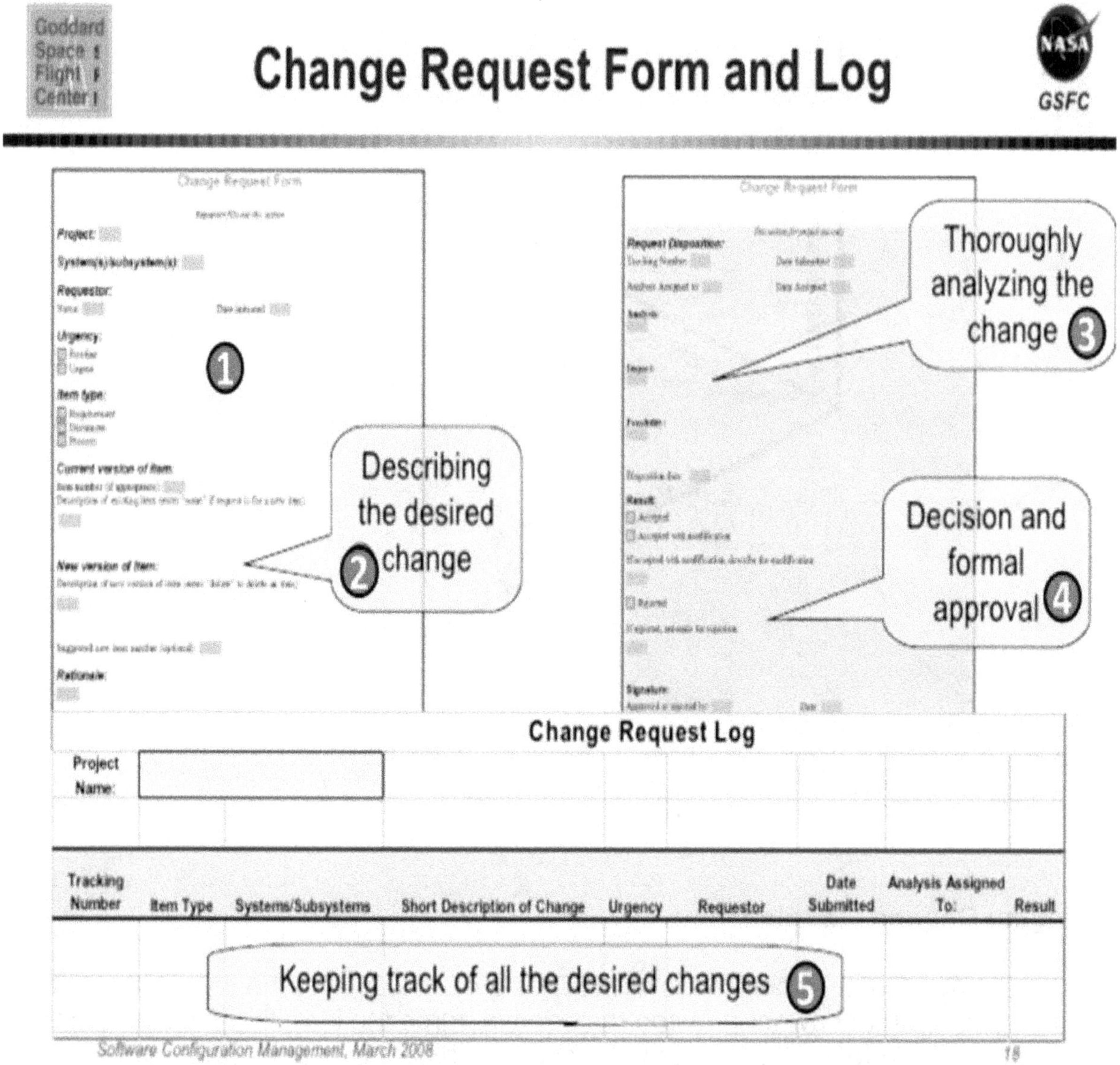

Figure 127: Change request Form and Log; Change Request Form from NASA (Owners Internal Change Management Database).

By default; the Z axis would impact costs. Moving to a multi-dimensional tesseract, the changes in terms of any of the above fields would be observable, plus the impact the change order might have on the business case is illustrated, in the event the project went significantly over budget and/or was late in finishing. Moving from the traditional 2D view to a multi-dimensional approach create possibilities of using VR or AR software or simulated using Systems Dynamics rather than Monte Carlo Simulation offers (see Figure 128).

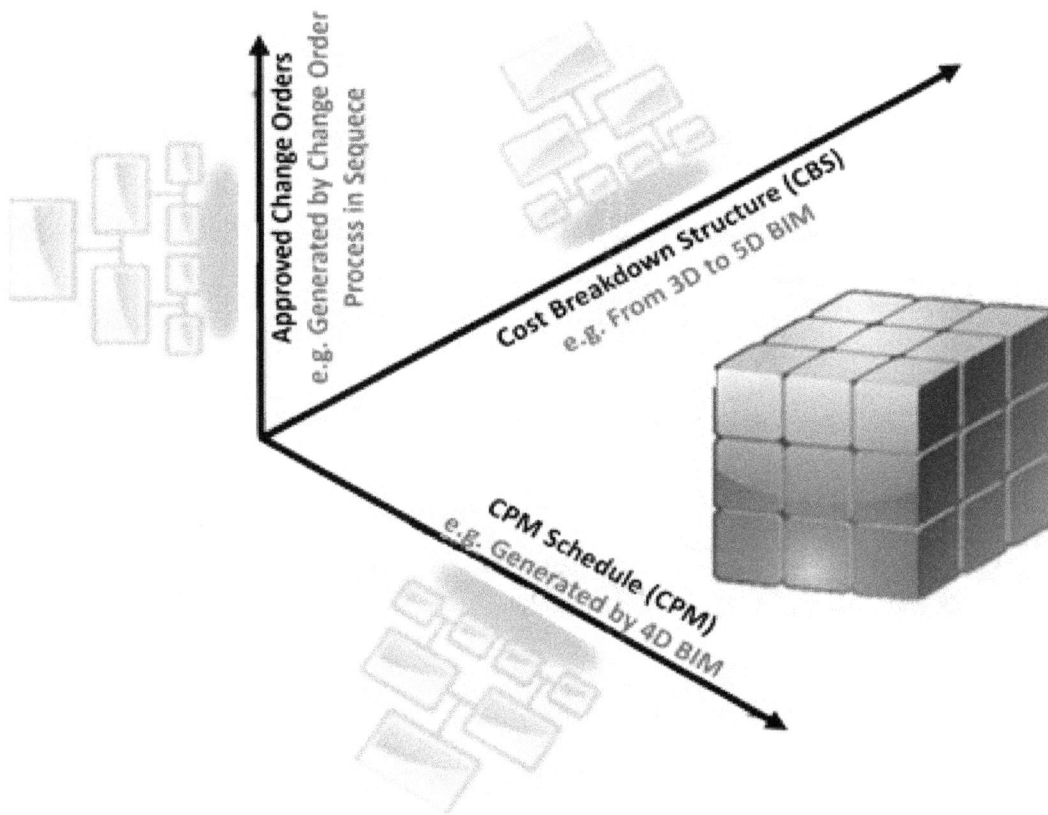

Figure 128: Owners Possible 3-D approach and View using APCO X CPM X CBS

From the modern contractor's perspective of change orders, most contracts have late-delivery penalties. The contractor isn't worried about the costs of the actual change orders, which should be recoverable when the change order is approved. The potential impact the change order will have is on the dynamic scheduling of other sequential or collateral work, causing the contractor to be penalized for missing a contractual completion date. (Savvy contractors should include a 'potential change' in the final delivery date if the contract mod is significant enough to cause delays to avoid Owner-imposed fines and penalties.)

Change Order Log

SUMMARY SHEET				
① Project	ABC Hospital, P-1234	② Total Number Of CO's to Date		5
Customer	ABC Health	③ Current CO Outstanding Duration		10.67
Architect	XYZ Designers	④ Average CO Closure Rate		7.5
Engineer	123 Engineering	⑤ Average Dollars Attributed to CO's		$7550
Drawing Version	2	⑥ Current Potential Exposure of CO's Related to Unresolved CO's		$37,750
Report Run Date	20-Dec-06			

⑦ CO CRITICAL INFORMATION							
CO NO.	CO TITLE	ORIGINATION DATE	DATE FINALIZED	CLOSED?	DAYS OUTSTANDING	FINALIZATION DATE	TIED TO RFI? (#)	COST / (CREDIT)
1	Error in Duct Size	1-Dec-06	7-Dec-06	Yes	Closed	5	#2	$2,000
2	Conflict with joist	2-Dec-06	15-Dec-06	Yes	Closed	10	n/a	
3	New Equipment: Carrier vs. Trane	1-Dec-06		Pending	14	n/a	#10	$50,000
4	Cut Refrigerant Lines	6-Dec-06		Pending	11	n/a	#11	$750
5	Deletion of West Wing HVAC	12-Dec-06		Pending	7	n/a	#13	$(15,000)

Figure 129: Change Order Log Example

Figure 129 (above) denotes critical information from a Contractor that differs from that required from an Owner. As Contractors are concerned about prompt payment for approved change orders, as well as the impact to the contract completion date, their 3-D model may well look something like what we see in Figure 130 (below) Change Order Log from the Contractor's Change Management Database. Slow payments for change orders have an impact on the contractors' cash flow, which in turn impacts the number of resources for activities in the schedule related to late payment penalties. Contractors can optimize the allocation of scarce or limited resources for not only funding of the project, but also for people (salaries, overhead, and administrative support).

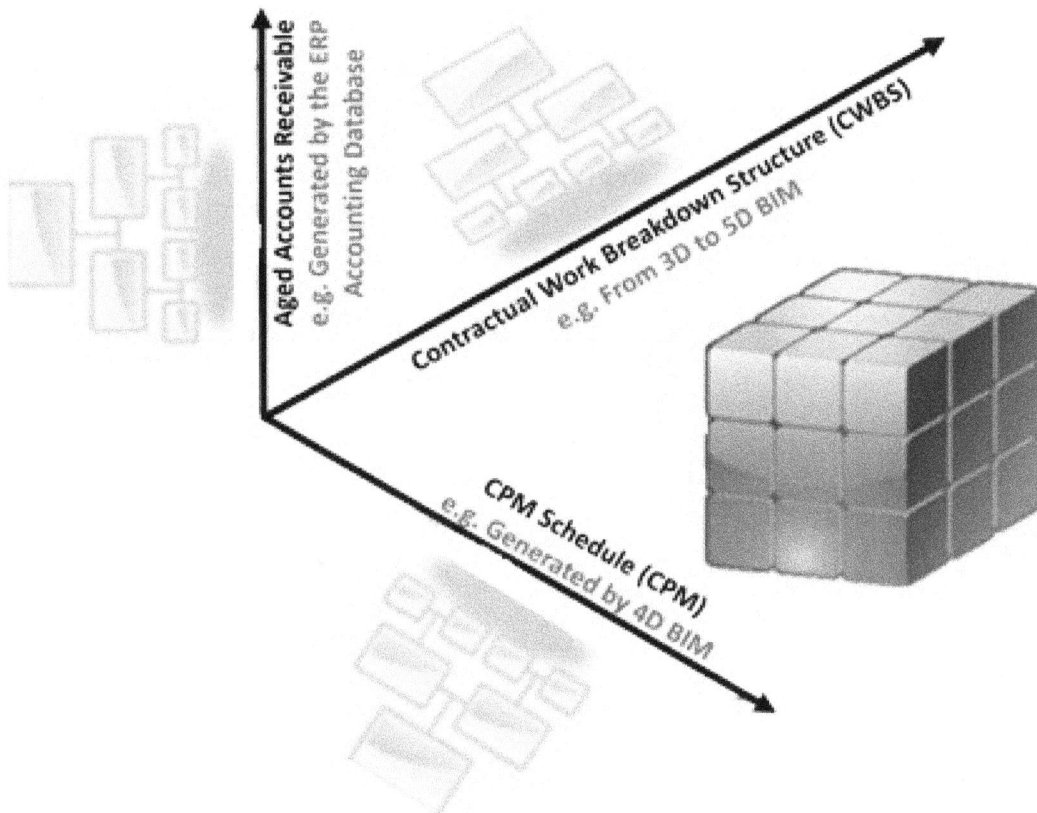

Figure 130: Possible 3-D view of Change Orders from the Contractors Perspective using AAR X CPM X CWBS.

Resource Management

The following are definitions related to resource management.

- Asset - Human, financial, physical, and/or knowledge factors that provide a firm the means to perform its business processes; synonymous with resources.
- Asset Management (Resource Management) - the process of using a company's resources efficiently and effectively, including tangible resources (e.g., goods and equipment, financial resources, and labor resources).
- Asset (Resource Categories) - assets or resource categories required to initiate, plan, execute, control and close projects successfully, including:
  a)   Physical (buildings, equipment, tools, etc.)
  b)   Financial (cash and near cash instruments)
  c)   Human (people)
  d)   Knowledge or Information (proprietary designs, cost, and productivity data)
  e)   Intangible (organizations brand image or reputation)

Knowing the five categories of assets or resources required for project managers, when creating a multi-dimensional Resource Breakdown Structure, start with the WBS that defines 100% of project requirements for the project lifespan. Thus the WBS forms one axis. Knowing resources will be used over time; the second axis needs to be time. Thus the 2-D Resource Breakdown Structure will be RBS = WBS X CPM. Using the five categories mapped to the relevant BIM Databases or OmniClass Tables, choose from any of the following resource parameters for the 3-D structure (as demonstrated in Figure 131):

Physical Assets (plant, equipment, tools, etc.)

- OmniClass Table 11- Construction Entities by Function
- OmniClass Table 13- Spaces by Function
- OmniClass Table 23- Products
- OmniClass Table 35- Tools
- OmniClass Table 41- Materials

Financial Assets (cash and near cash instruments)

- Costs from 5-D BIM
- Human Assets (people)
  Human Assets (Managers, Crews, Support Staff)

- OmniClass Table 33- Disciplines
- OmniClass Table 34- Organizational Roles

Knowledge or Information Assets (proprietary designs, cost information, productivity information)

- OmniClass Table 36- Information
- OmniClass Table 49- Properties
- 2D BIM Technical Specifications

Intangible Assets (organizations brand image or reputation)

- 6D BIM- Sustainability

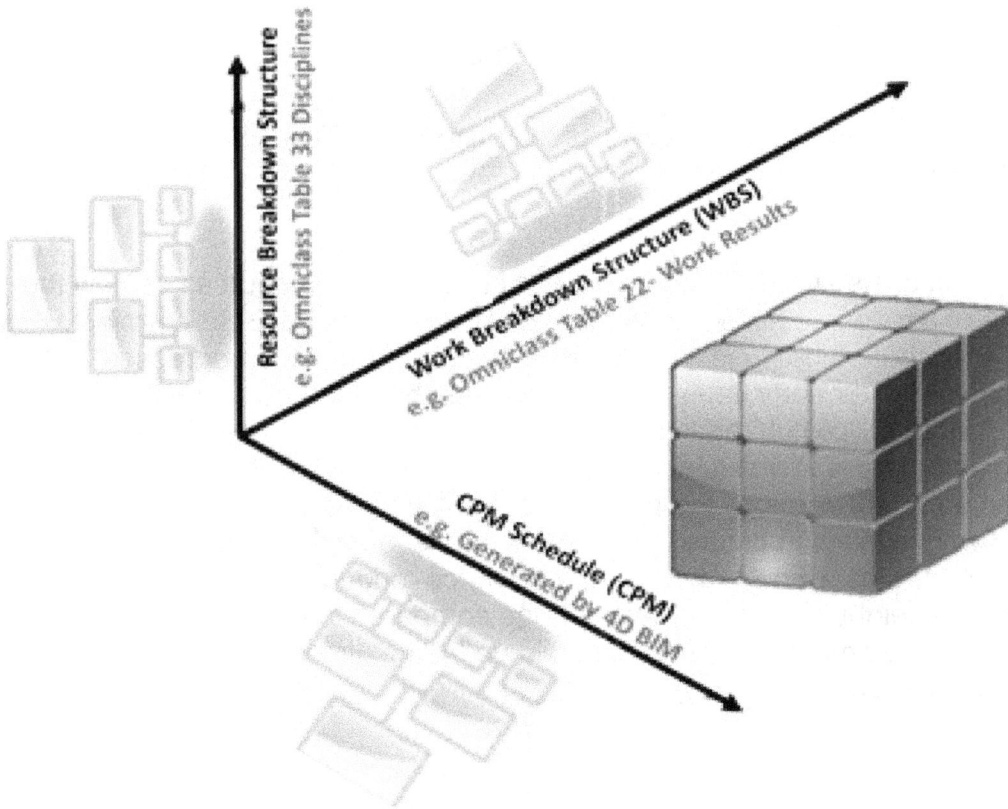

Figure 131: Showing RSBS (OCT33) X CPM X WBS = Human Resource Breakdown Structure (HRBS)

Using this model, create a 3-D resource histogram generated by all scheduling software packages, review any combination or permutation of resources using a 3-D approach. To review all resources (e.g., materials, equipment, and people) together, move to a multi-dimensional tesseract perspective. From a mathematical perspective, to produce a complete multi-dimensional, concatenate project resources:

- Activities (ABS)
- + Costs (CBS) (BoM/BoQ from 3-D X Unit Cost Database)
- + Sequence (4-D BIM)
- + Logic (4-D BIM)
- + Duration (BoM/BoQ from 3-D X Productivity Database)
- + Resources (RBS) (Materials, Equipment, and People)
- + Risk Contingency

equals

- Cost and Resource Loaded CPM Schedule

Once the cost and resources are developed and loaded into the database, there are two ways the project managers/project team normally look at that data:

- As an "S Curve" (Cumulative costs over time- BCWS or PV)
- As a Resource Histogram

Ignoring costs and focusing on human or equipment resources, review the conversion of a resource histogram from a 2D to a 3-D model. Before project work begins, a snapshot of the project becomes a baseline. As work progresses, not all activities start on their early dates, and this causes the resources allocated to each activity to "hang" or "pile up" against the data-date or time-now line. This phenomenon where the data-date is pushing incomplete work is known as a Bow Wave. A Bow Wave is an early warning sign the project may run into problems unless buildup of unfinished work is bled off before it converts into a tsunami at the end of the project. Figure 132 illustrates a Bow Wave using a resource-loaded schedule, but only in a 2-D format.[146] The height of the bow wave is huge compared to the available pool of manpower (or equipment). Viewing the build up in one dimension limits the ability to analyze it completely.

---

[146] Guild of Project Controls, Module 6.6- Allocating Resources http://www.planningplanet.com/guild/gpccar/allocating-resources

RESOURCE GRAPH

2016

| May | | | | June | | | | July | | | | August | | | | September | | | | October | | | |
| 02-05 | 09-05 | 16-05 | 23-05 | 30-05 | 06-06 | 13-06 | 20-06 | 27-06 | 04-07 | 11-07 | 18-07 | 25-07 | 01-08 | 08-08 | 15-08 | 22-08 | 29-08 | 05-09 | 12-09 | 19-09 | 26-09 | 03-10 | 10-10 | 17-10 | 24-10 | 31-10 |

Data Date or Time Now Line

Target Completion Date 31 October

Peak Manpower Requirements

"Bow Wave"

Mean Manpower Requirements

Available Manpower

| Peak Units: | 1,440% | 1,440% | 545% | 245% | 235% | 220% | 210% | 360% | 265% | 265% | 60% | 150% | 150% | 150% | 115% | 115% | 115% | 120% | 100% | 215% | 215% | 115% | 15% | 15% | 115% | 115% | 110% |

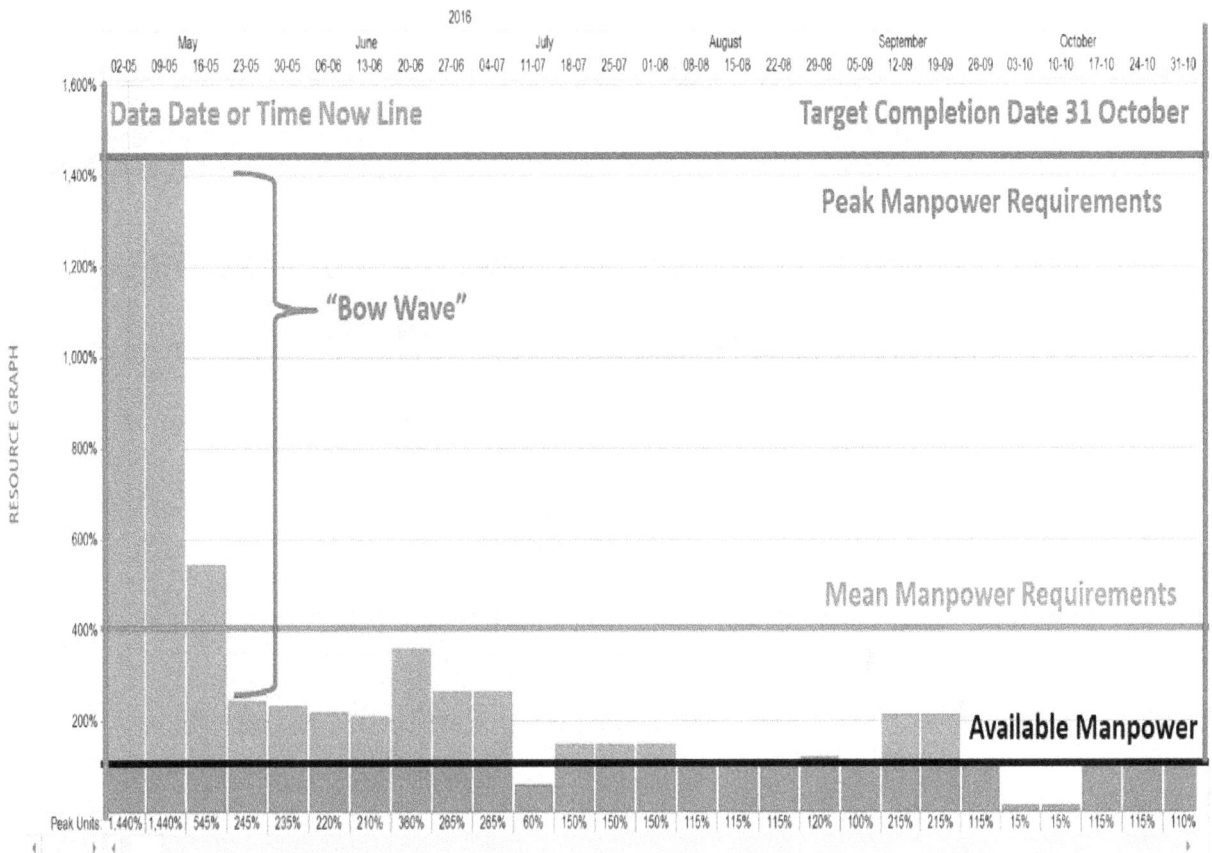

Figure 132: "Bow Wave" shown in the 2D format

Figure 133: Bow Wave in three-dimensional viewpoint

Viewing a Bow Wave in three dimensions would provide a better analytical viewpoint.[147,148]   Figures133 and 134, shows that viewing the impact Bow Wave (wake) has on resources and project activities from multiple perspectives can be invaluable in managing project resources more effectively. Analysis and viewpoint can also prove helpful in claims analysis, as measuring or validating any cumulative impact is difficult.

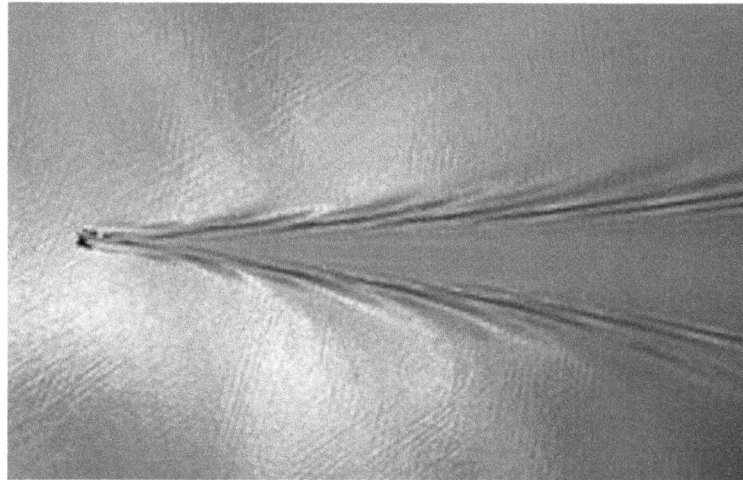

Figure 134: Real "Bow Wave" shown from an overhead perspective

Managing Claims – Explanation

The field of forensic claims uses Time Impact Analysis (TIA) methods is well-developed with multiple approaches as shown in Figure 135 (below). While multi-dimensional analysis could be applied to observational and modeled approaches, the modeled approaches seem to be the most logical to convert the traditional 2-D approach (normally the ABS on the Y axis and CPM on the X-axis) into a 3-D model.

Forensic Schedule Analysis Methodologies			
Observational	Static Logic	Gross	As-Planned vs. As-Built
		Periodic	As-Planned vs. As Built
	Dynamic	Contemporaneous	Contemporaneous Period

---

[147] *US Navy Stock Photo https://goo.gl/oU40rJ*
[148] *Wikipedia Public Domain "Wave" https://goo.gl/MlMtzW*

Forensic Schedule Analysis Methodologies			
	Logic	As-Is	Analysis (Windows)
		Bifurcated Contemporaneous	Bifurcated CPA
		Recreated / Modified	Recreated CPA
Modeled	Additive Model	Single Base	Impacted As-Planned
		Multiple Base	Retrospective TIA
	Subtractive Model	Single Simulation	Collapsed As-Built (Single)
		Multiple Simulation	Collapsed As-Built (Multiple)
AACE International www.aacei.org			

Figure 135: Various Time Impact Analysis (TIA) Methods used by Forensic Claims Analysts

Claims are often shown and analyzed using a 2-D model (as planned vs. as built) bar-chart view. It is worth exploring the potential of 'added value' being able to look at the impact of change orders or other delays in multiple dimensions as shown in Figure 136).[149]

---

[149] Livengood, John (2014) "Construction Claims A to Z" CDR 1484 AACE Symposium Bangkok, Thailand

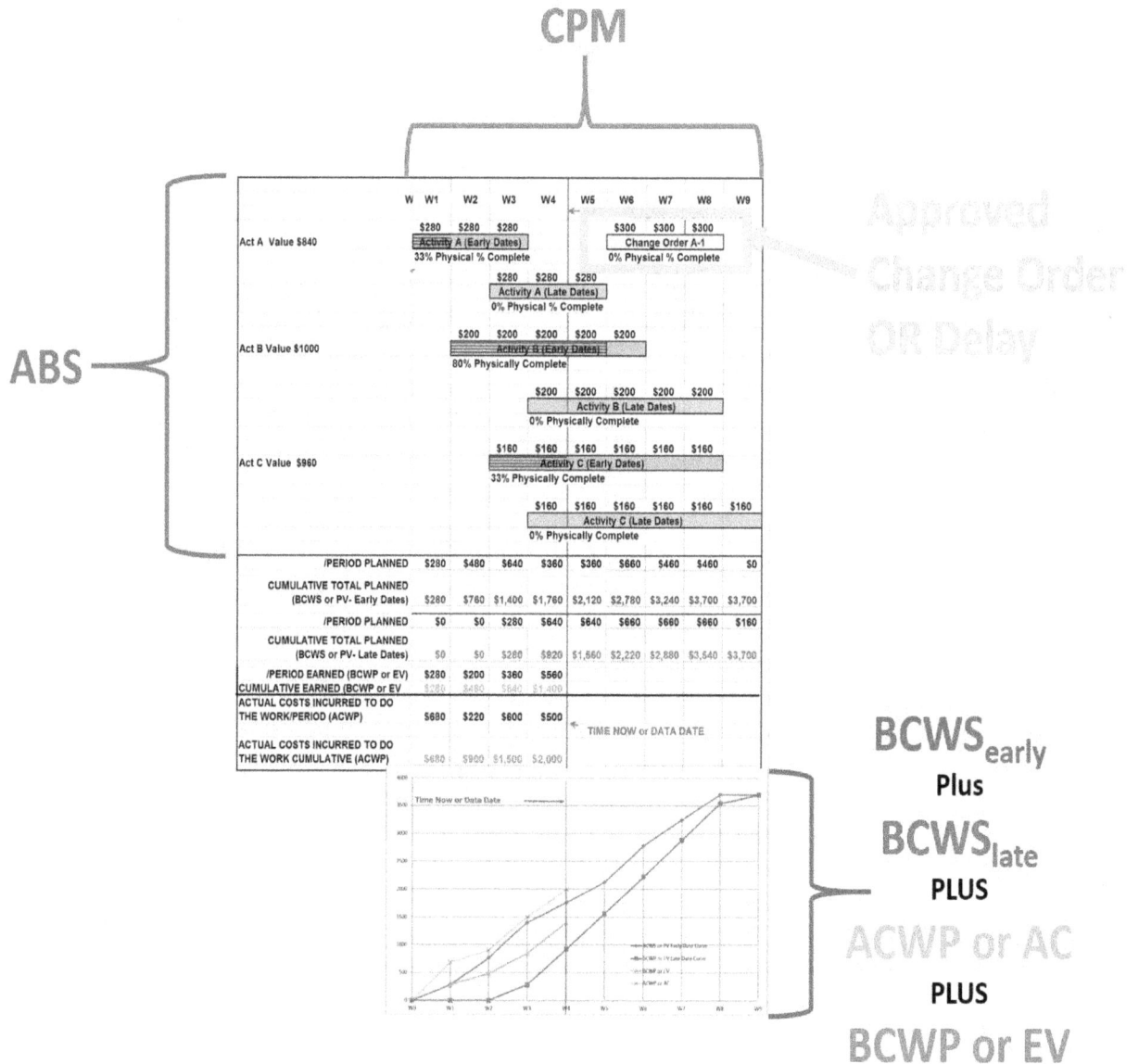

Figure 136: Potential Multi-Dimensional model showing ABS x CPM x BCWS x ACWP x BCWP x ACO/D

The traditional 2-D model to communicate and analyze impacts of change orders is a tested and proven approach. To explore how to turn a 2-D model into a 3-D model, the simple approach would be to compare only the change orders against the original baseline, resulting in a 3-D model similar to Figure 137 (below):

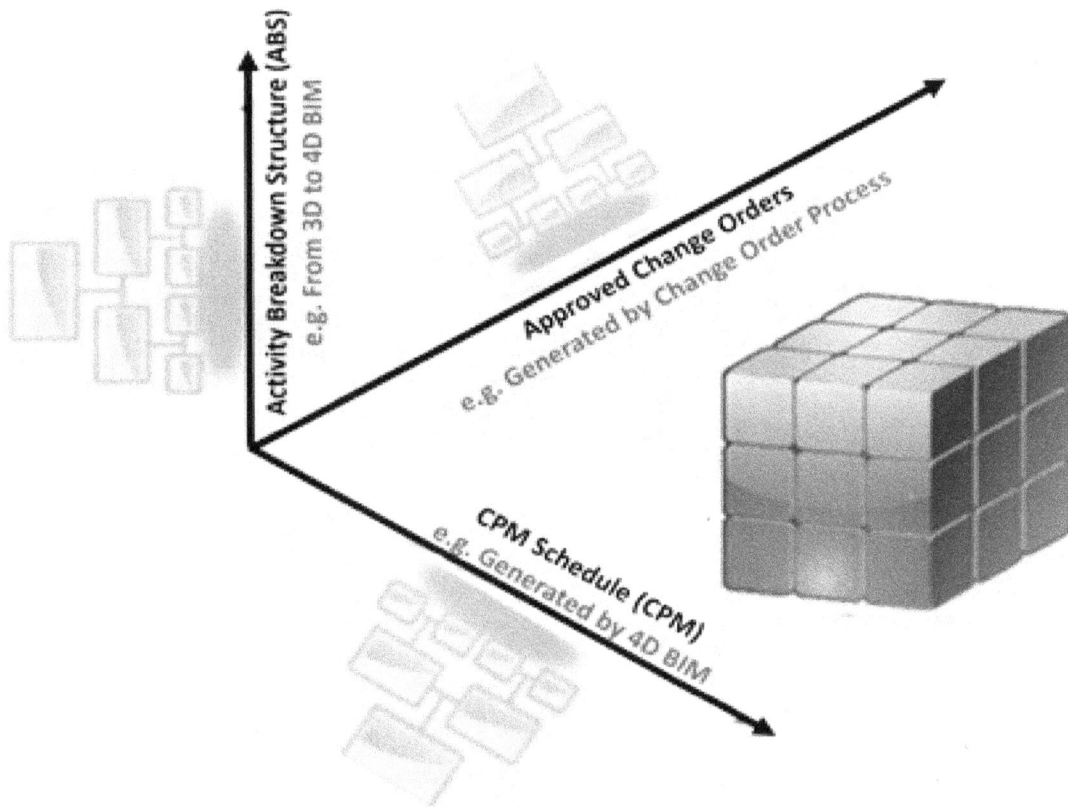

Figure 137: Simple Change Management (3-D model) using ABS X CPM X ACO

A simple 3-D model will be unlikely to represent an improvement over the traditional 2-D approach shown. When the BCWS adds early and late dates (ACWP and BCWP), the resulting tesseract model enables analysis of impacts using eigenvalues and eigenvectors. The tesseract may prove helpful for analysis, especially if there is a substantial number of change orders.

The Cumulative Impact concept recognizes that whenever there are a series of change orders, the impact to the project is more than just the summation of the costs (time and money) caused by each change order. There is a premium to that accounts for inefficiencies and workflow disruptions to be added to the summation of the impacts of all change orders. The concept of cumulative impact is recognized by contractors, owners, and the court system, who try to quantify the 'premium' should have and will remain a challenge. The theory is that creating a multi-dimensional tesseract model and applying eigenvalue analysis, the analysis may quantify the cumulative value.

Imagine being able to view a tesseract to determine relationships between the "as planned" activities and "as built" activities, Animate those activities, and then walk a judge or a jury through the process using virtual reality. While a dream at this point, creating virtual walkthroughs are being done today to help with the design process. So virtual walk-throughs are equally feasible to use in resolving claims or disputes?

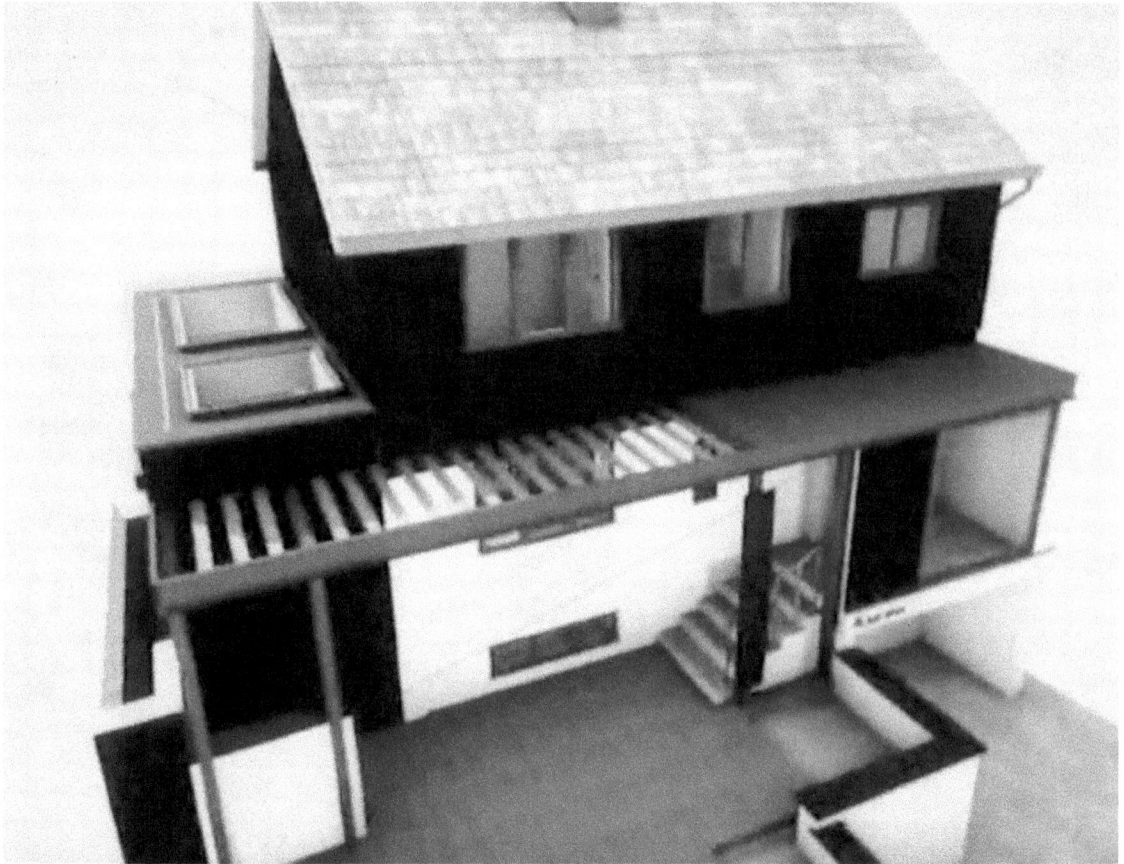

Figure 138: MVL Architects

The construction of the house (Figure 138),[150,151] by MVL Architects, using 3-D BIM and Animation Software, raises the question, "what prevents us from applying the same animation used to illustrate the construction processes, and applying that same approach to both time and cost impact analysis?" The use of BIM and simulation software is in its infancy, but using a multi-dimensional approach to the project management processes should enable better project management by architects and engineers applying the design. The same theoretical approach shown in Managing Resources or Managing Change would a starting point.

---

[150] *MVL Architects Building Information Modelling. (2011). Retrieved from http://www.mvl-architects.co.uk/examples%20of%20bim%20models.html*
[151] *MVL Architects Contemporary House Refurbishment Surry BIM Model. Retrieved from https://youtu.be/6TgA-3FquUl*

The Unfolded Tesseract Hypercube from a Stakeholders Perspective

The unfolded Tesseract (eight faces) is demonstrated in Figure 139.

The folded hypercube

8 cubital faces
The Unfolded hypercube

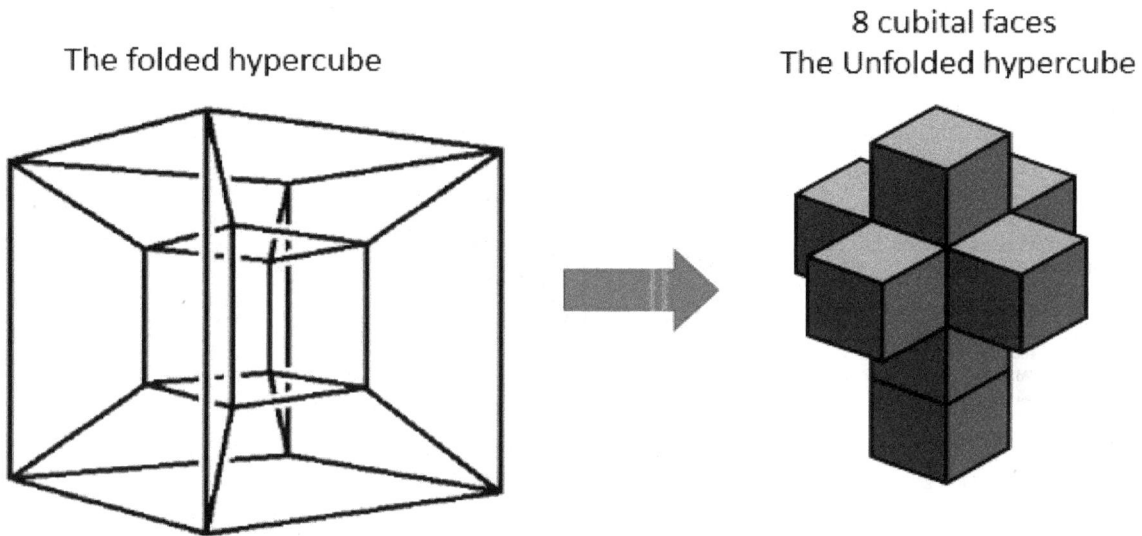

Figure 139: The Tesseract

With it unfolded, there is the possibility to reason in three dimensions. To see the full animation from folded to unfolded hypercube and back again, view these videos.

https://www.youtube.com/watch?v=BVo2igbFSPE

https://www.youtube.com/watch?v=4TI1onWI_IM

https://www.youtube.com/watch?v=4URVJ3-D8e8k

Stakeholders need to be able to see and understand the Tesseract unfolded. The Stakeholders' can view the model as shown in Figure 140 constructed with the unfolded theoretical Tesseract.

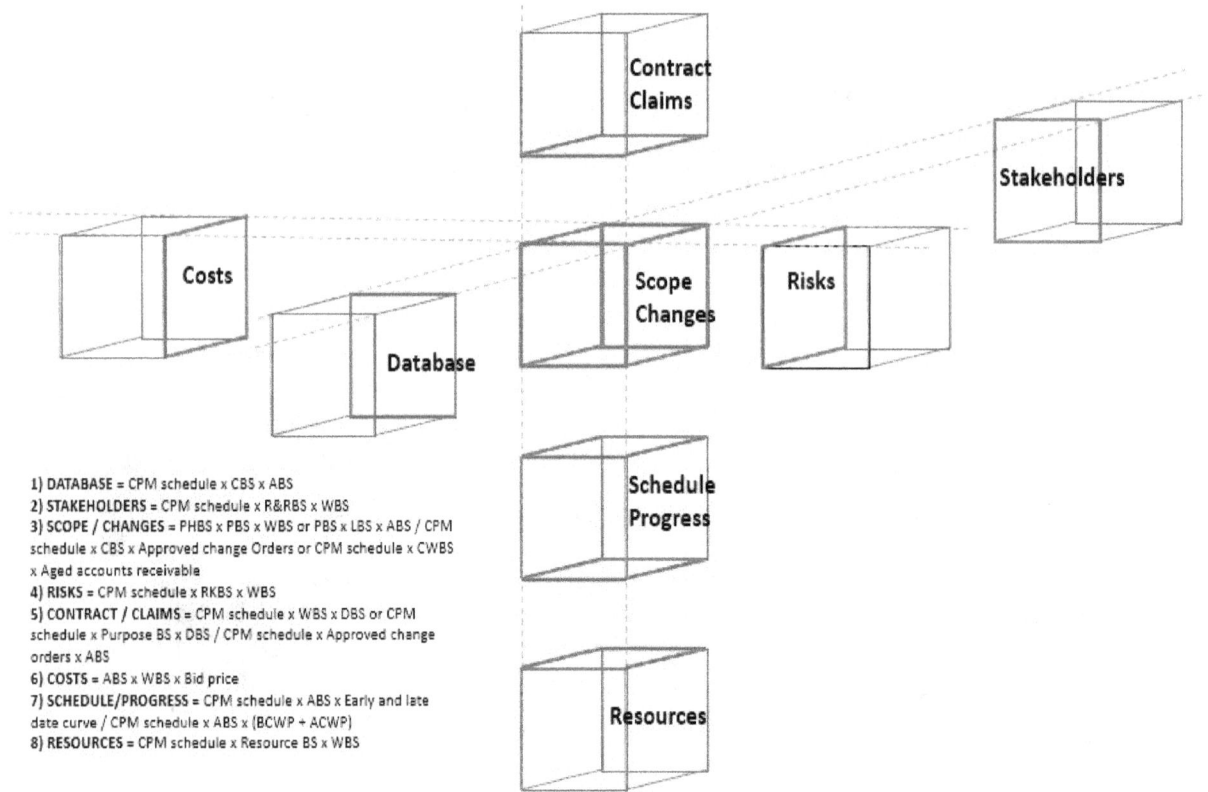

1) **DATABASE** = CPM schedule x CBS x ABS
2) **STAKEHOLDERS** = CPM schedule x R&RBS x WBS
3) **SCOPE / CHANGES** = PHBS x PBS x WBS or PBS x LBS x ABS / CPM schedule x CBS x Approved change Orders or CPM schedule x CWBS x Aged accounts receivable
4) **RISKS** = CPM schedule x RKBS x WBS
5) **CONTRACT / CLAIMS** = CPM schedule x WBS x DBS or CPM schedule x Purpose BS x DBS / CPM schedule x Approved change orders x ABS
6) **COSTS** = ABS x WBS x Bid price
7) **SCHEDULE/PROGRESS** = CPM schedule x ABS x Early and late date curve / CPM schedule x ABS x (BCWP + ACWP)
8) **RESOURCES** = CPM schedule x Resource BS x WBS

Figure 140: Tesseract unfolded in a Stakeholders perspective

Star Tetrahedron

Another modeling can be completed, as shown in Figure 141.

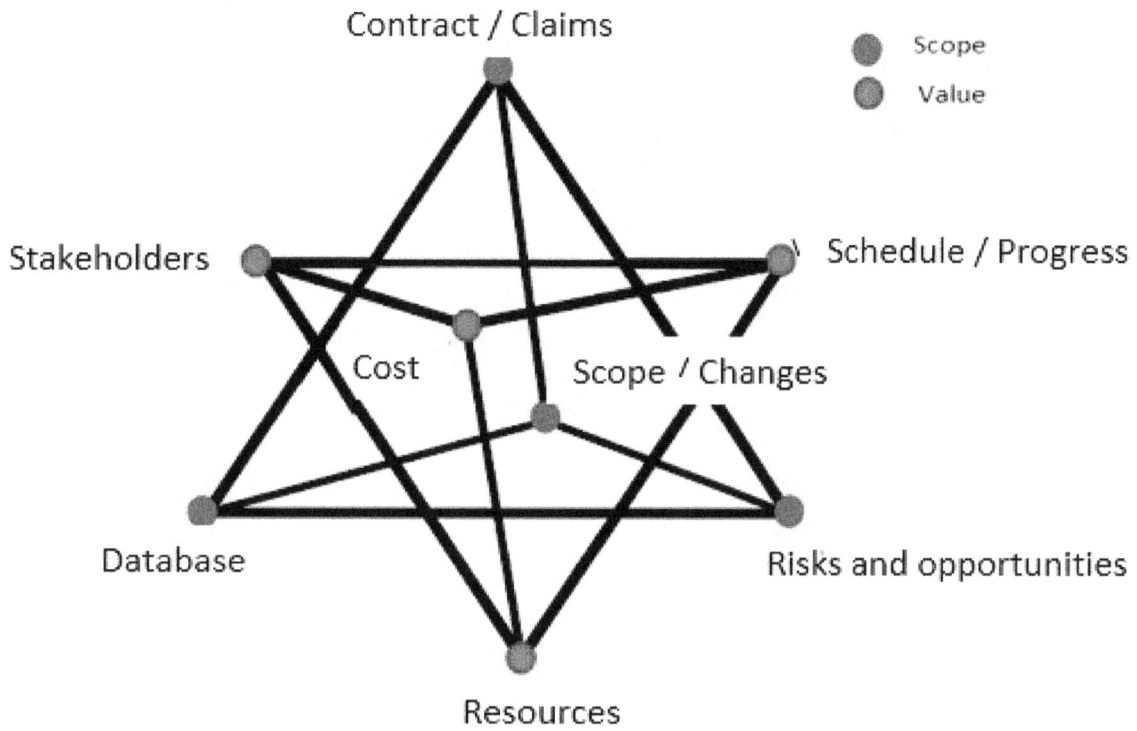

Figure 141: Star Tetrahedron for Stakeholders needs

Conclusion

This book was conceived by three global practitioners who have long rallied against the concept of single-dimensional or flat-file WBS structures. The authors predicted the practicality and utility in multi-dimensional, relational, or object-oriented WBS coding structures being the future of planning. Their belief was strong enough to utilize multi-dimensional WBS structures in their consulting and training engagements.

While the three author's perspectives have been honed through real-life applications … trial-and-error proceed what did and didn't work, resulting in this book. The author's explored the history showing the evolution of multi-dimensional WBS structures from the 1950's onward, but also analyzed external works that might support the adoption of multi-dimensional WBS structures. This research led to the work of Theoretical Physicist, Garrett Lisi, and more specifically, his work in Deferential Geometry and the algebraic mathematics underlying Fractals and Mandelbrot Sets. For academics, the door has been opened for further research on WBS as a Fractal formation, where the relationships between different levels can be defined by a mathematical formula and whether those formulas repeat as the scale increases or decreases. While not designed as an academic treatise, this is why Eigenvalues and Eigenvectors also have been included in the book.

Having raised the theory of algebraic relationships between WBS elements, on a more pragmatic, practical perspective, the authors also reviewed various construction project management literature and invested a considerable effort to show how those documents are developed and validated through the use of data identified and coded using the multi-dimensional coding structures. Having explored the history and the state-of-the-art of construction industry project management, the authors end the book by looking into the future with the understanding that the key to data exchange in the construction and project management fields is based on having standardized coding structures.

Artificial Intelligence (AI)

The use of Autonomous Machines (e.g., driverless machines) is growing in mining and other industries requiring heavy equipment. Figure 142 is courtesy of Rio Tinto and Matt Alderton in the article, "The Robots Are Coming! Driverless Dozers and the Dawn of Autonomous Vehicle Technology in Construction."[152] Reinforcement of this reality can be found at the Caterpillar Equipment company's homepage.[153]

---

[152] Alterton, Matt (May 3, 2018) "The Robots Are Coming! Driverless Dozers and the Dawn of Autonomous Vehicle Technology in Construction *Retrieved from:* autodesk.com/redshift/autonomous-vehicle-technology-in-construction/
[153] *Caterpillar: cat.com/en_US/articles/customer-stories/built-for-it/thefutureisnow-driverless.html*

Courtesy Rio Tinto

Figure 142: Autonomous Machines

Drones

Drones are already being used in electric power transmission, road work, pipelines and other applications where the work is spread out over extensive distances making it hard to analyze progress using time-lapse or other observational methods. In Figure 143, we can see the three major applications drones used: 3-D Modeling, Progress Modeling, and Orthomosaics.[154]

---

[154] *Patteron, J. (2018, Sep. 5). An Aerial View of the Future – Drones in Construction. GeoSpatial World. Retrieved from https://www.geospatialworld.net/blogs/an-aerial-view-of-the-future-drones-in-construction/*

1. 3D-MODELLING

3D models of large areas or objects can be easily created using drone technology and be combined with ground-based laser scanning and conventional surveying.

2. PROGRESS MONITORING

Drones are one of the best ways to monitor progress on a project. They provide managers with data to track workflow, manage resources, reduce downtime and keep projects on schedule and within budget.

3. ORTHOMOSAICS

High-resolution aerial imagery can be captured on the whole project area and all the images can be merged to form a seamless mosaic. This data can be used to understand the development area and measurements can be taken from it.

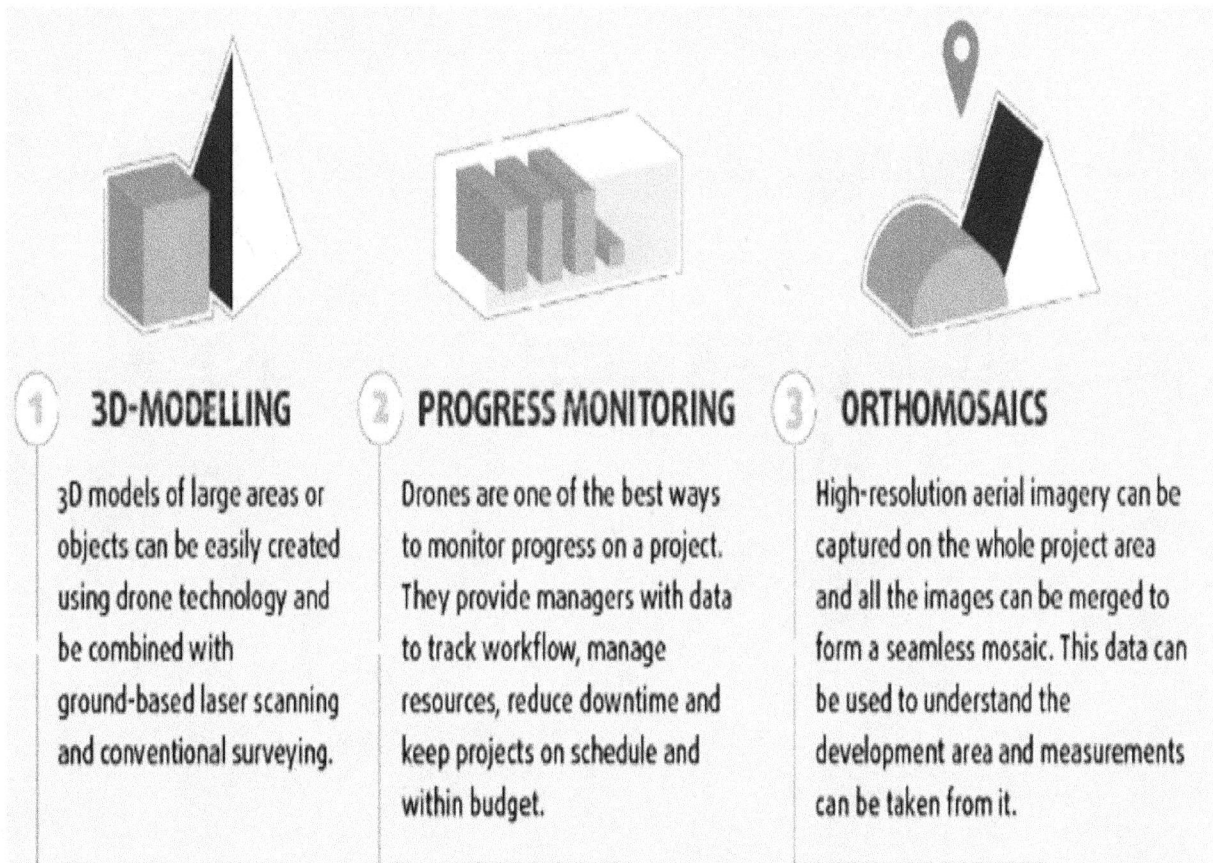

Figure 143: Drone Capabilities

A video from Airway-Bechtel provides an overview of how Orthomosaics can be used to expedite decision-making, particularly in project management and/or project management areas of control. As we can see from Figure 144, available storage areas are easy to identify, analyze, and inventory.[155] Any inspection processes can be completed faster, cheaper, and potentially more accurately using drone technology than by using the more traditional shoes on the ground methods (Airway Aerial Data: airware.com/en/industries/construction/)

---

[155] *Airway-Bechtel Video (n.d.) https://www.airware.com/en/industries/construction/*

Figure 144: Orthomosaics

Time Lapse Photography

While this technology is not new, it is gaining increasing utilization as a productivity and delay-analysis tool. The classic case study is the detailed look at how the Chinese were able to construct a 57-story building in 19 days (Figure 145).[156] [157]

---

[156] *Extreme Building in China - 57 Stories in 19 Days! Time-lapse March 19, 2015* https://www.youtube.com/watch?v=acLSbNxUP3s
[157] *Extreme Building in China - 57 Stories in 19 Days! Time-lapse March 19, 2015* https://www.youtube.com/watch?v=acLSbNxUP3s

Figure 145 - Illustrating the Use of Modularization (Assemblies) to Expedite Construction

Facial Recognition Software

Biometrics is a highly contentious subject being used at airports, immigration checkpoints, and even via closed-circuit television (CCTV) in the United Kingdom. China has taken it to higher levels, where citizens are being graded on their daily behavior and manners. In terms of construction project management, facial recognition is being used to identify who is on the job site (time-keeping and validation purposes, as well as security on-site). It is being taken to a new level to measure who is working on what tasks as well as their production and output.[158]

---

[158] NEC Corporation. (2016, Jul. 21). Video on Face Recognition Solutions – NeoFace (NEC official). Retrieved from https://www.youtube.com/watch?v=K4u4DpI6NKk&feature=youtu.be

Figure 146: Biometrics

Big Data

Big data refers to the management of bulk data. This enables transparent and accountable information sharing on platforms and processes. This encourages collaborative and inclusive decision-making processes. Advantages of the construction industry include improved analysis and prediction.[159] There is a huge demand from organizations such as RS Means Estimating Handbook (Available: https://amzn.to/2tEZvk2), General Construction Estimating Standards (Mechanical and Electrical) by The Richardson Rapid System (Available: https://amzn.to/2ECon2l), and Spon's First Stage Estimating Handbook by Bryan Spain (Available: https://amzn.to/2Vifqki), and other cost estimating and productivity analysis databases for localized cost and productivity data. While databases exist, they tend to be based on single region practices. These single-regions can include the United States or the United Kingdom and do not reflect differences in crew composition and levels of automation, and fewer differences in pay. This is one of the more important opportunities for those transitioning from the traditional roles of quantity surveying (QS) positions that are being automated to a more fully integrated, end-to-end roles of that as a BIM Consultant. [160]

---

[159] Sandle, T. (2018, Mar. 11). *Digital technologies could unlock billions for construction. Digital Journal.* Retrieved from http://www.digitaljournal.com/business/digital-technologies-could-unlock-billions-for-construction/article/517011#ixzz5bWPzY3M3

[160] Panchal. *Building Information Modeling Services – New Zealand, Silicon Engineering Consultants, Ltd. Suite of Professional Services Provided by BIM Consultant* https://www.slideshare.net/siliconecnz/building-information-modeling-services-new-zealand

1D	2D	3D	4D	5D	6D	7D
Scratch Point	**Vector**	**Shape**	**Time**	**Cost**	**Performance**	**Facility Management**
Research	**Production**	**Representation**	**Production**	**Production**	**Results**	**Applications**
• Existing conditions	• 2-D Drawings	• Renderings	• Model Federation	• Quantity extractions	• Known Alternatives	• Life-cycle BIM strategies
• Regulations	• Documentation	• Walk-throughs	• Virtual Construction	• Details Cost Estimation	• Assortment	• BIM As-Builts
• Weather simulations	• Views and Plans	• Laser Scanners	• Scheduling	• Fabrication Models	• Audited BIM Model (BPA Project)	• BIM embedded Q&M Manuals
• Sun Orientation	**Implementation**	**Implementation**	• Project Phasing	**Contracts**	• To Be Optimized	• COBie data population and extraction
• Functional Program	• BIM Object Creation	• BIM Object Creation	• Time-Lining	• Fees Comparison	**Value Engineering**	• BIM Maintenance Plans & Technical Support
Implementation	• Para-meter-ization	• Visual Programming	• Construction Planning	• Trade Selection	• Simulations	• BIM File hosting on Lend Lease's Digital Exchange System
• Consulting	• File Management	• Clash Detection	• Equipment Deliveries	• Logistics	• Energy Performance	
• BIM Execution Plan	• Communications	• Model Checker	• Visual Validation	**Sustainability**	• Systems Performance	
• Server Depository	**DS Development**	**Final Documentation**	**Systems**	• LEED Evaluation	• Construction Performance	
• Software	• Room Data Sheets	• Detailed Design	• Pre-Fabrication	• Life-Cycle Cost	• Architectural Performance	
Concept Design	• List of Deliverables	• Assemblies	• Structural Construction	• Comparative Study	**Save Estimation**	
• Strategies	• Scope Definition	• Structural Design	• MEP Construction		• Comparative Cost	
• Area Estimation	• Materials	• MEP Design	**Simulations**		• Construction Benefits	
• Cost Estimation	• Structural Loads	• Specifications	• Life-Cycle Simulation		• Owner Benefits	
• General Volumetry	• Energy Loads	**Sustainability**	• Sun Simulation		• Timing Risk	
• Accessibility	**Sustainability**	• Insulation Values	• Wind Simulation		• Selected Items to be Optimized	
• Viability	• Life-Cycle Estimation	• Sun Protection	• Energy Simulation		**Re-Design**	
	• Construction Solutions	• Daylight Requirements	• LEED check		• Certified BIM Model	
	• Primary MEP systems					
	• Energy Production					
	• LEED Strategies					

Figure 147: Suite of 'End-to-End' Services Provided by the BIM Consultant

Standardization

Standardization (modularization[161]) is researching, analyzing, identifying, and implementing efficient resource management. Advantages are a simplification of operations and supply chains. Seeking standardized methods for any industry minimizes waste and helps facilitate innovation and sustainability. One example of a standardized building module was the previously mentioned example of a Chinese 57-floor building constructed in 19 days.

The key to enabling data transfer and data exchanges between the various programs lies in the standardization of the coding structures, upon what this book was predicated. Barring future revelations, the most likely standardized coding structures are going to be coming from CSI as the most well developed and evolved. Whether any competition is established from other standard-setting entities or different parts of the world, remains to be seen.

For now, CSI's 15-Dimension model seems to be the industry standard. The real challenge for construction and building organizations is whether to adopt the CSI coding structures straight away and modify costs, productivity, and accounting databases to conform to CSI – or – will companies maintain current databases and write a translator program to convert existing data to CSI codes. Both strategies are employed, but this probably will only be a 5-10 year transition as more organizations purchase 4-D, 5-D, and 6-D BIM software with partnering databases. The creation, updating, and maintenance of localized cost and productivity databases offer an opportunity for those transitioning out of being Quantity Surveyors (QS) or Cost Estimators to becoming BIM Consultants.

---

[161] Sandle, T. (2018, Mar. 11) Digital technologies could unlock billions for construction. Digital Journal. Retrieved from http://www.digitaljournal.com/business/digital-technologies-could-unlock-billions-for-construction/article/517011#ixzz5bWZNkFVq

Predictions from the Authors

1. Crews and construction management/project controls will be connected in real time using mobile devices, allowing for crews' communications of issues or concerns in executing plans so management can communicate plan changes almost instantly https://solutions.borderstates.com/how-mobile-devices-are-revolutionizing-the-construction-industry/

2. Safety, health, and environmental (SH&E) managers will have real-time access to each worker's body temperature and heart rate to location; employees may swap out in shifts related to heat-related environments or inclement weather based on physical conditions relayed back to central control (command and control rooms) https://www.sciencedirect.com/science/article/pii/S0926580516303946

3. Three-dimensional scale models will be promulgated via wireless devices and printed using 3-D printers in the field to use in construction execution https://www.thebalancesmb.com/3-D-printing-construction-industry-845342

4. Specialized building components and tools to install them may be printed using 3-D printers in real time as crews create what they need as it is needed — particularly for specialized components or tools https://www.thebalancesmb.com/3-D-printing-construction-industry-845342

5. Facial recognition connected to 4-D and 5-D software enables a control center to monitor progress, cost, and productivity data; enabling Event Chain Methodology as the primary construction risk management methodology and real-time adjustments to crew composition and resource allocationhttp://auroracs.co.uk/wp-content/uploads/2015/04/13883-Aurora-MobileClocking.pdf

6. Workers wearing augmented reality visors have Building Information Modeling (BIM) data overlaid onto their real-world view of the site, giving a detailed plan and the information that used to require paper documentation and plans https://www.youtube.com/watch?v=8IY4qaVvR8c

7. Powered exoskeletons will enable workers to lift larger than usual loads, minimizing fatigue and decreasing injury rates from jobs requiring repetition (e.g., bricklaying) as well as automated using machines https://www.youtube.com/watch?v=sn7qETycSUs and https://exoskeletonreport.com/2016/04/exoskeletons-for-industry-and-work/ and https://youtu.be/GIhttsAM5YQ

8. Powered equipment will require fewer operators, and for the short term, equipment operators and other tradespeople are going to be in high demand to teach the machines (computers) tacit knowledge https://blog.obie.ai/3-ways-to-capture-the-tacit-knowledge-inside-your-employees-head-d593aa5c8934

9. The design-to-bid cycle will be shortened as project managers move away from traditional design>build (DB), engineer, procure, and construct (EPC), and design>bid>build (DBB) toward Integrated Project Delivery (IPD) or Hyper-Tracking where each project team member has input during design phase, and compensation is based on the success of the finished project (team members have equity positions in the projects) (see Figure 148 ??) https://info.aia.org/SiteObjects/files/IPD_Guide_2007.pdf

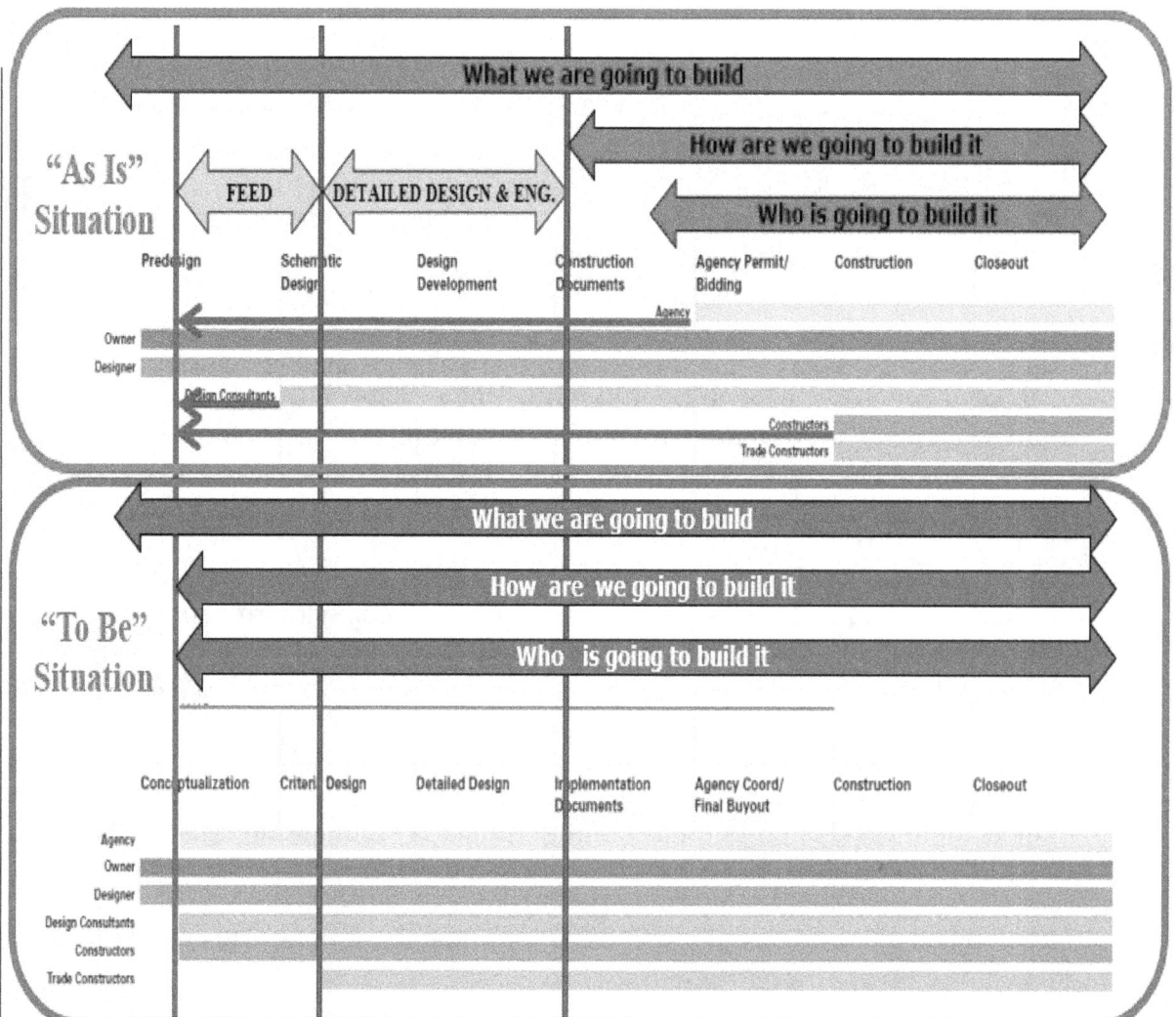

Figure 148: Accelerated Design Cycle Using IPD Approach

Consistent with the move towards standardization, Smart (or E-Contracts) in construction will become prevalent (referred to as 'Industry X.0'). Contracts will be based on blockchain execution, and the process is based on digitalization instead of paper-based.[162,163]

---

[162] AIA Integrated Project Delivery Approach. (2007). Retrieved from https://info.aia.org/SiteObjects/files/IPD_Guide_2007.pdf
[163] ENSTOA. (2018, Aug.) Can Blockchain Fix the Construction Industry's Productivity Problem? Retrieved from https://enstoa.com/sites/default/files/whitepapers/Can%20Blockchain%20Fix%20The%20Construction%20Industry%27s%20Productivity%20Problem_0.pdf

APPENDIX

Eigenvectors and Eigenvalues Summary

Introduction

Eigenvalues and Eigenvectors subject is used for the study of particular Axis of an application. When there is an application with rotations of vectors, the idea is to treat an Eigenbase (square diagonal matrix with Eigenvalues, so, an easy to use base compared to the original base) and then come back to the original base to easily obtain the transformation of the application. EigenVectors and EigenValues are used in matrices reduction concept.

Change of base of a linear application (general case):

X is one column matrix in a base B and A square matrix of this base B.
f is a linear application such as : f(x)=a.x
In the base B, f: Y=A.X
X' is one column matrix in a base B.'
In the base B', f: Y'=A'.X'
If P the "passage matrix" from the base B to the base B', resulting in X = P.X' with a P square matrix containing the components of B.'
In B': A'=P^{-1}.A.P (to refer to the mathematical demonstration)
A' is the matrix off relative to the base B.'
A' is similar to A.

It is possible to create an optimal change of base by using EigenVectors & EigenValues.

Definition of the EigenValues & EigenVectors:

A square matrix A (n lines, n columns) or a vector, and a column matrix X.
A linear application f: f(X)=A.X
The Eigenvalue of A a scalar λ such as it exists a vector X checking A.X = λ.X.
X is the Eigenvector of A.

The process to obtain the EigenValues & EigenVectors:

First, find the Eigenvalues. To find the Eigenvalues λ of A, calculate the determinant of (A- λ.I), and see the values of λ such as Det (A- λ.I)=0. I is the identity matrix. The result is several EigenValues. Once Eigenvalues λ are obtained, write for each Eigenvalue found: A.X = λp.X, with p the variable Eigenvalue, and search the coordinates of XP. This results in the Eigenvectors XP.

There is one family of Eigenvector per Eigenvalue; it is called the Eigensubspace. If a base of Eigenvectors and Eigenvalues exists, then A is diagonalizable. Search P (the passage matrix) from the base B to the base B' (base of Eigenvectors), and it's reverse P^{-1}, with P containing the Eigenvectors, and we calculate: A' = P^{-1}.A.P.

A' is diagonal; it is the matrix of the linear application associated with A but expressed in the base B.'
A is similar to matrix A'.
The diagonal coefficients A' are the Eigenvalues of A.
Go in the base B'; to solve the application, come back to B, as shown below:

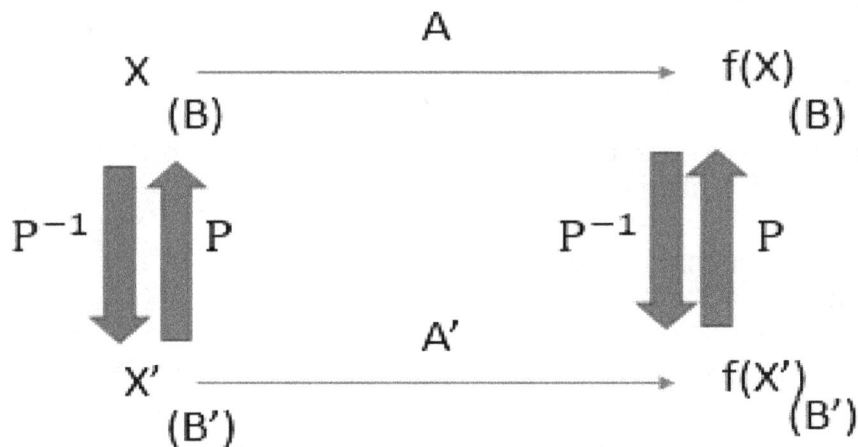

Figure 149: Change of base

Examples:

Example #1: $Y=A^{n}.X$
In the base B, it is complicated to calculate $Y=A^{n}.X$
In the base B', write: Y'= A'.X,' calculate it (A' is a square diagonal matrix composited with λp, calculate Y') and come back to the base B by doing: X'=Y'.P
Write: X=v, resulting in Figure 149 below, in base B (O, x, y):

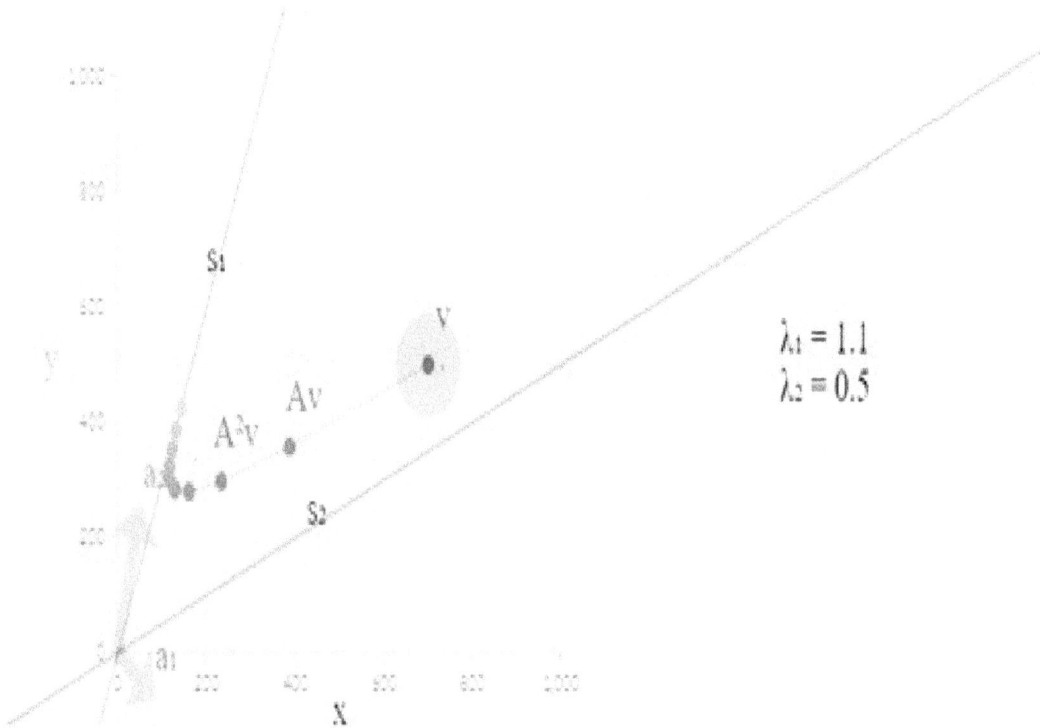

$$\lambda_1 = 1.1$$
$$\lambda_2 = 0.5$$

Figure 150: Example 1a

Put A on an Eigensubspace (S2), with $\lambda 2=0.5<1$; the sequence evolves: it converges to 0.

(To put it A on an Eigensubspace (S2) is equivalent to a change of base, use the base B' (S2): A becomes A'.)

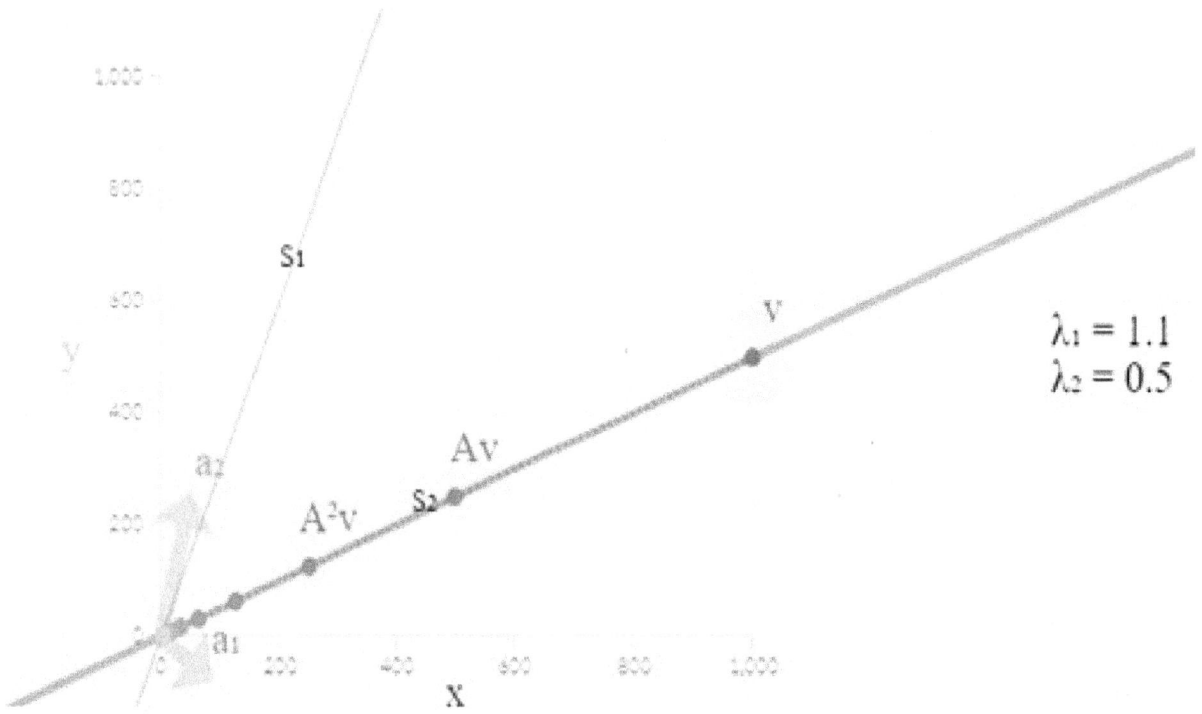

Figure 151: Example 1b

Same thing if we put A on (S1), with λ1=1.1>1, obtain the graph below:
The sequence evolves: it divaricates to ∞.

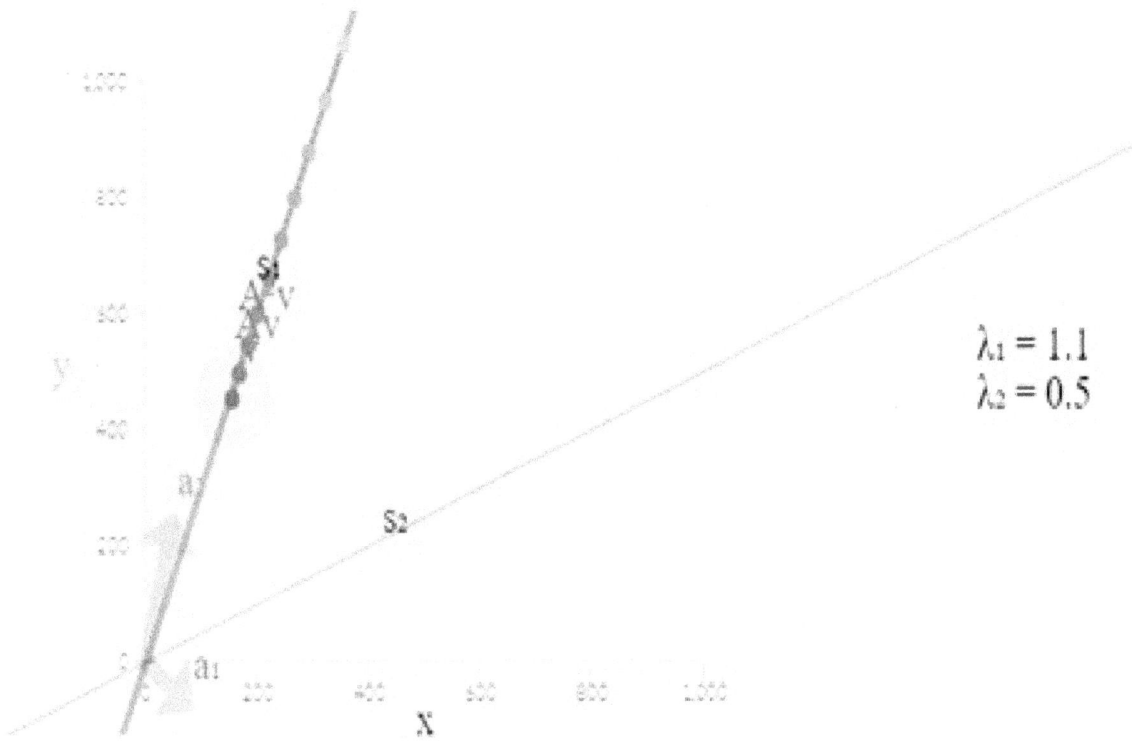

$$\lambda_1 = 1.1$$
$$\lambda_2 = 0.5$$

Figure 152: Example 1c

<u>Example #2:</u> Fibonacci sequence (1+1+2+3+5+8+13+…)
The result evolves by reasoning on an Eigenvectors subspace, as follow:

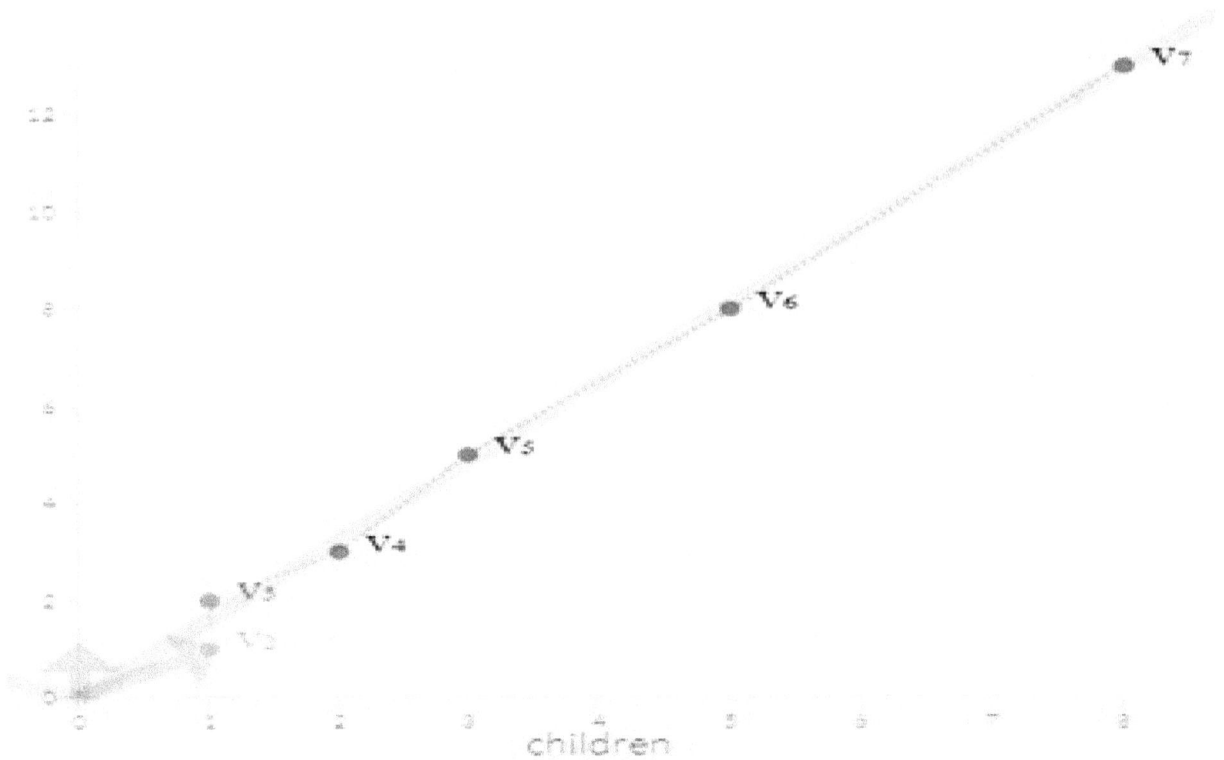

Figure 153: Example 2

Conclusion:

Eigenvectors don't rotate. Find the Eigenvectors of an application and its Eigenvalues, then dispose of an easy coordinate system (a new base) to work with. In this new base (which is on one Eigensubspace), multiply the vectors A by a scalar, to find the value of the application. There is no more rotation in this new base; that is why it is easier to use. On the Eigenspace, we can see how an application evolves.

REFERENCES

Codd E.F., Codd, S.B., and Salley, C.T. (1993). *Providing OLAP (On-line Analytical Processing) to User-Analysts: An IT Mandate.* Codd & Date, Inc.

Flatscher, W. (2014, Oct. 29). *S Curves.* ConCost. Retrieved from http://www.concost-ae.com/blog/why-do-i-never-see-a-correct-evm-s-curve

Pareek, D. (2007). Business Intelligence for Telecommunications, 294. *CRC Press.* ISBN 0-8493-8792-2.

Godinot, M. (2003). *The Work Breakdown Structure Matrix: A Tool to Improve Interface Management.*

ABOUT THE AUTHORS

Paul D. Giammalvo, Ph.D.

Dr. Paul D. Giammalvo, CDT, CCE (#1240), MScPM, MRICS, GPM-m, Ph.D., is Senior Technical Advisor (Project Management) to PT Mitratata Citragraha. (PTMC), Jakarta, Indonesia (www.build-project-management-competency.com). He is noted for the development and presentation of graduate-level, blended-learning curricula designed for mid-career, English as Second Language (ESL) professionals to develop competency in the building industry for local organizations. For 20+ years, Paul has been developing and delivering Project Management training and consulting throughout South and Eastern Asia, the Middle East, West Africa, and Europe.

Paul is active in the Global Project Management Community by playing an active leadership role in the Association for the Advancement of Cost Engineering International (AACEI; http://www.aacei.org). He is active in International Project Management Association (IPMA) member organizations, including The Green Project Management Association (GPMA) http://www.greenprojectmanagement.org where he serves on the Certification Board of Directors and American Society for the Advancement of Project Management http://www.asapm.org serving as Director of Marketing for the Board of Directors. Paul served the Board of Directors of the Global Alliance for Project Performance Standards (GAPPS), www.globalpmstandards.org, Sydney, Australia and is an active regional leader in the International Guild of Project Controls (www.planningplanet.com/guild).

Dr. Giammalvo spent 18 of the last 40 years working on large, highly-technical, international projects, including prestigious projects as the Alyeska Pipeline and the Distant Early Warning Site (DEW Line), upgrades in Alaska and the Negev Airbase Constructors, Ovda, Israel and the Minas Field in Rumbai, Sumatra, with a client list that includes Fortune-500 telecommunications, oil, gas and mining companies, the United Nations' Projects Office and other multi-national companies, non-government organizations (NGO) and Indonesian Government Agencies.

Dr. Giammalvo has an undergraduate degree in Construction Management, a Master of Science in Project Management from George Washington University, and was awarded his Doctorate of Philosophy in Project and Program Management from the Institute Superieur De Gestion Industrielle (ISGI) and Ecole Superieure De Commerce De Lille (ESC-Lille).

Jean-Yves Moine

Project planning consultant, Jean-Yves Moine, is an engineer who graduated from the Centre d'Etudes Supérieur Industriel (CESI), and worked in project control for more than 15 years in prestigious French companies, with successively larger and more complex projects in different sectors in France and abroad. He is a subject matter expert and consultant in the 3-Dimensional Work Breakdown Structure at the heart of project control.

During his different career accomplishments, he developed this model and approach to structuring project schedules quickly and productively in the 3-D WBS method in collaboration with Xavier Leynaud. Most of Jean-Yves subject matter expertise is in establishing a 3-D WBS at the beginning of the project and then a linked system to manage costs and time. His professional knowledge of project management theory enabled him to write four books published by the French Normalization Association (AFNOR). He published a fifth book, 3-D Project Management – The Project Cube (March 2012) at Cépaduès, as the French editor.

Moine has published articles in project management journals of the Association French Normalization Organization Regulation (AFNOR) and the French Project Management Association magazine. He has provided international lectures about the 3-D WBS method. Because of his subject matter expertise in many large companies, he also has an in-depth knowledge of project management tools like PRIMAVERA P6, Microsoft Project, and TILOS. Moine is a specialist in Project Management (time, costs, and risks).

Today, Moine is retired and concentrates on his chess-playing skills. He can be contacted at jean-yves.moine@outlook.fr

Xavier Leynaud

Xavier Leynaud started his career in the oil and gas sector, working for Bouygues Offshore (now Saipem) as a planning engineer on some of the largest Engineering, Procurement & Construction (EPC) projects the company had at the time. He was then hired by a Project Management Consulting Company where he stayed for 15 years, working mainly for infrastructure, construction, rail, water management, waste management, and software sector projects. During those years, he provided subject matter expertise consulting on project control (planning, cost, documentation, configuration, contract). He became managing director of the industrial and services of the consulting company and was eventually responsible for Project Management Software implementation activities.

During the early years in his career, he met Moine and started to work with the 3-D WBS methods and concepts - primarily in the rail sector, water, and waste management sectors. After 15 years he has accepted an opportunity with Alstom Hydro and joined the group as a Director in charge of project planning and load management.

After four years with Alstom Hydro, he started a private consulting company specializing in forensic and project management consulting. He now manages a firm that specializes in forensic planning, quantum, and complex project management issues and provides subject matter expert (SME) consulting for both national and international clients. He is frequently an expert witness in judicial and arbitration procedures.

Xavier graduated in 2016 from Paris 2 Pantheon Assas for the "International Construction Contract" law degree and is IPMA (International Project Management Association) PPMC (Project & Portfolio Management Consultant) since April of 2018.

He can be contacted at xl@leynaud-associes.fr

ABOUT THE BOOK

This book is targeted towards building and construction planning and project managers who are professional practitioners developing cost estimating databases or with strategic goals towards integrating Building Information Model (BIM) with Enterprise Resource Planning (ERP) systems. This book outlines, details, and explains how an excessive number of changes in the planning – including change orders, legal claims (contracts-related), and scheduling overruns can be avoided by adapting and using the 3-D Building Information Model. This book analyzes and explains the process of making the switch from single-dimensional (1-D or 2-D) flat-file Work Breakdown Structures (WBS) to multi-dimensional WBS and CBS that are suitable for relational and object-oriented databases.

This book provides a paradigm shift in thinking for intermediate- and advanced-level planning and project managers to accelerate small to large building and construction projects. The purpose of this book is to introduce a 'better way of planning' to pull organizations out of the cost-burdensome single-dimensional WBS/CBS planning stages of construction planning into a more cost-efficient practice of cost estimating using databases or integration of BIM with ERP. This solution is ideal for BIM developers, BIM consultants, and as an introductory textbook solution for students and course curriculum developers targeting Construction Database Creation and Management on a graduate level.

www.ingramcontent.com/pod-product-compliance
Lightning Source LLC
Chambersburg PA
CBHW081358270326
41930CB00015B/3339